Room for Diplomacy

Room for Diplomacy

Britain's Diplomatic Buildings Overseas 1800-2000

Mark Bertram

with a Foreword by
Lord Hurd of Westwell

Spire Books Ltd
PO Box 2336, Reading RG4 5WJ
www.spirebooks.com

Spire Books Ltd
PO Box 2336, Reading RG4 5WJ
www.spirebooks.com

Designed by John Elliott

ISBN 978-1-904965-32-9

Contents

The price of presence: the Royal Standard
flying at the Moscow embassy during HRH
The Duke of Gloucester's visit in 1986.

Foreword

BY THE RT HON LORD HURD OF WESTWELL CH CBE

In my first foreign posting in 1954 I lived in one of the bungalows which the Boxers besieged during their attack on Peking in 1900. In my last posting in Rome my office looked along the aqueduct in the garden of the Villa Volkonsky which we had taken from the Germans by way of reparation at the end of World War II.

Neither of these buildings now serves the purpose which I remember. Mark Bertram's fascinating account of the British diplomatic estate overseas underlines the many changes of need and fashion which guided those responsible for its upkeep and administration. In days of plenty the accent might be on emphasising the best in British architecture, as illustrated for example by the work of Lutyens in Washington. At other times we were emphasising our Imperial strength, as in Peking and indeed Kabul. More often however the accent has been, as of now, on the need to keep costs under control. The Treasury has never sympathised with the argument that Britain's diplomats need to keep up a certain style if they are to do their job properly. As Mark Bertram shows, the buildings in which they live reflect the anxieties or ambitions of each decade. On the whole he believes that those responsible did a good job – but the struggle and the arguments continue.

Douglas Hurd.

For
all my colleagues and our predecessors,
most of whose names this book is too short to include,
who worked hard and long, sometimes in extraordinary circumstances,
buying and selling, designing and building, maintaining and furnishing
diplomatic and consular buildings.

Preface

It struck me as odd, throughout my long involvement with Britain's diplomatic buildings overseas, that so little information was available about their history, either collectively or individually. Between consulting dry registers for a few hard facts and absorbing diplomatic anecdotes for questionable impressions, there was little information available, and none readily so. I resolved quite a few years ago to try and fill the gap, and this book is the result.

Since the 1870s, when the British government first became fully engaged in the search for suitable accommodation overseas, and still today, each property acquired was the best compromise thought to be achievable at the time between three competing considerations: what function was to be housed, what property was available, and what was affordable. None of these was precisely identifiable. Functionality depended on perceived future operational requirements. Availability was confined to four options, sometimes in combination: a building that could be bought and adapted, a site that could be acquired and built upon, a property that the host country might be persuaded to grant, and a property that could be leased for whatever term of years. Affordability depended on the Treasury's assessment or whim in the prevailing financial climate. With all these variables, it is not surprising that Britain's diplomatic buildings are a mixture of old and new, large and small, grand and humble: each is the chosen compromise in a unique set of circumstances. How long each remains in the diplomatic estate is one of the best measures of its success.

The story of these buildings needs to be told primarily in the institutional terms of the Foreign Office which needed them, the succession of Works departments which provided them, the Treasury which paid for them, and Parliament which kept an eye on their general suitability or otherwise. These institutions had relatively static outlooks towards the buildings: the

Foreign Office sought to keep up with, or ahead of, the standards of rival countries; the Office of Works was suspicious about the Foreign Office's requirements; the Treasury was sure that all buildings were more expensive than necessary; and Parliament was frustrated that it did not have more direct control. Within these relatively static institutional outlooks, of course, were the varied and changeable views of individual office-holders, each with their own job to do and their own opinions. The resulting patchwork of relations between, for example, London and abroad, diplomats and estate managers, ambassadors and architects, incumbent heads of mission and their successors, has always been a rich one.

Diplomatic buildings had a cachet from the outset by virtue of their location, size, emblems and the allure of being invited within. Nevertheless, the Office of Works regarded them as an unwelcome burden and treated them little differently from the general run of its civil projects in the UK. It was not until the 1920s that serious attention was paid to the actual architecture of diplomatic buildings. Nor until the 1950s that new buildings began to be considered as architectural opportunities for reflecting and projecting British national aspirations. The advent of looking for embassies to be national architectural icons is even more recent.

While some institutional and personal outlooks have changed surprisingly little over the last 200 years, the world, of course, has changed almost out of recognition. There are more than ten times as many countries enjoying diplomatic relations now than there were in 1800, a thousand times as many diplomats posted around the world, all able to communicate with their home governments in a millionth of the time. It is perhaps a surprise that diplomatic accommodation remains a necessary commodity at all and that forecasts of its extensive redundancy have proved wrong. Looming present-day cutbacks may force the pace towards fewer and smaller diplomatic buildings. If so, some of those in this book may find new lives in new uses. They would not be the first. The consulate at Amoy, for example, is now Xiamen's coin museum, the residence in Rio de Janeiro is the headquarters of the city's Municipality, and the consulates in Fez and Zomba are parts of hotels. In Shanghai, the former consular supreme court is now a smart restaurant managed by the new Peninsula Hotel next door and the consul-general's residence is about to become an expensive retail outlet: times change.

It was my original intention that this book should include a catalogue giving more details about the buildings mentioned here, as well as about those that I have excluded. Space, however, dictated otherwise and the catalogue will instead appear as a sister volume, currently in preparation.

Acknowledgements

This book has been more enjoyable, and taken much longer, to piece together and write than I expected. My first acknowledgment and my deepest gratitude is to my wife Vanessa for her patience and support, for doing lots of things that I should have done, or at least helped with, and for her resilient computer and image-handling skills. Many of my family, friends and colleagues have been consistently polite in enquiring about my progress with this book while plainly wondering why anything should take quite so long. I am grateful to all of them for their forbearance, and especially those who have additionally and kindly fed me, put me up, and buoyed me up.

This book has grown out of my working career and my thanks therefore extend beyond those who have helped me directly with it to those who were so good to me over an even longer period. I will restrict myself to mentioning only two. To Sir Roger Carrick I owe the most: he taught me to understand the Foreign Office in 1983 and has been unfailingly supportive and kind ever since. And Sir Curtis Keeble, who died in 2009, who ran him close for wisdom and wit, as well as patience in introducing this naive architect to what both would call the 'real world'.

The FCO, and particularly Sir Peter Ricketts and Professor Patrick Salmon, has encouraged me in this venture and given me plentiful access to material, some of which it did not know it had. Numerous others have given me help, advice, sources and ideas during the preparation of this book. They include Hugh Arbuthnott, Richard Burton, Sherban Cantacuzino, Sophie Carter, Roy Coombs, Andy Cornell, Alfred Coutts, Jane Crawley, Kate Crowe, Jim Daly, Stephen Day, Sarah Doig, Sir Simon Gass, Geoff Gillham, Alasdair Glass, Keith Hamilton, Peter Harris, Lady Ruth Hawley, Grant Hibberd, Ron Hills, Jim Hoare, Michael Holmes, Edwin Keates, Clive

Lacey, Sir Michael Llewellyn Smith, Jeremy Melvin, Richard Muir, Jeremy Neate, John Owen, Malcolm Reading, Steven Richmond, Derek Savage, Ann Snow, Dame Veronica Sutherland, Francis Walley, Stephen Whittle, Mark Willingale, Sir Andrew Wood, and Tristram Woolston. I am grateful to them all.

A splendid revelation to me has been the endless willingness of library staff to engage in esoteric pursuits. I cannot praise The National Archives too highly for its efficient and painstaking approach to every enquiry and service. For much the same reason, I have relished the time I have spent in the libraries of the Athenaeum, Cambridge University, the Royal Engineers at Chatham, and the Royal Institute of British Architects, and I extend thanks to them all.

I am most grateful to Lord Hurd for his Foreword, for there is nobody with greater experience of the diplomatic estate and the job it has to do, nor from such a variety of viewpoints as diplomat, Minister of State, and Foreign Secretary. Geoff Brandwood, John Elliott and Linda Hone at Spire Books have brought this book to fruition with enthusiasm and energy: I am immensely grateful to them.

Crown copyright material appears by courtesy of The Controller of Her Majesty's Stationery Office at The National Archives. The credits for the illustrations, listed at the end of the book, make clear by whose kind courtesy each appears, and I thank those individuals and organisations. Finally, I should say that the views expressed in this book are my own and do not represent those of Her Majesty's Government.

Notes on Nomenclature

I should explain a few conventions and short cuts that I have adopted in the interests of simplicity and readability.

Departments in London

The Foreign Office lasted from 1782 until it became the Foreign and Commonwealth Office in 1968, after which I have called it the FCO. The Office of Works lasted until 1941: I have avoided, except in quotations, the frequent alternative title of Board of Works. The Office of Works became the Ministry of Works in 1941 and I have called it that until 1972 (although there were variants during the mid-1940s and the 1960s) when it became the Property Services Agency, which I have called the PSA.

Diplomatic and Foreign Office terms

An embassy was originally the ambassador and his entourage, and they lived in an embassy house. In the same house was the chancery, where the ambassador's official staff worked. Slightly less important than an embassy, a legation was a minister and his entourage, living in a legation house. Both were missions, which is why the buildings were sometimes called mission houses. Legations became extinct in the 1960s with the result that diplomatic representation in a capital city was afterwards invariably an embassy, however small. As missions took on wider responsibilities, the expansion of offices led in the 1930s to their being housed separately from the mission house in a building called the embassy offices, soon shortened to embassy and thereby supplanting the original meaning of the word. The mission house, once the offices had moved out of it, came to be known as the head of mission's residence.

Consulates were a simpler matter: they retained a separate identity and consuls occupied separate premises from diplomats until after the First

World War. High commissions are, from most points of view, embassies in Commonwealth countries. The generic term for any British representation overseas, whether embassy, high commission or consulate, is a Post. There are two other peculiarities worth noting. The Foreign Office's 'chief clerk' matured from a quill-pusher in 1800 to the equivalent of a director of corporate affairs nearly 200 years later without his name being changed. And 'ingoings' are the adaptations made to a newly acquired building to turn it into a workable diplomatic building.

Cities

Where a city has been re-named, I have adopted the changed name after the date of change: Constantinople therefore becomes Istanbul after 1930. Likewise where spelling or transliteration conventions have changed, except in the case of the Chinese consulates which remain in the nineteenth-century 'Post Office' romanisation system, like Amoy, as being more recognisable to most readers than the current *pinyin* romanisation, Xiamen.

Measures, dates, currencies and costs

I have converted all measures to either imperial or metric so as to assist the reader to grasp the size, for example, of a plot of land in Hungary that was recorded in square fathoms or of a piece of Shanghai that was '2 mow 2 fun 7 le and 2 haou' in extent. I have not converted imperial and metric measures to each other. Only two key conversions need bearing in mind here: there are about 10 square feet to a square metre and about 2.5 acres to a hectare. All dates are converted to the Gregorian calendar so as to avoid confusion about when the 4th moon of the 493rd year of the Chao Hsien Dynasty might have occurred. Where only one date is given for a building, that is the date of its completion or occupation.

All currencies are converted to pounds sterling at the rate prevailing at the time of a transaction, to avoid the uncertainties of silver ingots, napoleons and Mexican dollars. This creates a risk, since many of the costs of older projects appear so small, of assuming that the Treasury was being unreasonably churlish in objecting to their expenditure. I had hoped to give a better idea of the scale of these projects by giving revaluations in 2010 cost terms but could find no method of doing so that was not as misleading in a different way.

1

First Ownerships
1800–1815

Diplomatic background before 1815

Modern diplomatic relations between countries have been evolving since the city states of Venice, Florence, Naples and the Vatican were competing for power in the fifteenth century. Their rulers communicated with each other by sending and receiving ambassadors. During the sixteenth century there was so much traffic of ambassadors between the states that the rulers found it preferable to post a single ambassador permanently in one anothers' capitals. Thus the concept of the resident embassy was born. An ambassador, appointed to serve for two years in a foreign place, would be briefed by his ruler on the business that he wanted transacted and the reports, or despatches, that he wanted to receive, particularly about political intelligence that the ambassador had garnered.

The first English ambassador resident abroad was John Shirwood at Rome in 1479, and the first to a secular court was John Stile at Madrid in 1509. By the end of the sixteenth century, resident embassies had become the normal channel through which major European states conducted their international relations with each other and with the Ottoman Empire in Constantinople. Besides Rome and Madrid, England had resident ambassadors at that time at Constantinople, Paris, Vienna and Venice. An ambassador was the personal representative of his sovereign, who gave him a credential letter to present to the sovereign at whose court he was to reside. Resident embassies were generally reciprocal: hence the exchange of ambassadors signifies the establishment of diplomatic relations and their withdrawal signifies a break in them.

As the number of resident ambassadors in a capital increased, questions inevitably arose about precedence among them and the countries that they represented. This conundrum was eventually resolved in 1815 by the Regulation of Vienna which required precedence among ambassadors to be determined solely by reference to the length of time that each had resided in that capital and without any reference to the power of his country. Other hierarchical questions of ceremony, the elaboration of entertainment and the grandeur of an ambassador's residence could not be so neatly resolved. The result was often competitive ostentation between diplomatic missions to establish superiority and to impress the host state. Resident embassies therefore became expensive enterprises. So expensive that, during the eighteenth century, a hierarchy of more economical resident diplomatic missions emerged. Ambassadors continued to head the most important missions but envoys, ministers, residents and agents headed progressively less important missions.

This hierarchy was formally codified by the Regulation of Vienna and by amendments agreed a few years later. To distinguish between resident ambassadors and ambassadors visiting on special missions, the former were called ambassadors 'extraordinaire' (French having become the language of diplomacy), and this rank alone had the right to seek audience of the host sovereign. The appellation 'plenipotentiary' was included in the title of diplomats if they had full powers to negotiate on behalf of their sovereign. All British ambassadors had these powers, hence their usual full title of 'ambassador extraordinary and plenipotentiary'. Below ambassadors came a tier that combined several previous ranks, including legate, that was called 'envoy extraordinary and minister plenipotentiary', or minister for short. As Sir Humphrey Trevelyan summarised it, 'the nice gradation of … the extraordinary and plenipotentiary at the top and the ordinary and impotent at the bottom'.[1]

The mission that an ambassador headed was an embassy, the collective noun for himself and his entourage, and a minister headed a legation. At the time that the regulations were drawn up, Britain had only a handful of ambassadors and nearly 20 ministers, practically all in Europe. The building in which an ambassador or minister lived and worked was called the embassy house or the legation house: he worked in his study in the main part of the house and his diplomatic staff, if any, worked in a room, called the chancery, tucked away elsewhere in the house. Appropriation of the words 'embassy' and 'legation' to describe the building in which the mission was housed, rather than the mission itself, hardly occurred before the twentieth century.

British diplomats, whatever their rank or posting, were appointed under systems of patronage. The sovereign's patronage gradually gave way to political patronage, with the increased risk that a senior diplomat would be replaced upon a change of governing party in London. Members of Parliament were allowed to accept diplomatic appointments without resigning their seats. Given that, in the nineteenth century, a senior ambassadorship was regarded as being on a par with membership of the cabinet, Members of Parliament kept a keen eye on these opportunities. Others were reluctant ambassadors who only accepted resident roles overseas in the hope of later securing a better job at home. Diplomats were drawn principally from the aristocracy and the landed gentry: only they could afford sufficiently to supplement their official salary to run a mission that would command the attention and respect of the court to which they were accredited. The head of mission was entirely responsible for housing his mission. He invariably leased one of the grandest houses that he could afford from a noble family in the host capital and paid the rent from an allowance within his salary. The sovereign, and later the British government, did no more than provide him with a large quantity of silver, and sometimes gilt, plate (i.e. tableware); a large bible, an altar cloth and some furniture for an embassy chapel; and a royal coat of arms to install above the door.[2]

The diplomatic corps, which comprised all serving British diplomats, was informally structured and loosely managed. The resident mission was its basic structural unit. The head of mission, whether ambassador or minister, was for a long time alone in being formally appointed and paid. Later, the government posted an official secretary to each mission, and in due course paid his salary. The secretary's main role was to act as chargé d'affaires during the head of mission's absences: between these times he had little, if anything, to do. All other members of a mission's staff, like attachés, private secretaries, interpreters, protégés and servants were selected and paid by the head of mission. Together with his family, friends and relations, private household and retainers, and a chaplain, an ambassador might take to his post a party of twenty or more people. Most attachés did simple chores in the chancery in return for the hospitality given them by their head of mission, although a few of them became officially paid after 1815. The secretaries and attachés often lived in the mission house: even if they lodged elsewhere, many a head of mission insisted that his staff should lunch and dine at his table. The mission therefore operated much like an extended family. At the end of a head of mission's posting, everybody except the secretary, and everything except the archives, would move on to his next post or back to Britain, and his successor would start all over again.

The first permanent embassy houses – Constantinople, Tehran and Paris
Ambassadors and ministers rented their own mission houses. Throughout
the eighteenth century, successive British ambassadors to the Ottoman
Empire rented the same house in Constantinople from the Timoni family
near the top of the hill in Pera, an aristocratic suburb on the north side of
the Golden Horn. By 1799, when Thomas Bruce, seventh Earl of Elgin,
arrived as ambassador, this house was too decrepit to be habitable. Elgin
was fortunate in being able to lodge for his first two years in the empty
French embassy house but was obliged to move out when the French
mission returned at the end of 1801. Elgin lamented that he had then had
to move 'to a wretched house the habitation of M. Pisani [the embassy's
chief dragoman/interpreter]. It is far from sufficient to contain all my family,
several of whom are distributed in other buildings, a circumstance of great
danger, and inconvenience'.[3] Elgin therefore set about procuring a suitable
embassy house for the future. His efforts led to the British government's first
purpose-built diplomatic building, and to transforming the way that senior
British diplomats would be housed.

With Anglo-Ottoman relations in an excellent state after the defeat of
the French at the Battle of the Nile in 1798 and their subsequent expulsion
from Egypt, Sultan Selim III offered to present a site to King George III
and to build on it a fitting permanent house for the British ambassador. He
therefore bought and handed over to Elgin the decrepit old Timoni house
and land that the embassy had formerly occupied for a century. Elgin had
two reservations about the Sultan's offer: the site was not large enough to
protect a future house on it from the spread of a neighbourhood fire, and
the Turks lacked the skills to build on it an embassy house of the type and
quality that he thought fitting. The Sultan's response was to offer Elgin a
handsome sum of money with which both to enlarge the site and to build
on it a house according to Elgin's own ideas of how it should be. Thus
challenged, Elgin sketched out the design of a building based on what the
neoclassical architect Thomas Harrison had recently built for him at the
Elgin family seat at Broomhall, in Fife. He then entrusted detailed design
work on it to a Roman architectural draughtsman, Balestra, whom he was
employing in Athens in connection with his project for the 'rescue' of the
antiquities.

Elgin described the Sultan's offer to the Foreign Secretary, Lord Hawkesbury,
and explained the need for a 'fixed establishment', or permanent home, in a
country 'where personal violence is almost unrestrained, epidemical diseases
are prevalent, ministerial Houses (which are respected) certainly ought to
be so capacious as to afford an asylum, and to comprehend all the persons

requisite for the public business or the minister's private service. All other foreign missions have accordingly fixed habitations here…'.[4] Elgin had heard, indeed, that the lack of a suitable house in Constantinople had led to worthy candidates declining offers of appointment as British ambassador to the Sublime Porte, as the Grand Vizier's headquarters were referred to. Elgin seems neither to have sent any drawings to Hawkesbury nor to have received any reply: he pressed on with the project.

In a long despatch in November 1801, Elgin made far-sighted practical recommendations to ensure that the new palace, as it was now described, would be well managed and a success for future embassies. The British government, he argued, as owner of the land and house, should allot an annual sum for its upkeep and repairs. Rather than each ambassador providing all of his own equipment, as was then the requirement, certain items should be appropriated to the embassy: Elgin suggested that the government should buy and send out good and substantial furniture, including for the chapel, as well as a service of plate, royal pictures and a set of full liveries. And he argued that the government should also buy a summer residence to enable the ambassador and his staff to escape from the heat of Pera to the relative cool of the Bosphorus shore for the hot months. It so happened that the house he had leased the previous summer was on the market and he recommended its purchase. 'In fact My Lord, this has appeared to me so obviously essential, that understanding the house was on the point of being sold, I have individually given a commission to secure it. But of course Government is not on that account under any obligation to stand by my bargain'.[5] And nor did it.

By January 1802, Balestra had advanced the designs for the new palace, the old Timoni buildings on the site were being demolished and materials for the new house collected. Elgin submitted to London a long and varied list of items to be procured from England. It included mahogany dining tables 'of a full breadth' for 80 people, with 80 mahogany chairs with dark blue leather seats and brass nails; 24 handsome gilt armchairs with red damask or velvet to suit the throne in the audience chamber; mirrors and chandeliers; locks and hinges on good and sound principles for 150 doors; Wilton carpets; water closets; an iron balustrade of a light pattern for a balcony of 200 feet to extend all along the garden front; and four tons of nails. The foundation stone was laid on 18 January 1802 at a ceremony with a huge Turkish official attendance. Elgin reported the Captain Pasha, admiral of the fleet, as saying 'that it was not in the power of language to convey an adequate idea of the obligations Great Britain had rendered to Turkey', and then releasing from their chains all of his 150 or so Maltese slaves, some of whom had been held for 50 years, and handed them to British protection.[6]

The shell and roof of the large new building were nearly complete when Elgin left Constantinople in January 1803. But construction and financial problems, disquiet in London about profligacy, and a year-long suspension of Anglo-Ottoman diplomatic relations caused so many delays that the palace was not completed until 1808 **(Fig. 1.1).** The Reverend Robert Walsh, chaplain to the embassy, described the house in the 1820s.

> The palace stands nearly in the center of a demesne, including a lawn and garden of about four acres, enclosed from the streets by a high and substantial wall. It is an oblong quadrangular building of three stories, surmounted on the roof by a lofty kiosk, or square cupola, which commands a most extensive view of the Bosphorus, Sea of Marmora, Constantinople, and the surrounding country. It also gave light to a large hall below, which occupied the center of the building, and round which the apartments were situated. One of them is the grand hall, or reception-room. At the end stands the throne, as the representative of majesty, which no one occupied, till the arrival of the unfortunate Queen Caroline [at the time of her visit, the exiled Princess of Wales], who, in her Oriental wanderings, had visited Constantinople. During her short sojourn she visited the room every day, and, as an old domestic informed me, was frequently seen weeping, with her head resting on her hands, sitting on the steps of this throne.[7]

1.1. The 'English palace' at Pera, started by the seventh Earl of Elgin in 1801 to a design that he based on his Scottish home.

Elgin's English palace was thus the first diplomatic building overseas to be owned by the British government. Although three times extensively rebuilt as a result of fires, the house remains in use as the British consulate-general in Istanbul.

The second building to come into the government's ownership, again through construction, was at Tehran. Unlike Elgin, who went to Constantinople as one of a long succession of resident British ambassadors, Sir Gore Ouseley was the first resident ambassador to be appointed to Persia in 1811. And, unlike Elgin's palace which took eight years to complete, Ouseley was able to move into his new house within a couple of years of his arrival. He had the advantage of taking with him to Tehran the Foreign Office's authority to obtain a grant of land from the Shah and to spend £8,000 on building and furnishing an embassy house. This arrangement seems likely to have owed its simplicity and generosity to the support of Charles Arbuthnot, who had spent the years 1805-7 as ambassador in Constantinople battling to complete Elgin's palace and being forced to dig deep into his own fortune to do so. Arbuthnot was now joint secretary to the Treasury and in a position to help others avoid the financial penalty he had suffered. The Shah duly stripped one of his generals of his land and presented it to Ouseley. It lay just south of the main bazaar and became known as the Bāgh-I Īlchī, Garden of the Ambassador. The area is still sometimes called that today.

The scholarly Ouseley was his own architect, and had previous experience. Ten years earlier, as a major serving in India, he had designed for the Wazir of Oudh the Dilkushā palace at Lucknow, modelling it on Vanbrugh's Seaton Delaval in Northumberland. The site in Tehran was awkwardly shaped, hemmed in by mud houses and bisected by a public street but Ouseley managed, with simplicity and elegance, to lay out an axis that controlled the siting of his tall single-storey house, and a number of ancillary buildings, courts and gardens **(Fig. 1.2)**. The house itself was approached through an entrance building, across a rectangular grassed court, and up a wide, shallow flight of steps on to a terrace with a classical portico supported on six slim columns. The new house was clearly designed to project the authority of His Majesty's ambassador. Its strong appearance and formal plan arrangement contrasted sharply with the muddle and mud of the surrounding native area. Over time, some of the huddles of adjacent buildings were bought direct from their owners and converted for chancery and consulate, quarters for attachés, and stabling.

Ouseley and his staff moved into the completed embassy house in December 1813. It was the first house that any foreign mission had been allowed to build in Persia and it drew admiring remarks from the outset.

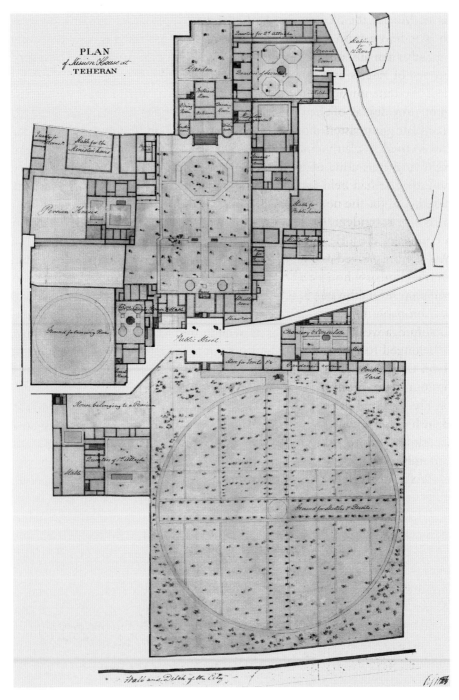

1.2. Site plan of the legation buildings at Tehran, surveyed by a Monsieur Bovagnet in 1860. Sir Gore Ouseley's original embassy house is at the top, with formal rooms grouped round a large terrace, and private quarters in the adjacent courtyard building. A public street bisected the site.

James Morier, the official Secretary of embassy, wrote four days after moving in 'The house, with its white columns and its clean, tall facade glitters more brightly than any other building in Tehran … it stands out among the mud houses of rascals and fishwives which surround it'[8] **(Fig. 1.3).** Ouseley described the impact of his entertaining style on his first Persian ministerial guests 'my display of chandeliers and lustres with spermaceti candles, and my fine plate quite astonished them – but a good English grate and a rousing fire seemed to claim almost equal admiration'.[9] Ouseley left Tehran in the following year: none of his successors until 1944 carried the ambassadorial rank that he had held, but he bestowed a fine legation house on them that lasted, just, for the next 50 years.

In Paris, resident ambassadors had rented their own embassy houses for a couple of centuries before Arthur Wellesley, newly created first Duke of Wellington, arrived as ambassador in August 1814 and walked straight into the first embassy house to be bought by the British government. Wellington had seen several houses in Paris in June, of which he liked best, but thought was probably too large, 39 rue du Faubourg St Honoré, which Quentin Craufurd, a wealthy dilettante Scot who lived in Paris, had taken him to see. It belonged to Napoleon's youngest sister, Pauline Borghese, who had put it on the market because she doubted that the restored Bourbons would honour their promise to let the Bonapartes keep their property. While briefly in London in July, Wellington had arranged in principle for the British government to buy a permanent home in Paris for the embassy. Charles Arbuthnot, still at the Treasury and a close friend of the duke, almost certainly assisted in this arrangement, as he had for Tehran.

Wellington left it to Sir Charles Stuart, the minister in Paris, to decide

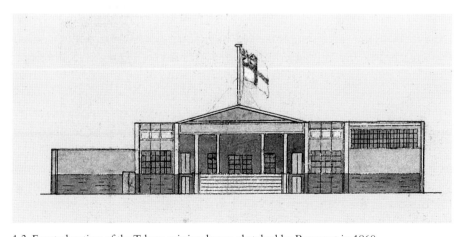

1.3. Front elevation of the Tehran mission house, sketched by Bovagnet in 1860.

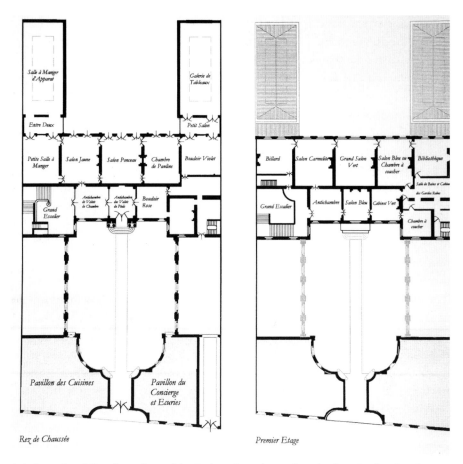

1.4. Ground and first floor plans of the Paris embassy house, bought from Pauline Borghese in 1814, with room names at that time. The site has an average width of 35 metres and is nearly 200 metres long. (North is to the bottom.)

which house the government should buy. Stuart, like Wellington, favoured Pauline's house and appointed Quentin Craufurd to negotiate its purchase. Craufurd and Stuart were both connoisseurs and collectors and it was their recommendation that led to the inclusion in the sale of many of the house's contents. Pauline was at the time in Naples, on the way to joining her brother on Elba, and relied on her Intendant General, J-P.L Michelot, to negotiate for her. She wanted a million francs for the house, its contents and the stables round the corner on Rue d'Anjou, but was in a poor bargaining position. Craufurd negotiated Michelot down to 861,000 francs (about £46,500 at the time) and the principals accepted that figure. The deal was sufficiently done for Wellington to move into the house on the day of his arrival in Paris on 22 August 1814 and was finalised on 24 October. The purchase, which was made in several instalments, was funded by the King's civil list and Wellington received the Prince Regent's 'gracious approbation of the terms of the contract with which you have entered in H.R.H. name'.[10] It was a splendid purchase and the house remains to this day one of the jewels in the crown of Britain's diplomatic buildings overseas.

The house was almost 100 years old at the time of its purchase. By the 1720s, the rue du Faubourg Saint Honoré had become one of the most desirable streets in Paris and some of the finest *hôtels particuliers* to emerge from the Regency period were rising along it. The Charost family built no. 39 between 1722 and 1725. Their architect, Jean Antoine Mazin, was relatively new to fashionable house building but what he may have lacked in spatial ingenuity he made up for in more solid construction than most of his peers. Even so, the Hôtel de Charost must have been in a sorry state when Pauline Borghese, just re-married and short of funds, bought it with borrowed money for 300,000 francs from the duchesse de Charost in 1803. With the aid of fashionable architects, Pauline transformed the appearance of the house through new decorations, introducing the deep hues of the Napoleonic era, and furniture commissioned from leading designers and craftsmen.

With the proclamation of the First Empire in 1804, Pauline became an Imperial Princess and her house an official royal residence. In 1809, Napoleon paid off her debts and settled a substantial income on her. She could now afford to commission the architect P-N. Bénard to enlarge her apartment on the ground floor by building two wings projecting into the garden, the eastern for a dining room to seat 60 people and the western for a picture gallery in which she hung 175 paintings from her Borghese husband's collection in Rome. (He, when in Paris, was confined to the lesser of the two first-floor apartments.) Pauline herself lived comparatively little in the house and she never saw it again after she left Paris in June 1812 **(Fig. 1.4)**.

Wellington only lived in the house for five months, during which he used it royally. He left in January 1815 as British Plenipotentiary to the Congress of Vienna and in March, after Napoleon landed back in France, went to Brussels to assemble an Allied army. The embassy house was put into the care of the bankers, Perregaux. The battle of Waterloo was in June; Stuart returned to Paris as ambassador and re-opened the house in July; Napoleon went into exile in August; and Wellington became Commander-in-Chief of the Army of Occupation in October. For the three years of this appointment, he lived close to the Hôtel de Charost in the house that is now the American embassy. He then returned to politics in England.

Consular background before 1825
As the role of diplomats developed in the fifteenth and sixteenth centuries, so did that of consuls emerge at seaports in the Mediterranean and Baltic to regulate merchant shipping and arbitrate commercial disputes. By the seventeenth century, British consuls were to be found in most parts of the world as British merchants followed the fleet to open up new markets. Consuls became officials of the state, or public servants, in 1649 when Cromwell's Act of Parliament constituting the Council of State authorised the employment of consuls to 'advise, order and direct concerning the entertaining, kepeing, renewing or settling of Amity and a good Correspondencie with Forreigne Kingdomes and States, and for preserving the rights of the people of this Nation in Forreigne parts, and Composeing of their differences there'.

Although some consuls were drawn from the same levels of society as most diplomats, most of them were made of rougher stuff, had fewer resources and had to reside in more challenging places than diplomats. Three types of consul emerged: salaried, unsalaried and Company. By 1790, about 60 salaried consuls and vice-consuls staffed about 45 consulates, roughly two-thirds of them around the Mediterranean. There were at least as many unsalaried consuls around the world who funded their consular activities by levying their own fees or trading on their own accounts. The Company consuls were employed by the trading companies, chiefly the Levant Company in the Ottoman lands and the East India Company in Asia, to which the British government had delegated responsibility for the staffing and funding of consular representation in their areas of monopolistic influence. Each consul derived his authority from a patent, called an exequatur, issued by his host country's head of state: the exequatur ensured that the consul's powers would be recognised throughout his consular area and guaranteed him certain rights and privileges.

The organisation of consuls and their work was astonishingly haphazard, unjust and disorderly. Consular posts often arose for ill-defined reasons, guidance was minimal, there was no career structure, and no means of forcing the retirement of played-out men. Most of the appointments, especially to the pleasanter posts, were in the private patronage of the Secretary of State, and jockeying was required to get on the list that he kept. In the least-favoured posts, the consuls were responsible for finding their own replacements. Members of Parliament had to resign their seats before taking up consular appointments, which few therefore did. Once arrived at a Post, and that fact confirmed to London, there was no obligation upon the consul to report anything further. Salaries, if paid, varied widely and often bore no relation to the demands of the job. Although salaried consuls were not permitted to trade, they had a general permission to act as agents for the Post Office, Lloyds and the mail steamers. Unsalaried consuls were left to act largely at their own discretion, which was often an unsuitably flexible instrument for a public service. British consuls did not have to be British: in several Levantine cities, local families passed the office of vice-consul from father to son for generations.

Leave was in theory available, most of it unpaid, but no travelling expenses were payable, even from the Far East. Some consuls therefore remained at their Posts for decades at a time. Many of their locations were remote, lonely and unhealthy, and some were dangerous. The files are full of harrowing letters from neglected and sick consuls and the cursory, unsympathetic bureaucratic replies they eventually received from London. Mortality rates for consuls and their families were extraordinarily high. Consuls had to find whatever accommodation they could, and it was often awful. Such allowances as were payable to rent and staff their consulates were only lightly controlled so that some consuls spent as little as possible and pocketed the balance, which made matters worse. Furniture bought from allowances was too easily regarded as the consul's personal property, which he sold either to his successor or into the local market to help fund his return to Britain.

No serious attempt was made to bring order to these chaotic circumstances until George Canning, Foreign Secretary, introduced a Consular Act in 1825. It described the principal duty of a consul as 'to protect and promote the lawful trade and trading interests of Great Britain by every fair and proper means'. The Act transferred the costs of the consular service from the sovereign's civil list to a departmental Vote, which parliament could scrutinise. Other intentions of the Act included creating a proper consular service and a consular department within the Foreign Office to administer it; ending the practice of consuls trading on their own accounts and introducing prescribed scales of chargeable fees; and defining the hierarchy of appointments, with consuls-general as the most senior officers, consuls in the middle and vice-consuls as junior officers. These admirable provisions of the 1825 Consular Act laid the foundations for an efficient Consular Service but they took almost 50 years effectively to fulfil.

The consular corps was separate from the diplomatic corps and the two corps rarely overlapped, geographically, functionally or socially, before about 1800: nearly all diplomats were in capital cities and consuls were mainly in seaports and trading posts. Diplomatic work was definably different from commercial and consular work, and consuls were in all respects subordinate to diplomats. Where members of both corps were posted in the same city, at Constantinople or Lisbon for example, the embassy or legation and the

1.5. A site close to the old sea-gate at Tunis was occupied by the British consulate from about 1650 until 2004. The consulate building shown in this 1990s photograph was built in 1915, to replace a predecessor of 1830.

consulate were separately housed in different parts of the city. No wonder that DCM Platt called his 1971 pioneering study of British consuls *The Cinderella Service*.

The consuls who came closest to being diplomats, or vice-versa, were those posted in North Africa along the Barbary coast, where parts of what are now Libya, Tunisia and Algeria were autonomous provinces of the Ottoman Empire from the sixteenth to the nineteenth centuries. Tripoli, Tunis, Algiers and Tangier were the home ports of the pirates who ventured in their corsairs as far as Iceland to raid coastal towns, capture merchant vessels and take Christian prisoners for ransom. British consuls were first appointed in these ports in the middle of the seventeenth century to work for the suppression of this piracy and later to ensure supplies to Gibraltar and the fleet. The role of these consuls tended to be as much diplomatic as consular because of the continuous potential for political upset with the local rulers and possibly with Constantinople.

The Barbary consuls were the first to receive regular salaries and allowances as though they were diplomats: these were fixed by 1754. The rulers, who had uncommonly close contacts with the consuls, were the first to provide them with permanent consulate houses. The first recipient of all was probably the consul at Tunis, to whom was ceded in about 1650 the use of a building just inside the walls, beside the sea-gate: the Bey kept the building in good repair in return for a rent **(Fig. 1.5)**. In Tripoli, a building was granted by the reigning Karamanlis family under a perpetual lease in 1742 at a fixed and invariable ground rent. In Tangier, the Sultan donated a building in 1783, for which he also paid the costs of maintenance. These arrangements were never clearly set out and recorded but the consul in Tunis explained the background in 1877 that

> owing to the rules observed by the Tunisian Govt. when the Christian powers first appointed Consular officers in the Regency it furnished them with houses as guests for which they pay an annual Rent. All the Consulates therefore appertain to the Govt. but by prescription each Consulate is considered to be especially destined as the residence of the Consul of the nationality to whom it was originally given.[11]

With this form of tenure, which amounted to a perpetual lease provided that the political balance was not destroyed, the Barbary consuls were relieved of the need to find and manage their own accommodation long before any head of a diplomatic mission. Although these properties were never owned by the British government, some of them proved long lasting. The Tunis site, first occupied in about 1650, was only handed back to the Tunisian authorities at the beginning of the twenty-first century. The Tripoli site also served well: the British consulate occupied it from 1742 until evacuating the city in 1940.

The leased Barbary consular houses were obviously of traditional local arrangement: two floors looking inwards over a square open courtyard surrounded by a veranda at first-floor level. Entrance, stables, stores, servants and kitchen were on the ground floor; the consul's reception rooms and bedrooms, and his office with a vice-consul and clerks, on the first floor. The Tripoli house was described, at the end of the nineteenth century, as having an aggressively blank exterior but 'inside it was a delightful Moorish palace, with patios and hanging galleries, bananas, palms and flowers, rich carpets, and an array of curiosities, classic and mediaeval'.[12]

Background to the Foreign Office

The diplomatic and consular corps both long pre-dated the Foreign Office. Throughout the seventeenth and eighteenth centuries, diplomats and consuls conducted most of their dealings with London through the sovereign's two secretaries of state and their under-secretaries. One of the secretaries of state ran the Southern Department and administered foreign relations with the southern, predominantly Catholic, European Powers, as well as covering Irish, American and Home affairs. The other ran the Northern Department and administered foreign relations with the northern, predominantly Protestant, European Powers. The workload of the two departments was rationalised by the reforming Civil List Act of 1782 when the Southern Department became the Home Office, and foreign relations were brought together in the Northern Department, which became the Foreign Office. Only Irish and colonial affairs did not fit into this arrangement and instead devolved upon the elder of the two secretaries of state. A third secretary of state, for war, was appointed in 1794 and colonial affairs were transferred to his responsibility in 1801.

From 1782, therefore, the diplomatic and consular corps, although each retained its separate status, were both administered by the same secretary of state in the Foreign Office. Early Foreign Secretaries were supported by two under-secretaries. The practice became for one of them to be a permanent official, still referred to today as the Permanent Under-Secretary, and the other to be the Secretary of State's own political appointee who could act for him with greater confidentiality. In 1797, the Foreign Office comprised 24 staff: the Secretary of State, the two under-secretaries, two assistant under-secretaries, the chief clerk, nine subordinate clerks, and some domestic staff including chamber keepers and a lamplighter. Salaries were low but the staff had various other emoluments, including a share of treaty presents each time that a treaty was signed. The most curious of the arrangements was the agency system under which members of the Foreign Office privately undertook to attend to the affairs, and perhaps interests, of individual diplomats and consuls overseas, including collecting and forwarding their client's salary and allowances and handling his mail, in return for regular payment not exceeding one per cent of the client's salary. These agency fees added appreciably to the income of the clerks, especially the chief clerk, and were not abolished until 1870.

In its early years, the work of the Foreign Office was mainly confined to Europe. Most of the relations with Turkey and the Ottoman Empire were in the hands of the Levant Company until it was wound up in 1825, and with India and the East in the hands of the East India Company until it was likewise wound up in 1858. The pace of life was not fast: nor did it need to be. It took three days for a despatch to reach London from Paris and six weeks from Constantinople, meaning that three exchanges a year with the ambassador in Turkey was the practicable maximum. Even so, ambassadors and ministers frequently complained of the lack of answers or instructions from London. Practically all of the business done by the Foreign Office was done by the Secretary of State himself, generally working at home. The secretaries organised the paperwork: it was no part of their task to offer advice to the Foreign Ssecretary. The clerks did the copying, in manuscript, and the filing. The chief clerk gradually became responsible for all of the non-political business of the office, including expenditure, accounts, records, passports, internal management and discipline. The Foreign Office was housed in an increasing variety of converted and often ramshackle town houses in the Whitehall area from its formation until the completion in 1867 of the 'kind of national palace' that it still occupies today.[13]

The first half of the nineteenth century witnessed the Crown's gradual withdrawal from active political life, the emergence of an alternating two-party system of government, and the refinement of a permanent and professional civil service. These developments led to the decline both of patronage and of the role that the private wealth of diplomats played in running Britain's diplomatic effort. The Foreign Office gradually gained ascendancy, both political and financial, over the diplomatic and consular corps. Interchange of personnel between the three bodies began in the middle of the nineteenth century but each corps retained its formal independence from the Foreign Office until well into the twentieth century.

By 1815, the Treasury found itself the owner of three embassy houses – in Constantinople, Tehran and Paris – but it made no arrangements to ensure that these large and expensive buildings would be kept in good repair. As it was, the ambassadors met the costs of unavoidable maintenance work, generally carried out badly and expensively by unsupervised local artisans. The ambassadors were sometimes successful in recouping the costs from the Foreign Office or the Treasury but London had no idea whether a piece of work had been worthwhile or well done, or was a reasonable charge on the king's purse, or what future costs might be in store.

The Treasury's rude awakening to the financial implications of the government owning civil property overseas occurred in Paris about ten years after the purchase of Pauline's house. Her architect, Bénard, had made two such large openings in the south wall when building her new dining room and gallery wings in 1810 that in 1822 the vaults beneath began to subside and the house to crack. Local architects, Damèsme and Bonnerie, propped up the structure with timber as best they could. In 1824, the ambassador asked for an estimate for a more permanent restoration and sent the resultant figure, about £3,600, to London. The Treasury was alarmed and turned to the Office of Works for advice.

2

Enter the Office of Works 1824–1856

Background to the Office of Works

The origins of the Office of Works lay in the medieval royal household, in which it was responsible for the construction and maintenance of royal castles, fortifications and other 'King's Works'. By the early seventeenth century, the Office of Works was headed by a Surveyor-General and he controlled a substantial and diverse design and construction workload. Inigo Jones held this post from 1615 to 1643, during which he most famously built the Queen's House at Greenwich and the Banqueting House in Whitehall Palace. After the Restoration, the Office of Works began dealing with major public buildings in London, and undertaking construction works associated with state ceremonial occasions like coronations and royal funerals. The Surveyor and the Comptroller, the two leading professional staff, were appointed from among the leading surveyors (a term which still included architects) of the day. Sir Christopher Wren was Surveyor from 1669 until 1718 and John Vanbrugh was Comptroller from 1702 until his death in 1726. Robert Adam and William Chambers were jointly appointed architect of the King's Works in 1761.

Under the same Civil List Act that brought the Foreign Office into existence in 1782, the Office of Works was remodelled within the reorganised Royal Household. Chambers was promoted to a new Surveyor-General role, in which he completed his masterpiece, Somerset House, the year before his death in 1796. He was succeeded by James Wyatt, whose chronic administrative shortcomings, coupled with his enormous private workload, left the Office of Works in a state of chaos when he died, penniless, in 1813. In consequence, an Act of 1814 remodelled the Office, and the Treasury saw fit to decree that it be headed by a full-time Surveyor-General who was not a surveyor by profession. Colonel Benjamin Charles Stephenson was appointed to this role, answerable to Parliament through the Chancellor of the Exchequer. His staff comprised an assistant surveyor, a cashier, ten or so clerks, and five clerks of works. To provide professional architectural input, the Treasury appointed three 'attached architects', each of whom would receive a retaining fee and a percentage on official work carried out under his direction: John Nash, John Soane and, 25 years younger, Robert Smirke. Nash saw their division of work this way, as he reportedly told Soane: 'Our appointments are perfectly constitutional. I the King, you the Lords, and *your* friend Smirke the Commons'.[1] These three architects, though distracted by their large private practices, undertook most of the Office of Works' commissions between 1815 and 1835. Nash was the most prolific: he laid out the whole Regent's Park and Regent Street area and designed the extensive terraces, as well as Clarence House, Buckingham Palace, Marble Arch and much else. Soane was comparatively inactive as an attached architect. Smirke's Office of Works commissions included the British Museum and the Post Office.

Stephenson's assistant surveyor, the only full-time architect in government service, was Robert Browne, succeeded in 1823 by Henry Hake Seward. Neither was a match for the attached architects who, being men of importance in their own right, had direct access to sources of influence and were in consequence hard to control. The assistant surveyor role became little more than a channel of communication between the Treasury and the attached architects. Meanwhile, Stephenson's own responsibilities as Surveyor-General widened. Although the 1814 Act had provided for the revenue departments' buildings to be placed under the Office of Works, the Treasury did not enforce this provision. When, however, in 1825 the central portion of the vast London Custom House by David Laing collapsed from foundation failure only eight years after its completion, the Treasury entrusted the rebuilding to the Office of Works and Smirke. The Office's responsibilities were further extended in 1828 when the tasks of supplying furniture, fittings and supplies (like coal, wood, oil, candles and soap) for official buildings were transferred to it from the Lord Chamberlain's Department.

The attached architect arrangement was discontinued in 1832 when the Office of Works became part of the cumbersome Office of His Majesty's Woods, Forests, Land Revenues, Works and Buildings. Stephenson was promoted to a Commissioner in the enlarged organisation, and Seward became Surveyor of Works and Buildings, succeeded by William Southcote Inman in 1844. James Pennethorne, Nash's professional heir, became the sole architect and surveyor in 1845, working on commission.

Maintenance at Paris, 1824-1856

When the Treasury turned to the Office of Works in 1824 for advice on the extent of restoration work necessary at the embassy house in Paris, it was the first time that it involved the Office in a civil building overseas. The Office responded by asking Robert Smirke to visit Paris and report on the state of the house. He found that there was a considerable maintenance backlog and he particularly warned that work was urgently required on the two wings. This work was approved by the Treasury but, before it could be carried out, Lord Granville succeeded Sir Charles Stuart as ambassador and was much more concerned about what he saw as deficiencies in the furnishing of the house, to which 'it does not appear that the attention of Mr. Smirke has been particularly called.' Granville therefore asked for another visitor to come and advise on putting 'the hotel in a condition fit for the residence of His Majesty's Ambassador'.[2] Lewis Wyatt, a nephew of James Wyatt and a clerk of works in the Office of Works, was accordingly sent to Paris in early 1825. He concluded that about £25,000 would be required to restore the house and stables, repair and replace furniture, and build the chapel that the ambassador had requested at the end of the garden.

The Treasury was aghast and decided to sell the house straightaway. Granville dissuaded it from that course by rubbishing the estimate and pointing out, in any event, that renting a suitable alternative house would be much more expensive. The Treasury instead limited expenditure to £12,000 for the house and furniture and forbade the chapel. Louis Visconti, later the designer of the Nouveau Louvre, was appointed as architect and the restoration of the two wings went ahead. Visconti also added a new glazed gallery that ran alongside both wings and linked them across the garden front of the house **(Fig. 2.1).** The outturn cost was about 50 per cent more than the Treasury had stipulated. Granville and Visconti both apologised and the Treasury accepted Granville's later offer to pay £1,500 himself for some of the furniture. He was highly pleased with the architectural outcome and celebrated with a ball in January 1826. Lady Granville, sister of the Duke of Devonshire and used to the scale of Chatsworth, wrote in letters home that

> My house ... looks more brilliant and enormous than I can describe. I have asked eleven hundred and fifty, and as the Russians and several great mournings in private families have brought me a number of excuses, I have

2.1. The garden front of the Paris embassy house, formerly Pauline Borghese's *hôtel particulier*. She enlarged her apartment on the garden side of the ground floor by building the two projecting wings in 1810, between which Visconti built the glazed gallery in 1825.

no fear of a crowd. We open the *rez de chaussée* – the *serre* with a carpet doubled of scarlet cloth, eighteen lustres with lamps and six divans, the same temperature as the rooms, with all the doors and windows taken off in the ball and drawing rooms. Three *salons au premier*, five whist-tables in the *salon vert*, *écarté*, newspapers and books of prints in the state *couleur de paille* bedroom. A buffet below in the first dining room till supper. At one the large dining room open with hot and cold supper.[3]

Chastened by the costs of the house, the Treasury posted the Hon. Frederick Byng to Paris in 1830 to keep a tight rein on expenditure and supervise the accounts. With the appointment the following year of a new local architect, I Silveyra, to carry out regular inspections and supervise all repair works, it looked as though effective management might be in place. But in 1835, Granville, at the start of his third incumbency as ambassador, called for an estimate of the cost 'for rescuing the interior of the hotel from its present degraded state'.[4] Silveyra reported that the building fabric was mainly in adequate condition but the bitumen with which the wings had been roofed only ten years earlier should be replaced, and about £1,000 needed to be spent on the interiors. This time it was the Foreign Secretary, Lord Palmerston, who decided that the embassy house should be sold: over £30,000 had been spent on repairs since it was bought 20 years earlier. Granville again successfully contested this conclusion and Palmerston reluctantly authorised £2,500, a third of which was for roofing the wings in copper (which he insisted be bought in England).

The outturn cost in 1839 was once more about 50 per cent greater than the authorisation. Granville's apologies and explanations this time failed to carry conviction. The Treasury proposed to the Office of Works that it should, as an experiment, take over responsibility for the Paris house. The commissioners agreed on condition that the same arrangements would apply in Paris as already governed their management of public buildings in England. This meant that all works should be properly estimated and requisitioned, all accounts should be rendered quarterly, no exceedings entertained unless pre-agreed, and an English architect should make periodic inspections. The Treasury and Palmerston readily agreed to this stern regime. Granville, in his fifteenth year as ambassador, and correctly assuming that fault was being imputed to him, agreed grudgingly.

The Office of Works asked the architect Decimus Burton, whom it regarded highly for his reliability and professionalism, to report. He first visited Paris in June 1840 and his findings were thorough but not dramatic. He had found no plans of the house, so had made nine drawings of his own; he thought a new inventory was needed, not least to distinguish between the ambassador's and the government's items; he proposed that 'articles only for fully and handsomely furnishing the Reception rooms [should be] supplied by Government and that those required for the domestic apartments [should be] provided by the Ambassador and ... be taken at a valuation by his successor'.[5] Palmerston pressed for Burton's recommendations to be put into effect but, before they could be acted upon, Granville was succeeded in late 1841 by Lord Cowley, brother of the Duke of Wellington, who considered the house to be in such bad condition 'that it was impossible to live in it'.[6] Cowley and Burton accordingly adjusted the programme to suit Cowley's revised priorities and the next ten years saw a relatively stable managerial routine. Burton, as supervising architect, made annual inspections, reporting to the commissioners after each visit and providing them with an estimate of the costs of repairs which it would be sensible to carry out during the following year. Silveyra prepared and oversaw the contract work. Burton was making arrangements for his 1851 annual visit when he was told by the Office of Works, without explanation, that no official inspection would be required that year. He regretted 'only the circumstance of having been uncourteously displaced, without the usual favour of an explanation or notice of any kind from the Board'.[7]

The tendency for ambassadorial views to oscillate resumed after Burton's departure. The Marquess of Normanby, who succeeded Cowley, moved the chapel from the state dining room to the ballroom, only to be succeeded in 1852 by Cowley's son, who argued the case for returning the chapel to the dining room on the grounds that it was more seemly for worship to share space with eating than dancing. More fundamentally, however, the younger Cowley found huge fault with the house and prompted the Foreign Secretary, fleetingly the Earl of Malmesbury, to tell the Office of Works that he knew from his own inspection of the house that 'the present state of the Embassy is so indecently dirty as to render it unfit to be inhabited by Her Majesty's Ambassador, and, in truth, reflects but little credit on the British nation; and that it is important that no time should be lost in remedying this evil'.[8]

The Office of Works was nonplussed. The First Commissioner, Lord John Manners, tried pleading economy measures but suggested that Benedict Albano, a London architect who had proved his worth to the Office of Works at Madrid, should visit Paris straightaway to survey and report. Albano put in hand another programme of repairs, mainly to the interiors and furnishings. He discharged Silveyra and the upholsterer, Isouard, and remained in Paris himself as resident architect for the next two years, during which the interiors of the house moved another step away from clean Empire towards enriched Victorian, a process of which Queen Victoria approved when she visited the house in August 1855. Not long after Albano departed, Henry Hunt was sent from the Office of Works to survey the house in 1856. Not for the first time, and far from the last, a new visitor from London reported, or was persuaded to report, that much needed to be done to the house.

Fire at Pera and planning new embassy house, 1831-1843

While the Paris embassy house was presenting maintenance problems, a far greater difficulty had beset Elgin's palace at Pera in Constantinople. The ambassador, Sir Robert Gordon, gave a grand *fête* on the Giant's Mountain on 2 August 1831, and all the domestic staff had left the palace to attend. The Rev. Robert Walsh, obliged to attend a funeral on that day, remained at Pera. When he first saw the fire, it was consuming just a few houses down the hill about half a mile from the embassy but, when he returned from the funeral,

> I found the fire had travelled so fast that it had arrived at the palace-gate before me, having nearly consumed all the intermediate houses in its way. ... [A] fierce and sudden gust of wind seemed to drive the whole body of fire directly on the palace. It came on roaring like a vast furnace, and enveloped us all in a dark and lurid-looking flame. When the obscurity dispersed all the trees of the garden and the edifice itself burst into a vast and sudden blaze. Accompanied by one of the officers of the Acteon I now ran back

to the palace, in the hope of saving the archives, ... but [the door] was fast locked. We made several attempts by rushing against it to burst it open, but it resisted all our efforts. The flames were now roaring out of the windows, and having no hope of being able to render any service in this way, I hastily left the palace to look after an object [his daughter] even more precious to me than the archives of an empire. I had scarcely found her, terrified and alone, when the roof of the palace fell in with a crash. A vast column of smoke and flame ascended from the centre, and in twenty minutes from the time the fire seized it, the noble palace was no more.[9]

Four months later, John Henry Mandeville, the acting minister, reported to Palmerston that the title deeds to the embassy house were burned in the fire but he had recently received re-confirmation from the Sultan that the land was British property. Mandeville thought that the foundations of the palace, on which Lord Elgin had spent so much of his financial allocation, were perfectly good. He mentioned that, although the fire had been so severe that no public property could be saved, 11 pieces of melted silver dug out of the ruins had been deposited with a bank in Galata. Twelve years later, upon learning that the bank had failed and the sacks were back in the chancery, the Foreign Office asked for the silver remains to be sent back to London, where they eventually arrived in May 1846. The rebuilding of the Pera palace took considerably longer.

Sir John Ponsonby arrived in Constantinople as ambassador in 1832 and chose to live on the Bosphorus at Therapia in the summer residence that the Sultan had made available to the embassy in 1829 and into which Gordon had moved after the Pera fire. Plans and estimates by Signor Peverata, the embassy's local architect, for rebuilding the embassy house at Pera were sent to the Treasury in early 1833, but were not followed up and Peverata died soon afterwards. Ponsonby was comfortable at Therapia and in no mood to hasten rebuilding at Pera. But the Treasury and Palmerston were looking further ahead and, in March 1834, despatched to Constantinople an officer of the Royal Engineers, Captain Harry D. Jones, to prepare plans and estimates for three options. These were to rebuild on the same site at Pera; to build anew on a site close to Pera, funded by the proceeds of selling the Pera site; and similarly on a site at Therapia, to be designated by Ponsonby.

Jones reported later in 1834 that he had been unable to find a suitable site to buy in the immediate neighbourhood of Pera, and so had only pursued the other two options. His main concern, however, was that it was practically impossible to make estimates in the local circumstances.

Under this despotic Government, the Public Departments only are engaged in the erection of large edifices of a permanent nature, and where detailed

> estimates are never required ... Such undertakings [as ours] are considered by
> the Persons employed as so many favourable opportunities for reimbursing
> themselves for the losses they have sustained by non-payment for Work
> performed for individuals holding high situations under the Government: it
> is therefore evident, that the actual cost of a Building, or the prices paid for
> the Materials, are not to be obtained ...[10]

Jones therefore recommended using direct labour, with the British
government ordering materials and supervising construction, in preference
to letting contracts. He submitted the best estimates that he could manage
in the circumstances: £22,454 3s.11¾d. (the apparent accuracy resulting
from un-rounded arithmetical conversion of piastres) for a new house on
the former site at Pera, and £21,770 17s.0d., excluding the cost of land,
on a new site at Therapia. London preferred the Pera option and Jones
was sent back to Constantinople at the end of 1834 to develop his plans
further, consider how supervision would be managed and to update his
estimate. He found himself with no option but to increase his estimate for
rebuilding to about £35,000. The Treasury decided this was too much to
submit to Parliament for approval, and Jones was recalled. Ponsonby was
also objecting to any new building but failed to specify his reasons, despite
repeated requests from Palmerston to explain his thinking.

It took six years for Palmerston's patience to snap. In June 1841, he wrote
to the Treasury, during a diplomatic crisis with the Turks, that

> It appears to Her Majesty's Government that the time has now arrived when
> it is absolutely necessary that the British Embassy at the Porte should have a
> Residence within such an easy distance of Constantinople as to admit of HM
> Ambassador having frequent personal communication with the Ministers
> of the Sultan. ... The execution of Captain Jones' plans was suspended, in
> consequence of certain objections stated by Viscount Ponsonby. ... I regret
> to have to state ... that I have not received from Viscount Ponsonby the
> required information, ... I have accordingly to request your Lordships to
> direct the Commissioners [of Works] to select some competent Architect to
> proceed to Constantinople to make arrangements not only for building a
> permanent Residence ... but also for the temporary accommodation of that
> Embassy in Pera ... until the new House is fit to be occupied.[11]

The commissioners promptly selected William James Smith, the assistant
surveyor for the Crown estates in London, for the task. He had started his
architectural career in private practice and had joined the Office of Works
as a professional assistant in 1830. He spoke French and Italian, and had a
Spanish wife. Smith worked quickly on arrival in Constantinople in 1841.
Within a month or so, and despite lack of cooperation from Ponsonby, who

was on the point of leaving, leases were signed on two adjacent stone houses in Galata Serai, the old commercial town below Pera. The larger house was for residence and the smaller for chancery, both on extensible three-year terms. Smith was instructed to remain in Constantinople until Sir Stratford Canning, on his second appointment as ambassador, arrived in early 1842. In March, Smith and Canning concluded that the existing Pera site was no longer suitable for the new house because 'buildings not of the best character have been erected around and completely overlook it'.[12] Fortunately, Smith had found what he thought was a good alternative site of about 15 acres next to the Armenian cemetery and an infantry barracks at the entrance to the town of Pera. He judged that sale of the existing Pera site, which was about five acres, could fund both the purchase of the alternative site and the construction of a new building on it. Canning supported this change of plan to Lord Aberdeen, Palmerston's Tory successor as Foreign Secretary, helpfully theorising that

> To procure a place of residence already provided with suitable buildings is altogether out of the question. To find a site entirely free from inconvenience or objection is also not to be expected. The question is a mere balance of convenience and inconvenience, in which our object must be to secure as little of the one and as much of the other as possible.[13]

Aberdeen gained the Treasury's approval to the exchange of five-acre sites, and told Canning that the Sultan's unambiguous consent to the sale of the Pera site must be obtained so that it would fetch full market value. He urged Canning to keep building costs down and, in perhaps the first guidance ever issued about the image that new embassy buildings should project, warned him that the government 'do not see any occasion that the residence of the Embassy should be built with a view to ornament the Turkish Capital or to attract the attention of passengers on the Bosphorus'.[14] The Office of Works likewise cautioned Smith from spending too much 'on account of Architectural Decoration'.[15]

Smith returned to London in late 1842 and faced a barrage of questions about his expenses and why he had taken so long to get home. He said that he had redesigned the embassy house while quarantined in Malta, solved a family property problem while in Barcelona, and regretted that Mrs Smith had been in delicate health. At the end of November, he was instructed to take his design forward into working drawings and to produce an estimate of cost. At this juncture, the Office of Works asked its consultant architect, Charles Barry, then hard at work on designs for the new Houses of Parliament, to comment on Smith's proposals for Pera. The extent to which Barry caused Smith to modify his design is uncertain, but unlikely to have been more than minor. The strong probability is that, when Barry saw it, Smith's plan was already based on a courtyard, as had been Elgin's, and his design expressed in a renaissance revival manner, and that Barry suggested various alterations informed by his recently completed Reform Club building on Pall Mall, in London. The only firsthand mention of any design contribution by Barry appears to be a minor item in a collective and retrospective fee account rendered five years later, in 1848, 'for advice and assistance to altering and modifying Mr Smith's Design'.[16] On estimated costs, Barry thought that Smith's estimate of £46,000 was ample. A figure of £45,000 was therefore adopted and, assuming that sale of the Pera site would yield £12,000 more than the cost of acquiring the identified new site, an estimate of £33,000 was laid before Parliament. Aberdeen approved the design in April 1843, and asked for immediate progress. By that time, and without alteration to the estimate, an attic floor had been added to the building.

Rebuilding Pera embassy house, 1843-1856
Smith returned to Constantinople in July 1843 as the superintending architect: arrangements were made for him to be supported by a clerk of works, Luke Richardson, and two foremen for masonry and carpentry work. Soon after his arrival, Smith found that the Turkish government had withdrawn the alternative Bosphorus site in order to build a cavalry hospital on it. Smith and Canning earmarked a third site, this time of ten acres, in November 1843 but the Turkish authorities soon vetoed its development. Eventually, in June 1844, it was decided to revert to the existing Pera site, where Smith's design could be comfortably sited to rest much of its weight on Elgin's original foundations **(Fig. 2.2)**. The new building was to rise four storeys to about 70 feet at the cornice. In appearance, this 'quoined, rusticated, urbanely attired building was little different from its fashionable Italianate contemporaries in England'.[17]

Smith took possession of the site on 21 August 1844, almost exactly 13 years since the day of the fire. Construction started quite well although Elgin's foundations were soon found inadequate and had to be excavated more deeply and expensively than estimated. The First Commissioner and principal officers of the Office of Works in London from the outset nagged Smith for information, explanations and proposals. He begged them to let him proceed with less hindrance.

I need not remind the Board that the difference in the method of executing

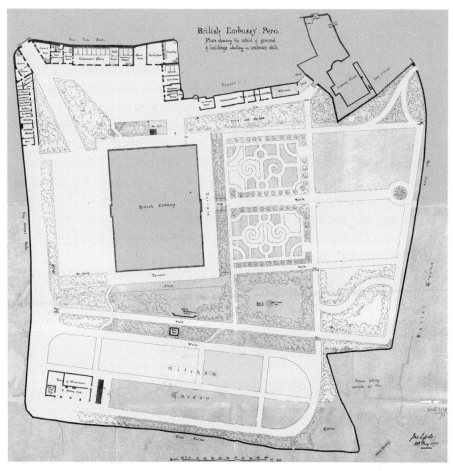

2.2. Site plan of William Smith's Pera embassy buildings, completed in 1856, with the house built partly on the foundations of Elgin's former palace. The embassy chapel is in the north-east corner. Drawn by John Lessels in 1871.

works in Turkey and in England is so exceedingly great that to attempt a reform in their system, in that respect, in an isolated instance and by a stranger, would be fraught with immense labour and, comparatively speaking, almost unbounded expense. I therefore am still of opinion, and would beg leave to propose, if it meets with the Board's approbation, to carry on the works … in the manner practiced here, and which has been adopted in the erection of the French and Russian Palaces, by the respective architects … [18]

Smith's difficulties mounted over the stonework. He had expected to obtain, and had priced for, good stone from a local quarry but access was now denied him because the Sultan's building works required all of the quarry's output. The best alternative he could find was a limestone from a quarry five hours' journey away: although the samples he sent home were unfavourably reported upon by the Museum of Economic Geology, Smith had no option but to use this stone. He found that the local labour was much less skilled than anticipated, mainly because the Sultan's building managers were luring away the better craftsmen, if not literally carrying some of them off, especially once they had been trained by Smith's English foremen. Valuable raw materials were wasted by unskilled craftsmen. Meanwhile, Smith was scheduling materials from England: '10,000 ft. of cast lead 7 lbs to the foot, exclusive of waste' and '80,000 3½ in. cut floor brads, 28 lbs per thou" and the like.[19]

Canning was sturdy in support of Smith, including when the consul-general, John Cartwright, acting for London as paymaster, complained that Smith did not provide him with enough evidence in support of claims for payment. In early 1845, he went so far as to accuse Smith of shady dealings: Canning instituted an enquiry which cleared Smith. By August 1845, one year into the job, the external walls were up to the first storey; by May 1846, many of the walls were up to cornice level and the ceiling of the saloon was being constructed; and by October 1846 the slaters were at work on the roof. At this juncture, Smith, having had no leave for over three years and feeling sick, was given permission to go to Carrara to sort out marble supplies for the grand staircase and take some recuperative leave.

Around this time, Smith was asked by the Turkish government to 'make designs' for a military hospital. With Canning's agreement, he submitted a design. He was then asked to superintend the building of his design, and trusted that the Office of Works would have no objection to this, given that 'the time which this service will occupy will be about an hour, once or twice a week, on my road to the Palace in the morning, and I hope I may be allowed to add that I have accepted it for the purpose only of being agreeable to the Turkish Government and without any thought of, or agreement for remuneration.'[20] London agreed. Thus started a sideline for Smith that did much more to secure his reputation in Turkey than building the English palace.

Smith returned from leave in spring 1847 in better health and spirits. The main structural works were by now complete, no mean achievement in 30 months with all the difficulties. 1847, however, was also the year in which progress stalled and recriminations began. With the hulk now in place, Canning began to see the need for extras, the most inconvenient and expensive of which were fireproof iron window shutters on two whole sides, for which he procured the support of Palmerston, now Foreign Secretary again. A fire in the autumn seriously damaged some of the outbuildings and destroyed materials from England, for which replacements would take months and months to arrive. Other delays were incurred by many of the *papier mâché* architectural enrichments for the state rooms arriving crushed. At the end of 1847, however, the chief obstacle to progress was financial. Smith submitted in December his estimate that completing the palace would bring the total cost of the project to about £17,000 more than the original provision of £45,000. Additionally, arranging the gardens and repairing the burned outbuildings would together cost a further £11,000. This forecast of overspend came as a significant surprise to London. Palmerston called for an enquiry and the Office of Works turned to Charles Barry again for a review of the history of the project. His report in August 1848 concluded that

> when the disadvantages and difficulties which the Architect has had to contend with, such as … [extensive list of examples] … , I must fairly say, that under these circumstances, I am surprised to find the works have been executed at a cost so little beyond the amount of the original Estimate … which, in my opinion, could not have been effected but for the judgement, discretion and constant vigilance that must have been executed on the part of the Architect.[21]

Barry's sturdy support did not stem the mounting criticisms of Smith. He retained, however, the support of Canning, who successfully pressed Palmerston to obtain a further vote of funds to keep the work going. Smith was also personally buoyed up by a request in March 1848 from high in the Sultan's court to 'allow two or three young Turks to be placed under my directions to obtain an insight into an art of which I am so humble a follower'.[22] The Office of Works again agreed that he could accept this role, which carried no payment, provided that it did not interfere with his official duties.

Canning and his family moved into the second floor of the unfinished building in October 1848, soon after his return to Constantinople after a two-year absence **(Fig. 2.3)**. His support of Smith waned from that date, as he looked for signs of progress to an early completion and saw only delays, with Smith appearing to lose resolve. Canning began to suspect that Smith and his foremen were no longer giving the palace their full attention because they were working on the side for Turkish clients. He sought to reduce the scope of the undone works by arguing for the omission of the glazed iron roof that was yet to cover the courtyard, claiming that it 'would in all likelihood turn out to be as inconvenient as it is unnecessary'. He got his way (only for it to be re-introduced in the 1860s by one of his successors).

Very little progress was made during 1849. Money was tight; work was

2.3. Garden front of William Smith's Pera house. The inscription beneath the cornice reads ÆDES LEGATIONIS ANGLICANA ÆDIFICATA VICTORIA REGNANTE ANNO DOMINE MDCCCXLIV, the year that its construction started.

sometimes suspended by London until more satisfactory explanations for cost exceedings had been provided; glass and other materials, some ordered two years previously, had not arrived from England; and Smith was finding the management of all the bits and pieces of finishing the building, and preparing for its furnishing, less to his taste and abilities than the excitement of walls and roofs. Smith was also by then responsible for work on other Office of Works projects in Constantinople. For the embassy, he was managing the leases of the temporary embassy buildings in Galata, surveying a newly donated summer residence at Therapia, and designing and rebuilding St Helena's chapel next to the Pera site. For the consulate-general at Galata, he was designing and supervising new buildings for the consulate, hospital and prison. It is not clear whether Canning was fully aware of these official distractions. There is no doubt, however, that his increasing suspicions about the Turkish client distractions were justified. Smith was steadily taking on more work from them, including possibly for Sultan Abdülmecid himself, without any longer seeking the agreement of the Office of Works and the ambassador to do so, doubtless because he knew that it would not be given now that the palace was so seriously in delay. Worse, Smith was no longer refusing offers of payment or gifts for his work for Turkish clients.

'The gentlemen attached to HM's embassy' followed their ambassador into occupation of the unfinished building in time for the winter of 1849–50. Canning was planning to use the state rooms on the first floor in April 1850, although much of the furnishings and furniture for them had not yet even been ordered from London and would take almost a year to arrive from the date of order **(Fig. 2.4).** The Foreign Office explained Palmerston's views on the scale of provision, namely that 'the Articles supplied should be handsome and substantial, but not of elaborate workmanship; that what is strictly necessary should be supplied, but that nothing superfluous should be provided; that the House should be furnished by the Public with all permanent things; but that linen, china, glass, and kitchen utensils should be found by the occupant'.[23] Canning was highly gratified that his recommendation that he be provided with an organ passed Palmerston's test of necessity.

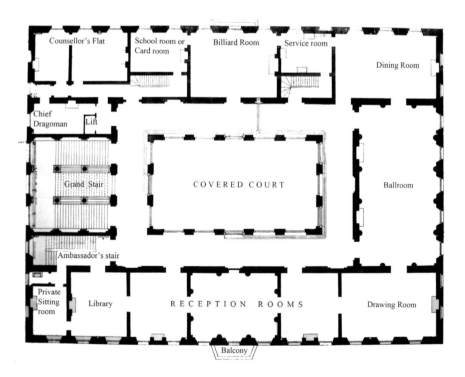

2.4. First-floor plan of William Smith's Pera house showing room use in 1906. The main reception rooms overlook the garden and the Golden Horn. (North is to the right.)

Smith was evidently on occasions still trying to placate Canning: he had to apologise to the Office of Works in October 1850 for having spent £150 on meeting, without its authorisation, several requests by Canning. As a result of this loophole, the Foreign Office's discretion to order work was removed and the full financial responsibility for Pera and Therapia accommodation was put entirely under the Office of Works' control. By then, Canning and Smith were no longer in direct communication and correspondence was only through Count Pisani, the head dragoman. Canning gave his version of Smith's and his foremen's activities and shortcomings at great length to Palmerston in December 1851. Smith gave his side of the story to the Office of Works the following month, and described the schemes he had done for the Sultan, the grand Vizier, the Porte and individual pashas and beys in the employ of government. Most of it, he said, less than truthfully in the light of Pisani's later enquiries at the Porte, without remuneration.

Smith seems to have been oblivious of the ambassador's operational requirements, which were the sole reason for building the house. In February 1852, he complained that four unfurnished rooms on the principal floor that he had been asked to hand over before they were quite ready had been used 'for dancing and dinner parties' and that nearby rooms had been used as sculleries, causing excessive dirt and filth which he felt bound to report to London. Smith also complained, in writing, to Pisani that the ambassador had told one of Smith's foremen that he would have to vacate the rooms he was occupying in the palace to make way for their intended purpose as the laundry. Canning's subsequent letter to the Foreign Secretary, briefly Granville, brought matters to a head.

> On returning this year for the fourth time to Pera [from the summer residence at Therapia], ... we called upon Mr Smith to give up to us [the area] which was intended expressly for the Laundry. He made difficulties on the ground of [there] being no other place on the premises for the Clerk of Works ... . At the end of six weeks ... I thought myself justified in apprizing Mr Smith's man ... of my intention to take possession of the rooms occupied by him, unless he left them in the course of a few days. His notification of this occurrence to Mr Smith produced the letter to Count Pisani. ...
>
> It remains for me to add that I have reason to complain of Mr Smith in other matters besides that of the Laundry. ... I have to request that these circumstances may be considered with reference to former parts of my correspondence ... . On every ground both of public interest and official consideration it is time that Mr Smith's conduct should be brought to some conclusive test.[24]

Besides Canning's onslaught, Smith was defending himself against an engineer sent to improve the heating works who alleged irregularities by Smith, and against others who accused him of improperly disposing of some surplus leaf gold. After enquiry, the Office of Works exonerated Smith but concluded that it was time to withdraw him from Constantinople. It agreed that he could return home by easy stages so as to improve his health, and it gave him back his previous job in London. Smith left Constantinople in May 1853 after ten years in the city. The Office of Works sent Robert Hayden to complete and furnish the Pera building, and an architect, Henry Pulman, to take over all the consular works at Galata. It continued to seek Smith's advice in London about all aspects of the works and furnishings in Constantinople for the next two years. The total cost of the house, including furniture, turned out at about £80,000: the Treasury ruled that the Office of Works should remain responsible for the maintenance of the building and grounds. The embassy house was finally occupied in all its glory in 1855. Canning, ennobled in 1852 as Viscount Stratford de Redcliffe, celebrated its completion, as well as the ending of the Crimean War, with a huge ball on 31 January 1856, at which Sultan Abdülmecid was guest of honour.

By the 1850s, with the Pera embassy house having been out of action for twenty years, the Tehran house deteriorating quickly, and no end in sight to the expensive maintenance nightmare of the Paris house, the British government's ownership of diplomatic buildings hardly looked like a promising proposition for the future.

3

The Treasury Tightens its Grip 1852–1876

The Office of Works, 1852-1876

The Office of Woods, Forests, Land Revenues, Works and Buildings, created in 1832, was split in two in 1851 in response to parliamentary concern that the sovereign's land revenues were being used to finance public works without any parliamentary control. One half, the new Office of Woods, Forests and Land Revenues, was left free-standing to administer the Crown's estate. The other, the Office of Parks, Palaces and Public Buildings, was put under direct Treasury control. Five centuries of the 'King's Works' thus came to an end. In 1852, by the Commissioners of Works Act, this half was reconstituted as the Office of Works with wide powers to manage its properties and to purchase, lease, exchange and sell land, with the consent in each case of the Treasury. It was headed by a First Commissioner, who was to be a Member of Parliament so that he could both answer for the government on public building issues and contribute to debates on behalf of the public. There was never any intention that he should have an interest in architecture, planning, building or the arts. The First Commissioner chaired a Board of several other ministers ex-officio but, for all practical purposes, the Board was the First Commissioner acting in concert with the secretary, who was the permanent administration head of the Office of Works.

The responsibilities of the Office of Works were gradually extended to cover other public buildings funded by Parliament, such as the Houses of Parliament, the Royal Courts of Justice and county courts, arts and sciences buildings, national museums, customs houses, coastguard buildings and post offices. Most government offices in the early 1850s were in lamentable

51

condition: departments tended to rent expensive, cramped, inefficient and unhealthy townhouses that mocked the dignity of their function. The general case for better public buildings had by and large been accepted by 1852 but it took the far-reaching 1854 report by Stafford Northcote and Charles Trevelyan on the organisation of a permanent civil service to set out the managerial and economic rationale for the government to build for itself.

Northcote, formerly private secretary to Gladstone and a secretary of the 1851 Exhibition, and Trevelyan, assistant secretary to the Treasury, also published a report into the management of the Office of Works. They thought that it was paying too much rent for government offices and they were 'induced to believe' that it would be more economical to build new offices instead. They recommended centralising the management of departmental buildings in the Office of Works, because 'Nothing conduces more to economy and efficiency than the consolidation of duties which are strictly analogous to one another, and a proper classification of the public expenditure, so as to bring all that belongs to the same category under one point of view'.[1] In 1856, Trevelyan made the case for the quality of public buildings in London, contending that

> As it costs little more to build handsome public offices than unsightly public offices, [it is] very desirable on general national grounds to take this opportunity of embellishing the town … . I consider that we have a very important national duty to perform in this respect; this city is something more than the mother of arts and eloquence; she is a mother of nations; we are peopling two continents … and we are organising, christianising and civilising large portions of two ancient continents, Africa and Asia; and it is not right that when the inhabitants of those countries come to the metropolis, they should see nothing worthy of its ancient renown.[2]

On the professional side of the Office of Works, Northcote and Trevelyan were disappointed by the performance of the Surveyor of Works, William Inman, and recommended that 'the greatest care should at all times be taken in supplying the important post of Surveyor of Works by the appointment of gentlemen of sufficient eminence as architects to be able to maintain a proper degree of authority in acting on behalf of the Board of Works in cases where it is brought into communication with the leading professional men of the day'.[3] Sir Benjamin Hall (after whom the bell, Big Ben, was nicknamed) became First Commissioner in 1855, the fourth in as many years and the first to have any effect. He found in the Office of Works an idle and decayed organisation, seriously ill-equipped to manage the large programme of works in hand, not least Barry's Palace of Westminster and Houses of Parliament, which was at last nearing completion. Hall brought in a new surveyor, Henry Hunt, an early and influential proponent of quantity surveying who had advised Barry on costings for the Palace of Westminster. Hall, preparing to embark on a new government offices building programme, wanted to buy designs from the market through competition rather than rely on the in-house James Pennethorne.

Despite Hall's vigorous efforts, however, there was no real improvement in the management of major projects over the next decade, during which four more First Commissioners came and went. In 1868, Gladstone appointed Henry Layard as First Commissioner, in the expectation that he would bring administrative reform to the Office. Layard had had an extraordinarily varied and colourful career, including as archaeologist in Ottoman lands, under-secretary in the Foreign Office, an outspoken Member of Parliament, and art collector. He quickly identified the need to attach to the Office of Works an eminent architectural adviser who could revise consultants' schemes and control their costs in a way that Hunt and Pennethorne had failed to do. The Treasury agreed but Layard appointed a man who proved entirely unsuited to the job: a friend of his, James Fergusson, who made his money as an indigo planter in Bengal before turning to architectural history and writing. Layard, with his own vision of improving London with major new public buildings crushed by expenditure limits, departed after less than a year. He went first to Madrid as ambassador and, later, to Constantinople.

Layard was succeeded by another quarrelsome, but very different, man, Acton Ayrton. He promptly dismissed Fergusson, retired the exhausted Pennethorne without replacement, and acceded to Treasury pressure to appoint a director of works to oversee all the professional and technical work of the Office of Works. Captain Douglas Galton, a Royal Engineer whose job as head of army finance at the War Office had just been abolished, was accordingly appointed in 1870: he was well-connected, a leading sanitary engineer and an ally of Florence Nightingale. Ayrton, in a provocative throw-back to the days of professional men at the top of the Office, and despite Treasury opposition, permitted Galton some freedom from the writ of the secretary, George Russell. Scornful, too, of expensive consultant architects, he preferred work to be done in-house: no matter if it was of inferior quality provided that it was good enough. On these terms, Galton was quickly effective in reforming the professional and technical side of the Office of Works but, in his ardour to separate executive from clerical business in the office, he allowed the number of staff to increase in his first four years from 85 to 150.

These arrangements lasted until the change of government in 1874, when Disraeli became Prime Minister again. His appointment of Northcote as Chancellor of the Exchequer made it inevitable that the Treasury would become more interventionist in respect of the Office of Works. It set up a committee, against the wishes of the First Commissioner, now Lord Henry Lennox, to enquire into the operations of the Office. This committee quickly concluded that the director of works should be fully subordinate to the secretary, a conclusion that Lennox refused to implement. Disraeli, describing the Office of Works as 'an Augean stable, which must be swept clean',[4] appointed as Secretary Algernon Mitford, then aged 37 and with a successful fifteen years in the diplomatic service behind him. When Lennox refused to give Mitford clear seniority over the director of works, the Treasury took the matter to a cabinet committee where, of course, it won. Galton retired early and his post was abolished in 1875, concluding 25 years of chaos in the Office of Works. The demand for buildings had been unaffordable; the desirable extent of their public ownership contested; the type of leadership that the Office required elusive; the balance between consultant and in-house designers unclear; competitions badly handled while the Battle of the Styles raged; project management (though it was not called that) weak; and Parliament increasingly asking awkward questions.

The Royal Engineers
Throughout this period, the Office of Works might be excused for regarding the Treasury's periodic demands that it pay more attention to the Foreign Office's building requirements overseas as a tiresome distraction, particularly because it had no staff to deploy who had any experience of working in foreign parts. There was, however, in the army's Corps of Royal Engineers, a seemingly plentiful supply of able men upon whom the Treasury, and later the Office of Works, could call to undertake construction assignments overseas. Its officers were energetic, well-educated, widely travelled, managerially competent, used to command in both military and civil situations, and often familiar with structures and buildings. Since 1812, many of the young officers just out of the Royal Military Academy at Woolwich had been taught construction for a year at the Royal Engineer Establishment at Chatham. When, in 1822, the design and construction of barracks at home and abroad was transferred from civilian professionals to the Royal Engineers, Woolwich added an architectural course to its training, the first in the country to supplement the normal apprentice and articled-pupil arrangements through which architects were trained. In addition to barracks, the Royal Engineers were often deployed at home to build prisons and hospitals and, most famously under the influence of Henry Cole in

the middle of the century, the South Kensington (later the Victoria and Albert) Museum and the Royal Albert Hall. Assurance was one of the Royal Engineers' hallmarks: it explained why, in India for example, 'a captain of engineers blithely took on a cathedral'.[5] They were prized for their ability to work with teams and for getting things done on time and to budget – unlike the 'art-architects', as they were called at the time, who always wanted more of everything.

A dozen or so Royal Engineer officers made their mark on diplomatic and consular building programmes during the nineteenth century. The captain who was sent to Constantinople in 1834 to report on rebuilding the embassy house at Pera after the 1831 fire, Harry Jones, was among the first. He was then 43: he had joined the Royal Military Academy at Woolwich at 14, was a first-lieutenant at seventeen, served throughout the Peninsular War, was on a special mission to New Orleans during the Anglo-American War, and instructed at Chatham before being selected to visit Constantinople. Twenty years later he was back in Constantinople as commanding Royal Engineer. He was knighted in 1855, and awarded a Doctorate of Civil Law by Oxford University in 1856.

Tehran 1830-1876

The Royal Engineers' next involvement with diplomatic buildings was in Tehran. The house that Ouseley completed in 1813 in the centre of the city was unbearably hot in summer and the legation escaped to the slightly cooler foothills of the Elburz mountains for five months each year. In the mid-1830s, the Shah issued a *firman*, or decree, granting quasi-manorial rights over the village of Gulhak to the British minister and his successors as their summer quarters. Gulhak was about seven miles north of Tehran and at about 700 feet greater altitude. For the next 25 years or so, the British legation annually pitched its summer tents in the village of Gulhak. Lady Sheil, a minister's wife, described her accommodation during her stay at the camp in 1850:

> Ours is certainly a camp on a large scale. We have sleeping-tents, nursery-tents and my private sitting-room-tent, all enclosed in a high wall of canvas, and forming the *anderoon* [women's quarters]. Then detached are the dining-tent, drawing-room tent, and tents for each of the gentlemen of the Mission. To me it looks very magnificent, yet I am told that it is paltry in comparison with the good old times that are gone. From the size of these tents, some of them being thirty feet in length, their double roofs and double walls several feet apart, I had anticipated a comfortable residence during the summer. But I am disappointed beyond measure; the dust and heat being intolerable in spite of a stream of water which I had caused to flow through my tent.[6]

When Charles Alison arrived as minister in 1860, after long service in Constantinople, he was able to rent about 20 acres of garden at Gulhak, which the Shah was induced in 1862 to present to the legation as a free gift. As a 'slight return for this munificent donation' Alison presented the Shah with one of the large mission tents. He lost no time in seeking the Treasury's approval to spend £2,000 on building a permanent summer residence on the new site. To frame this estimate, he consulted Captain John Champain, a Royal Engineer recently arrived in Tehran to command a small group of British military officers seconded from the Indian Army to the Indo-European Telegraph Department to build an alternative line to India across Persia. The Treasury nevertheless asked for more details 'on consideration of the deceptive nature of general estimates for buildings in foreign countries.'[7] Alison managed to satisfy it and the project, comprising minister's house with chancery, three staff houses, stabling and domestic staff quarters, went ahead, not least because the total cost was less than that of 'a new set of tents' and the costs were anyway to be shared with the Government of India (**Fig. 3.1**).

Land in Persia was of little use unless it had accompanying water rights. These entitled the owners of the rights to a regulated quantity of water from the *qanats* that brought it underground from the hills to the vegetated or populated areas, where they surfaced to feed a distribution system of small streams or rills. The administration of water rights was as important as the administration of land title and the two were always registered together. Since water was scarcer than land, land was often bought solely for the water rights that it carried. A *qanat* was owned by an association of shareholders who collectively held 240 shares, each share being worth one hour's flow of the *qanat's* water every ten days. Each shareholder was liable for annual cleaning and clearing of the *qanat* and any extraordinary works to improve the supply. Disputes, unsurprisingly, were common because water assets could be so easily purloined. An 1894 report on the water supply of the (by then enlarged) Gulhek compound described the legation's shareholding in three *qanats* that served the area. The legation owned one fifth of the shares, numbering 48, acquired thus: 12 with the land presented by the Shah in 1862; 4 bought in the late 1880s; and 32 bought with more land in 1890. By 1913, mainly as a result of a further purchase of land in 1906, the legation owned 74 $^{13}/_{60}$ shares, which entitled it to a flow of 74 hours and 13 minutes every ten days.

Encouraged by the success of his new and permanent summer residence, Alison turned his attention to improving the deplorable conditions at the Bāgh-I Ilchī house in Tehran. He employed Monsieur Bovagnet, a resident

3.1. Small painting of the recently completed Tehran summer residence at Gulhak, looking north to the Elburz mountains, by Lieutenant Pierson in 1865. Arched verandas to each floor were built across the front of the house in 1896: it continued to be used as the summer residence until the Second World War.

French civil engineer, to advise him. Bovagnet reported in detail, including

> The neighbouring streets are narrow, abound in wells and holes, and have generally an open sewer in their centre. The nearest gate, being the only one by which caravans are allowed to enter the town, is constantly choked with camels, mules and apes. It is therefore almost impossible to reach the Mission door in a carriage.[8]

Bovagnet's recommendation was firm: the legation should move. Good sites for new buildings were now available because the Shah had begun demolishing Tehran's old walls to enable the city to expand in an orderly way. The attention paid in London to Alison's arguments in favour of a move was much assisted by his long friendship, from their joint service in Constantinople, with Henry Layard, now under secretary in the Foreign Office (and soon to become First Commissioner at the Office of Works). By 1867, London had agreed to the expenditure of £20,000, plus the sale proceeds of Bāgh-I Īlchī, assessed as £12,000, to buy a new site in Tehran and build a new legation on it. In 1868, Alison identified a good 16-acre rectangular site, previously occupied by factories and barracks, on what

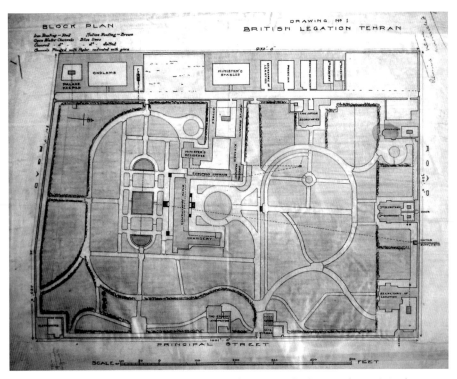

3.2. Pierson's 1868 layout for the new Tehran Ferdowsi site. The legation house is in the centre, with five European adobe houses round the perimeter. The main entrance is bottom-centre. A service strip of stables and local quarters runs along the top side. (North is to the right.)

became Ferdowsi Avenue, between Artillery Square and the new Shemiran Gate: the price was 20,000 tomans, about £8,000.

Alison arranged that Henry Pulman, William Smith's successor as resident architect in Constantinople, should be the architect for the new legation buildings but Pulman died of typhoid soon after arrival in Tehran. Alison therefore turned again to the Royal Engineers in Tehran, now commanded by Captain Robert Murdoch Smith. He was at the start of his 20-year stint in Tehran, during which he suffered the awfulness of seven of his nine children dying – three of them on three successive days. Murdoch Smith arranged for the India Office to release Lieutenant Henry Pierson from his telegraph group to superintendent the design and construction of the new legation. Pierson, not yet 30, had a gilded record: head boy of Cheltenham College, star graduate of the Royal Engineers' courses at Addiscombe and Chatham, a good linguist, admirable chess player, musician and oarsman. His record in the field, in Sikkim and Oudh, and his exertions on telegraph duties, were also widely praised. Pierson began his new task by making a rough sketch of how the legation buildings might be disposed about the site on Ferdowsi Avenue, and had it drawn up by an Austrian engineer in Tehran called Gasteiger **(Fig. 3.2).** He contacted the Treasury, which introduced him to the inconveniences of public accounting:

> [The Lords Commissioners] think it advantageous to inform you that they are not prepared to interfere with any arrangement as to the plan or elevation which may be decided upon by H. M. Minister and yourself, but that it must be distinctly understood that My Lords cannot consent to any expenditure for the building (including of site) beyond the … total sum of £32,000. … You will understand, however, that any portion of the £8,000 to be voted in this year, 1869-70, which may not be expended before or by the 31st of March 1870 will have to be surrendered to the Exchequer, and cannot be carried in aid of the expenditure for the following year.[9]

Although Pierson's original sketch became the adopted layout for the compound, he required architectural advice for the legation house itself, sited near the middle. During his leave in London in the summer of 1869, Pierson commissioned for this purpose James William Wild, an architect working at the South Kensington Museum, an organisation with which the Royal Engineers had had close links since the Great Exhibition. Wild, who had spent some of his early professional years travelling in the Levant, had built St Mark's church in Alexandria in 1846 and, when Pierson approached him, was working as the fifth architect to be asked to prepare designs for a British consulate in Alexandria. Wild's health was not good, and he no longer travelled, but he was well equipped to work up Pierson's outline plan for the legation house into a full architectural scheme. Alison was also on leave in London during the summer of 1869 and may have helped with briefing Wild, as may have Henry Layard **(Fig. 3.3).**

3.3. James Wild's sketch for the legation house at Tehran, 1869, looking south-west. An eclectic mix of an Early Christian clock tower at the end of the chancery wing; a Cairene entrance portal; an open kiosk above the hall; and a Byzantine chapel for the Oriental Secretary's office.

The Office of Works was in no way involved with the pre-construction stages of the Tehran project, and had no desire to become involved with its superintendence. The Treasury, however, asked it to take on responsibility for procuring in the UK all the materials which Pearson would require to be sent to Tehran. These included the iron for the roof, for which Pierson had commissioned drawings from a W. Dempsey and written the specification himself. He required that no part of the roof should weigh more than a camel's load of four hundredweight and the parts would be fit to be 'put together on their arrival by an ordinarily intelligent smith'. Pierson made sure that long-delivery items were tendered and ordered as soon as possible, including a flagstaff, iron gates, rainwater goods, ironmongery and so on. A turret clock with four seven-feet. dials and a four-hundredweight. bell was tendered to nine suppliers in London, and won by Dent. By the time that he left London in November 1869, Pierson had in his hands Wild's sketch for the main house: detailed plans followed in January 1870.

Murdoch Smith had overseen the construction of a boundary wall around the site while Pierson was in London. After his return, construction work on the compound made relatively good progress and, by the end of spring 1871, the brickwork and masonry of the legation house itself were complete except for the upper cornices and parapets which were awaiting the arrival of the iron roof. The five detached and semi-detached houses for secretaries and staff were roofed, with plastering in progress, and would be occupiable only a few days after the grates and ironmongery arrived from England; the servants' quarters, stalls, cook houses and other dependencies were all well in hand.

Early in 1871, the Treasury decided to transfer to the Office of Works, with effect from 1 April, the full financial responsibility for the Tehran project. This sparked the Office of Works' suspicion that the project might be heading for an overspend. The Office suggested that it should also take direct control of the project on site but the Treasury wisely wanted Pierson to retain that responsibility. This put the Office of Works in a difficult position, especially as prices were increasing, the rate of exchange was worsening, the cost of carriage had doubled, and obstructions by the Persian authorities were plentiful. Pierson maintained that 'the original design is so moderate and unambitious in extent' that he still hoped to complete it within the estimate, though he suggested some precautionary savings, including transferring some of the charges to the furniture account, a wheeze which the Office of Works refused.

The residence roof, however, was causing great difficulty. It was shipped from Glasgow in early 1871, weighing 65 tons and comprising 1,900 sections, some of which were lost overboard while being transhipped into small boats at Bushire. Much of the cast-iron guttering had also been broken from, Pierson presumed, bad stowage. And, as Pierson complained to Alison, the overland journey from Bushire was not going well either:

> The first caravan of 270 camels ... left Bushire on 18 March. The second caravan of 97 camels left 21 days later both under a contract to reach Teheran (a distance of 750 miles) in 70 days. ... Up to the present date (26 April) these caravans have not got further than Konartakhte about 70 miles from Bushire, having been detained there for more than a month by officials in charge of the tolls.[10]

The Shah had agreed that no tolls or customs should be levied and Alison swung into action. A few days later, Pierson reported

> In consequence of Mr Alison's remonstrances, the Persian governor of Kazeroon sent officials to Konartakhte to release our caravans from their detention at the toll house. These officials carried out their orders, but at the same time exacted a considerable amount of blackmail from the camel drivers. The caravans then proceeded on their way and a few stages on were attacked by bandits, who stripped the camel drivers of all their remaining cash, took their donkeys and clothes, and two of the packages belonging to the mission buildings containing, I believe, screws and nuts for the roof. One of the camel drivers was shot in the affray.[11]

Whereupon Alison sent a mission courier to protect the march of the caravan, which eventually reached the building site towards the end of June 1871. Although Jonathon Mustill, the foreman for the roof who accompanied it from England, suffered badly from the travelling, he and a Sergeant Hockley succeeded in putting the roof framework together by mid-August, when the lack of white lead delayed bolting-on the covering plates. Meanwhile, however, a much more serious problem had developed as a two-year drought over much of Persia brought cholera and starvation to Tehran. Prices rose, commerce was paralysed, cash was short and labour was weak. Pierson had no option but to close down the site for the winter of 1871-2, denying himself any chance of completing the project within the three years he had planned. Murdoch Smith sent him off on a six-month tour of telegraph installations.

Pierson was back in charge of the Ferdowsi site in May 1872 and the legation was able to occupy its new accommodation on its return from Gulhak in the autumn of that year (Fig. 3.4). All of the compound was

3.4. Garden front of the Tehran legation house. Curzon described in 1899 'a lovely garden, where swans float on brimming tanks of water and peacocks flash amid the flower beds'. Huge wisterias drape the 50-metre length of the terrace.

by then complete except for the interior of the legation house. None of the woodwork, plasterwork and decorations had started because persistent sickness had put Wild far behind programme in supplying the necessary details. The death of Alison in April 1872 slightly obscured the embarrassment of the delay. Pierson met Wild and the Office of Works in London in December 1872 to try and advance matters and decided to design the plasterwork for the ceiling in the central hall himself for execution by the excellent Persian plasterers available. Although he claimed to be satisfied with his efforts, he did not pursue them because his work 'stands out in some contrast to the more restrained, classical decoration' of Wild: a Royal Engineer, it seems, was finally beaten.

Pierson left the project in August 1873, regretful that he could not see the state rooms through to completion, and Murdoch Smith was to keep an eye on the final stages. But two more setbacks upset that plan. It was another six months before some of Wild's designs arrived, and extremely heavy snowfalls and rainstorms in the early spring of 1874 caused severe damage to the state rooms' roof. Upon realising that the project would drag on, the India Office withdrew Murdoch Smith from the project, and the Office of Works sent Caspar Purdon Clarke, who worked closely with Wild at the South Kensington Museum, to take over. Clarke arrived in August 1874 with instructions to design everything that Wild had not yet sent. It took him nearly two years to complete the state rooms, even using as many local substitutions as he could for work that was originally planned to come from the UK **(Fig. 3.5).** The total cost of the Ferdowsi compound when Clarke left Tehran in July 1876 was about £46,000.

Clarke went on with his career in London to become, 20 years later, Director of the South Kensington Museum: he was knighted in 1902 and died in 1911. Wild became Director of Sir John Soane's Museum in Lincoln's Inn Fields in 1878, and remained there until his death in 1892. Pierson was denied a long career: he was secretary to the Indian defence committee in 1877, military secretary to the viceroy in 1880 and died suddenly from dysentery while commanding a field force of Royal Engineers on the North-West Frontier in 1881, at the age of only 41. But the sheer resourcefulness of his achievement lives on in Tehran, shaded by those that remain of the 1,500 plane trees that he planted in the early 1870s.

3.5. The Tehran state dining room today, much as Caspar Clarke left it in 1876. Winston Churchill celebrated his 69th birthday in this room on 30 November 1943 with Roosevelt and Stalin during the Tehran Conference.

Alexandria 1859-1870

While Alison was making considerable progress with new buildings at Tehran through the 1860s, his opposite number in Egypt, the consul-general at Alexandria, Robert Colquhoun, was making no headway at all. Colquhoun arrived in Alexandria in 1859 and straightaway adopted the idea of building a new consulate-general on vacant land next to St Mark's church, which had recently been completed to the designs of James Wild. Colquhoun submitted the case for a new building to London and appended an outline plan of how he thought it should be. This was a large hollow rectangle on two floors, characteristic of European-developed urban buildings of the time in Alexandria, sometimes called *okelles*, which had arcaded courtyards of commercial activities on the ground floor and residential flats on the upper floors. Colquhoun, however, was not working to any agreed brief and the Treasury ignored his proposals, asking instead in 1860 for a statement of need, schedule of rooms, and estimates, and when 'this information shall have been all obtained My Lords propose to instruct the Commissioners of Works to put themselves in communication with the Foreign Office in order to prepare instructions for some competent Architect or Surveyor' to visit Alexandria and produce a design.[12]

With the traumas of completing the rebuilding of the embassy house at Pera less than ten years earlier in mind, the Foreign Office had a better idea, '... bearing in mind the great expenditure which resulted from the employment ... at Constantinople of an Architect from this country, Sir John Russell [Foreign Secretary] would submit for the consideration of the Board of the Treasury whether it might not be on the whole the most economical course to authorise Mr Colquhoun to employ an Architect on the spot...'. The Treasury, after consulting the Office of Works, asked that Colquhoun should indicate whether competent local architects existed in Alexandria, to which came the reply that 'several Architects, especially one, and an Ionian subject, who has studied in Italy and has been here eight years, very actively employed ... I should pronounce capable'. His name was F. Sofio. Colquhoun estimated that the total building cost would be about £12,000, and '... having a little knowledge myself of Architecture, I shall bring to bear my personal knowledge in making sketches of what I think may be best adopted for the situation, climate etc so that no time should be lost after HMG shall have sanctioned the works'. Sofio produced a three-storey design, planned almost identically with Colquhoun's first proposal, which Colquhoun unsurprisingly endorsed and sent to London. Soon after, Colquhoun was asked by the Prussian consul-general if a young architect, Carl Heinze, lately arrived from Berlin where he had been a pupil of the

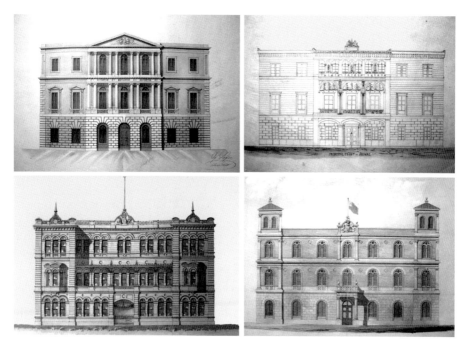

3.6. The main elevation, facing the square, of four successive proposals by different architects for a new consulate-general in Alexandria. Clockwise from top-left: by Sofio, Heinz (both 1860), Donaldson (1862), MacDermott (1867). None was built.

celebrated Stüler, could hand in a set of plans. Colquhoun thought Heinze's rough sketches evinced such taste that he told Heinze to produce a set of drawings straightaway and he sent these to London with another supportive letter.

The Office of Works estimated that Sofio's building might cost about £60,000 in Alexandria, and marginally preferred Heinze's scheme. It reacted to both, though, by sending an eminent British architect, Thomas Donaldson, a safe choice, to go to Alexandria and produce a design and estimate of his own. Donaldson came up with a simpler and smaller design, still based on the *okelle* plan form, which he estimated at about £23,500. The Treasury said this was still too much to lay before Parliament. The Foreign Office advised applying to Parliament for the £12,000 that Colquhoun had first proposed and then letting him 'do the work without further interference by the Board of Works, and in fact under our own orders which of course would bind Mr Colquhoun and his local architect not to exceed the grant of Parliament'. Donaldson was in touch with Layard, then at the Foreign Office, but could not entice him to take any interest in the Alexandria scheme. More than two years were then spent considering whether to

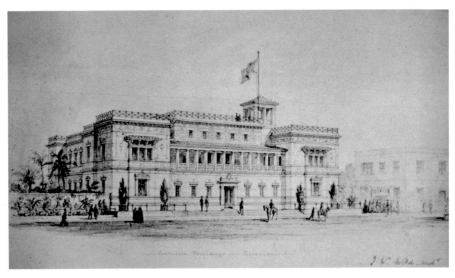

3.7. James Wild's unbuilt proposal for the Alexandria consulate-general, 1869. He exhibited this drawing at the Royal Academy in 1870.

include a new courtroom in the building because the tenancy of the present one was soon to expire. The Foreign Office wrote to the Treasury in May 1865 that 'the cause of this delay has been the utter impossibility of coming to any practicable conclusion so long as the Treasury insisted upon the interference and superintendence of the board of works, and Lord Russell is so fully satisfied that nothing will result from the employment of a board of works architect...'.[13]

Colquhoun had now left Alexandria and Colonel Edward Stanton, his successor, did not take long to conclude that the building requirements had altered. In April 1867, he sent two designs to London, A and B, by an engineer called Martin Macdermott, both with rather clumsily adapted *okelle* plans and heavy-handed elevations **(Fig. 3.6)**. Stanton recommended Scheme A, for which the estimate might be reduced to about £23,000. A Foreign Office annotation, dated March 1868, on the file states 'These plans were rejected at first sight.'[14] Stanton asked Wild in June 1868 to produce a design and send it to the Foreign Office. Wild skilfully and diligently did this, and informed the Foreign Office about a year later that his estimate for the cost of the building was about £15,000 **(Fig. 3.7)**. The Treasury invited Stanton's observations in August 1869 on Wild's plans which, it became apparent, he had not seen, an oversight that laid him open to accusations of having wantonly commissioned work from Wild. The scope of Wild's design was substantially less, and its sophistication considerably more, than any of the previous designs, though the essence of an *okelle* remained in his courtyard plan. By this time, however, everybody had lost interest in the whole idea of building in Alexandria, and it was not until 1903 that a site was bought and a building completed on it, designed in-house by the Office of Works.

Constantinople 1866-1876
As in Tehran, both the summer and winter embassy houses in Constantinople required radical action during the 1860s and early 1870s: the summer one at Therapia because the current house was tumbling down and the winter one at Pera because another fire, in 1870, caused great damage.

It is unclear which house on the Bosphorus Elgin recommended to the Foreign Secretary in 1801 should be bought as the summer embassy for Constantinople. In the event, the practice continued of renting a *yali*, as a timber mansion built on the Bosphorus waterfront was called. The promontory on the west shore just to the north of the village of Therapia was one of the most favoured spots because it caught the coolest breezes blowing directly from the Black Sea. In 1829, the British ambassador, Sir Robert Gordon, was given the use of a house there by the Sultan. The deeds to this property were destroyed in the Pera fire of 1831 and Gordon, because he needed to live at Therapia all the year round while Pera was being rebuilt, anxiously asked the Sultan for a duplicate copy. A letter from the Sultan in August 1831 could have left him in little doubt about the answer to his request.

> Whereas the relations of the sincere friendship and the effects of the strict amity firmly existing between my Empire and the Court of Great Britain are, through the good intentions of both sides, more and more increasing; and whereas particularly the fair and righteous conduct which the Ambassador Extraordinary and Plenipotentiary of Great Britain presently residing at Constantinople, the most distinguished among the grandees of the Christian Nation, Robert Gordon, whose end may be happy! has, in conformity with his natural sagacity and that wisdom which characterises him, displayed in the performance of his functions, ... We have been pleased to give a house situated at Therapia ... [as] the peculiar dwelling of the said Ambassador, as well as that of his successors ... and an Imperial Title dated [March 1831] has been delivered in consequence ... . But the said House has been burnt, God having so decreed, and he has asked for a new one. We have consequently caused the present title to be delivered.[15]

Some years later, it transpired that this property had originally belonged to some Catholic Armenians from whom the Porte obtained it either by confiscation or a forced sale at the time of persecution of that sect after the Battle of Navarino in 1827. The British government therefore returned the property to the Sultan once interim premises for the mission at Galata had been leased by Smith in 1841. Six years later, and in honour of Queen Victoria's birthday on 24 May 1847, Sultan Abdülmecid presented the ambassador with another site at Therapia, comprising four *yalis* and some disused factory buildings that had belonged to the Austrian Danube Steam Navigation Company. Smith surveyed these buildings and arranged some improvements to them, and the ambassador subsequently spent his summers in the best of them, while chancery and his staff sojourned in the others **(Fig. 3.8)**

In January 1866, a Major Edward Gordon (no relation to the former ambassador) was appointed as the superintendent of British government buildings in Constantinople, reporting to the Treasury instead of to the Office of Works. Asked for a report on the future of the Therapia buildings, Gordon observed that 'In front of the Ambassador's dwelling are the most unsightly

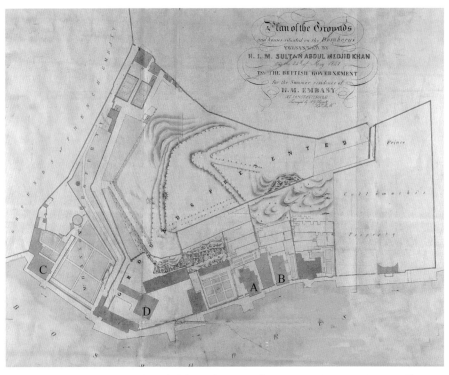

3.8. Survey of the site that Sultan Abdülmecid presented to Queen Victoria in 1847 at Therapia, on the Bosphorus, for the embassy's summer residence. Drawn by Lieutenant Glascott RN, 1847. Building A served as the summer palace, and B was occupied by the attachés. (North is to the right.)

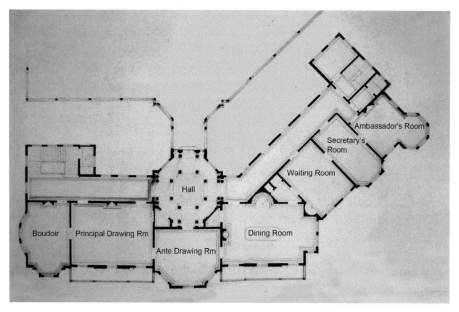

3.9. First-floor plan of the summer residence built at Therapia in 1870 on the site presented in 1847. The design was credited to George Stampa. The steep contours behind enabled a bridge from the upper hall to the hillside to shade the main entrance beneath.

ruins of a factory, which add greatly to the general air of desolation pervading the whole of this property …' and concluded 'To speak plainly and in a few words, I should say that the work most urgently required is *an entire New Embassy*,' which he estimated to cost about £14,000.[16] He suggested that the money could be appropriated from the receipts of the Constantinople Post Office. Once he was disabused of such a convenient course, he included £14,000 in his annual Estimates bid for 1867, strenuously supported by the newly arrived ambassador, Henry Elliot. The Treasury agreed to proceed, and was content to leave all design aspects to Elliot, within a maximum of £10,000 and subject to approval by the Foreign Secretary and the Treasury.

The origin of the design of the summer embassy is unclear but the probable course of events was Gordon asking a London architect, E. J. Eardley Mare of King's Road, Chelsea, to prepare a set of plans, much as Pierson approached Wild two years later. Mare's scheme was approved in London. Elliot, however, found fault with it and asked a local architect, George Stampa, to revise or redesign it. Certainly, the drawings that Elliot sent to London in August 1868 were credited to George Stampa, who was paid five per cent plus expenses to act as architect. Mare learned three years later that he was not to be paid for his earlier design because Gordon's original letter to him had clearly stated that no fee would be payable if the scheme was not accepted. Mare argued in vain to the Foreign Secretary that, as his plans had been approved and submitted to Parliament, he was entitled to the usual commission of 2½ per cent. It remains unclear whether the basic design was Mare's or Stampa's. Either way, it was an attractive architectural solution **(Fig. 3.9).**

Frederick Guarrancino, a vice-consul, was put in charge of the building contract, which was won by Haggi Meguerditch Calfa. In early 1869, the Treasury asked that the furniture should be supplied through the Office of Works in London, but Guarracino won the argument that it would be cheaper to procure it locally. The new building was occupied in May 1870, at the start of the summer season **(Fig. 3.10)**. Lady Annie Brassey, passing by with her husband in their steam yacht *Sunbeam* a few years later, noted

> We dropped anchor about five … and at 7.30p.m. we went to dine at the English Embassy. It is built of wood outside, but within you enter a marble hall, and go up a marble staircase, along a corridor with marble columns, filled with plants. The rooms are handsome, and the effect is very good. [17]

Within months of the new Therapia summer embassy being brought into occupation in mid-1870, the Pera embassy house was all but destroyed by another fire. The building had been considerably criticised by its occupants since its expensive completion in 1855, and had required a good deal of maintenance, especially to leaking roofs. The Office of Works was alarmed in 1862 that the ambassador and Henry Pulman, the then-resident architect, were proposing to spend too much on it in preparation for a ten-day visit by the Prince of Wales. It wrote to the ambassador:

> After the Expenditure which has been incurred in building and furnishing the Embassy …, HM's Govt. cannot suppose that any outlay is necessary in order to render habitable such a portion of the rooms as may be required for the personal accommodation of H.R.H. … and they are not prepared to sanction an outlay of more than £100 at the utmost. Y[our] E[xcellency] has been apprised of Her Majesty's wish that the Prince should go in the quietest manner to the Embassy …[18]

Sterling efforts by the crew of HMS *Antelope*, a visiting paddle sloop, in helping to fight the latest fire eventually succeeded in containing it and saving the archives and plate. The Chancellor of the Exchequer, Robert Lowe, commiserated to Edmund Hammond at the Foreign Office '… I dare say we shall have to rebuild the former House but I should like to pause

3.10. The summer residence at Therapia from the Bosphorus in about 1900: it was destroyed by fire in 1911. The wooden chapel to the right was built in 1882.

upon it as it is sure to be burnt down again'.[19] The Office of Works primly sought to distance itself: '... this Board is not responsible for, and has no duties to perform, in connection with [this building], with the exception of an examination as to the arithmetical correctness of the quarterly accounts sent to their Department by the Treasury'.[20] Nevertheless, the ambassador, Henry Elliot, suggested that someone from the Office of Works should survey the damage.

The Treasury sent William Crossman, a Royal Engineer, to Constantinople at short notice to report. Meanwhile, Frederick Guarracino set about finding and renting a house as an alternative winter residence until Pera could be re-occupied. Crossman found that the damage at the embassy was not as bad as had been feared. The external and courtyard walls were good but the main cornice showed signs of weakness. The whole of the building above the ground floor was completely gutted and nothing remained but the bare walls and damaged stone staircases but, on the ground floor, only two rooms were totally destroyed. Strangely, there was hardly a broken pane of glass in the recently installed roof over the court. Elliot wondered whether some of the embassy's ground at Pera should be sold to raise money for the repairs although that would increase future fire risks. Crossman made his recommendations in July: the house should be fully restored and made fireproof, for which his rough works estimate was £50,000; the ground floor should be prepared for the ambassador that winter; and no land should be sold.

While in Constantinople, Crossman went to see the new Therapia building. He thought highly of it: 'The arrangement ... is excellent, nothing could be better; the kitchens, stables and outhouses are very good.' He was surprised that the house could have been built for £10,000. On the other hand,

> The Contractor, I believe, did lose by it, and on inspection I find that although the framework is strong and has proved itself to be so by withstanding a very heavy gale of wind without vibration, all the internal and external fittings – doors, windows, window shutters, locks, bolts and ironmongery of every kind are of the most inferior description. The house has only been occupied five or six weeks, and many things require repairs already.[21]

Some of the contractor's outstanding claims were finally settled in 1875.

Concurrently with Crossman's inspection of the Pera damage, Elliot sought a report from two local architects, George Stampa and H. A. Goebbels. The latter signed himself 'Architect attached to the Prussian Ministry of Public Works, actually on a mission for studying and preparing plans for the erection of a new Embassy in Pera for the North German Confederation'.[22] Their conclusion was the same as Crossman's. In October 1870, doubtless as the result of another Crossman recommendation, the Office of Works was asked by the Treasury to resume full responsibility for all the buildings at Constantinople. John Lessels, a Scottish architect in its employ at Windsor, was therefore sent to Constantinople to gather information and costs for rebuilding the Pera house.

Meanwhile, the Turkish government had produced a plan for reducing the damage from future fires by widening the wretchedly narrow lanes throughout the Pera district. The plan required landowners to cede strips of land around their perimeters up to five metres wide. This cession, to which the British agreed in April 1871 on condition that the Porte would pay for rebuilding the boundary walls on their new lines, required many of the stables and other outhouses to be moved. Lessels prepared a scheme that re-sited some of the outbuildings in the north-west corner on either side of two new gatehouses and most of the stables and stores in the south-west corner in a courtyard development, in the middle of which he proposed a large underground water cistern. To provide for a servants' hall and secretaries' kitchens, both of which used to be in outbuildings, Lessels proposed adding a rounded ground-floor extension to the northern end of Smith's building.

Lessels' proposals were all agreed and he left Constantinople in August 1871 to begin, with two staff, drawing up the schemes in London and arranging tenders for the materials to be sent from Britain. Big items among these were iron girders to insert beneath the floors to render the whole building more fireproof, and the iron for a replacement glazed roof. Lessels completed this work in December 1871, estimated it all at £38,000, to which the Treasury agreed, and forecast that it would take two to three years to complete. He returned to Constantinople in 1872 as surveyor overseeing all of the embassy and consular buildings in the city. Charles Rapson assisted him as clerk of works on the Pera restoration. The project started reasonably well but by mid-1875 had slowed almost to a halt while awaiting Treasury approval to exceed the estimate. Elliot began to feel as persecuted as Canning had: 'There has certainly been no saving to Government in the dilatory way in which these works have been carried on, but a great deal of annoyance.'[23] All was finally completed in 1876, with only a £1,500 excess of the works estimate: another £10,000 was spent on furniture. Lessels returned to Windsor, and was promoted to Surveyor of what was called the Country District.

These building sagas at the winter and summer mission houses in Tehran and Constantinople illustrate the halting and unenthusiastic response by the Office of Works to pressures from the Treasury to become more involved with diplomatic buildings overseas. It was already over loaded with its own problems at home. And major diplomatic missions in important capitals were not the only overseas pressures during the third quarter of the nineteenth century. The demands of consulates – smaller Posts in remoter places – were also bearing down on the Office of Works.

4

Consulates 1850-1900

The Consular Service

The Consular Act of 1825 paved the way for an efficient consular service to emerge over time from the prevailing chaotic arrangements. Its necessity was explained to consuls, who then staffed well over a hundred consulates:

> the System under which the British Consular Service abroad has hitherto been conducted has been so little settled or uniform, the Duties and Position of Consuls so undefined, and the manner in which they were remunerated, partly by Salary and partly by Fees (the legality of which latter was liable to question), so unequal and uncertain that it became apparent that some fixed and general System ought to be adopted for the regulation of His Majesty's Consular Service.[1]

The fine intentions were extraordinarily difficult to implement in the circumstances of the time, and progress on them was scant for the first 25 years, and halting for the next 25. Regular enquiries by Select Committees and in Parliament into the costs, appointments, inequities and locations of consuls had few effects. The newly-created Consular Department in the Foreign Office lacked vigour and failed to provide the focal point intended for the fragmented General Consular Service. Although the principle of a qualifying examination for admission to the service was established in 1856, in the wake of the main Northcote and Trevelyan reforms, there was little agreement about the kind of consul required and therefore about which subjects candidates should be examined in. Indeed, when the case for specialisation in consular work was being debated in 1856,

Palmerston, by then Prime Minister, argued that 'The duties of Consuls, though very important and involving a great number of details, do not require any particular education or avocation. A man of good sense is able, with very little application to discharge the various functions which a Consul has to perform'.[2] Two years later, Lord Strangford, who had served in Constantinople, emphasised that relations with Turkey were of such importance that Consuls there should be 'the most perfect and the highest type of English manhood'.[3]

Concurrently with introducing the Consular Act reforms in 1825, Canning, Foreign Secretary, caused the Levant Company to be wound up because its monopoly of trade with the Ottoman Empire was inconsistent with the government's policy of expanding British commerce through free trade. The Company's consular establishments were transferred to the Foreign Office, including considerable property assets at Constantinople and Smyrna. Their staff constituted the Levant Consular Service, part of the General Consular Service until 1877, and then a separate Service of its own.

Through its new responsibility for the consulates in the Levant, the Foreign Office became more directly involved with all the ramifications of extra-territoriality. This was a system that the Ottoman rulers had developed of granting certain freedoms, called privileges or capitulations, to foreign trading companies to the extent that foreigners could behave almost as if they were in their own country and not on the Sultan's territory. It permitted foreign nationals to trade, travel freely, be exempt from local taxation and be subject to the justice of their own consular courts. From the Sultans' point of view, extra-territoriality began as a convenient way of relieving them of responsibility for the behaviour of weak but useful groups of Christian foreigners. As the strength of the Sultans weakened, however, foreigners took such advantage of the arrangements as to distort the operation of the local political, economic and judicial systems. Widespread abuses became institutionalised, especially through the mechanisms of protection by which a foreign consulate would treat another foreigner, a Turkish protégé or almost any local inhabitant as its own national if he had purchased a *berat*, or patent of protection, from that consulate.

The sale of *berats* naturally provided consuls (and ambassadors) with useful extra income. *Berats* themselves were officially outlawed early in the nineteenth century but corruptions of a comparable kind remained endemic. By 1850, there were 50,000 Europeans in Constantinople, all regulated by their own national laws and united in their disrespect for the Turks. Extra-territoriality was not finally abolished in Turkey until the Treaty of Lausanne in 1923. Until then, the British consular network in the Ottoman lands required its own courts and prisons, managed its own post offices and, in the larger maritime consulates, administered its own seamen's hospitals and dispensaries. It was, for example, these consular buildings in Galata in Constantinople that claimed some of the attentions of the resident architect William Smith in the 1840s and practically all those of his successor, Henry Pulman in the 1850s.

The first Chinese consulates

All the extra-territorial imbalances that had developed in the Ottoman lands were reflected and embedded in the treaties that were negotiated in the middle of the nineteenth century with the Chinese and Japanese governments – long known as the 'unequal treaties'. The Treaty of Nanking, which ended the First Opium War in 1842, and was ratified the following year, began the process in the Far East. It handed Hong Kong, 'fragrant harbour', to Britain and designated five ports that were forced to open to world trade and in which foreigners would have extensive extra-territorial rights. The Foreign Office brought the China Consular Service into existence in 1842, independent of the General Consular Service, in order to staff the treaty ports: it grew into the Far Eastern Service to embrace Japan, Korea and Siam. Extra-territoriality was abolished in Japan in 1899 and in China in 1943, a full century after the Treaty of Nanking.

The first five treaty ports – Canton, Amoy, Foochow, Ningpo and Shanghai – were spaced along some 800 miles of China's south-east coastline **(Fig. 4.1)**. The Treaty of Nanking permitted the establishment of British consulates at each of these ports. The consuls reported to the Chief Superintendent of Trade, initially stationed in Hong Kong, who in turn reported to the political department at the Foreign Office, by-passing the Consular Department. The treaty ports developed at different rates. Canton was already a trading centre, extensively used by the East India Company until it lost its monopoly of trade with China in 1833. The consul in 1843 rented a comfortable building designed for occupation by foreigners but it soon burned down and he was forced to move the consulate into boats. Shanghai raced ahead and never lost its substantial lead among treaty ports: it grew into the largest extra-territorial international settlement, with a British Supreme Court as part of the consulate-general. But Amoy, Foochow and Ningpo saw little trade for the first ten years or so, and their consulates were established only slowly. The first consuls rented what little and wretched accommodation they could find or were allocated. Their life was hard and unhealthy, and their jobs exceedingly difficult in the face of official obstruction, seething local resentment and unfriendly incidents designed to

4.1. Map of China showing cities in which British consulates were established during the nineteenth century. Many also closed before the end of the century.

upset them. Within just over three years, the first four British consuls on the China coast had departed: two by dying, one through resignation in disgust, and one was removed for inadequacy. During the early years at Amoy, three successive consuls died in harness.

Rutherford Alcock was 35 when he was appointed as the first consul at Foochow in 1844. He had been a surgeon with the British forces in Iberia but a muscular trouble in his hands forced him to give up that career in favour of consular work. At this he excelled, and he spent the next 27 years of his career in China and Japan. On his way to Foochow in 1844, Alcock was detained in Amoy for a year or so as acting consul. Among his preoccupations was, in the words of his biographer,

the future residence of the consul. Trifling as this last may seem, it was a matter of no small consideration in China, where, to paraphrase Polonius, the dwelling oft proclaims the man. … It was one of the innumerable devices of the Chinese authorities for degrading newcomers in the eyes of the populace to force them to live, as at Canton, within a confined space or in squalid tenements. Mr Alcock knew by instinct the importance of prestige, while his Peninsular training had taught him the value of sanitation. Following these two guiding stars, he overbore the obstruction of the officials, and not only obtained a commodious site but had a house built to his own specification during his temporary incumbency of the office.[4]

Alcock's house at Amoy was on Kulangso, a small island in the harbour which had been occupied by the British during the First Opium War. The consular office was in the town, and on its staff as an interpreter was a bright 16-year-old boy, Harry Parkes, who had arrived in Macao from England three years earlier and taught himself Chinese. Alcock took Parkes under his wing and these two formidable characters were to work in tandem through much of the next 40 years as the backbone of the Far Eastern Consular Service. At Foochow, where Alcock (with wife and family in tow and with Parkes as interpreter) eventually arrived in 1845, the first consulate was in the grounds of a Buddhist temple within the walled city, three miles from the island of Nantai, the business centre. Alcock soon moved the consulate to high ground on Nantai, where it commanded superb views and was healthy.

At Shanghai, the first consul, Captain George Balfour, who lived in a rented house, laid out a large area of land with zones for residential quarters, cargo handling and godowns (warehouses). The Chinese authorities permitted the British to manage this area themselves and it became in 1846 the first British extra-territorial settlement on the China coast, with its citizens, including numerous Chinese, living under British law. Between 1851 and 1861, the Chinese government permitted the British government to buy additional land from its Chinese owners to hold in perpetuity in accordance with Chinese law. The British government divided the whole area into lots, and sold 99-year leases on the lots to British traders by auction, charging them a ground rent sufficient to cover the land tax that it had to pay to the Chinese government. This procedure for establishing land tenure underlay the development of all the later concession areas. It also gave British consuls the opportunity to select for themselves the most desirable site within a concession area on which to erect the consulate buildings **(Fig. 4.2)**. Generally speaking, the best sites in river port concessions were on the bund, the road and jetty strip that ran along the riverside: elsewhere, the best sites were likely to be found a little above the town, where the congestion and smells were less. The stage was now set for the construction or purchase of permanent consulate buildings on land with secure tenure. The first such buildings were almost certainly designed by the Surveyor-General's department in Hong Kong and built in 1849 in the Shanghai compound: a house with offices for the consul, and two houses for vice-consuls.

Nothing else seems to have been built at the first five treaty ports before the Second Opium War began in 1856 and the troops of Britain and France, in pursuit of new commercial concessions from China, seized Canton. The war came to an end in 1858 with the signing of the Treaties of Tientsin, under which China was obliged to open seven more designated ports to Britain, France, Russia and the USA. The choice of ports illustrated how the traders had penetrated wider and deeper into China. Swatow, on the coast between Canton and Amoy, and Taiwan (later called Tainan) on Taiwan island, were in the region of the first ports but Chinkiang, Hankow and Kiukiang were river ports on the lower Yangtze River; Chefoo was at the north-east tip of the Shantung peninsular; and Newchwang was in Manchuria. China, however, refused to ratify the Treaties of Tientsin and hostilities were resumed in 1860. This time, British and French forces took Tientsin, which was the river port that served Peking, occupied Peking and, enraged by the Chinese seizure of Harry Parkes and others while under flag of truce, burned down the Imperial Summer Palace. China capitulated and signed the Peking Convention in 1860, which ratified the 1858 Treaties of Tientsin. In spring 1861, Parkes himself had the satisfaction of establishing the consulates

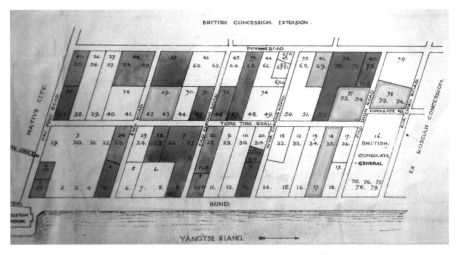

4.2. Diagram of the British concession area granted at Hankow in 1861, with lots auctioned to trading companies. The British consulate was on the bund at extreme right, next to the Russian concession, and the custom house was at extreme left, close to the native city.

4.3. Shamian Island, Canton (now Guangdong), from the air, about 1920. Originally a sandbank in the Pearl River, the island became the concession area in 1842 and was progressively developed over the next 80 years.

at the three Yangtze ports. The Peking Convention additionally designated Tientsin as a treaty port, and for the first time established the right of Western diplomatic representation in Peking. The first buildings to be erected after the Second Opium War were on Shameen Island at Canton in the late 1850s, designed by Charles Cleverly, the second Surveyor-General to serve in Hong Kong **(Fig. 4.3)**. By 1864, these had been followed by buildings at Kiukiang and Hankow, both on the bund in the concession areas, and at Foochow, where Nantai Island in the middle of the river became the foreign settlement. Two sets of consular buildings were also bought in the early 1860s, at Amoy and Swatow. The six-acre compound at Amoy, above the beach on the southern side of Kulangso Island, was so close to meeting the consulate's accommodation requirements that the buildings may well have been built by the vendor, Tait and Co. to the consul's specification. At Swatow, a large house on the bund for the consul and the offices, and a smaller one further back for the assistant, were bought from the American vice-consul **(Fig. 4.4)**.

Crossman and Boyce
By 1865, there was a dozen or so consulates and subsidiary vice-consulates established in China. As trading companies arrived and prospered, they built godowns and other premises for themselves. With other merchants prepared to speculate in property, rental markets developed for expatriates, enabling the consuls and their staff at some posts to move into more acceptable

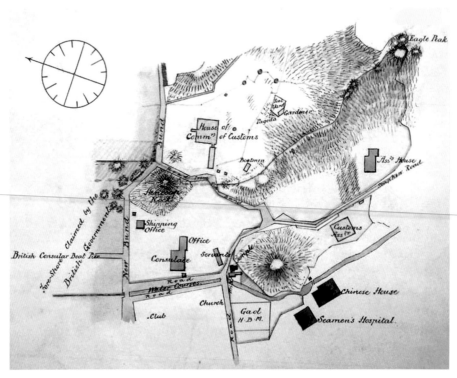

4.4. An 1889 sketch plan of the British consular compound at Swatow. The consul's house faces the bund, with boat pier directly opposite, with shipping office and assistant's house close by. The gaol, seamen's hospital, customs, church and club are all in the same enclave.

rented premises than their predecessors had endured. At other posts, active planning was in hand for starts to be made on building new consulates, not least because rents were rising dramatically. The Treasury, however, was concerned that some of the money that it had authorised was being spent less than wisely by consuls, and disturbed to learn that several consuls had kept for their consulates, if not for themselves, the proceeds of the sale of surplus land. The most notorious example was in Shanghai where, without any reference to the Treasury, almost half of the 15-acre consular compound was sold in nine lots for about £60,000, a colossal sum. The Treasury thought first of sending an architect to inject discipline into the consulates' building programmes but concluded that no civil service architect could be spared and that a private practitioner would be too expensive. In consequence, it reverted to its successful practice of asking the War Office to lend a Royal Engineer whom the Treasury could send to the Far East to sort matters out.

Captain William Crossman was put forward. At 36, he was the

quintessential all-rounder Royal Engineer. After the Royal Military Academy, he was commissioned into the Royal Engineers at 19, worked on the organisation of the Great Exhibition, superintended the construction of public works in western Australia, where he was also a police magistrate, and served at the War Office under the inspector-general of fortifications on surveying and designing new defences along the south coast of England. As a young captain, he was sent to Canada in 1861 to help with military preparations and became secretary to the royal commission on the defences of Canada, visiting every post on the frontier.

The Treasury briefed Crossman by letter in February 1866 while he was staying at the Junior United Service Club in London for the week before his departure. He had been nominated, the letter said, 'to report upon and make general arrangements for the construction and maintenance of consular and judicial buildings in China and Japan.' The Treasury listed the consular projects it thought it had sanctioned and spelled out its credo that 'accommodation should be confined within the strictest limits of economy compatible with the requirements of the public service and the convenience of the officer [consul]'. The Treasury gave Crossman a ringing, rare and enviable endorsement: '… My Lords believe that the Public interests will be best served by entrusting you with large discretionary powers, and they do not doubt that Their confidence will be justified by the results.'[5]

The day before his departure, Crossman was promoted to local rank of major. He arrived in the Far East in May 1866, going first to Hong Kong, where he consulted the acting Surveyor-General, Wilberforce Wilson, who had been organising some of the new consulate projects either directly from Hong Kong or through consultants in Shanghai. The military in Hong Kong agreed to loan Crossman a number of Royal Engineer non-commissioned officers to supervise works at the consulates, and the admiral agreed to convey him where practicable between consulates. Crossman was supplied with £10,000 by the 'officer in charge of the Treasury Chest' for works expenditure. For building materials and fixings to be supplied from Britain, Crossman was to apply to the Treasury, which would arrange for one of the surveyors at the War Office to procure and send the items. The Foreign Office would inform the ministers at the recently established legations at Peking and Tokyo, and all the Far Eastern consuls, about the importance of Crossman's role and the authority he carried: he was not to be regarded as subservient to the two ministers and any serious argument with either of them would be settled in London.

Crossman settled himself into Shanghai, the most central and developed of the consulates, quickly established his authority and visited every consulate within his first year. He laid down the pattern of accommodation for current and future consulates in the Far East. For three and a half years he worked energetically and effectively, bringing to bear a rigour and expertise that had been sorely missing, and laying down designs, practices and procedures that would long outlast him **(Figs. 4.5 & 4.6)**. He put maintenance work in hand that he judged necessary, assessed the future demand for buildings, advised whether they could be bought or rented or would have to be built, selected sites and produced outline designs for new buildings, and established liaisons with contractors, customs people and the business fraternities. Crossman proved skilled at reconciling the operational priorities of the ministers at Peking and Tokyo, the basic requirements of

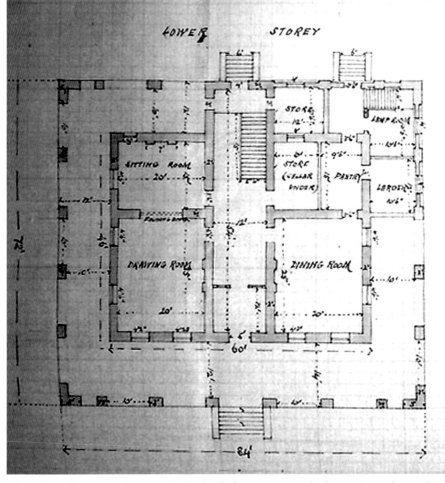

4.5. William Crossman's 1867 notebook sketch for a new consular house at Foochow, subsequently built. A simple and typical house plan, mainly surrounded by veranda on both floors, derived from East India Company and Royal Engineer precedents.

4.6. Main front of the consul's house at Foochow, developed from William Crossman's sketch of 1867, on high land on Nantai Island. The consular offices were in the Assistant's house in the same compound.

the consuls in their often difficult circumstances, and the financial resources allocated to his programmes by the Treasury **(Fig. 4.7)**. There were few rules to guide him at the outset but it helped that the consular staff were all salaried members of the growing Far Eastern Consular Service: he was spared having to negotiate with trading consuls. Six months after his arrival in Shanghai, the Treasury answered a query from him with 'My Lordships are unwilling to give any directions to you which might fetter your judgement and they leave it to your discretion, on which they have every reliance, to carry out such arrangements …'.[6]

Crossman also groomed his successor, an assistant surveyor, Robert Henry Boyce from the Civil Branch of the Royal Engineers Department, who joined him in Shanghai in 1867.[7] Boyce was four years younger than Crossman: he lacked Crossman's easy authority and far-sightedness, and had a tendency towards the doctrinaire, but he shared his determination and energy. When Boyce joined him in Shanghai, Crossman moved from a room in the vice-consul's house into a whole house that he rented off-compound. He and Boyce lived on the first floor, while the ground floor was given over to their office, in which a Mr Donaldson, initially taken on as a temporary clerk, worked mainly as a draughtsman. They worked hard together for two

4.7. Drawing of the garden front of the consulate at Kiukiang, built in the early 1860s on an acre of land on the bund.

years before Crossman departed in September 1869 to resume his military career, which included assistant director of works for fortifications at the War Office, and commanding Royal Engineer of the southern military district. He made several visits for the Treasury or the Office of Works to diplomatic properties during the early years after his return to London, including to Constantinople in 1870. He was knighted in 1884, resigned the following year, sat as a Liberal MP for Portsmouth for seven years, and died in 1901.

Boyce stepped into Crossman's shoes in 1869, and was transferred to the staff of the Office of Works in 1871 when the Vote for the consulates in the Far East was transferred from the Foreign Office to the Office of Works. Boyce remained in Shanghai until 1876, when he was succeeded by his assistant F. J. Marshall, and returned to London where he spent the rest of his career working as the principal architect/surveyor for the diplomatic and consular estate worldwide **(Figs. 4.8 & 4.9)**. Upon his retirement in 1899, he undertook a tour of inspection of all Posts in the Far East to make recommendations about future policy for the management of the legation and consulate buildings. His resulting report remains the most accurate summary of the accommodation at the 60 or so Posts in the region.[8]

Compounds and bungalows

Whereas sites and houses were the customary development blocks of European and other developed cities, in the Far East the sites were mostly compounds and the houses were mostly bungalows. A compound provided a secure, healthy, communal, uncrowded, fairly self-sufficient living and working environment for expatriates and their trusted staff in countries where safety and health were not otherwise to be found. They derived from the military cantonments in India which were established to keep troops away from the native city so that the smells, noises, thieves and diseases could not intrude but not so far away that it was inconvenient to venture into those cities on business or to keep order. Compounds tended to be of a generous acreage because space was rarely at any premium and the officers who laid them out were used to their scale.

A bungalow, both the word and the form, derived from *bangla, banggolo* or similar, being the indigenous hut of Bengal. It was free-standing, close to square in plan, with a large room in the middle and a wide covered veranda all round to protect the walls of the room from rain: it sat on a low brick plinth and was covered by a single pyramidal thatched roof. At the end of the eighteenth century, north-east India was home to a huge number of

4.8. Main entrance, off Yuen Ming Yuen Road, of the British Supreme Court at Shanghai, designed by William Crossman in 1867 and rebuilt by Robert Boyce after a fire ravaged the compound in 1870.

4.9. The consul-general's house at Shanghai, designed by Robert Boyce and built soon after the compound fire in 1870.

European expatriates, predominantly East India Company employees and military. Unlike settlers, who were prepared to build permanently and with their own hands, traders and soldiers were transients and preferred to rely on local ways and labour force for their dwellings. They adopted the form of the local hut, which was so successfully adapted that by 1810 it had become the norm for expatriate accommodation throughout India, irrespective of other indigenous forms. The square plan became a rectangle with a line of two or three inter-connected rooms; the front, generally south, veranda grew deeper and the others narrower; and bathrooms and store rooms fitted neatly into the corners. The front veranda, a relaxing retreat from both sun and rain, was the focal point of expatriate living: entry, meeting-point, and communal sitting and play area. The veranda was also a bridge for the expatriate mind, between inside and outside, shade and brightness, privacy and duty, and between memories of far-off home and the realities of here and now. The rear veranda developed as the servants' access from their quarters and the kitchen, always apart from the bungalow for fear of fire. These bungalows – 'bungle-ohs!', as Edwin Lutyens called them – were often quite large, with walls that might be 15 feet high. The most likely internal features were a *chandry*, a stretched sheet of fabric over a room, and a *punkah*, a swinging fan on a frame.

The Royal Engineers and the East India Company's engineering departments and, after 1854, the three Presidencies' Public Works Departments introduced improvements to bungalows. Terms like 'engineering vernacular' and 'Military Board style' were coined to describe the appearance. More elaborate bungalows of brick or even stone became achievable even with unskilled labour. Flat roofs were introduced, and tiling replaced thatch on pitched roofs. Architects became involved in fashioning the veranda arches and pillars, roofs became more elaborate, and clerestory lights were inserted to improve ventilation by raising the main roof above the veranda roofs. These 'classical' or *pukka* bungalows evolved an upper floor, with stairs connecting the ground and first-floor verandas, both with balustrades, arches and pillars. By mid-century, the term 'bungalow' had lost its one-storey connotation in the Far East. The first bungalow to migrate to England, where the term has always precluded an upper floor, was built in north Kent in 1869. Well before then, however, variations of the Anglo-Indian bungalow were being pre-fabricated in Britain and exported to companies, and consuls, abroad. These export models were not designed to sit on plinths, which would have meant extensive site work and unpredictable fixing details, but were fully framed so that they could sit on either short brick piers or, especially in malarial areas of Africa, stilts.

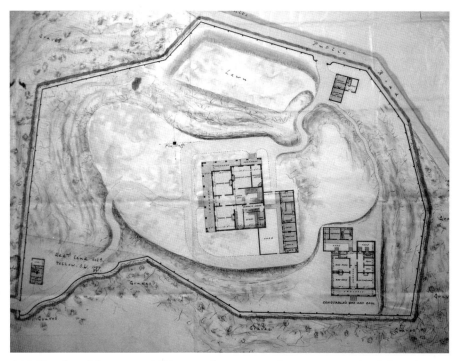

4.10. Site plan of the two-acre Wuhu consulate compound in 1887, atop a low hill overlooking the Yangtze River. The consul's two-storey house and office is in the centre, with flagstaff nearby, with the constable's one-storey quarter and gaol, with two cells, behind it.

Bungalows, like barrack blocks and prisons, were researched and refined by Royal Engineers on their construction courses at Chatham, with special emphasis on designing against the spread of disease. Crossman and Boyce were therefore familiar with the form when they arrived on the China coast, and they developed their consulate designs, and particularly their use of brickwork, from 'classical' bungalow precedents. Their consulates were generally of brick, on two floors, sited in walled compounds of a few acres that also included single-storey offices, local staff quarters and outbuildings. The consulates at Chefoo, Tamsui and Chungking, each at some distance from the native town, were typical **(Fig. 4.10).** The exceptions to compounds were in the concession areas where the consulates were beside godowns, customs house and merchants' residences and there was safety in numbers in the not infrequent event of local uprising. Wherever the concession area lay alongside a river, as was the case at Shanghai, Canton, Ningpo, Swatow, Tientsin, Chinkiang, Hankow and Kiukiang, each consulate would have its own tall flagpole and large flag to signal its position to captains sailing up the river. Wherever the consulate was sited, and since the consul's work consisted mainly in upholding British interests, the consulate buildings needed to demonstrate that Britain was confident and strong, and to look superior to other nations' consulates. To a large extent, Crossman and Boyce succeeded.

Later Chinese consulates
By about 1870, as Crossman was leaving Shanghai, the direct trade between England and China was increasing but the coasting trade in the hands of British merchants was being lost to cheaper Chinese operators. With reduced numbers, too, of British residents at the smaller ports, the workload of some consuls was decreasing. Their lives must have been exceedingly dull and lonely for much of the time. In some ports, there might be as few as ten ships appearing a year and perhaps only two other Britons in the town, most likely a missionary and the customs man (for, quirkily, the Chinese Imperial Maritime Customs Service was predominantly managed by Britons from its founding in 1854). There might be several other consuls, French, German or American most likely, but social life was exceedingly limited except for the occasional and well-documented excesses, especially when visitors appeared.

A Select Committee of the House of Commons, in the course of a wide enquiry into Diplomatic and Consular Services in 1870-2, probed whether some of the consulates could be closed or their staff reduced. Crossman, who had submitted two memoranda to the Committee and was called to give evidence, recommended fewer but better-paid consuls. His memorandum on staffing concluded that, excluding Shanghai, there were in

4.11. The Wenchow consulate, completed in 1892, stood on Conquest Island, in the centre of the Ou-Kiang river, opposite the city.

China 35 consular officers (consuls, vice-consuls, interpreters and assistants) serving 102 branches of British business houses, 52 missionaries and 209 British subjects engaged in trade, a figure that 'does not include women and children, but only men following some definitive pursuit; there are, of course, in addition, many stray individuals at the ports, such as tramps, deserters etc. ...', plus another 160 or so British subjects in Chinese employ, mostly with the Customs.[9] Crossman was questioned about whether it was worth the British government owning buildings in China. Aware of the fierce current debate about whether the government should own legation houses in Europe, Crossman chose his words carefully: '... as a general principle, it is wrong for the government to hamper itself anywhere with more buildings than are absolutely necessary; but in China and Japan it was very difficult to rent buildings except at most exorbitant rates, and it was cheaper to build than to hire', especially because the lessee had to pay for the repairs on hired properties.[10]

In these circumstances, the only new consulates to be established between about 1863 and 1876 were three vice-consulates at deeper anchorages downriver from Canton, Foochow and Tientsin to serve the new and larger ships that drew too much water to reach the consulates. These were at Whampoa, Pagoda Island and Taku respectively. The Chefoo Convention of 1876 opened four more ports to trade: Wuhu and Ichang on the Yangtze (and Chungking, far further up the Yangtze, was opened in 1890 by an additional article to the Agreement); Wenchow, another south-east coastal port between Foochow and Ningpo; and Pakhoi, far south on the Gulf of Tongking and close to French-dominated Indo-China. By 1875, however, the expense of building the infrastructure of concession areas had become so great, and Chinese nationalist sentiment so evident, that the British government withdrew from holding or managing new settlement land: it was henceforth leased or bought by the merchants direct from its Chinese owners **(Fig. 4.11)**. The Sino-Japanese War of 1894-5 over the Korean peninsular ended with the treaty of Shimonoseki of 1895 which forced China to recognise the independence of Korea, cede Formosa (Taiwan) to Japan and open up several more of its own ports to foreign trade. These were Hangchow and Soochow, both in the Yangtze delta area on the ancient 1,100-mile Grand Canal, and Shasi, less than 100 miles down river from Ichang on the Yangtze. Three more treaty ports – Szumao, Wuchow and Tengyueh, all in the south-west – were opened before 1900.

Non-China Far East consulates
The Americans were the first in 1854 to force open the door into Japan's ports. The British signed a convention at Nagasaki later in the same year, giving access to Nagasaki and Hakodate for repairs and supplies but no rights to reside or trade. In 1858, again shortly after the Americans, the British signed a treaty that provided for the appointment of a 'Diplomatic Agent' to reside at Edo (renamed Tokyo, 'eastern capital', in 1868 with the restoration of the Meiji dynasty) and for five ports to be opened for commerce on much the same extra-territorial terms as in China. These were Hakodate, at the south tip of Hokkaido; Kanagawa, the port for Edo; Nagasaki, on the west side of Kyushu, the southern island; Niigata on the west coast; and Hyogo, the port for Osaka.

Alcock was appointed Britain's first consul-general in Japan in 1858 and he oversaw the establishment of the first consulates. At Hakodate, he managed to lay claim, after a great tussle, to the best of the four available temples. 'On the ninth day after my arrival … a fine flag-staff, with the assistance of the *Highflyer's* men, was got up, and the Union Jack was hoisted with a royal salute from the squadron, to mark the first time the flag had floated over a British consulate in the port'.[11] At Kanagawa, it suited the Japanese better for the foreigners to settle on reclaimed land at the nearby village of Yokohama, lying below the huge outcrop that was later called the Bluff. The first site here was leased in 1863 and used for consulate, quarters and gaol but a fire swept through much of Yokohama in November 1866 and destroyed the consulate. Another site was immediately leased on which new offices were built and occupied in 1870. At Nagasaki the first consulate was also in a temple, the Myogoji temple. It had its drawbacks with just two small rooms, plus bathroom and kitchen, and only paper windows to keep out intruders, but a permanent consulate was completed in the settlement in 1864. The port at Niigata never really took off: the consulate eventually opened in 1869 but in that year the only trade had been with other Japanese treaty ports and there were only 17 resident non-Chinese foreigners, none of them British.

The first trade treaty between Britain and Siam was negotiated in the 1820s, but it was not until 1855 that a more solid basis for relations was negotiated when Sir John Bowring, Governor of Hong Kong, accompanied by Parkes, was received by King Mongkut. A treaty in that year granted Britain the right to trade throughout the kingdom and to establish consulates. Charles Hillier arrived as the first British consul the following year, and in 1857 King Mongkut gave a piece of land by the river in Bangkok for a British consulate site, which was slightly enlarged soon afterwards to about seven acres. The consul to whom it fell to lay out this compound was Sir Robert Schomburgk (sic) who arrived in Bangkok in December 1857 at the age of 53, having previously been a traveller, writer and collector but was best known for having surveyed and marked out the boundaries of British Guiana. His plan for the Bangkok compound was straightforward: the residence faced the river, which was also the main means of access, with the office and houses for UK staff behind, and quarters for local staff at the back **(Figs. 4.12 & 4.13)**. It was fitting that this fine large site was laid out by an experienced surveyor, in contrast to the earlier, larger and better-located site at Shanghai, on which all the early buildings were just strewn about.

Bangkok was not a treaty port in the full China coast sense but the principle of extra-territoriality was established, and hence the need for consular

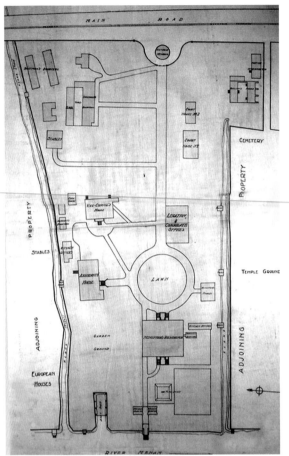

4.12. Sir Robert Schomburgk laid out the Bangkok compound in 1858 with the formal approach from the jetty on the river, at bottom. By the time that this plan was drawn in 1895 road access had been introduced, at top, with the entrance marked by a statue of Queen Victoria.

courts, constables' quarters and gaols. The Siam Consular Service, mainly on account of the difficult language its staff had to master, was a small and self-contained branch of the Far Eastern Service, with few career prospects for its members. Chieng Mai, the first vice-consulate, was established in 1882 at the behest of the Government of India, which contributed towards its upkeep and sent a guard of 20 Gurkha troops to protect the vice-consul. He sent them back after a few years for being more trouble than they were worth. The Siamese government, having found foreign consular courts irksome in Bangkok, was unwilling to see them in the north and instead established an International Court, applying Thai law, in Chieng Mai in 1886. Subsidiary vice-consulates to Chieng Mai, permanently staffed with consular assistants and visited regularly by the consul and the judge, were established at Lakhon, Nan and Phre in the 1890s.

The most well-known Siam consul was William Alfred Rae Wood. He was born in 1878, went to Dulwich College, and was sent to Siam as a student interpreter in 1896. He served successively in Bangkok, Chieng Mai and other vice-consulates before returning to Chieng Mai in 1913. He knew that his marriage to a Siamese girl would blight his promotion prospects but had gone ahead anyway. In consequence, he retired out of Chiang Mai as consul-general in 1931. He lived the 39 years of his retirement on his estate near Chieng Mai, publishing an entertaining, revealing and politically incorrect collection of memoirs in 1965. 'It is not a very pleasant job, hanging a man, but it was all part of the day's work for a British Consul in Siam when I was young,' he wrote, though he admitted that he had never had to do it himself. The Chieng Mai consulate kept elephants for many of its transport needs. Wood could not resist describing the enraged elephant that 'seized the man in its trunk, and this time drew his body two or three times on to its tusks, passing them through him. It was the most fearful sight I have ever seen. The elephant finally flung away the dead and shapeless body and went quietly down to a stream near by, where it calmly proceeded to wash its tusks.'[12]

Korea was the fourth and last country to be serviced by Far Eastern consuls, after China, Japan and Siam. The first British treaty with Korea

4.13. Garden front of the consul's house in Bangkok, built in the 1860s, with flagstaff and the river beyond.

4.14. The consular house in Seoul, designed by F.J. Marshall in Shanghai and built in 1891.

was signed on the beach at Inch'on, the port of Seoul, in June 1882. It had been negotiated by Vice Admiral George Willis and was quickly condemned on all sides. The British government entrusted Parkes, by now the minister in Tokyo, to re-negotiate the treaty from scratch, and Parkes sent William George Aston to Seoul to do so. A new treaty was signed in November 1883, to come into force in April 1884. Aston, a bachelor, stayed on in Seoul as consul-general and managed to persuade the Treasury to buy the Korean house that he was leasing. It consisted of six separate buildings and his successor complained that the dining room was an isolated tenement 20 yards from the drawing room, with no covered communication between. 'One always suffers by following bachelors', as the rueful accommodation adage has it.[13] A new house, designed by Marshall, the Office of Works' surveyor at Shanghai, was authorised in 1890 and completed the following year **(Fig. 4.14).** King Kojong, who had a palace next door, took a great interest in the building and wanted Marshall to build him another like it within the palace grounds. Boyce, back in London, and unused to hearing such praise, commented wryly to the Secretary in August 1892

It is so seldom that we have the pleasure of reading such kindly acknowledgements of the efforts of the Board's officers it is therefore all the more gratifying. I would willingly advise the Board to accede to the King's request but in the face of Mr Marshall's representations of excessive work I fear any further addition such as this … would too seriously interfere with his official duties.[14]

Chemulp'o, the chief seaport of Korea, and Pusan, at the head of a good harbour on the south-east coast, were both opened to foreign trade in 1883. A lease was taken on a good site on high ground at Chemulp'o and a single-storey bungalow was built on it in 1897. Nothing was bought or built at Pusan until 1902.

Persian consulates
Consulates were established in Persia long before the Far East but, though they were numerous during the nineteenth century, their buildings counted for less and were, anyway, mainly the responsibility of the government of India and not of Britain. The Sheikh of Bushire agreed in 1763 that the East India Company could establish a trading post, called a factory, at Bushire, near the head of the Persian Gulf, and he paid for its construction and gave the company a garden and burial ground as well: a simultaneous decree exempted the company from all customs duties, and gave it other privileges. The company transferred its Persian headquarters to Bushire in 1778 and the city became the principal British commercial and political centre in the Persian Gulf. The political resident, a senior company officer, became the most important Briton in Persia. Even after 1811, when Sir Gore Ouseley arrived in Tehran as Britain's first ambassador to Persia, the resident in Bushire remained a significant figure. The over-riding British concern was that Persia should be kept independent and resolute to deter interference in India by France, Afghanistan and, above all, Russia.

The international jockeying for position in Persia, which Rudyard Kipling popularised as the Great Game, lasted throughout most of the nineteenth century. The Persian consulates were essential pieces in this game. The first two were established in 1841 when the Persians permitted consuls at Tehran and Tabriz, then Persia's major commercial city, in return for Persian consulates in London and Bombay. In Tehran, the consulate was probably housed beside the legation at Bāgh-I Ilchī. In Tabriz, it was in the house that the Shah had 30 years previously confiscated from its owner and assigned to Ouseley for his periodic visits to Tabriz to be close to the Crown Prince: it was large and rambled around three courtyards, and remained in consular use until 1926.

In the Treaty of Paris of 1857, which ended the Anglo-Persian war of 1856, the Persians conceded 'most favoured nation treatment' to the British, which meant that the Foreign Office could locate consuls wherever it wanted, a privilege hitherto reserved for the Russians. A consulate at Resht, on the Caspian Sea, was the first direct result in 1857: the city was the centre of the important silk trade and a good place from which to observe Russian activities. The consulate was housed in a building leased from the Persian government, and bought from it in 1898. Twenty years after Resht was established, the Persians recognised the resident at Bushire as also the consul-general for the Fars region, with the result that a consulate was opened near the residency in Bushire.

Meshed, in the north-east, besides being the holiest and most politically important city in Persia, was well placed to collect intelligence about Russian military activities across the border. A consulate opened there in 1889. George Curzon, future Viceroy and Foreign Secretary, then travelling around Persia and writing occasional articles for *The Times*, passed through Meshed that year and was dismayed by the poor showing of the consulate. In a piece for *The Times*, he called on the British government to provide for the maintenance of the consul-general 'in a style and in quarters better fitted to represent to the native mind the prestige of a great and wealthy power'.[15] The result was the acquisition of an eight-acre site and the completion on it in 1893 of a full set of consular buildings, designed in Royal Engineer tradition for construction with local materials. The principal buildings stood on platforms well clear of the ground, with brick piers and mud wall panel infilling, all plastered and distempered. Verandas had plastered piers. Roofs were flat with pole joists, lathed and built up with mud above and plastered below.

With the opening of a consulate in Isfahan in 1891, there were, by 1900, six consulates in Persia (which was to rise to 18 in 1921). Yet, even as late as 1886, there were only about 70 British people resident in all of Persia, and more than half of them were working on the Indian Telegraph line. Clearly, the main purpose of the consulates was hardly consular.

Consulates elsewhere
By the mid-1850s, the British had established consulates at coastal trading ports around the coast of sub-Saharan Africa. Within the next 60 years, the European powers colonised all of Africa except Ethiopia and Liberia and had penetrated deep into the interior. *The Foreign Office List* of 1865 described David Livingstone's consular district as 'the territories of all African Kings and Chiefs in the interior of Africa, not subject to the authority of the King of Portugal, or of the King of Abyssinia, or of the Viceroy of Egypt.' There was no need for the European powers to establish legations in Africa because diplomatic relations were conducted between their own capitals.

But they established consulates in the more important of each others' new possessions: the British had consulates, for example, at Lourenço Marques, the capital of Portuguese East Africa; Boma, the capital of what became the Belgian Congo; and Dakar, in France's Senegal. British consulates that were established in territories that had not yet been formally colonised by Britain, Zanzibar and Zomba for example, became the stations of the various commissioners later appointed to administer these possessions, an activity that the Colonial Office took over from the Foreign Office in 1854.

Consuls in Africa, in common with other consuls in the General Service, were left to find and manage their own accommodation as best they could. London was never keen to provide capital funds for the General Consular Service unless such expenditure could not, or could no longer, be avoided. It much preferred consular accommodation to be rented by consuls, like diplomatic accommodation by diplomats, and paid for through financial allowances. Real hardship, however, resulted when a consul could find nothing remotely suitable and affordable to rent and could not muster influential support, as could diplomats in similar circumstances. 'I venture to hope that I may not be considered importunate in urging that the question of providing a Consular Residence may be brought before the Lords Commissioners of the Treasury as soon as possible' politely wrote an increasingly desperate consul from Dakar in early 1895.[16] This evoked from the chief clerk's section a request for more information. After that had been carefully presented but only cursorily considered, the consul received a reply 15 months later that 'I am to inform you that the Office of Works after carefully considering the circumstances of the case, are not disposed to waive in regard to this house the objections they entertain to the purchase of property of the kind by H.M.'s Government.'[17]

There was another side of the story. London, and particularly the Office of Works, was sceptical about the reliability of the estimates that accompanied proposals. 'The savings promised in these cases are never realised – or are swallowed up in expenses not entered in the account. … It is quite certain that the moment we become owners of the house we should be pressed to make alterations and do repairs that would alter the aspect of the Profit & Loss account…' wrote Henry Primrose, Secretary at the Office of Works, in 1890 when first resisting buying a good house in Lourenço Marques at a bargain price.[18] Costs were bound to exceed estimates in circumstances like this: the Secretary suggested adding automatic margins to the architects' estimates to cope with their optimism. London was also weary of successive incumbents' widely different views about the acceptability of particular properties. 'Experience shows that what one consular officer approves his

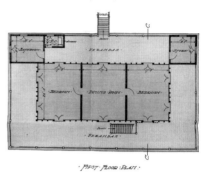

4.15. Drawings of 1906 for the proposed consulate at Monrovia, to be sent from England in mainly prefabricated from. On the main floor, a bedroom on either side of a dining room: below, the consul's office and a store.

successor condemns' was a typical comment, and not, of course, applicable only to consuls.[19]

London's scepticism looks cavilling in the context of consuls' dire predicaments. The First Commissioner concluded to the Treasury, when a later consul at Dakar returned to the charge in 1903, that 'we entertain very strongly objections to adding to our building responsibilities abroad, i.e. at remote and isolated stations like Dakar.' Charles Hardinge, in the Foreign Office (and later its permanent under-secretary), was more realistic: 'There can be no doubt that the present accommodation is quite inadequate; and [the Foreign Secretary] considers that it is precisely at remote and isolated stations where the absence of proper sanitary arrangements renders prolonged residence injurious to health, that it is most necessary for HMG to provide the Consul with a house.'[20] He won the day.

Other arguments were won too, with the result that about 15 consulates were built in sub-Saharan Africa between 1850 and 1910. Identifying the best site at which to buy land and put up a consulate was one of the most far-reaching tasks for a consul, whether in Africa, China or elsewhere. He needed to consider the lie of the land, where to catch the breezes when hot but find shelter from the gales, avoid proximity to unhealthy local dwelling places, be within practicable reach of his interlocutors, and take account of the likely future development of the town. The African consuls were not supported, as consuls were in the Far East, by visitors from the Office of Works until after 1900. 'The fact is we haven't the machinery to do this kind of thing', the Office of Works lamented in 1905 when faced with the prospect of building a consulate at Stanleyville, 1,500 miles up the

Congo river.[21] Most of the consulates that were built in sub-Saharan Africa, however, were procured by the Office of Works and, in varying degrees, built with materials and fittings shipped from Britain. Supplying the structures, parts and fittings for complete bungalows, ready for re-assembly on site, was an active industry in Britain serving a burgeoning demand for expatriate residential quarters throughout the colonies. Designs were straightforward, there was little room for argument about them, siteworks were basic, and an employee of the supplying firm was generally sent with the shipment to supervise assembly on site **(Fig. 4.15).**

Of the complete bungalows sent, the Fernando Po consulate appears to have been the first in 1856, followed by Old Calabar in the 1860s, Tamatave in 1886, Beira in 1890, Boma in 1903, and Leopoldville, Stanleyville and Monrovia in 1907. Bungalows built with local materials and by local contractors but with significant quantities of parts and fittings sent from England were Lourenço Marques in 1885 and Monrovia in 1908. These bungalow plans were typically three rooms in a row, surrounded by a deep verandah with its main sitting-out area protected by mosquito screening. They were simple but not small: the structures were timber-framed, and

4.16. The consulate at Boma, capital of former Belgian Congo, was exported from Glasgow in 1903 and erected on a 34-acre hillside site looking over the Congo River. The veranda was the hub of expatriate bungalow living.

sat either on low stone or concrete pads or on posts or piers tall enough to provide additional accommodation below the main floor **(Fig. 4.16)**. Access to the verandah was by timber stair, and the kitchen and servants' quarters, built from local materials, were a short distance to the rear. Monrovia, and its identical twin Stanleyville, based on an 11 feet grid, was seven bays wide and four bays deep, giving three rooms of 17 feet width and 22 feet depth. Other consulates – Johanna in about 1850, Zomba in 1887 and Dakar in 1908 – were designed with no prefabrication in mind, and were therefore freer in their planning, especially if brick or stone was locally available as the basic construction material. The Zomba plans indicate that it might originally have been the most architecturally attractive of all the African consulates. It was probably designed by the consul, Albert Hawes, and was certainly built by Messrs Buchanan Brothers, who occupied adjacent land. The house had five rooms in a row on both floors, with a verandah along both sides **(Fig. 4.17)**. With local construction, the list of fittings to be imported from Britain was relatively short. Any imports, though, could still be expensive when heavy duties were levied by a strict and preferential colonial regime: appealing to the colonial master's capital was rarely of much use. The British ambassador in Paris, for example, was instructed to seek from the French Ministry for Colonies a waiver from import duties on British goods being supplied for the new consulate in Dakar but the French government refused to interfere with colonial decrees. The Portuguese were

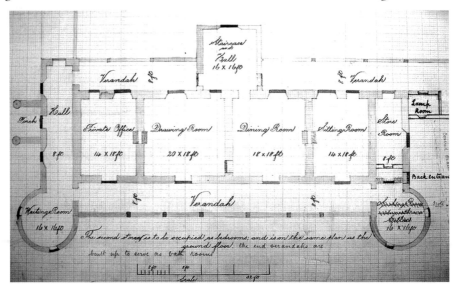

4.17. Ground-floor plan of the consulate at Zomba, of solid construction and completed in 1887. The building became the first Governor-General's residence on the creation of the Protectorate of Nyasaland in 1891, and is now part of an hotel.

Proposed New Consulate

Noumea New-Caledonia

WORKS. 40/273

4.18. Robert Boyce's proposed redesign of a French architect's proposal of 1891 for a consulate at Noumea, in New Caledonia.

so consistently unhelpful in sorting out some site tenure issues in Luanda that a frustrated officer in the British embassy in Lisbon told the Foreign Office Consular Department in 1921 that 'This Embassy has been trying for nineteen years to rouse the Portuguese molluscs out of their lethargy and to circumvent the obstructions placed in our path.'[22]

Five of the sites acquired freehold by the British government at Addis Ababa, Lourenço Marques (now Maputo), Luanda, Monrovia and Dakar remain in use today as British embassies. That they do so is testament to the skill with which the sites were first selected by the consuls. At Addis Ababa, Maputo and Dakar the consular buildings themselves, built over 100 years ago, remain in British diplomatic use. The house in Zanzibar presented by the Sultan in 1841 still stands, but is no longer a consulate, and subsequent Agency buildings are still recognisable. The consulate in Zomba is now the heart of the Hotel Masongola. Otherwise, the old African consulate sites and buildings have been sold or handed back and information about their fates is scant.

Three consulates that were built on small Pacific Islands – Tahiti, Noumea and Apia – in the second half of the nineteenth century illustrate a quieter world. Land in Papeete was granted in 1837 by Queen Pomare, on which a consulate was built in 1850. The project slightly overspent and the consul asked the Foreign Office to sanction the excess of £340 that he had incurred in building his small and distant consulate. The reply in October 1851, signed off by Palmerston as Foreign Secretary, contended that

> [t]he cost in this instance appears to me to have been excessive; for the best London House, built of brick and slate ought to be built and finished ready for furnishing for sixpence a cubic foot, measuring the height up to the top of the upright exterior walls, and their junction with the roof; while the Consular Residence at Tahiti, which is only a thatched Cottage, contains 13480 cubical feet, and has cost 11,780 shillings, being little short of a shilling per cubic foot. … Nevertheless under the circumstances which you have represented I am willing to allow you the difference …[23]

The municipality of Noumea granted a site, free of charge, in 1877 on which to build a British consulate. The building had tortured origins. The Treasury sent the designs, produced by a local architect, J. Coursin, to the Office of Works for observations. Boyce high-handedly sent a revised plan and specification to the consul, which prompted a 15 page letter from Coursin, disputing Boyce's proposals and wanting more fee **(Fig. 4.18).** Boyce replied that both the scheme and the fee should be reduced. The consul responded five months later to the effect that the Boyce plan was unworkable and sent another. After threats to sue and an intervention by the Secretary, quite a pleasing consulate resulted but the price went up from an estimate of £2,200 in 1890 to almost £5,500 by the time that the building was completed in 1895. In contrast, the consulate at Apia, where land was bought in 1886, was completed the following year for £1,000.

The need to build consulates peaked during the second half of the nineteenth century. In the twentieth, some would need rebuilding, many would close and new ones would be established, but the emergence of property markets in developing cities, and the greater availability of premises to buy or lease, reduced the requirements to build anew.

5

Legation Houses 1850-1900

At mid-century, France and Turkey were the only two countries in which Britain was represented by a resident ambassador, and the two embassy houses at Paris and Pera were owned by the British government. There were 23 legations, headed by resident ministers, all of them in Europe except for Mexico City, Rio de Janeiro, Tehran and Washington. None of the legation houses was owned by the British government.

Peking and Tokyo
With the negotiation of the right of diplomatic representation at Tokyo and Peking in treaties with Japan and China in 1858 and 1860 respectively, Britain quickly established legations in these two capitals with Frederick Bruce, youngest son of the seventh Earl of Elgin, as minister in Peking and Rutherford Alcock as minister in Tokyo.

Peking was the earlier legation to settle into permanent premises because a provision of the Convention of Peking obliged the Chinese to assist towards this end. Bruce wrote to Prince Kung, in effect the governor of Peking, in November 1860 that 'Several houses have been inspected in the last few days, but with [one] exception … which is more or less suitable, all have been found either too small or in such disrepair as to make them untenable'.[1] The exception was the palace that belonged to the Duke of Liang, the descendant of a former Emperor, that lay to the south-east of the Forbidden City, in an area where visiting foreign envoys were customarily lodged and which became Peking's legation quarter. A rent of 1,000 taels per annum was agreed, with British rehabilitation of the palace being in lieu of the first two years' rent. Since the Duke of Liang was 'absent on the

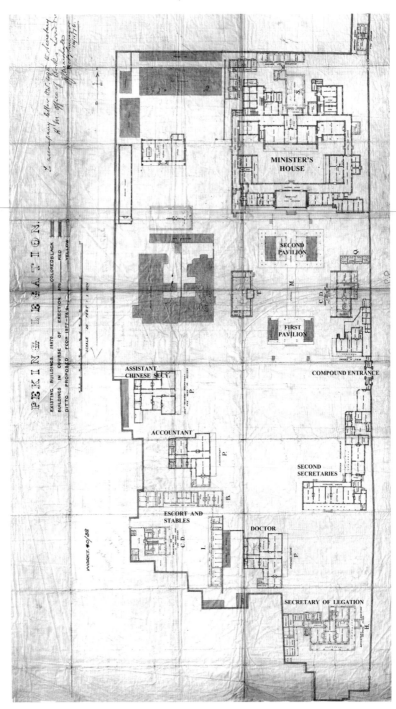

5.1. An 1876 plan of the seven-acre Duke of Liang compound in Peking. The canal road and entrance are on the east side. The duke's palace had been converted to an operational minister's house by the extensive enclosure of corridors. The shaded buildings were under construction.

public service', Bruce asked Prince Kung to confirm the deal, which he did the following day. Bruce went to Tientsin for the winter, leaving the legation Secretary, Colonel Neale, in charge of bringing the Liang palace into habitable order. He returned to Peking to take up residence in March 1861.

The Liang compound, of about five acres, was rectangular in shape, with its long axis running north-south, surrounded by a massive wall over four metres high **(Fig. 5.1)**. Along the eastern boundary was a canal that ran south from the Forbidden City to the Tartar or Manchu city, and on the western boundary were the Imperial Carriage Park and an open area called the Mongol market. The compound's northern neighbour was the Hanlin academy, faded by then from its heyday as Imperial China's highest academic institution, and its southern neighbours were Chinese dwellings and shops. The gatehouse into the compound was off the canal road, near the south-east corner. The palace itself, which became the minister's residence, was north from the gateway: a traditional Chinese building with a series of courts divided by handsome timber open pavilion structures roofed with green glazed tiles **(Fig. 5.2)**. It was all on one floor, and re-planned as far as practicable for its diplomatic entertaining role by enclosing some open pavilions and connecting them with corridors so as to form a large dwelling

5.2. The first pavilion on the route to the minister's house in Peking. To its left, a flanking pavilion that was converted to a church: to its right, another that housed the archives.

around a central courtyard. The interiors of the state apartment were handsome, with the ceilings highly decorated 'with gold dragons within circles on a blue ground, which again are in the centre of small squares of green, separated by intersecting bars in relief of green and gold' **(Fig. 5.3)**.[2]

As staff numbers grew, especially of Chinese teachers and their young British student interpreters being trained to serve in the increasing number of consulates, the compound was extended. Between 1860 and 1875, five separate pieces of adjoining land were bought direct from their owners, bringing the area of the compound up to about seven acres. The old Chinese houses were either converted or replaced with new European-style buildings designed and supervised by William Crossman. A house for the Secretary of the legation was fashioned from an assemblage of small old Chinese houses on the west side of the compound, nearly opposite the entrance gatehouse. The area to the west of the palace housed the students' quarters and a Chinese building in the middle was divided into a reading room, billiard room and hall with a small stage. A bowling or skittles alley ran along the wall with the Imperial Carriage Park, and a fives court was nearby. The west pavilion of the palace itself was converted to a church, and the

5.3. Entrance hall to the minister's house in Peking.

east pavilion used as escort quarters. The so-called bell tower, which looked more like a tall pavilion than a tower, was built in 1887 to mark Queen Victoria's Golden Jubilee. The British compound, the largest in the legation quarter, was the main focus for the 40 years from 1860 of the diplomatic community's frenetic social life, acted out in the midst of Peking's smells, squalor and official Chinese aloofness.

The Tokyo legation took much longer to settle into permanent premises. When he arrived in Tokyo in 1859, Alcock selected a temple called Tozenji as the first legation because it was the largest of the four he was offered and was convenient for both the bay, in case there was a need to evacuate by sea, and the road to Yokohama and Kyoto: besides, he was much taken by its beautiful Japanese garden. Temples, with their many rooms and spacious grounds, and often with special apartments set aside for visitors, were the most practicable buildings for westerners to adapt to their use, even if they had to share the grounds with the Buddhist monks. So frequently, however, were foreigners attacked, sometimes fatally, that many of the diplomatic missions withdrew to the relative safety of Yokohama.

The worst attack on the British legation was in July 1861, after which the Japanese guard was increased to 500, and later supplemented by British forces from China. Nevertheless, the legation staff had to withdraw to Yokohama, and demands came from London for a more defensible site for the legation. The Japanese produced one in a new diplomatic quarter at Gotenyama, and undertook to build on it at Japanese expense a strong legation to British designs, with walls, ditches and stockades. In January 1863, however, the incomplete buildings were burned down and the British decided to remain at Yokohama, using Tozenji on essential occasions, until they were better accepted, or could be better defended, in Tokyo. When Tozenji deteriorated beyond use, another temple near Sengakuji, at Daichuji, was used instead by legation visitors from Yokohama.

Harry Parkes succeeded Alcock as minister in Japan in 1865 and jibbed both at the indignity of being excluded from the capital and at the wastefulness of time spent travelling between Yokohama and Tokyo. He persuaded the Japanese government to erect a temporary one-storey timber legation in a courtyard in front of the Sengakuji temple, into which parts of the legation moved in November 1866. For a spell, 'HM Legation Sengakuji' was the letterhead. Crossman condemned this hutment structure as only suitable for bachelors, and then only in summer, but it had perforce to remain the British base in Tokyo for a further seven years. Meanwhile, Crossman helped to improve the legation's accommodation in Yokohama, where it was located on the Bluff, completely separate from the consulate.

By 1871, Tokyo was becoming safer for foreigners and Parkes decided that it was time to move the legation permanently from Yokohama. He had for years been keeping an eye out for a suitable eventual legation site in Tokyo and in 1871 earmarked a plot outside the Hanzomon Gate in Kojimachi, close to the Imperial Palace. Robert Boyce inspected this site, which was rectangular and a little under nine acres, in May 1871 and pronounced it suitable, although not ideal. He straightaway drew up proposals for setting out the compound, and outlined designs for the minister's residence, chancery offices, several single-storey houses for UK staff and ancillary buildings **(Fig. 5.4)**. Parkes endorsed these plans and Boyce sent slightly more developed versions of them to London in November 1871. The Office of Works tinkered with them and secured the Treasury's approval: the residence was estimated to cost about £8,000 and all the rest about £18,000.

A temporary lease was taken on the Kojimachi site in May 1872. Boyce returned in August 1872 to set up contractual arrangements for the buildings but found that, in Parkes' absence on leave, second thoughts were the order of the day. The newly-arrived *chargé* had doubts about building a residence in Tokyo, not least because a railway had now opened that brought the door-to-door journey from Yokohama down to an hour. Plans were put on hold until Parkes' return to Japan early in 1873, when he put paid to all the second thoughts and work on site started in March 1873. Parkes had, however, concluded that a pavilion should be included in the residence plans to serve as a ballroom but the Treasury refused. The contract itself proceeded relatively smoothly but the legation kept changing its mind about the scope

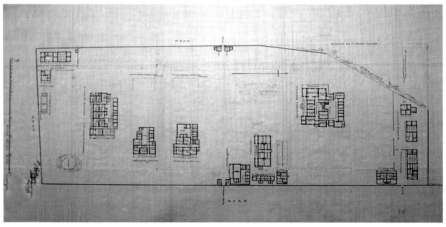

5.4. Robert Boyce's 1873 plan for laying out the nine-acre Tokyo compound. The five central buildings are, from left to right, students' quarters and vice-consul's house, Japanese secretary's house, secretary of legation's house, chancery, and minister's house. (North is to the right.)

5.5. The entrance front of the minister's house at Tokyo, designed by Robert Boyce and completed in 1875. A large room for dining and balls was added to the west (left) side in 1912. The house was destroyed in the Great Kanto Earthquake of 1923.

of what to build in the light of staff changes and of the Japanese Secretary, Ernest Satow, insisting on living off-compound. Relations between Parkes and Boyce also grew strained about what had and had not been agreed about the residence.

The compound was ready for occupation in January 1875 and the new buildings were roundly criticised by their first occupants for all manner of inadequacies, although they were built to plans that they or their predecessors had approved. Boyce sorted out most of the problems before he left Shanghai in 1876. The buildings' appearances were included in the criticisms but gradually their brick suburban demeanour became a source of comfort and pleasure, especially to many British visitors **(Fig. 5.5)**. Parkes left Tokyo for Peking in 1883 (and died there two years later). The 1872 temporary lease of the compound was superseded by a new one in 1884 which granted tenure in perpetuity in exchange for an annual rent of six silver yen per hundred *tsubo* (about 3.3 square meters, the area of two tatami mats) – the equivalent of £200 per annum for the whole compound. In 1894, the tower which Boyce had built at Parkes' request at the residence to provide a cool sitting area with a good view of Mount Fuji, collapsed, despite much binding around with iron straps, as a result of the frequent earth tremors: an omen. In 1901, when the addition of a ballroom was finally

111

approved, the minister of the day decided that an internal re-arrangement within the house had rendered it unnecessary.

From the mid-1890s, ambassadors leased an idyllic summer retreat west of Nikko, at the edge of Lake Chuzenji, looking across at Mount Nantai. It was a two-storey, shuttered Japanese timber house, then about a seven-hour rail and track journey from Tokyo. The ground landlord, the Imperial household, leased the site of about half a hectare on five-year renewable terms. Sir Ernest Satow, who became minister in 1895, commissioned Josiah Conder to rebuild the house. Conder had come to Japan in 1876 at the age of 24 on appointment as the professor of architecture at the Imperial College of Engineering and later ran a successful architectural practice in Tokyo: he was one of the foremost influences in introducing Western architecture into Japan. The house served as a summer retreat for embassy staff until 2010.

Legation houses in Europe
Building the Tokyo legation was unopposed by those in London who objected to the principle of government ownership because there was self-evidently no alternative to building and because Boyce handled the whole project as though it was just a large consulate. The expensive problems of Paris and Pera, however, had strengthened the case against ownership elsewhere and explained why none of the legation houses in Europe had been purchased. Ministers continued to be paid allowances towards leasing their own legation houses and carting about with them their own furniture and chattels. If an incoming minister was not taking over the lease of his predecessor's house, he would make enquiries about other available houses owned by noble or wealthy families in advance of his arrival through a personal acquaintance, a court official, or the secretary of the legation. Negotiations would then be with the owning family's appointed agent. A minister, especially one from Britain, was a good catch as a tenant: he could be expected to keep the house in reasonable condition, he might be easy to over-charge, and he might assist financially with capital repairs when they could no longer be put off.

A legation house needed to be quite large because a senior envoy might well take with him a party of anything between ten and twenty family members and staff. The house needed a few rooms to accommodate the chancery, where the officially paid legation secretary and the attachés would work: it could be tucked away because the minister did all his work in his study and never visited the chancery. Grand houses worked well as legation houses because much of a minister's role was to engage with the courtly life of his host country and most such houses could readily cope with any entertainment from small dinner party to large ball. Ministers and their wives, often aristocrats with a townhouse in London and a seat in the country, took the management of large households in their stride, often much eased by having brought with them their own senior domestic staff. Once a legation was installed in a suitable house, it often suited both landlord and successive ministers to keep renewing the lease. Thus had ambassadors occupied the Timoni family's house in Constantinople for over 100 years. At the opposite extreme, the ten ministers at Washington in the 60 years after 1815 had had to move the legation house more than ten times.

The costs of running a mission were increasing as the century wore on, the salaries and allowances paid by the Treasury were falling behind, and ambassadors and ministers were less prepared, or less able, to dig so deep into their own pockets to sustain the standards of their missions. The Treasury's first involvement with the accommodation problems of a European legation was at Madrid in 1846 when the lease of the house which successive ministers had occupied for decades in Calle de Alcalá was coming to an end. The minister, Henry Bulwer, who had served as embassy secretary at Constantinople and knew that the government could own a mission building, failed to persuade the Treasury that it should buy the Madrid house. But, for the first time, the Treasury was prepared, if Bulwer could find another suitable house, for itself to be designated the lessee instead of the minister. Bulwer therefore found 9 Calle de Torija for the legation and leased it for ten years in the Treasury's name. The Treasury sent the lease to the Office of Works in 1850 because, by then, the rent was being charged to the Office's diplomatic buildings Vote and the Office would be responsible for whatever negotiation with the landlord would be necessary as the lease expiry in 1857 drew near. In the event, the Office of Works, in agreement with successive incumbents, renewed the lease in 1857, 1867 and 1877. In 1886, by which time opposition to the government owning houses abroad had waned, the Office of Works decided to buy the freehold of the Madrid house for £12,000 instead of renewing the lease.

The waning of opposition was gradual. In 1861, the Select Committee on the Constitution and Efficiency of the Diplomatic Service included among its recommendations 'that, whenever it is practicable and fit, a residence for the term of years should be secured for the British Embassy or Mission …'.[3] Sir Andrew Buchanan, who arrived at The Hague as minister in 1861, was an early beneficiary of this recommendation when he was authorised to negotiate a 21-year lease on the house at 12 Hooge Westeinde from the Jesuit Fathers. The case for government leases was further helped by the unifications of Italy and Germany, in 1861 and 1871 respectively, because they significantly reduced the number of legations in Europe. Another help was the retirement in 1873 of Edmund Hammond, who had been the permanent under-secretary at the Foreign Office for almost 20 years and was a stalwart opponent of owning permanent houses, as well as of almost all other reforms. The Select Committee of 1872 on Diplomatic and Consular Services went so far as to recommend that permanent houses should be provided for missions abroad. This did not end the argument, and indeed the First Commissioner of the Office of Works at the time, Acton Ayrton, was still opposing government ownership, but it shaped the rest of the debate.

The lease of the legation house in St Petersburg – or rather, the huge legation apartment on the first floor of Prince Soltykoff's house overlooking the Neva – renewed by heads of mission since at least 1865, was the next to be put on a more permanent basis. In 1875, an Office of Works surveyor concluded that there was a better deal to be done than the ten-year lease negotiated by the minister in 1873. He renegotiated it to run from 1875 on the basis that Soltykoff would put parts of the apartment into proper order in return for a higher rent: this incentive was repeated in 1879. The work to be done this time included re-papering the state rooms, which paved the way for a new kind of debate now that the public purse was paying for items that heads of mission would previously either have put up with or paid for themselves. The ambassador, the Earl of Dufferin, wanted silk covering instead of paper in the boudoir and drawing room. The Treasury, while agreeing with everything that the Office of Works had provisionally negotiated, jibbed at the silk. 'My Lordships cannot agree to charge the public with such expenses as £600 or £800 for covering the walls of any of the rooms with silk, and, in negotiating with the proprietor, you will be careful not to allow the demand for any such expense to be introduced'.[4] On furniture, 'They are of opinion that expenditure out of Public Funds should be limited to moveable furniture, which is substantial and handsome, without being in any degree extravagantly expensive'.[5]

The pattern of the Office of Works taking over the lease of a legation house and later buying it applied, after Madrid, to six more European legation houses in the second half of the nineteenth century. In Lisbon, a rambling house on Rua de San Francisco de Borja in Lapa, a smart suburb on a steep hill rising from the Tagus just west of the city centre, was first leased by ministers in 1833, then by the Office of Works, and was bought in 1875, the first European house to be bought since Paris in 1814. The ambassador, the Earl of Lytton, straightaway added a ballroom wing in rather the same relationship to the house as Pauline's ballroom at Paris, where he had recently served. His haste resulted from wanting it ready for the Prince of Wales's visit to Portugal later that year. The wing was so badly built that, as soon as Lytton departed to be Governor-General of India a couple of years later, it had to be demolished and rebuilt properly.

In Copenhagen, the old house at 26 Bredgade, on the corner with St Anna Plads, was first leased by ministers in 1854, by the Office of Works in 1879 and was bought in 1898 for about £22,000. In Athens, the fine house on the corner of what became Euripides and Dragatzani Streets, on the north side of the Square of the Mint, was leased by ministers from about 1859, by the Office of Works in 1885 and was bought in 1899 for about £14,000. In Brussels, the Hotel de Rodes, on the corner of Rue de Spa and Rue de la Loi, was probably leased by ministers before 1875 but in that year was taken on a ten-year lease by the Office of Works, and bought in 1887 for about £14,000.

The other two leased, and later bought, European mission houses were at Rome and Berlin: both were larger and more contentious. Rome joined united Italy in 1870 and immediately became its capital. The Italian Ministry of Foreign Affairs moved from Florence in 1871 and the following year the minister, Sir Augustus Paget, moved the British legation to Rome. After a difficult search, he took a five-year lease from Baron de Reinach on the house next to Michelangelo's Porta Pia to serve as the legation house, although it had no ballroom and was too small to fit in the chancery. Three years later, Paget wrote to the Foreign Secretary, the Earl of Derby, explaining that, although his lease did not expire for another two years, he was acting now because he knew how dreadfully difficult it would be to find another house in the event that renewal of the lease proved impossible.

> Even supposing that my landlord will be disposed to renew upon the same terms I must frankly aver that the house as it stands at present, although not a bad house for a private gentleman, is by no means fitted for the permanent residence of the British minister. In the first place it is undoubtedly an inconvenience having the Chancery in another part of the town, next there is no possibility of giving a ball or a large entertainment, the dining room is on the ground floor, and by reason of the drawing rooms being on the first floor with a staircase of 51 steps to get to them, the only room to receive in before dinner is my own writing room, also on the ground floor, which is neither large enough nor properly adapted to the reception of a numerous and formal dinner party. All these defects however could be remedied … should Her Majesty's Government be disposed to purchase it, and to go to the necessary expense of building and altering, and it is this proposal that I am now solicitous of submitting to your Lordship, it being in my opinion very desirable to take time by the forelock as my landlord, Baron

> de Reinach, a banker at Frankfort bought the property on a speculation and
> may at any moment dispose of it.[6]

Paget recommended buying the buildings and half the land for about
£23,000 and spending an additional £10,000 on the necessary additions
and alterations. He pointed out that the interest foregone by the government
from making this capital purchase would be less than the allowance of
£1,200 per annum that he received for housing the legation. He hoped that
the government would despatch to Rome 'some fit and competent person
to pronounce a judgment' upon his whole proposal. The Treasury at first
simply said that the costs were more than it was prepared to incur, but later
agreed that a qualified person should visit. The Office of Works sent Charles
Stephenson, a consultant surveyor. Stephenson concluded that the costs were
a 'fair and proper sum' and that purchase was a more economic proposition
than paying a rent allowance. The Treasury accepted this advice and the
purchase deed was signed in 1877. Building works on the new ballroom and
chancery wing started soon afterwards and worked out satisfactorily.

Without informing London, Paget concurrently and privately leased
from Reinach the half of the land that the British government had not
bought, so as to preserve the whole of the magnificent garden for the use
of the embassy (to which status the legation had been raised in 1876). Five
years later, and with Paget still in post, Reinach's heirs wanted to terminate
this lease so as to develop their half of the garden. After a tussle, the Treasury
agreed to buy about a fifth of the heirs' land so as to shield the residence
garden from their adjacent development. A young third secretary in the
embassy, Gerald Portal, lamented to his sister in April 1882, 'Our government,
with their usual economy, are going to allow this Embassy to lose half of its
splendid garden, which is the greatest blessing to us all … . They are going
to begin to cut down a wood and avenues of old ilex above 300 years old
tomorrow. It seems an awful shame. We also lose the only lawn tennis court
which is in the shade.'[7]

Berlin became the capital of the united Germany in 1871, and Odo
Russell, later Lord Ampthill, was the first British ambassador. Russell leased
the house at 544 Dorotheenstadt (later 70 Wilhelmstrasse) from the Duke
of Ujest soon after his arrival. The Office of Works, again using Charles
Stephenson to report on the house in 1876, affirmed its suitability and
negotiated a ten-year lease from that year. Seven years later, the Duke of Ujest
became the sole proprietor of the house and proposed to sell it for what
it cost him, £64,375, and gave the British government first refusal. Boyce,
recently returned to London from the Far East and now the Office of Works'

5.6. The Berlin embassy house at 70 Wilhelmstrasse, leased in 1872, bought in 1884, and destroyed by bombing in 1944. It was designed by August Orth in the 1860s and known as the Palais Strousberg after its owner. The present embassy offices, completed in 2000, stand on the same site.

first full-time surveyor/architect to be engaged solely on diplomatic and consular work, was despatched to make a recommendation. His conclusion was that, unless Ujest would reduce his price to £50,000, it would be more economical to buy a site and build a new embassy on it. Ujest declined to reduce his price, and the Treasury authorised the purchase of an alternative site in Thiergarten that Boyce had identified as suitable.

Boyce, perhaps used to simpler property issues of the Far East and to sparring with Parkes, had clearly over-stepped the mark. His cost calculations built no contingency margin into the construction costs of a major new house and there was no assurance that the ambassador could remain in his present house until a new one was constructed. Worse, Boyce had not discussed his recommendation with the ambassador. Ampthill strongly objected: the Duke had now dropped his price by £3,000; other parties, doubtless rival embassies, were interested in buying the house; and the Thiergarten site that Boyce had identified would simply not do. An Office of Works official annotated '… the great difficulty is one of valuation. Lord Ampthill, strongly supported by Lord Granville [Foreign Secretary], urges the purchase at a price considerably in excess of what the professional officer of the Board considers the house to be worth'.[8] The First Commissioner

117

over-ruled Boyce's advice and supported purchase to the Treasury but warned about expensive improvements that would need to be made to the sanitary arrangements in the house. The Treasury dropped the idea of the Tiergarten site and authorised the purchase of Ujest's house. Ujest hoped the government 'will suit their own convenience in regard to the time, and mode of payment….'.[9] The Office of Works took some advantage of this leniency, partly because a low payment in the current year would enable them to fund some consular residences on the west coast of Africa. The deed of purchase was signed at the end of 1884, three months after Ampthill's death at his post **(Fig. 5.6)**.

The first legation house to be built by the British government in Europe was at Vienna. The initial proposal was that a *bauverein,* or building society, should construct a house which the British government could then take on a long lease at a rent less than the ambassador's current rent allowance. On his arrival in Vienna as ambassador in late 1871, Sir Andrew Buchanan, by now one of 'the shire-horses of the Victorian diplomatic corps',[10] found that the owner of his leased residence on Herrengasse was keen to see him out of it within a few years. Buchanan, well aware of the debates in London about owning houses, identified both a suitable *bauverein* and an able, busy and fashionable architect, Viktor Rumpelmayer, an Austrian born in Bratislava. The Treasury was wary of Buchanan's proposal: 'the party to be contracted with is a Bauverein, a Building Society (chiefly rich Jews) at Vienna. They speculate in land and in the erection of buildings'.[11] The Chancellor of the Exchequer, Robert Lowe, was nevertheless minded to go ahead despite the advice of some officials. The First Commissioner, the inflexible Ayrton, was implacably opposed to the idea. He knew he could not win an argument with the Chancellor, so he refused to take part in the debate. The Treasury therefore dealt with Ayrton's director of works, Douglas Galton, through the Secretary in the Office of Works, George Russell. Russell informed the Treasury

> that the First Commissioner adheres to his opinion that it is not desirable that he should interfere with a service that is being carried on by their Lordships. The First Commissioner is unable to perceive how it was necessary in point of time to adopt the course which has been pursued and he has directed their Lordships' letter and its enclosures to be handed to the Director of Works. The First Commissioner is not in a position to express any opinion upon their Lordships proceedings and he regrets that the business of the Office does not in his opinion admit of the Director of Works proceeding to Vienna at the present time.[12]

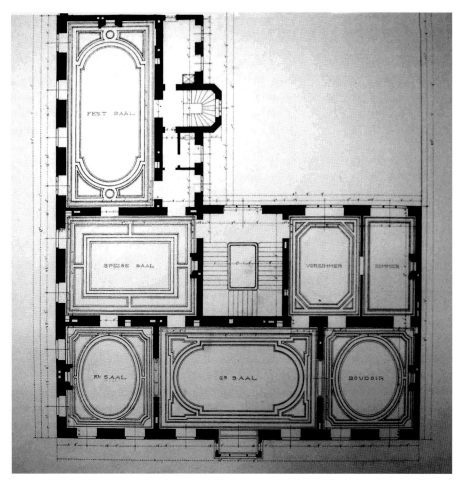

5.7. Viktor Rumpelmayer's plan of 1873 for the first floor of the Vienna embassy house. The rooms are, clockwise from the stair: ante-room, a private room, boudoir, large and small drawing rooms, dining room and ballroom. The chancery was on the ground floor below the small drawing room.

To which the Treasury riposted to Ayrton that it had 'not discharged your Department from its ordinary duty of superintending, and providing in your Estimate for, the execution of works approved by this Board'.[13] At this juncture, Gladstone transferred Ayrton to another role, that of judge-advocate-general. Not for nothing was the front cover of the Treasury file on Vienna annotated in manuscript 'Control of – and protests of – Office of Works'. Meanwhile, the pragmatic Galton had visited Vienna and found, rather to his surprise, that the *bauverein* project was feasible – so feasible, in fact, that he recommended that the Office of Works should buy both the land and Rumpelmeyer's house once the *bauverein* had built it, rather than lease the result from the *bauverein* **(Fig. 5.7)**. The scheme proceeded on that basis, although there were a few hiccups to come. The ambassador wanted to widen the site by six feet so as to lengthen the chapel and improve the public rooms. Treasury reminded the Foreign Office that the proposed house,

> representing as it does an area about equivalent to that covered by one of the large central houses in Belgrave Square, is sufficient for the erection of a suitable Residence for Her Majesty's Ambassador. My Lords do not feel warranted in authorising the acceptance of the additional ground referred to … but would suggest a readjustment of the building plans as the best means of securing any improvements that may be thought desirable.[14]

Buchanan became impatient: he asked to be authorised, to save time, to complete the contracts without further reference home. His arguments carried no weight: the Treasury's internal minuting included '… the FO does not shine in negotiations about land and buildings, and has extremely vague notions of specific performance, as you will see if you compare page 12 within with what has been actually agreed to by us'.[15] Galton was satisfied that the proposal would make a suitable British embassy, but it would need managing well. He wrote, in no-nonsense Royal Engineer fashion,

> [I]t is manifestly undesirable to proceed in this matter without a clear understanding as to what is to be, 1, the cost of the ground, 2, the definite plan, 3, the materials for construction, 4, the extent of decoration and, 5, the cost of the building. Any loss of time, consequent on the delay required to place the business on a clear and systematic basis, will be more than repaid by the avoidance of extras, even if it should entail (which is not certain) the prolongation of the allowance for the hired house. And, until the plans, specifications, and estimate had been prepared and sent here for consideration, it would appear quite unnecessary for anyone to proceed to Vienna.[16]

The contract worked out well and, thanks to favourable movements in the rate of exchange, out-turned in 1876 within the £42,000 estimate that had been laid before Parliament **(Fig. 5.8)**.

Legation houses beyond Europe

The design and construction of the first legation house in Washington was concurrent with Tokyo and Vienna but the Treasury chose hardly to involve Ayrton or the Office of Works. When Sir Edward Thornton arrived in Washington as minister at the end of 1867, he resolved to establish a

5.8. The embassy house at Vienna, completed in 1875 to the designs of Viktor Rumpelmayer. The main entrance is at the right. The subsidiary entrance to the left was to the stables, yard and staff quarters: this block was demolished after damage in the Second World War.

permanent home for the legation by the time that the lease on his current house expired in 1872. After several years of making fruitless purchase proposals to the Treasury, Thornton proposed that the Treasury should buy a site and build upon it. The Treasury agreed in 1872 and Thornton bought a site (which he then conveyed to the Commissioners of Works) of about 30,000 square feet the following year on the north-west corner of the junction between Connecticut Avenue and N Street for just under $15,000. This site, ten blocks from the White House, was adventurously far north for the time.

Thornton commissioned plans from the architect John Fraser, of Washington DC and Philadelphia, who produced drawings for a fine house in a Second Empire style with a small wing for chancery offices. Galton was asked for his observations and found a good deal to fault in the minister's and Fraser's proposals and apparent under-estimate. As it turned out, construction went well in the hands of Robert I. Fleming as builders and the project overspent by only a little, with an outturn cost of about £31,000 **(Fig. 5.9)**. Thornton moved in during 1875. The house became the best

5.9. The legation house in Washington on Connecticut Avenue, designed by John Fraser and completed in 1875. This was the first permanent home for the legation in Washington after six decades of peripatetic leasing. A local paper likened its appearance to 'the rugged headland of some storm-swept cape'.

building in the vicinity of Dupont Circle, where many other diplomatic houses joined it over the years to create one of the most elegant residential sectors of Washington and a diplomatic hub. Thornton's house was also the first foreign-owned legation building in Washington.

The Cairo house, though not technically a legation house, came next. The Suez Canal opened in 1869 and came under British control in 1875 when the British government bought the Khedive Ismail Pasha's controlling shares for a huge sum. Nervousness about the safety of the canal after a nationalist revolt caused the British to invade Egypt in 1882 and establish a country-wide occupation. Sir Evelyn Baring was appointed in 1883 to manage this 'informal' British protectorate and, in effect, to become the ruler of Egypt. His lowly new title of 'agent and consul-general' reflected Egypt's continuing formal international status as a vice-royalty of the Ottoman empire: it hardly hinted at the diplomatic importance of Baring's role in seeking to put Egypt on to a sound financial and political footing.

On his arrival in Cairo, Baring rented a house on Maghraby Street (now

Adly Street) from a Mr Baird, but he and his staff quickly outgrew it and needed somewhere larger and better. Aware of this need, the local Church Committee in late-1885 offered first refusal for £6,000 of about 3,000 square meters of land that it owned, and on which a new agency could be built, between the church and the house that Baring was occupying. Mitford, Secretary at the Office of Works, talked this proposal over with Baring, who emphasised that any building should be done well and that a better chance was unlikely to arise. Although Mitford was one of those still opposed in principle to building government houses abroad, he was prepared to make an exception in the case of Cairo because he understood, as many failed to do, that leasing suitable houses was an inadequate policy if there were no suitable houses to lease. The Treasury authorised Boyce to visit Cairo and report, without any commitment whatsoever to spend the £20,000 or so that a subsequent project was thought likely to cost. Boyce supported all that Baring had said, negotiated the Church Committee's price for the land down to below £4,000, outlined a plan for the site, estimated a total of £27,000 for the whole project, and urged a speedy decision because the Church Committee was, allegedly, considering an alternative offer.

The Treasury rejected the project on grounds of expense in March 1886: 'It is of course necessary that H.M. Representative in Egypt and elsewhere should be properly housed but the experience of each year only confirms My Lords in the view that this end can be attained at far less expenses by means of suitable allowances than by provision in kind'.[17] Baring returned to the charge in a letter to the Foreign Secretary, fleetingly Stafford Northcote (by now the Earl of Iddesleigh), in October 1886. Baring set out in graphic detail the shortcomings of his house, and went on

> I receive at present allowances to the amount of £1000 a year. There are charges on these allowances amounting to about £600 a year leaving about £400 a year available for the payment of rent. The rent of my present house is £600 a year, being £200 more than the amount covered by the allowances. If such an arrangement were possible, I should much prefer the plan of drawing allowances and making my own arrangements for a house. But I can most positively assure Your Lordship that even if the Treasury were willing to increase the allowances, no suitable house is to be found in Cairo. ... If therefore anything is to be done, I submit that there is no alternative but to build a house. ... I need hardly say that, if the Treasury maintain [their] view, all idea of building an Agency must be dropped.
>
> I doubt whether there is any diplomatic post in which such heavy expenses are incurred [as] by H.M. Representative at Cairo. ... My present salary, exclusive of allowances is £5000 a year, and I can assure Y[our] L[ordship]

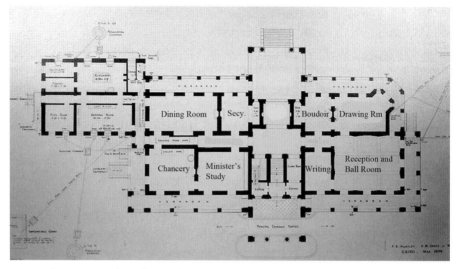

5.10. Robert Boyce's plan of 1887 for the Cairo agency building, with characteristic verandas and the service functions in a rear wing. The house was too small for Lord Kitchener, for whom a separate ballroom was built in 1913 and connected to the corner of the veranda outside the main reception room.

that considerable as that salary is, it would be impossible for me to maintain my present position properly, were I not possessed of a considerable private income. With every wish, however, to make use of my private income in a liberal spirit, I really must decline to bear so heavy an additional charge as would be thrown upon me by the proposal of the Treasury.[18]

The Treasury relented and Boyce revisited Cairo in February 1887. The Church site had gone but Baring had squeezed out of the Egyptians a 1.3-hectare site beside the Nile, in the aristocratic neighbourhood of Kasr al-Dubara. Boyce thought well of it: 'On its west side it has an uninterrupted view of the country across the river – the pyramids being well in sight – and on the opposite side the citadel'. Boyce agreed a price for the land, and recommended making an immediate start on fencing, levelling and collecting materials. He produced an outline plan, of which he said 'The building itself will be a rectangular one of easy and simple construction and so far as I can judge not in excess of the present and future requirements of the Post' **(Fig. 5.10)**.[19]

Baring put him in touch with Mr Crookshank, Director of Convict Prisons, who offered to procure stone, cement and lime through his depot at perhaps 30-per-cent discount to market prices: this buoyed Boyce's confidence that the whole could be achieved for the £30,000 by then accepted in principle by the Treasury.

As the result of a debate in Parliament, however, the budget was cut to £22,000. Boyce shrank the plan and sent it to Baring for comment. Baring said that to build such a small house would be a waste of money, adding that the French had just spent over £30,000 on their new house. The Treasury decided in July 1887 that 'My Lords are of opinion that it would be inexpedient to proceed with the scheme', and withdrew the £22,000 from the Vote.[20] Boyce pointed out that a watchman was needed to keep an eye on the stone and brick stored on the half-levelled site: that suggestion was also turned down, Baring let nearly two years pass before forcing the case open again. The Egyptians, he said, would now accept £2,580 for the site, instead of the £3,620 that Boyce had agreed, if the British government would promise to build. Boyce thought the house could be built for £25,000. The Secretary at the Office of Works, Henry Primrose, succeeding Mitford, weighed in

the Office of Works have always opposed the acquisition of official diplomatic houses in European capitals. But the arguments which apply to European cities do not apply to cities in the semi-civilised states. In these 'representation' is of infinitely more importance than in Europe, and in many cases it is almost impossible unless an official residence is provided. This appears to be the position in Cairo, and the political argument in favour

5.11. The agency building in Cairo, completed to Robert Boyce's design in 1894. Frederick Huntley, the resident architect and clerks of works, recorded his achievements in a bound volume that he presented to the Office of Works library.

of building is a strong one. On the other hand it is doubtful if the House of Commons is disposed to take this view …[21]

But it did. In May 1889, the Treasury agreed to buy the land at the lower figure but only in the next financial year, starting 1 April 1890: the Egyptian government agreed to this, and was now prepared to add to the plot, free of charge, a further 50-metre strip of previously reserved ground, thereby increasing the site from 1.3 to almost 2.0 hectares. Boyce was despatched to Cairo again to mark out the site and get things moving: he was not the man to resist pointing out that all the earlier collected materials had been stolen as he predicted would happen without a watchman. He had difficulty in making headway for want of both a good contractor to build a boundary wall and good superintendence. The local Department of Works could not help because it was low Nile season and its entire staff was fully occupied. The Office of Works therefore sent Frederick A. Huntley, one of its own assistant architects, to Cairo in October 1890 as resident architect and clerk of works. Construction of the house started soon afterwards and was completed in 1894, with a final total cost of just under £40,000 **(Fig. 5.11)**. Baring, raised to the peerage as Lord Cromer in 1892, occupied it until his departure from Egypt in 1907.

By 1900, the Office of Works was the owner or long leaseholder of a dozen or so mission houses in Europe. Today, Paris and Vienna remain in full use, each with, coincidentally, more recently acquired embassy offices next door. The sites at Berlin and Rome now both contain embassy offices, the former buildings on each having been demolished after serious bomb damage wrought by the Allies in Berlin in 1943 and Zionist terrorists in Rome in 1946. The house in Madrid was sold in 1909, Athens in 1938, Brussels in the mid-1960s, Copenhagen in the late 1970s, and Lisbon in 2006. The St Petersburg lease was given up in 1924 and The Hague lease was terminated in 1984. The buildings in Copenhagen, The Hague and Lisbon survive in other uses. Of Washington and Cairo, the two other major houses besides Vienna built before 1900, Washington was demolished in 1932 and Cairo survives as the ambassador's residence in Egypt: it is still sometimes referred to as *Bayt Al Lurd* – the Lord's house.

6

Order and Disorder 1875–1900

The arrival of rules

The first rules to apply to diplomatic accommodation overseas concerned silver plate. In the seventeenth century, the sovereign loaned silver to ambassadors and ministers as a perquisite of office. The arrangement clearly had some failings because, in 1688, the Secretaries of State were ordered 'to allow no ambassador to take official plate from the Jewel House unless he promised either to return it or buy it at the end of his mission'.[1] A better control system was introduced in 1816, beginning at Berlin, whereby plate was officially provided to eight missions in Europe under rules drawn up by the Treasury and the Lord Chamberlain's Department. These stipulated that the head of mission should be responsible for the safe custody of the plate described in the official inventory; should annually check the inventory and certify its completeness; hand the plate over to his successor; and make good any losses at his own expense.

As the Treasury's direct stake in the accommodation overseas grew during the nineteenth century, it enforced the same rules as governed other public expenditure. The Treasury categorised all public expenditure into Classes, sub-divided into Votes, and further into Subheads. Each year it presented to Parliament, for its discussion and approval, the Estimates of the sums that it had agreed with each department could be spent in the following financial year. Before 1842, all expenditure on diplomatic and consular activity overseas was within Votes held by the Foreign Office. A new Vote was 'taken', i.e. created, in that year specifically for overseas diplomatic accommodation to identify expenditure related to the Paris embassy house, and the Office of Works was charged with responsibility for this new Vote. It grew with the inclusion of the mission houses at Constantinople and Madrid in the mid-1840s, and in 1856 its scope was further widened to include all 'British Embassy Houses abroad'. The legation and consular buildings in China, Japan and Siam were transferred to this Vote in 1868, and the Tehran mission in the following year. Rents in China and Japan followed in 1872, and the Vienna and Washington legation houses in 1874. The Vote was accordingly re-titled in that year as 'British Embassy Houses and Consular and Legation Buildings'. Lisbon and various consular rents were added in 1875. Thereafter, all new responsibilities assumed by the Office of Works for diplomatic and consular accommodation overseas were included in this Vote. Its title was shortened to 'Diplomatic and Consular Buildings' in 1887, giving rise to the name 'dips and cons', by which the overseas estate was informally known for most of the next century.

Although the money approved for a project by Parliament through the Estimates procedure was allocated to the Office of Works as the Vote holder, the Office could neither incur nor commit expenditure on a project until it had been specifically approved by the Treasury. The Treasury therefore had a stranglehold on almost every accommodation decision. Annual Vote accounting in this way worked well enough for running costs like rents, maintenance and fuel, but it caused problems for capital projects. Before 1866, the full estimate for a capital project was voted at the outset of the project, even though the expenditure would be spread across subsequent years, with no repercussions if money was drawn down earlier than expected or, more likely, underspends were carried forward and spent later than expected. This arrangement obviously suited the Office of Works, particularly for its large projects at home, but it gave Parliament no opportunity to reconsider a capital expenditure decision unless more money was required than it had voted. The arrangement also gave a misleading view of the Vote in any one year, and hence denied proper control. The auditor-general therefore ruled in 1866 that underspends on capital projects had to be surrendered at the end of each financial year and the money re-voted. This change gave Parliament many more opportunities to adjust projects and programmes, and had a highly significant effect on their management.

The chief accounting problem that the Office of Works faced on overseas projects in the nineteenth century was a lack of control as a result of not being sure what expenditure was being incurred in its name. It therefore pressed for the introduction of procedures that were no different in principle from the stipulations that it had made in 1840 when first becoming involved with the Paris house. Before the Office could accept expenditure, it needed to know exactly what property the government owned, to dictate the terms of leases that were drawn up in the name of the Crown, to have opportunity (except in emergencies) to authorise purchases and construction work before they were incurred, and to have reliable accounts rendered to it at regular intervals. These were all thoroughly defensible strictures but they inevitably led to frustration and bureaucracy at home and overseas. Demarcation disputes were the most common. Was the Foreign Office or the Office of Works financially responsible for, for example, fire buckets, flagstaffs and their halyards, and mats for official boatmen?

Robert Boyce, the Office of Works surveyor, still in Shanghai in 1874, took it upon himself to draft, with London's support, a set of 'Rules and Regulations as to the Care of the Property of Her Majesty's Government at the Treaty Ports in China and Japan'. The document, based on Crossman's and Boyce's experience over most of the preceding ten years, was promulgated by the Foreign Office in December 1874: it ran to 48 rules under 32 heads. The gist was little different from any landlord/tenant lease: here, the Office of Works was landlord; the 'Assistant Surveyor' in Shanghai, mentioned in 16 of the rules, was the landlord's agent; the head of Post was the tenant of the offices and residence; and other entitled UK staff were the occupants of residential accommodation. Boyce's regulations set out the respective responsibilities, distinguished between the costs that the Office of Works would bear and those that would continue to fall on the Foreign Office or the occupant, and described the need for estimates of likely future costs. Furniture 'of a plain and durable description' was provided for all offices, court-rooms and gaols but not for any residential accommodation, which continued to be covered by allowances paid with salary.

Other rules committed the Office of Works to paying lodging allowances if that would be a more economical course than providing property itself; it would also pay for watchmen employed on the protection of consulate offices and grounds; for one 'extincteur' and at least 12 fire-buckets at each building; and 'where a fire-engine is stationed the officer in charge is to see that it is always in working order.' The initial supply and maintenance of boats and flagstaffs were not chargeable to the Office of Works. The Foreign Office ruled that 'new boats are to be of plain construction (substantial gigs), built of teak or other durable wood, copper riveted, about 26 feet in length, 5 feet 6 inches in the beam, 2 feet 2 inches in depth, square sterned, and fitted for four oars.' Consulates were not allowed more than three flags per annum: 'one flag (16 feet by 10 feet) for Sundays and holidays, and two flags (each 12 feet by 9 feet) for ordinary use.' These rules for China and Japan were barely amended over the next 50 years.

Boyce returned to the Office of Works in London in 1876 as the principal architect/surveyor for the overseas civil estate. He was frequently consulted by the Secretary, Algernon Mitford, whom he advised in a generally sensible but slightly dogmatic manner. Mitford usually took his advice. While visiting Constantinople in September 1877, Boyce found a huge muddle which he described to the Secretary.

> The immense building at Pera affords accommodation not only for the Ambassador and his establishment, but for five secretaries, one keeper of the archives and the Dragomen. All have their apartments lavishly furnished even down to the meanest servants and that not only with heavy articles of furniture but with bedclothes, carpets, rugs, indoor blinds etc and the Clerk of Works is continually being called upon to renew or repair this furniture no matter how trifling the service or how the injury was occasioned. ... A large portion of the sums for ordinary repairs [of buildings] has been spent upon services which, in my opinion, should properly be paid for by the occupant.[2]

Boyce found that there were no records, nobody knew what belonged to the government and what to the ambassador, and the seasonal moves between Pera and Therapia compounded the confusion. In respect of the ambassador's accommodation, Boyce thought that the government should pay or grant furniture allowances only for official and reception rooms that were beyond the requirements of a private gentleman, and should cease provision of bedclothes and minor domestic items. Boyce recommended that he should write a set of rules, based on the Far East rules, to apply to all mission houses. Mitford agreed: he had already had some tussles with various ambassadors, including one who had classified his servants as workmen so that they would be paid by the Office of Works. The Treasury also agreed with the idea of setting out some rules, but belaboured

> the necessity which has been supposed to exist for departing from [allowances] by the acquisition of Ambassadors' houses, with all the inevitable disputes. ... My Lords however express this regret only as explaining their desire to confine within the narrowest possible limits the intervention of the First Commissioner of Works.[3]

Boyce duly produced a draft set of rules, which the Treasury suggested should be sent to heads of mission for their observations. These gentlemen were neither slow nor brief in flattering, complaining, cajoling, boasting and questioning, each copying his thoughts to most of the others. Robert

Morier, for example, declaimed from Lisbon:

> I have observed that … great stress is laid on the providing of state bed-
> rooms, for the accommodation of distinguished guests. I cannot too strongly
> deprecate this innovation. … The supplying [of] rooms at the public expense
> in a Minister's house for distinguished guests may … be looked forward
> to as certain to create a large demand for such rooms, and the question
> would then necessarily arise as to who is to pay the cost of entertaining the
> temporary tenants of such rooms, … . The Minister cannot well refuse the
> use of the rooms to the persons for whose accommodation the public has
> provided them but, on the other hand, he can hardly be expected to provide
> these guests of the public, at his own expense, with the food, attendance,
> horses, and equipages which the latter would require.[4]

Boyce reviewed all the offerings, giving way at one point to his frustration
and cynicism in a note to Mitford:

> At the request of the Board, I, in conjunction with Mr Alston [Chief Clerk
> at the Foreign Office], prepared the draft Regulations and these have over
> and over again been discussed and remodelled and were, I understand, on the
> point of being approved when their consideration was further postponed
> until Lord Dufferin [who had just arrived at Constantinople] could report. As
> his Lordship has recently succeeded in obtaining authority for the necessary
> furniture to complete the furnishing of the state rooms at Therapia, and
> has, in consequence, expressed himself willing to abide by the regulations,
> I submit it is for the Treasury now to take the final step in the matter. Any
> hesitation would, I think, be got over by distinctly pointing out that the
> allowance clauses are only to come into force on the occurrence of new
> appointments.[5]

After nearly five years' gestation, the 'Rules and Regulations as to the
Occupation, Maintenance and due Preservation of Embassy and Legation
Houses, the Property of Her Majesty's Government' were finally issued by
the Foreign Office in November 1883. Some of the provisions were new: a
right of appeal beyond the First Commissioner of Works; and an obligation
upon the Office of Works to pay for redecorations but 'not oftener' than
once in seven years internally, and three years externally. The Office of Works
became responsible for furnishing 'the State rooms, that is to say, those rooms
that are required for State receptions, such as the principal drawing and
dining rooms, or rooms en suite, together with the staircase and corridor (if
any) leading thereto, the principal entrance and hall': it would also furnish
the chancery. For the avoidance of doubt, the State rooms in each of the

eleven mission houses then owned by the government were separately listed. Heads of mission would be paid allowances to cover the costs of many daily repairs. These were listed, as were the exclusions, which would continue to be paid by occupants, such as sweeping chimneys, replacing broken glass (unless broken by *force majeure*), and anything to do with kitchen gardens. A certificate was to be signed annually by each head of mission agreeing to be bound by the rules and recognising 'as a legal claim on me or on my estate the liability to repay to the Commissioners of Works the cost of making good such dilapidations as may be decided to be properly payable by me under the Rules'. The 1883 rules and regulations brought clarity and some order to the erratic arrangements that had grown up over half a century for the provision of diplomatic accommodation. They were updated, more in detail than character, in 1893 and 1897.

The Office of Works 1875-1900

Meanwhile, the last quarter of the nineteenth century had been relatively uneventful for the Office of Works. Three able and well-connected men, Algernon Mitford, Henry Primrose and Reginald Brett (Lord Esher from 1899), successively held the Secretaryship from 1874 to 1902, answerable to the succession over the same period of ten different Frist Commissioners, two of whom served twice. None seems to have rued the absence of the Director of Works post which was abolished in 1875 but, by the turn of the twentieth century, the argument had gained currency outside the Office that a senior professional man was needed to lead the increasing number of professional officers on the staff of the Office of Works, to give authoritative professional advice to the Secretary, and to watch over the increasingly complex works for which the Office was responsible. The problem that had arisen from the absence of this role was that Secretaries became more supportive of their lesser professional staff than the quality of their output merited, and more reliant upon them for professional wisdom than their standing in their profession justified. The wider world began to notice that the quality of the Office's work was lower than it ought to be. *The Builder* put it this way:

> If we are ever to have public buildings worthy of the genius of the English people, of a character proportionate to their influence and wealth, we must have a Government Department differently constituted to HM Office of Works, and possessing nobler aspirations than those which actuate and have too long actuated the Chiefs of that Office.[6]

Eventually, on Esher's initiative in 1901, the respected and forward-looking

Henry Tanner was confirmed in the role of principal 'Architect and Surveyor', at the head of a new Architects and Surveyors Division within the Office. A chief engineer was appointed in 1902 to head a separate Engineering Division in response to the rapid development of heating and lighting technology. These appointments did not go far towards addressing the main problem of not having a director of works and, with the principal architect and the chief engineer both reporting directly to the Secretary, they damaged co-ordination between the two disciplines and long delayed the advent of closer inter-professional working within the Office of Works.

The siege of the Peking legation quarter 1900
The twentieth century opened with the Boxer siege of the legation quarter in Peking. So-called after a flowery translation of their movement as the 'Society of Harmonious Fists ', the Boxers were intent on driving foreigners out of China. They had been spreading their attacks over North China throughout the early months of 1900 but the legations in Peking were slow to grasp that the attacks might turn upon them. Extra forces, including British marines, were eventually summoned from Tientsin and arrived on

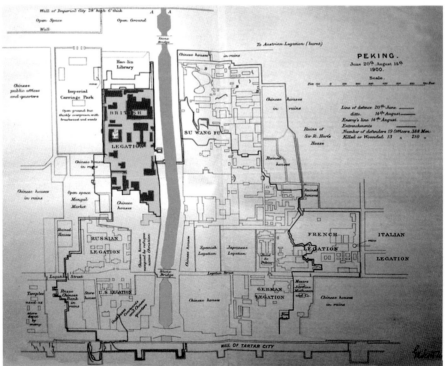

6.1. Plan by the Royal Engineers of the legation quarter of Peking after the Boxer siege, June–August 1900. The British legation compound, with its massive walls, was selected as the safest haven and it was here that most Westerners sheltered throughout the siege.

133

31 May 1900. Missionaries fled from the countryside into Peking, which was effectively sealed off from contact with the outside world on 10 June. Legation guards and the new troops began to clear lines of fire around the legation area in case of attack. On 19 June, the Chinese authorities declared a state of war and offered foreigners a safe passage to Tientsin the following day: few took up the offer. An ultimatum ran out at 4 p.m. on 20 June, at which time firing on the legations started and the siege began. It was to last for 55 days.

At the beginning of the siege, the legations' line of defence enclosed an area of about 70 acres with the canal dividing it roughly into two halves **(Fig. 6.1)**. The British compound was in the north-west of this area, the Russian and American legations in the south-west, the German and French legations in the south-east, and the Suwangfu palace in the north-east. The massive walls round the seven acres of the British compound, and the compound's fresh-water wells, gave it the best defence of any legation. The 11 resident ministers decided that the British compound, as the safest haven, would be the fallback for a last stand should one be needed. All foreign women and children were gathered there at the beginning of the siege, and missionaries and the foreign staff of the Chinese Imperial Maritime Customs retreated there soon afterwards. As a result, there were about 500 Westerners, including about 75 troops, over 350 Chinese and over 200 horses and mules in the British compound for most of the siege. In the outer legations there were about 400 troops, 400 Chinese servants and about 2,700 Chinese Christians. There was a crisis early on in the siege when it looked as though all of these might need to retreat into the British compound, but the danger passed. The chancery building was used as the hospital for the whole quarter, with its reading room as the operating theatre, and the residence as nursing wards.

The siege was relieved on 14 August by an international expeditionary force. By that time, the defenders had had to concede about 30 of their acres, mostly around the eastern edges: most of the ceded and surrounding areas were in ruins **(Fig. 6.2)**. The British compound fared much better although almost every building had been damaged by shot or shell, many of the trees had gone, the horses eaten, and the grounds dug up for filling sandbags, excavating shelters and making a burial ground. Much of the furniture had been destroyed, and 'the window Curtains in Minister's house and silk for Drawing room walls had to be cut up for sandbags'.[7] The casualties were borne by the troops: 13 of their 19 officers and nearly half of their 400 or so men were killed or wounded. The death toll of civilians in the British compound was fewer than ten, including four consular officers.

The trials, recriminations, farces, heroics and moods of over 800 people of different nationalities and callings crowded into seven acres for eight weeks under spasmodic fire and continuous risk are widely and contradictorily chronicled. A Royal Engineer shed a sarcastic sidelight on the efforts of one individual:

> There were no engineers, military or civil, among the garrison of the British Legation. There was, it is true, an architect and surveyor, whom we might have expected to take some share in the works of defence, but it is said that as far as works were concerned, he confined himself, with a singleness of aim in the discharge of his professional duties which is noteworthy, to writing down damages and dilapidations: It is to be hoped that the Chinese government will appreciate his accuracy.[8]

William Cowan, the traduced Office of Works architect in question, was stranded at the legation while making what he expected to be a short duty visit from Shanghai. He gave a fuller account, albeit rather a vague one, of his contribution during the siege to the Secretary of the Office of Works after he managed to get back to Shanghai in mid-September: 'I acted night and day as a Volunteer in defence of the Legation, and I also afforded Sir Claude MacDonald [the British minister] my professional services when called on'.[9]

6.2. Quarters damaged during the Peking legation quarter siege in 1900.

Once the siege was over, the legations determined that there would be no repetition in the future. They set about enlarging their compounds, and the legation quarter, by commandeering the surrounding areas of ruined Chinese offices, shops and houses. They then built a wall with gatehouses around the whole new legation quarter, and administered it much as if it was a concession area. Under the 1901 protocol that settled future arrangements, including compensation for the damage sustained, legations were able to bring in many more of their own troops. They built quarters for them on their recently grabbed land, for which they paid nothing, and they stopped paying the rent for their original legation areas. Hence, in 1901, the areas formerly occupied by the Hanlin academy (which the Boxers had set alight during the siege), the Imperial Coach Park, the Mongol market and former important Chinese offices were brought within the British compound's perimeter, increasing its size from seven to about thirty acres. The original compound, referred to as the civil area, was extended northwards, a large military area was created to its north-west, and a recreation ground to its south-west.

All the damaged buildings were made good soon after 1901 under Cowan's supervision, thanks to the Treasury agreeing a special grant of

6.3. Sketches of the four bungalows built as a summer retreat from Peking in the Western Hills. They were destroyed by the Boxers within months of their completion in spring 1900, and were never rebuilt.

£5,000 pending receipt of compensation monies from the Chinese. The War Office built barracks, potentially for up to 500 troops, on the new military ground. Their local commander wanted to build his own house on the site of the Hanlin academy, now part of the civil area, but the diplomats had their eyes on this site as an extension to the minister's garden. The commander retreated to the western end of the recreation ground, where a house for him was completed in 1906.

The Boxer rebellion put paid to the British legation's long-awaited permanent arrangements for getting away from the heat and chaos of Peking in summer. In the nineteenth century, the most common destination was in the Western Hills around the village of Fengtai, about 15 miles south-west of Peking. The legation would lease one of the many Buddhist temples for its sojourn: they were, in practice, walled compounds containing buildings for rent to foreigners, besides the monks' shrines and dwellings. Since the 1860s, the British minister had taken a temple large enough to house his family, temporary office, several student interpreters and other agreeable and impecunious junior staff. Other senior members of the legation took temples of their own nearby.

By the 1890s, other legations in Peking had established permanent retreats in the Western Hills and the British minister began arguing the case to London for similar provision. In this pursuit, MacDonald was eventually successful, though not before he felt he had cause to complain to a colleague about Boyce in London: 'The Autocrat Boyce, before whom the entire Diplomatic and Consular Body bow down, has been heard to say that he will see me d.....d before he lets me have a summer Residence or sanitarium or whatever I choose to call it '.[10] A site of about 30 acres, 7½ of them enclosed by a wall, was bought in 1897 for £381 about 12 miles from Peking on a bleak site about 200 feet above the plain. The Shanghai office of the Office of Works built four different bungalows here for the minister, three senior secretaries, a secretary's mess and chancery, and students' quarters, complete with stabling for 12 horses **(Fig. 6.3)**. The buildings were completed in spring 1900 and Lady MacDonald and family arrived for their first stay in them on 3 June. On the following day, the minister sent an armed escort to bring his family back to Peking. The Boxers burned down all of the bungalows the following week. The site was never re-occupied and was sold in 1923 to the Church of England Mission for the equivalent of its original cost.

7

Early Twentieth-Century Houses 1900-1915

The image of a mission house

By the start of the twentieth century the proposition was fully accepted that it was fairer and more efficient for the British government to own or lease its diplomatic and consular buildings than to rely on the resources and efforts of incumbents to find and rent their own accommodation. All of the eight embassy houses (five in Western Europe, St Petersburg, Constantinople and Washington) were already owned or long-leased, and about half of the 20 or so legation houses. The Treasury was prepared from about the turn of the century for new requirements to be met by the Office of Works buying, building or leasing accommodation. The Office of Works would also progressively take over all existing private leases over the next few decades. The Treasury's specific authorisations were generally grudging, and influenced much more by the economic facts of the case and the state of the exchequer than by any qualitative consideration of whether a British-owned or designed building would help project Britain's reputation or promote its influence and trade.

The use of style as an overt agent either to affiliate with a host country's culture or to project a British culture was not among London's priorities and heads of mission did not bring such considerations into their arguments. Besides cost, their concerns were confined to the convenience of location within a city; a building's capacity, in size and layout, to cope with the entertainment requirements of the head of mission and the reasonable expectations of his guests; and comparison with how rival countries were represented. In all of the arguments about William Smith's embassy and consulate buildings in Constantinople in the 1840s, 'nowhere in the documents relating to these commissions was national identity an articulated issue. Instead, function and institutional decorum were the main concerns'.[1] The closest that Britain came to a debate about how a new building should look was the series of proposals during the 1860s for the new consulate-general in Alexandria. There was certainly a relevant context for the debate because the Battle of the Styles was at its height in London and Sir George Gilbert Scott was being manoeuvred by Palmerston into changing his design for the Government Offices building from a Gothic to a classical style. But no discernible notice was taken of Alexandria, not even by the cultured Layard, who was a Foreign Office minister for some of the period. The battle of Alexandria was instead between the Foreign Office, keen to leave the choice of architect to the man on the spot, a kind of affiliation, and the Office of Works, with the Treasury standing behind it, keen to have tight financial control, which did not leave much room for projection.

Houses were bought because they met the requirements or could be adapted or extended to meet them. Purchasing was, by definition, an act of affiliation and the scope for projection of Britain was limited to internal decoration, works of art, furnishings, and, of course, the style, frequency and energy of the entertaining done by the head of mission and his wife. Houses were built because there was no other way of acquiring a suitable and affordable house. Their design and construction offered the opportunity for greater projection but it was hardly taken.

Once the need for a new mission house was agreed upon, the Office of Works and the Foreign Office usually succeeded in the end in reaching a mutually acceptable outcome. But suspicions ran deep, including at the highest levels. Whether or not to renew the lease on Prince Soltykoff's apartment in St Petersburg exercised the Secretary of the Office of Works, Lord Esher, in 1901. Esher felt driven to write to the Foreign Secretary, Lord Lansdowne: 'it is never safe to trust an Ambassador, either in building or buying an embassy, unless he be a *rara avis* of the Cromer [formerly Sir Evelyn Baring] type. The personal factor, convenience of a special household, number of children etc ... carries too much weight. Vienna is the great object lesson'.[2] The following month, Esher annotated a paper in manuscript: 'An Embassy should in the first instance be a house of reception and the transaction of business. The comfort of the Ambassador is a secondary consideration. If Sir Charles Scott [the ambassador] did not happen to be an Ambassador, he would be inhabiting a very ordinary house in South Kensington'.[3]

Legation houses in Europe

Nevertheless, it is some indication of the prudence of the decisions made that all of the six sites acquired for legation houses in Europe between 1905 and 1915 are still in the diplomatic estate 100 years later. Four were bought (Madrid, Oslo, Bucharest and Berne) and two built (Sofia and Stockholm). A seventh, at Cetinje, was remodelled but never used by a legation.

Madrid was the first legation house to be acquired in the twentieth century, to replace the old Calle de Torija house, leased since 1847 and bought in 1886. The ambassador, Sir Edwin Egerton, thought it no longer suitable and Sir Henry Tanner, principal architect of the Office of Works and recently knighted, went to have a look. He did not think the old house was dreadful but it was too congested, partly because 'the sides of the building are in narrow streets and on the side where the reception rooms are placed views of linen being hung at the opposite window to dry may be frequently enjoyed'.[4] Tanner liked a house that he saw on Castellana that would suit as a

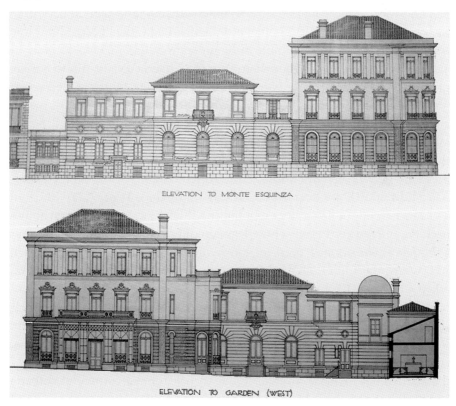

ELEVATION TO MONTE ESQUINZA

ELEVATION TO GARDEN (WEST)

7.1. The three-storey mansion at 16 Calle de Fernando El Santo in Madrid that was bought as the embassy house in 1905. Sir Henry Tanner added the narrow two-storey wing with dining room and kitchen on the ground floor, and with chancery on the first floor, reached by the domed circular stair.

141

replacement and was pursuing it when, two months later, he was summoned back to Madrid to see a better house that had come to Egerton's attention at 16 Calle de Fernando El Santo.

Tanner agreed that it was a preferable opportunity and reached terms with the owner, the Marquis de Ávala, that proved agreeable in principle to the Treasury. Sir Arthur Nicolson succeeded Egerton early in 1905 and favoured buying a cheaper house that had come on the market in the same street, but the Office of Works held firm and the purchase of 16 Calle de Fernando El Santo was completed in April 1905 for about £28,000. As well as the usual kind of alterations required – known as ingoings – to meet the needs of a legation house, it also required a new wing for the chancery, which Tanner designed **(Fig. 7.1)**. These works were first estimated at £14,000 but by the time that the embassy moved in during 1907, the cost had crept up to £26,000. The Treasury refused formal sanction for the extra expenditure. It reasonably complained that it would never have approved the project if it had known the cost would increase so much but, less reasonably, it compared the cost unfavourably with Rome and Vienna. The Office pointed out that they were 30 years ago, and quite different anyway.

A legation house was required at Oslo (or Christiania as it was to remain until 1924) in 1905 because Norway was separating from its civilised union with Sweden to become a fully independent country with a Danish prince as its elected king, reining as Haakon VII. An exceptionally good house, Villa Frognaes, completed in 1859, with six acres of land and views across the fjord, was available, and its purchase was relatively smoothly and quickly accomplished in 1906 not least because King Haakon's British father-in-law, King Edward VII, was keeping a close eye on progress **(Fig. 7.2)**.

Concurrently, a house was required in Bucharest, where Britain found itself the only major Power whose legation did not have a permanent home, although Romania had been an independent country since 1878. When J.H. Willis, the Office of Works architect resident in Constantinople, was asked why he had not visited Bucharest, he replied that the minister had not found any suitable property for him to inspect. Sir Schomberg McDonnell, successor to Esher as Secretary of the Office of Works, annotated 'Mr Willis should have gone to Bucharest: it is of no use to have the Minister looking for sites. The price becomes prohibitive directly it is known that he is in the market'.[5] Willis therefore visited in January 1907 and recommended that a house at 24 Strada Jules Michelet was the best on offer. He thought it might also be fairly cheap to buy because there were disputes among the owners and the court had ordered its sale at auction with a low reserve. Curiously,

7.2. Villa Frognæs was bought as Britain's legation house in Oslo in 1906. It was designed by a local German architect, Heinrich Schirmer, and built in 1856-9 for the banker, Thomas Heftye.

Willis neglected to mention that the house was already being leased as the consulate.

Acquisition was drawn out because the Office of Works had no spare money in its programme and the Treasury was not disposed to be helpful in the light of the Madrid overspend. When a purchase in Buenos Aires fell through in December 1907, McDonnell sought the Treasury's agreement to buy the Bucharest house instead. It agreed provided that the conveyance could be completed before the end of the financial year, only two months thence. The deadline was met. Conyngham Greene, the minister, afterwards wrote to McDonnell 'I cannot give you the vaguest idea of what trouble I have had with the whole negotiations and had I any idea of what brutes and liars these Romanians are to deal with I would never have embarked on it '.[6]

The legation house at Berne was the last to be bought in Europe before the First World War. Esme Howard arrived as minister in 1911 with nowhere to live because his predecessor, recently widowed, had spent his two years in Berne living in the city's leading hotel. Howard leased a house and came to like it so much that he recommended that London should buy it. London was prepared to buy a house in due course but preferred another, at 50 Thunstrasse **(Fig. 7.3)**. A significant argument ensued which the Office

7.3. The house at 50 Thunstrasse in Berne was bought as the legation house in 1913. A small chancery was built behind it in 1914, and the adjacent house bought in 1919. The present embassy offices were built on this site in the 1960s.

of Works won. The Treasury agreed to lease the Thunstrasse house in 1912 and buy it in financial year 1913/14 for £10,000. Howard retaliated in his autobiography

> The decision was made on the report of a young official [Allison, later chief architect] of the Office of Works, who was the only person sent out to examine the question. Perhaps if I had fought it, I might have got it reversed, but I foolishly thought that it was so much in my own interests that the dearer house should be chosen that I hesitated to show the necessary fighting spirit. As I was transferred to Stockholm immediately after the purchase was decided on, it was only my unfortunate successors that suffered. They have not hesitated to tell me what they thought of me, and I could but [sic] agree with them.[7]

When Willis was visiting Sofia from Constantinople in 1906, he learned that some years previously the Bulgarian government, nominally still then under Turkish suzerainty, had presented the British government with a site on which it could build an agency. No use was made of the site and the offer was, in effect, withdrawn. Willis therefore called on several Bulgarian ministers and they agreed to consider whether to renew the offer. The Foreign Office followed this up and the Office of Works asked the Treasury whether, if a new site was offered, it would support building a new legation house on it. It agreed, in principle. A year later the Bulgarians did offer another site: Willis inspected it on Christmas Day 1907 and recommended its acceptance. The actual transfer of the site did not occur until 1910 but, meanwhile, Thrift Reavell, an experienced architect in the Office of Works in London, visited Sofia twice and produced a design for a legation house which met with the approval of the minister **(Fig. 7.4)**. The estimate of £22,500, however, did not meet with the approval of the Treasury, which was expecting about £15,000. Sir Thomas Heath at the Treasury complained to McDonnell in May 1910:

> Their Lordships cannot but regard such a costly residence as being prima facie out of keeping with a salary of £1600, … They are of course aware that too much stress ought not to be laid on such a comparison, where houses have been bought standing; but even at such an important Embassy as Washington, where the salary is £10,000, a house appears to have been built by your Department for £31,000 pounds, or only about 50% over the cost now proposed [for Sofia].[8]

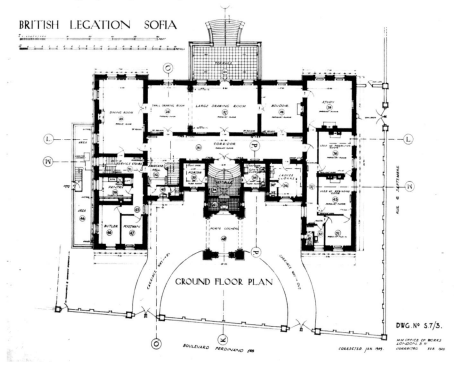

7.4. The Sofia legation house, designed by Thrift Reavell, was built in 1911-14. A simple and effective plan, with dining room, two drawing rooms, boudoir and study all facing the garden, and served by a wide corridor. The chancery was in the right wing, behind the study.

7.5. The garden front of the Sofia legation house, soon after its completion in 1914. An extra strip of garden, on the right above, was acquired immediately after the First World War from the adjacent German site.

McDonnell riposted that the £15,000 estimate was three years old and produced before any drawings had been prepared; wages had risen massively; the minister's rent allowance of £200 per annum covered only half of what he had to pay for his present inadequate accommodation; that Washington had been completed 35 years ago; and that if Washington was to be built in 1910 it would cost at least £60,000. The Treasury relented and work started on site in 1911.

Richard Allison, the newly promoted architect working on diplomatic buildings in the Office of Works, visited Sofia during construction in 1911 to assess the complaint by the minister, Henry Bax-Ironside, that the stables were about to be built too close to the terrace of the house, and to see an extra piece of land nearby that had been offered for the stables instead. He agreed with the minister, and together they called on the Bulgarian Prime Minister, Ivan Gueshoff, to thank him for offering the additional site. Allison recorded to McDonnell that Gueshoff 'hinted that in consideration of the gift of the Legation site, [Gueshoff] would expect a contribution from us for the benefit of the poor of Sofia on completion of the building and I understand from the Minister that this is a customary practice'.[9] To which McDonnell minuted, 'If the F. O. like to make donations to the poor we have no objection. It is not our affair'.[10] Work almost stopped on site in the autumn of 1912 as a result of the First Balkan War. At this time, Bax-Ironside had no stabling for his horses. He wrote in manuscript to Lionel Earle, who had recently succeeded McDonnell as Secretary at the Office of Works, 'I have one carriage in the Italian and one in the Servian [sic] Legations – my horses are temporarily in Bulgarian cavalry stables – favours which I cannot ask for beyond a limited time. … meanwhile we are living in the house of the Bulgarian Minister in London'.[11] Earle replied that he had no money to offer as he had been cut to the bone to fund the 'enormous naval demands'. The Sofia house was eventually finished in 1914 but hardly occupied before all the staff left when Bulgaria entered the First World War on the German side in October 1915 **(Fig. 7.5)**.

Howard was transferred from Berne to Stockholm in 1913, where, he later recalled in ambassadorial anecdotal mode, he

> found the Legation was situated in a first-floor apartment in the Strandvagen, having a beautiful view across a sheet of water to the Royal Palace, but hardly large enough for me, my numerous family, and the Chancery. It had, besides, the disadvantage of being situated over a grocer's shop which smelt strongly of cheese and bacon. This so outraged King Edward, when a year or two before on a visit to Stockholm he had dined at the Legation, that he had at once, on returning to England, insisted that a proper Legation should be built far from such perfumery.[12]

All the legations in Stockholm were in flats and the Swedish government was anxious to encourage the building of legation houses. It had offered in 1911 to sell a suitable site to the British government in an area beside the river and near the English church which it intended should become a diplomatic quarter. The lease on the legation flat was due to expire in 1914 and Allison had rather optimistically thought that a new house could be ready by then. A senior Treasury official, R.S. Meiklejohn, privately suggested to Earle in early 1913 that the Office of Works might consider buying the offered site in Stockholm from a forecast underspend in its Vote and soon afterwards, more privately, wrote that it would be desirable to purchase the site before the end of March 'if you can make out a colourable case that it's eminently advisable to get the site into your possession immediately'.[13] Earle did so the next day and Treasury, 'in the special circumstances', replied positively. Meanwhile, the Foreign Office concluded its own letter of support with the observation that 'as the future Queen of Sweden is an English Princess it is desirable on general grounds that the British Minister at Stockholm should be suitably housed.'[14] He was, because Allison had designed and supervised the construction of a handsome and efficient house into which Howard moved in 1915 **(Fig. 7.6)**. Howard recalled, with customary sting in the tail,

7.6. The Stockholm legation house, designed by Richard Allison, and completed in 1915. This drawing, by Palmer-Jones, was exhibited at the Royal Academy in 1916.

> The one great drawback of the new house was that the architect, not knowing Stockholm, had not recognised that the dining-room … [should be] a large room of noble proportions … which no gentleman can decently do without. How much more, then, is this the case where it may fall to the lot of the incumbent of a Legation to entertain kings. Now, the mind of the architect of the Office of Works was not tuned up to the proper pitch in the matter of dining-rooms, and he only calculated for dinner parties of sixteen, a sadly bourgeois conception of the requirements of a Stockholm dining-room.[15]

Montenegro became a kingdom in 1910, with Cetinje as its capital, and a minister, John Charles, seventh Count de Salis-Soglio, arrived in 1911 to head the British legation. For its accommodation, the Office of Works in 1912 bought a terrace of four small houses close to the royal palace and Julius Bradley, the Office of Works architect, remodelled them into a legation house. Work on site came to a standstill at the outbreak of the First Balkan War in October 1912 but direct labour, including Turkish prisoners, was later drafted in to complete the building in 1914, under the control of an Office of Works clerk of works, W.C. d'Harty, who was arrested and narrowly escaped internment. Allison happened to visit to make the final inspection of the works on the day that the First World War broke out. De Salis refused to move in and remained in his rented house until the legation was withdrawn in 1916. The ill-starred house was intermittently occupied by caretakers and a vice-consul until it was sold in 1928.

Legation houses beyond Europe
Several other legation houses were acquired in the decade or so before the outbreak of the First World War, most notably through the construction of new buildings at Addis Ababa and Mexico City. In 1896, Emperor Menelik II of Ethiopia had allotted one gasha of land (a variable measure, but approaching 100 acres) for a British agency at the foot of the Entoto Hills, 8,500 feet above sea level, just outside his then-new and still-tented capital of Addis Ababa. The boundaries of the land were defined by physical features: a spring, a prominent rock, a stone wall, a road, a creek and back to the spring. The upper part of the site was wood and scrub and the lower was thick grass. This allocation of land was not and, despite significant efforts, has never been consolidated by title deeds but, in recognition of receipt of this land, the British government for many decades exempted the Ethiopian embassy in London from paying the beneficial portion of the non-domestic rate.

Captain John Harrington arrived as agent in 1898 and stayed for ten years, his mission having become in 1903 a legation, the first in sub-Saharan Africa. Harrington built eight *tukuls*, indigenous circular thatched huts, connected by covered walkways, in 1900, at a cost of about £2,000 **(Fig. 7.7)**. In one of these *tukuls*, Wilfred Thesiger, the future explorer and travel writer, was born in 1910 to Harrington's successor. Besides the *tukuls*, the

7.7. The remaining few *tukuls* in the Addis Ababa compound, built in 1898 by the first agent, Captain John Harrington.

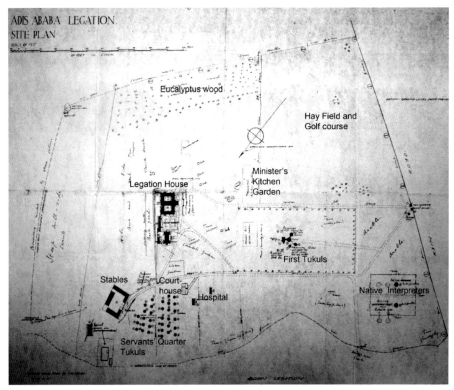

ADIS ABABA LEGATION.
SITE PLAN

Eucalyptus wood

Hay Field and
Golf course

Minister's
Kitchen
Garden

Legation House

First Tukuls

Stables

Court-
house

Hospital

Native Interpreters

Servants' Quarter
Tukuls

7.8. Plan of the Addis Ababa compound in 1921. At 87 acres, it was the largest piece of land in the British diplomatic estate. The land rises from the road boundary and entrance on the right.

compound had separate areas for the Sudanese and their households, the Abyssinian servants and their families, stables for 30 horses, other *tukuls* for harness room, fodder stores and quarters for men of the Aden troop; and a large grass field for the ponies. The first non–indigenous buildings, for escort quarters and stables, were erected in 1905 towards the north corner of the compound.

Plans for a more European-style legation, with residential accommodation for minister, secretary of legation and vice-consul, and legation offices, were prepared in 1908 by the architect Thrift Reavell in the Office of Works in London. The site was further up the hill than the *tukuls*: from its terrace, reached by a long flight of steps, was a magnificent view over the plain and the town **(Fig. 7.8)**. The residence plan, on a single floor, was rectangular and included two courtyards with a durbar hall between them. The vice-consul's house and chancery offices were in a similarly detailed building on the other side of a formal flower garden **(Fig. 7.9)**. This scheme was built under the supervision of d'Harty as clerk of works and completed in 1911 at a cost of about £21,000. The buildings were of local black stone, the roof originally of asbestos, and the internal timberwork of local cedar: the ironmongery was sent from Britain. D'Harty, able and diligent, also gave good advice to other bodies building in Addis Ababa, including the Ethiopian government which wanted to award him the Star of Ethiopia, third class, in recognition of his generosity.

Thrift Reavell was also involved in the design for the new legation building in Mexico City. In 1907, the minister, Reginald Tower, advanced three reasons to the Foreign Office for buying a site and building a legation: he was frequently having to move because his rent allowance was inadequate; Mexico was becoming a more prominent country; and a new legation would give pleasure to the Mexican government and the British colony in Mexico. None of these was perceived in London as a strong argument for a new building. Tower was nevertheless in touch with a syndicate called the United States and Mexican Trust Company which had acquired a large piece of land which it called the Cuauhtemoc Colony 'in the most advantageous and healthful quarter of the capital'. The syndicate had already invested in the Colony's infrastructure and was now selling plots for development. Should London agree to buy one, Tower recommended commissioning Charles Grove Johnson, a respected local English architect, to do the design. Both the Office of Works and the Treasury again said no.

Tower was persistent. Early in 1909, McDonnell annotated an internal minute 'Mr Tower might be asked to give prices per foot of land. It will keep him quiet'.[16] The suggestion was put less bluntly to the Foreign Office:

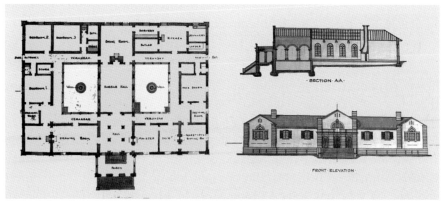

7.9. The legation house at Addis Ababa, designed by Thrift Reavell, completed in 1911. From the hall, with its four columns, the durbar hall and dining room are straight ahead; the drawing room and minister's quarters to the left; and his office and staff to the right.

7.10. The garden front of the legation house in Mexico City, completed in 1912, in the subdued and polite Office of Works' manner of the period.

whilst the Board [of Works] are not in a position of course to give any undertaking or to express any opinion in the direction desired by His Majesty's Minister, they think it would be extremely useful if he [Tower] would be so good as to correlate any information as to properties or sites in the market, which he can obtain, together with prices per foot of the land ruling in the Mexican Capital, and to forward such particulars for the Board's consideration.[17]

Tower responded inconveniently quickly and with unwelcome enthusiasm: there was no lack of sites but a shortage of money. While on leave in London in 1909, he brought to a meeting with the Office of Works a merchant called John Benjamin Body, who had a site to sell in the Cuauhtemoc Colony and was the representative in Mexico of Messrs S. Pearson and Son, a huge British contracting firm. He also brought Johnson, his preferred architect and one of very few reliable contractors in Mexico City. The Office of Works was finally impressed by Tower's arguments and the purchase of the site was competed in 1910. Tanner asked Reavell to produce an outline design along normal Office of Works lines, an arrangement with which

Johnson was entirely happy, but McDonnell later ruled instead that Johnson should have a clean slate as architect. His designs accordingly turned out to be much too elaborate and expensive. Tower enlisted Weetman Pearson, later the first Viscount Cowdray, to intercede with the First Commissioner, Lewis Harcourt. Pearson was less than persuasive: 'As Mexicans are rather impressionable and inclined to judge by outside appearances I should be inclined to strongly advise you to recommend a little extravagance in their own style, rather than something plainer and cheaper'.[18] The Office of Works was unmoved and sent H.N. Hawks, one of its senior architects, to Mexico to liaise with Tower and Johnson and come up with an acceptable design at affordable cost. He produced a good plan, which Pearson built for about £24,000: it was the first purpose-built legation in Mexico City, and was liked by its occupants from the outset **(Fig. 7.10)**.

The unsuccessful search for a permanent site or house in Buenos Aires shortly before the First World War featured a bizarre new element. In 1912, Louis Mallet, then an assistant under-secretary at the Foreign Office, proposed that Britain should cede the South Orkney Islands, off the tip of the Antarctic Peninsular, to Argentina in exchange for a site on which to build a legation in Buenos Aires. The Treasury thought this quite an appealing idea and the Office of Works was asked what sort of site in Buenos Aires should be requested in exchange for the islands. It said that one of its officers would need to visit Buenos Aires before it could pronounce. The Colonial Office, on the other hand, objected that as the Falkland Islands, to which the South Orkney Islands belonged, would suffer a loss of licence revenue from whaling companies, any legation site would be being acquired partly at the expense of 'the Colonial revenue'. The Foreign Office declined to regard that as a serious objection but helpfully suggested that cession might coincide with the start of a licensing year so that no refunds would be due. The ambassador, Sir Reginald Tower, recently arrived from Mexico, believed that the proposal would be viewed favourably by the Argentine government, and London asked him to test its stance. The Argentinians told him in 1913 that the islands were not Britain's to cede and there the matter rested for the duration of the war and beyond. In 1927, however, when the legation in Buenos Aires was raised to the status of an embassy and soon after the Office of Works had bought a suitable house in Buenos Aires, the Argentinians offered to resume discussion about the exchange. Earle showed the papers to the First Commissioner, Viscount Peel, as 'an interesting proposal'. Peel annotated that 'I should be reluctant to barter these islands for an Embassy site'.[19] The Admiralty was strongly opposed to the idea, and that was the end of it.

Summer residences

Permanent accommodation for four summer residences was acquired between 1905 and 1912: Peitaiho, built for Peking; Posillipo, donated for Rome; Ramleh, built for Cairo; and Petropolis, bought for Rio de Janeiro. Their acquisition was not part of any programme but in each case the result of a strong initiative. As permanent summer residences, these four joined Gulhak for Tehran and Therapia for Constantinople.

The attempt to build permanent summer quarters for the Peking legation, after the just-completed bungalows at Fengtai were burned down by the Boxers in 1900, began in 1905. Peitaiho, a burgeoning seaside resort about 200 miles east of Peking that had become accessible by rail, was overtaking the Western Hills as the legations' preferred summer retreat. Although all the foreign-owned houses in Peitaiho were destroyed in the Boxer uprising, by 1905 about 150 new ones had been built and were occupied each summer by merchants and missionaries. William Cowan was sent from Shanghai to look for a suitable site in 1905 on which to build what was then called a sanatorium for the British legation in the form of two bungalows, one each for married and unmarried staff. Sir Claude MacDonald's successor as minister, the cultivated (and unaccompanied) Sir Ernest Satow, was not interested in provision being made for a minister. Cowan selected two adjacent sites, belonging (as it happened) to Sir Claude MacDonald and a Mr Lees, that sloped down to the sea and together comprised about three acres. The Treasury agreed to their purchase but local complications delayed their acquisition until 1908, by which time the Treasury had put a limit on the cost of the scheme which meant that only one of the bungalows could be built in the first instance. Satow's successor as minister in 1906, Sir John Jordan, decided that he and his successors should have a bungalow after all, with the result that more land needed to be acquired. Fortunately, three adjacent plots, together comprising almost five acres, proved purchasable in the course of 1909 and four buildings were completed at a cost of about £8,250 in 1910. The site was superb and ran down to the beach but the buildings at first looked very raw: long and low rectangular timber bungalows, with pitched roofs and verandas on all four sides, well set apart from each other **(Fig. 7.11)**. They served their purpose well until 1937 when the embassy followed the Nationalist government as it was driven out of Peking by the Japanese invasion.

The fifth Earl of Rosebery, twice Foreign Secretary and Prime Minister once, in 1909 gave his beautiful estate on the western shore of the Bay of Naples to the Commissioners of Works to be the summer retreat for the British embassy at Rome. Rosebery had also been, for four months,

First Commissioner of Works in 1885. When offered that job by Gladstone, and in two minds whether to accept, Rosebery observed that it was 'not an attractive post, having neither dignity or importance, and is I think the least of all the offices, being only a sort of political football for contending connoisseurs'.[20] The estate that he gave was at Posillipo: it comprised six hectares of ilex groves and orange orchards and came complete with three houses and all their contents. Rosebery had coveted the property, then known as Villa Serra Marina, for a long time before he bought it from Gustave Delahante in 1897. Because he had numerous houses and made little use of the Posillipo estate, he let the consul at Naples, his close friend Eustace Neville-Rolfe, and his family live there instead. It was Neville-Rolfe's death in 1908 that prompted Rosebery's donation the following year.

Sir Rennell Rodd was the first ambassador to use the estate in 1910 and for the next few years most of the embassy moved there for about four months in the summer, leaving two staff by turns in Rome. 'Thus a succession of summers passed very happily until the outbreak of the Great War, when all pleasant things ceased perforce'.[21] Use of the villa was slight during the 1920s and, after Rosebery's death in 1929, the Office of Works could no longer justify the cost of its upkeep. The estate was handed back to the Rosebery family, which made a gift of it to the Italian government in May 1932. It is now the official residence of the President of Italy when he visits Naples.

Egyptian ministers and their senior staff migrated to Alexandria for the June–October period when Cairo was unbearably hot. The British mission went too. It was accustomed to renting suitable premises but Sir Eldon Gorst

7.11. Bungalows, seen from the beach, built at Peitaiho in 1910 as the Peking legation's summer retreat. They were used regularly until 1937, occasionally again during the 1950s, and were taken over by the Chinese authorities in 1959.

made a sufficient case in 1909 for buying a site and building a permanent summer residence. In that year, a site of about 0.3 hectare was bought from the Alexandria Water Company for about £1,000 at Ramleh in a district called Roushdie, about five miles east of the city centre. A two-storey house with a pleasing plan, including offices for chancery, was completed on this site in 1912 for about £10,000. Use of it, however, was contentious from the start. Gorst departed from Egypt before it was finished. His successor, Lord Kitchener, thought it inadequate and never occupied it, and it was let to the Red Cross instead. Sir Henry McMahon, who came next, wanted a different summer residence in Ramleh, and his successor, Sir Reginald Wingate, preferred to look for an alternative of 'sufficient importance'. The Ramleh house was not to find a grateful user until the 1960s.

Petropolis, about 40 miles north of Rio de Janeiro in the forested hills of the Serra dos Órgãos, was the summer residence of the Brazilian monarchy and aristocracy throughout the second half of the nineteenth century, and the legations naturally followed. In 1907 the minister, William Haggard, proposed buying the good villa that he rented in Petropolis, but the idea fell on deaf ears in London. He tried again when the owner of the villa died two years later and he saw the opportunity for a bargain. The Office of Works remained unimpressed: the Secretary minuted the First Commissioner, 'This is a typical instance of the recommendations which are thrust upon us by importunate ministers. Sir William Haggard has been occupying this house for some time; but he has not sent us plans, photographs or even details as to the extent of the grounds. Under these conditions I feel no desire to purchase'.[22] The Foreign Office persuaded the Office of Works at least to ask for the details which, when they arrived from Haggard, were really quite acceptable: the villa was built in 1897 and stood in about 2.5 hectares of steep and wooded countryside. Haggard was authorised to buy it for a maximum of £5,000, which he did in January 1910. He then infuriated London by pointing out, for the first time, that he needed to spend a further £200 on stables and servants' quarters.

In 1911, the summer residence for Constantinople, completed at Therapia on the Bosphorus in 1870, burned down so extensively that its reconstruction was ruled out. The newly-appointed Secretary, Lionel Earle, visited the site in spring 1914.

> On examining the problem of site for the new house ... I came to the conclusion that the old house ... had not been sited to the best advantage. It stood close to the road which runs along the Bosphorus with the garden, which runs up a steep incline, behind the house. I suggested that

it would be far better to place the house halfway up the hill, so as to get full advantage of the splendid view over the Bosphorus and Asia Minor, with the lovely sloping garden in front of the house, running down to the road. It meant, of course, a little walk up to the house for visitors, but this in the Ambassador's and my opinion did not outweigh the advantages.[23]

On Earle's return, the Office of Works architect, Thrift Reavell, developed an unexciting three-storey scheme for a terrace site on the hillside. But by then the First World War had started and all but imperative projects were put aside.

Among the non-legation buildings constructed in the pre-First World War period, the more significant included, in Egypt, a consulate-general, at last, at Alexandria in 1903, a consulate-general in Cairo in 1907, a consulate in Port Said in the same year, and a fine ballroom connected to the main house in Cairo in 1913 during Kitchener's 'governorship' of Egypt. The rebuilding of the 1830s consulate in the Place de la Bourse in Tunis was completed in 1915. There were also continuing projects for consulates in the Far East and Persia, and a few in Africa.

In-house and outside professionals
Private, or so-called outside, architects delighted in taunting the Office of Works about its new buildings in England, not least in the hope of steering more of its work their way. Leonard Stokes, President of the Royal Institute of British Architects, and 'no respecter of persons', according to the *ODNB*, wrote in March 1911 to the First Commissioner, Earl Beauchamp, claiming that using Office of Works architects was costing significantly more than outside architects and arguing against the Office increasing its staff to cope with the large increase in telephone buildings. He went a step further the following month, maintaining that 'that the bulk [of the Office's work] is quite second rate from an architectural point of view (forgive me)'.[24] Beauchamp replied that the Office of Works was answerable to Parliament and not to the Royal Institute of British Architects. In 1913, however, the year in which Sir Henry Tanner retired, the Treasury commissioned a report from a three-man committee chaired by Sir George Holmes, chairman of the Board of Public Works in Dublin, to enquire into the Architects and Surveyors Division and the Engineering Division of the Office of Works. The committee consulted several eminent private architects who said that the in-house architects had too many administrative pressures on them to do enough design work and they therefore relied too much on draughtsmen. The committee nevertheless defended in-house architecture in general terms, but recommended that the employment of outside architects for

large building schemes should 'depend on the circumstances in each case'. It made numerous recommendations, including, as one way of relieving architects of administrative and paper work, 'Impressing on Departments … the need for fully maturing their requirements for new works before requesting the Office of Works to prepare detailed plans'.[25] The committee introduced rules for the future recruitment of architects and for the gradation of architectural staff. It satisfied itself that the small part of the Architects and Surveyors Division devoted to foreign buildings, including establishments in China and Japan, was working fine: indeed, it doubted that the employment of private architects would be practicable in conditions obtaining overseas.

The committee was divided about 'the means whereby the technical divisions should be controlled by the Board': in other words, whether to bring back the director of works role in the form of a technical assistant secretary. The chairman, Holmes, who had a director of works under him in Dublin, favoured re-introducing the role. His two colleagues, both administrators, produced a rival memorandum against the role because they feared it would be impossible to define the respective functions of the lay and technical assistant secretaries and to assign a clear field of work to each. More fundamentally, they argued that 'the basis of the arrangement is that in the last resort the decision depends on the application of ordinary principles of administration and policy to technical questions, and that application is most conveniently made when a proposal comes before the Board [of the Office]'.[26] In other words, all decisions, however professional or technical, should be at the discretion of the Secretary and the First Commissioner.

Lionel Earle, appointed Secretary in 1912, relayed the Office of Works' advice to the Treasury on the rival memoranda as even-handedly as he could consistent with ensuring that he would not be landed with a technical assistant secretary. He recited the experiences that led to the abolition of the role in 1875 (37 years previously), and repeated the argument 'that the public interest is sufficiently served if the decision ... is arrived at on what may be called common sense principles, which do not depend on technical training'. Earle also deployed a more parochial argument: since a principal architect 'from outside good enough to succeed Sir Henry Tanner' would require at least £2,000 per annum, a technical assistant secretary would require a salary 'approaching if not equalling that of the Secretary [himself]. There are precedents in the Service for a higher rate of salary to a technical officer subordinated to a layman, but the arrangement is obviously one which should not be made if it can be avoided'.[27] Earle got his way, after which he appointed Richard Allison in 1914 to succeed Tanner, but at the lesser grade of principal architect.

8

Post-War and the 1920s

When a breach in diplomatic relations occurs between two states, including when war is declared, each asks a third state to protect its citizens and property in the territory of the state with which it no longer has diplomatic relations. Such property includes its diplomatic buildings. The third state is called the protecting power. The arrangement leaves both sides with a residual diplomatic channel of communication to the other. The protecting power can exercise its responsibility to the protected power in respect of diplomatic buildings by occupying vacated buildings or paying the wages of caretakers. More widely and recently, it can permit diplomats of the protected power to work in its own mission as an Interests Section. Sometimes, the same third state is asked to be the protecting power by both antagonist states. This was the case during the First World War when America, until it entered the war in 1917, was the protecting power both of Britain's interests in Germany and of Germany's interests in Britain.

Some civilities could continue as though there were no hostilities. Thus, in 1916, the year of carnage on the Somme, the Foreign Office could send a note to the American ambassador in London requesting him

> to ascertain through the United States Ambassadors at Berlin and Vienna whether the German and Austro-Hungarian Governments share the view of his Majesty's Government that the reciprocal arrangement of 1898 [by which each government paid a proportion of the other's embassy rates bill] has been terminated by the war. ...
> His Majesty's Government are ... prepared on the receipt of assurances of reciprocity from the Governments concerned, to authorize payment, in the

159

customary manner, to the local authorities in London of rates in respect of the German and Austro-Hungarian Embassies and houses up to the dates of the departure of the respective Ambassadors.[1]

The enemy government gave the necessary assurance and proceeded to assess its outstanding liability in respect of the empty British embassy house in Berlin. The Foreign Office subsequently sought reimbursement from the Office of Works of the £385 3s 6d that it had paid in respect of the empty German embassy premises in London.

Britain's diplomatic buildings emerged almost unscathed from the First World War, though the Berlin embassy building was damaged by fire during riots in 1919 and the ambassador was unable to re-occupy it until 1920. The embassy in Paris, fearing a German attack, sent 36 cases of plate and works of art to London in June 1918, via lorry to Le Havre and destroyer to Portsmouth, for safe-keeping in 'the Tube at King Edward Building'.[2] Most of it arrived back at the embassy the day before a dinner for H.M. the King at the end of November 1918.

Montgomery and Earle

Shortly before the war, a Royal Commission, chaired by Lord MacDonnell, was appointed to examine the civil service. It completed its report, and its recommendations were accepted in principle, in 1914 but action had to wait until the end of the war. One important recommendation was that the diplomatic service, which had avoided most of the Northcote-Trevelyan and subsequent reforms, should be amalgamated with the Foreign Office and brought fully within the civil service. By the time that the amalgamation took place in 1919, various of the MacDonnell recommendations had been diluted. The combined entity was granted a separate Order in Council which established it as the Diplomatic Service to staff both the Foreign Office in London and overseas missions, but kept it separate from the Consular Service and the Home Civil Service. The Foreign Office, in other words, was now staffed by diplomats who were different from normal civil servants.

The Royal Commission swept away many of the restrictions that had barred entry to diplomacy by individuals without private means: the property qualification of £400 was abolished, junior attachés no longer had to give unpaid service for two years, rent allowances were paid in addition to salary to enable staff to live within reasonable reach of the mission, and travel allowances were paid to cover the costs of an officer's family moving from London or between Posts. These new allowances were soon afterwards extended to the consular service as a result of a report in

1919 by Sir Arthur Steel-Maitland, junior minister in the Foreign Office, which also laid down the principle that consular offices 'should compare favourably with those of business firms of good standing'. The Treasury's 'natural desire to fix limits', on rent allowances for example, was overcome by the Foreign Office successfully arguing that the head of mission should decide what was a reasonable rent in the circumstances of his Post. As for heads of mission themselves, their salaries were relieved of some of the costs of running a mission by the introduction of a separate *frais de représentation*, an entertainment allowance, and by the Office of Works paying for the furnishing of all the rooms in their residences, not just the state rooms. All these new allowances helped but, as a former chief clerk dryly commented later,

> It must not be supposed that the new regulations met the views of every man in the Service, or that diplomats did not soon become so well accustomed to their new incomes as to find them at times too small. This was bound to happen, but the views of the man on the spot do not always carry complete conviction at home on the point of cost of living.[3]

In 1919, the Foreign Office appointed Hubert Montgomery as chief clerk, in which role he supervised the entire administration of the Foreign Office, including all aspects of its accommodation at home and overseas, for the next fourteen years. He had served several stints as private secretary and précis-writer to the Foreign Secretary before his appointment as secretary of the Earl Marshal's office that organized the king's coronation in 1911, which, in turn, equipped him to be what was soon afterwards called Marshal of the Diplomatic Corps. He was clearly a humane man of great common sense and vast administrative ability.

This did not rescue him, however, from the red tape imbroglio of 1922, a microcosm of Foreign Office attitudes at the time. H.M. Stationery Office wrote to the Foreign Office's superintendent of printing to say that it was unable to meet his indent for a supply of red tape because he had not explained why white tape would not do.[4] A Foreign Office under-secretary replied to the controller that 'the use of red tape tends to greater neatness and efficiency than is possible with the use of white tape', which became more quickly soiled. The controller replied that it would be unnecessarily expensive to arrange a special purchase just for the Foreign Office and opined that the increase in efficiency 'is, in fact, nil'. He would need Treasury authority to supply red tape. Montgomery doubted whether it was worth returning to the charge, although he thought 'elementary cleanliness' came before economy. Somebody else fumed 'this is the most objectionable letter that I have ever seen addressed to this department by another' and wanted to send this 'impertinent effusion' to Sir Warren Fisher at the Treasury. Montgomery did not demur. Sir Eyre Crowe, the permanent under-secretary, accordingly wrote to the head of the Treasury saying that the Stationery Office's arguments 'are difficult to beat in futility'. The supply of red tape resumed soon afterwards. The *Evening News* had great fun with the story.

Montgomery's tenure as chief clerk at the Foreign Office was concurrent with the second two-thirds of Lionel Earle's tenure as Secretary of the Office of Works, and with the whole of Richard Allison's time as chief architect. Earle retired in 1933, the same year that Montgomery was appointed minister at The Hague. Earle steered the Office of Works through the First World War, when the volume of work at home increased massively through carrying out programmes for other government departments. After the war, another reorganisation within the Office was precipitated by the arrival of a new First Commissioner, Sir Alfred Mond, who commissioned a report in 1919 from James Eggar, an acting assistant secretary, to look again at the arrangements that had been put in place following the pre-war Holmes report, including not appointing a director of works. Eggar recommended, against Earle's advice, the resurrection of the director of works role. Mond promptly promoted his architectural protégé, Frank Baines, into the role in 1920. Eggar also took an opposite view from Holmes on architects for diplomatic and consular buildings because 'I cannot help thinking that, for all new work, the Board would be well advised to employ as a general rule private architects resident and practising in the Country'.[5] Baines, however, only lasted for seven years: he was forced to resign in 1927 because he had entered into a large private contract to design Thames House South for Imperial Chemical Industries, then chaired by Mond. Earle lost no time in abolishing the director of works post.

Montgomery and Earle had had rather similar careers before their paths met in 1919. Earle, well connected and fluent in several languages, was private secretary to several prominent politicians before becoming Secretary. From the start in the Office of Works, he took a deep interest in the diplomatic and consular buildings: they were only a small part of his responsibilities but the opportunity to travel and to hobnob with leading figures, and the inherent interest of the problems, ensured a significant proportion of his time. He even recalled in 1935 that 'I spent many hours in studying and selecting designs, not only of furniture but of cretonnes, chintzes, curtains, etc. Invariably I went with my technical officers to the great carpet warehouses in the City to select carpets and rugs for the embassies and legations abroad'.[6] He could be stiff when he thought occasion demanded, as in a spat with the high commissioner in Egypt, Sir Percy Loraine, in 1931 against building more rooms for his domestic staff entourage when visiting the summer residence at Ramleh. Loraine concluded a letter with 'I would beg you to remember that I must be regarded as more or less competent to judge what are my obligations towards my position in general and towards my staff in particular'. Earle responded

> May I say at once that I have never questioned your competency to decide your obligations in relation to your staff; it is only when those obligations have to be translated into bricks and mortar charged to this Department's Vote that I am interested, and I have the responsibility, within the financial limits imposed by the Treasury, of taking a decision which is final unless the Foreign Office put up so persuasive a case on your behalf as to induce the Treasury themselves to over-ride me.[7]

Loraine climbed down and made do. One of Earle's deputy secretaries, Eric de Normann, wrote of him after his death: his 'experience as a man of the world supplemented happily the departmental knowledge of his officials. ... his tact and common sense, together with the gift of knowing where to go for advice, remedied a somewhat impulsive judgement'.[8] Earle was a driving force in establishing the Royal Fine Art Commission in 1924 and fostering it in its early years. He did not marry until he was 60 and divorced 11 years later. He also spent a fair part of his time on the royal residences, as instanced by a story that Thomas Jones, deputy secretary to the cabinet, heard from Stanley Baldwin and his wife, Lucy, in July 1932:

> Stanley Baldwin: 'The Queen and Lucy had a great pow-wow the other day while the King and I were dealing with affairs of State. They were making such a rattle that the King asked "What can they be talking about?" I said "I bet it is either maternity or Lionel Earle." It was Lionel Earle.'
> Mrs Baldwin: 'I wanted a frigidaire because the hot water pipes go through the larder. He said he hadn't one himself. And who is he I'd like to know! And the Queen said that he treats Her in the same fashion and that they have had Words. "So I go now to Ormsby-Gore [First Commissioner] and get what I like."'[9]

Earle and Montgomery co-operated well together for 13 years, easily the longest twentieth-century partnership between the two roles. There was a great deal of work to do: first of all, in housing the huge proportion of the Foreign Office's staff that had been spared for the Peace Conference at Versailles, for whom six Paris hotels were commandeered. A backlog of works had built up during the war, the new regulations about rents and furnishings had to be interpreted and implemented, and many more junior staff were being posted abroad to free the secretaries at missions from routine work. While the number of diplomatic missions was much the same before and after the war, at about ten embassies and thirty legations, the total number of staff overseas had increased from about 160 to 270. It was agreed in 1919 that 'Ambassadors would in rank and personal salary be in the same position as the Permanent Under-Secretary': there had been some slippage from their rank equivalence nearly a century earlier with cabinet ministers but being an ambassador was still a considerable role.[10]

Probably most valuably, from an accommodation point of view, Earle and Montgomery introduced a system of elementary programme planning to replace the pre-war focus on individual projects. They instituted an annual conference in November on the diplomatic and consular building programme as the centrepiece of this development. Projects, including purchases, were divided into four categories: category A to go into the next year's Estimate, in order of precedence; B to go into a five-year programme; C to be deferred

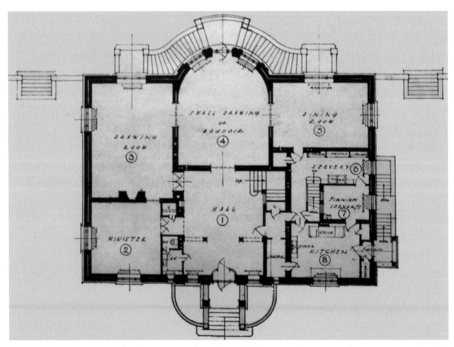

8.1. Ground-floor plan of Villa Damsten, bought as the legation house on the Kaivopuisto head-land in Helsinki in 1925. It was designed by Jarl Eklund and completed in 1918. An excellent plan for a medium-sized house.

8.2. The Thun palace in Prague, in the foreground, with the Royal Castle and cathedral behind. It was leased in 1919 and bought in 1926 as the legation house. The site is so steep that the building has five floors facing the courtyard at the front and only two facing the garden at the back.

for the present; and D to be postponed indefinitely, i.e. ignored. The focus was obviously on category A: much of the Estimate would already be filled by projects under construction so that there was always only limited room for new projects. The merits, demerits and progress of every project were discussed before it was assigned a category or a precedence, giving everyone attending the conference the chance to air their own priorities and *bêtes noires*. The results quickly found their way back to Posts, most of them to be received with a dismay that fuelled another round of lobbying.

Buildings in Europe

The re-arrangement of central Europe after the First World War brought independence, or returned it, to Finland, the three Baltic countries of Estonia, Latvia and Lithuania, Poland, Czechoslovakia, Hungary and the Kingdom of Serbs, Croats and Slovenes (called Yugoslavia from 1929). By 1920, British diplomatic representation was established at Helsinki, Riga, Warsaw, Prague, Budapest and Belgrade. An early pre-occupation of Earle and Montgomery was to provide legation buildings in all these cities. Suitable houses were

165

leased in Warsaw in 1919 and Riga in 1921, and bought in Helsinki in 1925, all without undue complications (**Fig. 8.1**).

The same could not be said of the acquisition of the legation house in Prague, although the outcome was particularly satisfactory. The Thun palace, including much of its furniture, was taken on lease in 1919 soon after the minister, George Clerk, arrived in Prague. Built on a steep hillside just below the Royal Castle, the palace had been reconstructed by the Thun family in an Italianate manner in the early eighteenth century (**Fig. 8.2**). The leasing arrangement suited Count Thun well because, unless he could keep his building in full occupation, the Czechoslovak government would take it over. The lease, however, was never actually signed because Thun argued over every detail: on the furniture schedule he wanted, for example, a professor to be commissioned, for a fee, to check on the state of the furniture quarterly. Clerk described Thun, in a private letter to Earle in January 1921, as

> an odd and unpleasant person, one of the few real Huns in this country, and now that things look fairly steady here, he bitterly regrets the moment of panic in which he gave up the house to us, and would gladly wriggle out. As it is, he is always playing mean tricks, taking off pictures and tables and rugs and so on. On the other hand, the more I live here, the more I feel that, with all its dilapidation and inconvenience, there is no Legation house in Europe to touch it, in its own peculiar way. You *must* come and stay with us in the spring.[11]

In 1923 Thun, now in debt, decided to sell the palace and gave the British government first option to buy it. He had initially thought it was worth 18 million crowns but asked for 15 million (approaching £100,000). Thrift Reavell, architect in the Office of Works, who had already inspected the palace twice and recommended its purchase, was sent a third time to report. He could find nothing more suitable than the Thun palace and warned that, if it was sold to anyone else, the new owner might eject the legation. This time he recommended purchase for not more than about 6.2 million crowns, less than half Thun's asking price. Since the gap was so wide, London was nervous about a rival purchaser but none appeared. Thun, increasingly pressed financially, grew ever more cantankerous, and was erratically advised by his lawyers and agents. Clerk, on the other hand, was supported by his dependable honorary legal adviser, Dr Boucek.

In August 1923, Clerk suggested that Thun might be interested in receiving a capitalised rent payment, explaining to Earle 'Forgive these suggestions of desperate and doubtful expedients to save the Palace, but the fate of myself and my successors, if we are turned out, is too dreadful to contemplate, and that prospect must be my excuse!'[12] That did not tempt Thun, but not long afterwards he let it be known that he would accept 12 million crowns and, a few weeks later, a fairly reliable source told Clerk that Thun would probably accept an offer of an immediate 10 million crowns. In October 1923, however, a 12 million crown formal asking price was accompanied by a demand for an answer in eight days and, if negative, for the legation to have vacated the palace by 1 January 1924.

Earle was evidently talking quietly to the Treasury. He was able to tell Montgomery in early November 1923 that he thought the Treasury might authorise expenditure of about £50,000 (7.75 million crowns), provided that the Foreign Office delayed pressing for expensive ingoing items like a lift and central heating. Earle thought it might help if the Foreign Office could save some rents by finding room in the palace for a couple of flats for UK staff. Montgomery accordingly offered these sweeteners to the Treasury. In December, Thun dropped his price for the palace plus all of its contents to 10 million crowns. In January 1924, his agent refused to accept the legation's normal quarterly rent advance because it should have vacated the palace at the beginning of the month. Boucek remonstrated successfully on behalf of the legation. The next quarterly rent advance was again returned, this time accompanied by an application to a local court that the legation was breaking the terms of its lease. Thun filed a court application to secure vacation by 14 July 1924. In mid-May, Clerk learned of Thun's possible preparedness to settle for 7 to 8 million crowns. By this time, an official administrator for Thun's property had been appointed by the competent court at the request of his creditors. Clerk received a summons, relayed by the ministry of foreign affairs, to attend a District Tribunal. He replied, magnificently:

> Neither I nor His Majesty's Government would desire to prejudice the question, nor to evade any just or proper discussion of the right of Count Thun to resume possession of his Palace, but I am constrained to confess that it is with some surprise that I have received a communication of the above nature from the Foreign Ministry of the Government to which I have the honour to be accredited. As you, Monsieur le Ministre, are aware, it has long been established as a principal in the comity of civilised nations that the official Representative of a Foreign Power is not judiciable in the local courts. ... I am therefore confident that the adoption of so different a procedure in the present instance must be due to inadvertence.[13]

In mid-June, Earle asked Clerk to offer up to 5 million crowns, which

Thun turned down. A new lawyer for Thun, Senator Soukup, sent a memorandum to the British Prime Minister, Ramsay MacDonald, pleading for his government to negotiate seriously. In mid-August, Clerk reported that Soukup had confirmed that 6 million crowns, exclusive of furniture, was likely to be acceptable to Thun, provided that the British government paid the transfer and additional value taxes. In October, Soukup said Thun would accept 6 million crowns plus payment of half the total tax bill and in December he accepted 7.27m million crowns (£46,000) for the palace, contents, and most of the taxes, to which the Treasury agreed, and the purchase contract was concluded in May 1925. The tax element of the sum was subsequently deducted from the British government's wider claim on the Czechoslavak government.

Various last minute wobbles, as so often, came into play: among them, Thun was, apparently, leasing to the German legation next door some washrooms in the palace that nobody knew about; and the Ministry of Public Instruction required from the British government a declaration that it would treat the building properly. Montgomery asked Clerk for more information about Soukup's role. Clerk replied privately that this request for information was

> one to which an official reply is difficult. His [Soukup's] services in connection with the purchase of the Thun Palace are not such as to lend themselves to explanation in full detail. They are, rather, 'imponderabilia' that cannot be definitely stated, but I realise that without Senator Soukup's assistance we should never have succeeded in pinning Thun down to the definite sale of the Palace. … it was only the constant pressure kept up by Senator Soukup, backed by his weight as a political force in this country and as Vice- President of the Senate that brought Thun to terms. Dr Boucek is away on holiday at the moment, but as soon as he returns I will … see if he can give me material for a more formal answer to your despatch, if you really must have one. You might send me a line as to this.[14]

Formal ownership of the Thun Palace passed to the Office of Works in January 1926. Boucek was given a silver inkstand and candlesticks, of the 'Privy Council' type, as a token of gratitude for his successful advices. He replied to Clerk in his best English that

> It was a great pleasure for me to work together with you in such a rather clumsy and difficult case and I am sorry that many and many of our people, in a responsible situation, had not the same opportunity as I had. They would have learned what it means to dispose of money trusted to a Government by the tax-payer.[15]

Montgomery stuck to his word: central heating was not installed in the palace until four years later. While the Prague saga was under way, the selection of a legation house to buy in Budapest was made by Earle himself in 1921. In his own words, 14 years later,

> I finally selected the Batthyani palace, which had many attractions, having a lovely view from the high ground on which it stands, for twenty miles up the Danube with distant hills. ... This old-fashioned house ... was occupied at the time by forty different families, among them two prominent people, ... the remainder being refugees from the territories taken from Hungary and given to Roumania. ...
> We bought the house, but it was many months before we could get delivery so as to do the necessary alterations. I finally had to travel again to Budapest, where I laid my grievance before the Prime Minister. He, Count Bethlen, was very sympathetic and helpful, summoned the Cabinet and they decided that the Municipality must find accommodation somewhere for the refugee families.[16]

Emptying the house of its squatters and completing the ingoing works took until late 1924 and cost about £25,000 – four times the purchase price. It is exceedingly unlikely that Earle would have approved such a grandiose, complicated and expensive project if it had been proposed to him while sitting at his desk in London. But, having made the selection himself, he doubtless felt bound to see it through.

The only city in Europe in the post-War period in which a suitable legation house could not leased or bought, but had to be designed and built, was Belgrade. This project progressed remarkably smoothly from purchase of the site in 1925 to occupation of the building in 1928. It was designed by Thrift Reavell, shortly to retire after a long and productive career with the Office of Works, and was planned very much along the lines of his successful Sofia house that had been built 15 years earlier. Earle insisted that Belgrade should be smaller than Sofia. The minister at Belgrade, Howard Kennard, whose Post was more important than Sofia, noticed the size discrepancy while his building was under construction, and made his dismay known to London, to no effect. Although the Office of Works had by then accepted responsibility for entirely furnishing the interiors of mission houses, it still did not regard the land around buildings as its responsibility and its architects never gave any real consideration to the design, let alone the planting, of gardens. The first occupants of a new building were surprised to find that they were expected to arrange and fund the garden themselves. Kennard did not shrink from this and pleaded to London that 'my proposals as regards the

8.3. The wooden house in Ankara at the top of the site which was selected for the future mission in 1926. It served as an over crowded legation house until 1930, and was not demolished until 1951. A small chapel was built on part of its site in 1963.

laying out of the garden and tennis court … may be approved. I have some slight experience in dealing with a sloping site gained at my country place in England and have found that it is essential if one is making a garden to have a level site'.[17]

From Constantinople to Ankara

The new Turkey was recognised in July 1923 by the Treaty of Lausanne, and Ankara was proclaimed its capital three months later. The Turkish government invited diplomatic missions in Istanbul (as Constantinople was officially re-named in 1930) to select sites in Ankara which it would then make available for embassies. The missions did not take this offer too seriously because the new government was widely expected to last for only a short time. When Sir Ronald Lindsay presented his credentials in March 1925, a six-strong party from the embassy in Istanbul hired two railway coaches – one a saloon for the ambassador's study and chancery and the other a sleeping car – to take them to and from Ankara and house them in a siding at Ankara station for nearly a week while they did their business. Lindsay gradually realised that at least a *pied-à-terre* would be necessary and in January 1926 he sent Alexander Knox Helm, the third dragoman at the embassy, and Hewlett Edwards, the Office of Works architect resident in Istanbul, to Ankara to look for a site. To be acceptable, it would need road access, its own water supply and a house already on it. Helm and Edwards reasoned that there would be good road access to whichever district the Gazi, as Helm referred to President Atatűrk, had chosen to live. This led them to Çankaya, where they spotted a good sloping site, with a wooden house at the top, that belonged to Salih Bey, the Gazi's former aide-de-camp.

Helm rented the property for immediate use, taking over Salih Bey's stores which included three-and-a-half tons of anthracite and a ton of coal, and settled on a purchase price for the house itself **(Fig. 8.3)**. This would be paid on completion of the acquisition by the Turkish government of the seven-acre site from Salih Bey and its transfer to the British government. Edwards said in his own report of this visit 'it must be assumed that Angora [Ankara] will eventually become the seat of the diplomatic representative'. The ambassador hoped not: 'I have never gone quite so far as this, but in my recommendations to Mr Edwards I have said – what for his purposes amounts to nearly the same thing – that in all we do about houses and sites, we must keep in view the terrible possibility that some day Angora may be the permanent residence of a regular British Mission.'[18]

The wooden house had a couple of reasonable rooms on the first floor, with four small bedrooms above and the coal cellar below. Its period as *pied-à-terre* for visitors from Istanbul ended when a counsellor, Geoffrey Knox, was posted full time to Ankara in autumn 1926, supported by two secretaries, one of them Helm. When the ambassador visited, the house was so crowded that 'even he, if we had eight people to dinner, had to get dressed in time so that we could turn his bedroom into a second sitting-room.' It was in this cramped run-down little old house 'that Turkish frigidity was broken down and – a good deal over the bridge table – the foundations laid of the renewed Anglo-Turkish friendship and of the later ... alliance.'[19]

London was unreceptive to Lindsay's pleas to build a proper building on the new site. In 1928, the idea emerged of quickly putting up one building that would meet all of the current working and living needs, including for the ambassador, in such a way that it could later be converted entirely to offices once a separate ambassador's residence had been built. It was referred to as the First Building. The wooden house would then become available for clerical staff. Edwards in Istanbul and F.L.W. Cloux, an Office of Works architect in London, did a skilful job of outlining and negotiating floor plans that would work for both the short and long terms. Their proposals were minutely examined: '... a card room for the Secretaries is omitted' Allison commented at one stage; two deputy secretaries, poring over the plans in London, talked of 'transposing the wine cellar'.[20] When building was about to start in early 1928, the Treasury decreed a delay for public expenditure reasons. Ankara was not alone to suffer. The ambassador, by now Sir George Clerk from Prague, weighed in mightily and the Treasury relented to the extent of permitting the foundations to proceed: unfortunately, that proved of little benefit because it was found that the building was oriented the wrong way round and the drawings needed correction.

Clerk argued that 'the Turk' might think that London was boycotting Ankara, the symbol of the regeneration of Turkey, unless something was seen to be happening. He toyed with the idea both of a transportable house from the United Kingdom and of an offer by Holzmann to put up a suitable building for £10,000, a quarter of the likely cost of the stalled First Building. The arguments ran throughout 1928 and well into 1929: the Italians were apparently intending to spend £200,000 on their new embassy; the War Office wanted more space for the military attaché, whose office in the just-completed Belgrade building was too small; Cloux visited and unhelpfully doubted whether Ankara would last as the capital. The Treasury finally agreed to proceed in mid-1929 within a sum of £30,000, excluding furniture. The building was ready for occupation in late 1930 **(Fig. 8.4)**. The main gate and lodge, and a greenhouse, were built at the same time. Clerk complained to Earle:

> Must I have a separate [flagpole] in the grounds? It does look so like a retired sea captain and I do not want to be reminded of Southsea or Cheltenham before my time comes to go and live there! I gather that there is no technical difficulty in the way of having one on the roof and, if the objection thereto is aesthetic, perhaps it would be less obnoxious if we had one at either end.[21]

The building worked well in its intended multiple use for the first three years. Clerk's successor, however, Sir Percy Loraine, was much less accommodating. Within months of his arrival in 1934, he and his domestic staff were in sole occupation of the building, while his secretaries had been given allowances to rent flats in the town and the offices had returned to the little wooden house up the hill.

South America

Besides Europe, the continent with the greatest need in the early 1920s of improved diplomatic accommodation was South America. All nine of Spain's South American colonies, and Portugal's Brazil, gained independent statehood between 1816 and 1830 and major powers, including Britain, established quasi-diplomatic missions in most of the capital cities. These were raised to embassy status during the first half of the twentieth century,

8.4. The multi-purpose First Building at Ankara, completed in 1930, intended by its Office of Works' architects as a 'simple unpretentious house of typically English character'. It had magnificent views across the developing city.

beginning with Rio de Janeiro in Brazil in 1919 and ending with Asunción in Paraguay in 1952. In 1922, Montgomery and Earle agreed that the Office of Works should take over from the Foreign Office responsibility for the leases of all the South American mission houses. The need to improve the operational effectiveness of these buildings in changing circumstances led them next to embark on a co-ordinated regional programme.

It started with a tour of inspection of South American Posts during the winter of 1923-4 by Cecil Simpson, a senior architect in the Office of Works, armed with an assurance of £25,000 from the Treasury to spend on buying suitable sites if any were to be found. Simpson did his best to find a way of reconciling London's belief that mission houses should not necessarily continue to accommodate the chancery with heads of missions' certainty that they should. London's case was first set out by McDonnell, Earle's predecessor as Secretary of the Office of Works, in 1912:

[I]n a City of this kind [Buenos Aires] the actual Legation [ie where the minister lived] might well be situated at some distance from the business centre of the town, and indeed in the suburbs or upon the outskirts, where a good site is obtainable, with a garden, etc. ... Meanwhile it should be possible to hire office accommodation in the centre of the town, to which the Minister could resort daily for the transaction of business. It would probably be combined with the Consulate, so that as far as possible all offices should be under one roof.[22]

Heads of mission were exceedingly reluctant to give up the convenience and efficiency, as they saw it, of having the chancery within their houses, even if the introduction of motor cars was reducing the journey time to and from a separate mission office. The incumbents accused London of not understanding local perceptions about location and size. Hohler wrote from Santiago in 1925:

It is important everywhere, but nowhere so much as in Latin countries which are affected by display – or by the lack of it – to a degree which is not understood in Europe. The mere fact that I have taken the Ariztia house, which is generally considered as one of the best in the town, has made a distinct and favourable impression in the town.[23]

Simpson sought a compromise. He looked in the better inner suburbs for houses that were large enough to accommodate both residence and offices and were not too far from the city centre for commercial visitors, but far enough out to provide, at affordable cost, sufficient land for a decent garden. If there was no such house available, Simpson looked for a site on which to build. The fluctuations in this debate contributed to the high incidence of false starts that resulted from Simpson's recommendations and decisions. Houses were bought at Buenos Aires in 1924 and Rio de Janeiro in 1928, both of which proved unsatisfactory and were later replaced. Sites acquired at La Paz and Santiago in 1924 were both eventually, and for different reasons, sold after alternative solutions were found. On the other hand, new legation houses were successfully constructed in Panama City in 1926 on land leased in 1921; in Montevideo in 1927 on land bought in 1923; and in Lima in 1932 on land granted by the Peruvian government in 1927. The Office of Works architects were responsible for the design of these three houses, as well as one for La Paz which was not built. They illustrate the high-water mark of planning a chancery within a mission house. At Montevideo, the chancery was accessed from the hall, and in the other houses it had a separate external entrance, as well as easy internal access from the head of mission's study **(Fig. 8.5)**.

At Lima, the site that Simpson originally identified was exchanged for another in 1927 for the nominal consideration of one penny. The Foreign Office asked the Office of Works for a new penny to be supplied. The Royal Mint said that no pennies had been minted since 1922 and there were 'valid

8.5. The proposed legation house at Montevideo, designed by Thrift Reavell and J.L.W. Cloux. This drawing was exhibited at the Royal Academy in 1925. The building was completed in 1927.

objections to striking a special coin for the purpose'.[24] The Mint could offer, however, an unused 1922 penny, two 1926 halfpennies or a 1926 silver Maundy penny. The 1922 penny was chosen and the Mint charged this sum to the Office of Works, which seemed to exercise the accounting ingenuity of its finance division.

Far East

Most heads of mission did not concede until after the Second World War that there were more efficient places for chanceries than inside their own mission houses. The dilemma never arose for those who had served in the compounds of the Far East, where many of the 'out-offices' had for long been separate from the residence. The head of mission worked in his own study, of course, but his staff in chancery or consulate were in separate buildings across the lawn or, as in the case of Bangkok, down the drive. By 1921, there was strong pressure to move the legation in Bangkok away from its old compound on the river, laid out by Schomburgk in 1857. That area of the city was now too overcrowded and polluted, and almost every other mission in Bangkok had already moved away. Cecil Simpson visited

175

early in 1921 and, strongly supported by the minister, Richard Seymour, concluded that the time had come to act. He was attracted by a site which was occupied by the Royal College of Pages but, soon after he left Bangkok, Seymour reported that Phra Pakdi Noraseth, a successful and cultivated businessman popularly known as Nai Lert, who had shown them some of the paddy fields he had drained in the Sapatoom area on the edge of town, had offered to exchange a large site there for half of the present riverside compound. The Treasury was sceptical, recalling a stipulation it made in 1908 that any move should be fully self-financing.

A few months and several discussions later, Nai Lert recast his offer: he would give the British government an option on about 11 acres of his site at Sapatoom free of charge in return for his being given an option, up to the end of 1923, to purchase the riverside legation site (except for a small piece that the British government wanted to retain for the Consular Shipping Office) for 1.1 million ticals (£117,000). Nai Lert was also content for the statue of Queen Victoria to be removed to the new legation site, as well as the iron gates and railings, and the flagstaff. This scheme held promise of being self-financing and pretty well satisfied London. The option agreement with Nai Lert was signed in March 1922. Robert Greg, who had recently replaced Seymour as minister, correctly forecast that Nai Lert would make every effort to exercise his right of option quickly, and he did – three months later. It would appear that the net effect of the transaction which Nai Lert master-minded was that the Siamese government bought back in 1922, as the site for a new Central Post Office, at least some of the site which King Mongkut had donated to the British in 1857.

In expectation of agreement, planning and design work had been put in hand promptly. Julius Bradley, the Office of Works architect in the Shanghai office, was tasked with preparing preliminary plans and arrived in Bangkok with them in June 1922. Greg was far from impressed and asked W.A.R. Wood, the consul-general at Chiang Mai, to discuss improvements with the Office of Works in London during his forthcoming leave. An Office of Works architect in London, Archibald Scott, accordingly took over the design work from Bradley and was shortly afterwards posted to Bangkok as resident architect, charged with tailoring the designs to local conditions, incorporating Greg's preferences where acceptable, and overseeing construction contracts.

The new compound was close to square in plan, each side about 200 metres long, with *khlongs* (drainage channels) along three sides and, to the north, a large rectangular drainage pond that Nai Lert had dug as a cistern to cope with the heavy rains. Bradley's layout of the new compound reflected the general disposition of Schomburgk's at the former compound (**Fig. 8.6**). The axis was a wide, formal and ceremonial route northwards from the main gates in the centre of the south frontage to a circular drive in front of the minister's residence, with two other buildings on each side for offices, consul-general's and vice-consul's houses, and students' quarters. Each of the five main buildings was of two storeys, with verandas round each floor. The first structure to be erected was a granite war memorial, designed by the Aberdonian sculptor Sir James Taggart, and commissioned by a trust formed for the purpose in 1919: it was dedicated on 10 October 1922.

The plans of the five main buildings were relatively easily agreed between Greg and Scott and construction started on them first. The ancillary buildings proved more difficult, not least because Greg saw less need of them. Scott explained to London that

> Mr Greg is naturally not keen on having so many native families close to his own residence, and he is still of the opinion that the Clerks should live outside the compound. The official servants and their families, who number about seventy altogether, are very well behaved on the whole, but the small babies which arrive at abnormally frequent intervals are apt to be rather noisy.[2]

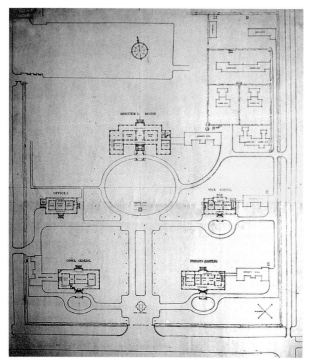

8.6. Layout of the new compound in Bangkok after the 1926 inclusion of the drainage pond strip at the top. The formal drive between entrance and the minister's house, with subsidiary buildings to the sides, reflected the layout of the former compound on the river.

177

The result was that all servants' quarters were pushed away from the main axis towards the compound perimeters. Another intrusion that Greg feared was also resolved. As Scott explained to London in November 1925:

> From the middle of October to the beginning of December, holiday makers from all parts of Bangkok … visit the pond [Nai Lert's cistern, next to the minister's garden] in motor cars and boats and spend the day bathing and canoe-racing and picnicking on the banks; and on Sundays during this period, from early morning till dusk the pond is crowded with overloaded boats and the banks lined four or more deep with a mob of noisy onlookers. … The pond is offered for T40,000, and while this far exceeds its market value, the value of our property would I think be increased by a greater amount by the inclusion of the pond, apart altogether from the abolition of the intolerable nuisance of the noisy Sunday crowds.[26]

London was anxious not to breach the self-financing principle by exceeding the 1.1 million ticals received from Nai Lert. Fortuitously, the need for a Shipping Office down by the river was receding and the part of the former compound that had been retained for it was now sold to an Indian merchant for 50,000 ticals, enough to buy from Nai Lert the 70-metre-wide strip of land, including the pond, that lay along the northern boundary of the new

8.7. The new Bangkok compound in 1930, with the war memorial inside the gates and the statue of Queen Victoria in the finally agreed position.

compound. The Treasury acquiesced 'although the price demanded for it appears ... a high one to pay merely for the preservation of amenities and T[heir Lordships] are disposed to doubt whether its purchase is politically expedient'.[27] As well as saving the minister's residence in perpetuity from noisy crowds on the pond, the new strip provided land on which to build quarters for clerks, gardeners and messengers.

The exact siting of the statue of Queen Victoria, and the vexed question as to whether she should look outwards towards visitors entering through the main gates or inwards towards the minister emerging from his residence, took a long time to agree. She finally arrived at the top end of the straight ceremonial approach, and looked outwards **(Fig. 8.7)**. A huge flagstaff that could be seen from the river was erected at the south-east corner of the compound.

Greg was posted to Bucharest before the residence was completed. Back in London, he called on Allison, who recorded that 'Mr Greg ... was somewhat critical on two or 3 points of detail and seemed to be of the opinion that the main house should have been larger'.[28] Another official, present during the call, recorded 'the impression left on me was that he had not been given as many opportunities for expressing his opinion during the progress of the work as he thought proper!' Greg's successor, Sidney Waterlow, arrived in Bangkok in July 1926 and was most enthusiastic about the new compound until he had to deal with the clerk of works, Mr Dunn, whom Scott had left in Bangkok to finish the works. Delays of several months in the arrival of the furniture caused more justified dismay, though the *punkah* over the dining room table was transferred from the former house **(Fig. 8.8)**. To cap it all, the doorway of the legation strongroom was too narrow for the safe from the old compound to be installed.

Waterlow finally moved in to the new house in September 1926 and, the following week, praised the new site and the wisdom of moving from the old compound in a long letter to the Foreign Secretary, Austen Chamberlain. Earle could not resist minuting the First Commissioner, Lord Peel, 'This should convince the FO that their representatives are not always wise in their views, as the last Minister kept on inveighing against the change of site etc.' Peel merely annotated 'an intelligent and discerning Minister'.[29] Waterlow also wrote effusively the following week to Scott. Photographs of the finished buildings caused a good impression in London: Earle showed them to Peel, who congratulated Allison and Scott personally. The total project fell only fractionally short of its self-financing target. In 1926, the new compound was among paddy fields several miles from the town. Nowadays it is an oasis near the centre of Bangkok's concrete jungle.

8.8. One of the cool first-floor verandas in the Bangkok minister's house, about 1930.

Britain formally recognised the independence of Afghanistan in the Anglo-Afghan Treaty of 1921, which also provided for each country to open a legation in the other's capital. Lt-Col Francis Humphrys, of the Indian political service, arrived in Kabul as minister early in 1922. He leased temporary accommodation for the legation while he found a site on which to build a permanent legation.

Humphrys' choice was a site of 26 acres about 2½ miles from the centre of Kabul. It comprised 12 individual plots which were bought by separate sale deeds by the Oriental Secretary, Sheikh Mahboob Ali, in his own name but '…on behalf of the British Legation and is the property of the British Government…'. The legation buildings were designed by Basil Martin Sullivan, a British architect who moved to India in 1913 when in his early thirties and spent most of his career working for the Punjab government, retiring as its superintending architect and town planner in 1938. He designed many of the public and civic buildings in Lahore and was, geographically, the closest British architect to Kabul. Sullivan laid out the main compound with the residence on a wide platform looking across a large formal garden to the mountains beyond. The residence, on two floors, looked huge on account

180

8.9. The legation house at Kabul, designed by Basil Sullivan and completed in 1927. A masterly exercise in projecting maximum power with limited substance. The other houses in the 26-acre compound were in much more of a Surrey idiom.

of deep verandas around every side, with a squash court at one end and a greenhouse at the other but in reality it was only one or two rooms deep **(Fig. 8.9)**. Legend has it that Lord Curzon, Foreign Secretary until January 1924, wanted the Kabul residence to be the best house in Asia **(Fig. 8.10)**. Sullivan went some way towards fulfilling that brief. But he apparently made

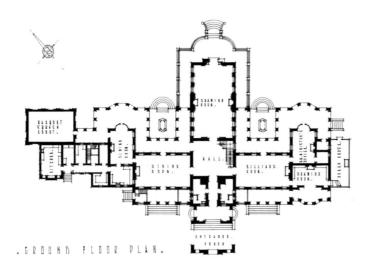

8.10. The ground-floor plan of the Kabul legation house.

181

one mistake: used to designing against the heat of India, where houses faced north to avoid the sun and catch the breeze, his north-facing Kabul houses caught instead the −25°C winds.

Separate buildings, out of site from the residence, included the chancery offices, detached houses for the counsellor, secretary and military attaché, lesser free-standing buildings for clerks' and superintendents' accommodation, and a village for stables and servants' quarters. Across the road, opposite the main gate, was a small compound of two acres for the hospital and the oriental secretary's residence. Construction of the compound took three years from 1924. Most of the building materials came from India and were carted from Peshawar by traction engines over the Lataband Pass. Rebellions, a local timber shortage, passport regulations and other interferences all contributed to the frustrations of building a palace in a remote location lacking local infrastructure. The leased legation premises in town were completely destroyed by fire in the autumn of 1926, mercifully not before some of the lesser buildings on the new compound were far enough advanced for the legation to move into. The cost of the land and buildings was about £175,000 in total, met from Government of India funds.

1928 and most of 1929 passed happily for the legation: wives and families were living comfortably on the compound and in the autumn of 1928 a large reception was held which Afghan ladies attended in European dress. The Emir was deposed in 1929 and fighting broke out between his supporters and those of his usurper. In mid-December 1929 the legation lay between the opposing forces and was cut off from the town and other legations. The staff, neutral onlookers, mainly took refuge in the residence because anyone appearing in the grounds was fired on. They watched as fire destroyed the military attaché's house on 19 December, and stray shells and bullets caused extensive damage throughout the compound. The indomitable Lady Humphrys recorded in her diary 'bullets in the squash court, 3 in the bedroom, 3 near my bed, 3 in our own bathroom, one missing the Minister by 6 inches'. It was she too who organised the tearing up of white sheets into strips to be laid out in block letters on the lawn so that, when other communications failed, messages could be read by aircraft flying up from Peshawar.

On 23 December 1929 began the world's first airlift:

It was carried out by the RAF using mainly Vickers Victorias and DH9As and flying in conditions of extreme cold and at altitudes for which the planes were never designed. First to leave were the British women and children … followed over the next two months by the rest of the British and foreign communities, 586 people in all.

The evacuation continued throughout the winter, even when the snow on the airfield had to be trampled down to allow the planes to land. ... Finally, on the 25th of February, the seven Victorias made their last trip to pick up the Legation staff; flying out of Kabul on the last plane was Sir Francis Humphrys, accompanied by his parrot and carrying the Legation Union Jack under his arm.[30]

Remarkably, no lives were lost. The legation staff returned three months later and had all essential services at the compound working again within a week.

Much else, of course, was in train at other Posts during the 1920s. A new consulate was built at Fez, in Morocco, which today is part of an hotel. The consulate that had eventually been built at Alexandria in 1903 began to show cracks only two years later and was finally abandoned in 1924. A new consulate-general building was erected on much the same site, but with better foundations, in the later 1920s. Unbuilt projects during this period included Allison's massive proposed lengthening in 1920 of Boyce's Cairo building to extend across the adjacent site, known as the Bacos site, that was acquired in 1916: this scheme was set aside in 1922. Concurrently, the architect W. J. Roberts, in the Shanghai office of the Office of Works, developed huge proposals for rebuilding most of the Shanghai compound, which were set aside as soon as they came to London's serious notice. By then, the two large projects at Tokyo and Washington were attracting most of the attention.

9

Tokyo and Washington
1923–1932

Sir Lionel Earle, Secretary of the Office of Works, and Hubert Montgomery, chief clerk at the Foreign Office, together oversaw, from start to finish, the two largest and longest projects of the inter-war years. These were the rebuilding of the embassy compound in Tokyo after the great earthquake of 1923 and building a new embassy in Washington to escape the congestion and noise of the 1875 house on Connecticut Avenue. The two projects could hardly have been more different: Tokyo was a modest in-house design mainly borrowed from the destroyed compound, Washington an inspired display of self-confidence with no precedent, by Britain's leading architect of the day. The Tokyo project started about a month before Washington. Both were seriously affected by the Treasury's stringency as the international financial climate worsened in the late 1920s.

Tokyo
The Great Kanto Earthquake struck the whole Tokyo and Yokohama area at about noon on Saturday, 1 September 1923, and fires raged through the cities for the rest of that day and night. The ambassador, Sir Charles Eliot, was on leave and most of the UK staff's families were still at their summer retreats away from the city. The chargé, Michael Palairet, was unable to get a wireless message to London and news of the fate of the embassy compound was not received there until five days later via the consul-general in Kobe: 'Following received from Embassy. Earthquake fire Saturday destroyed large part of Tokio, all embassy buildings uninhabitable and require rebuilding.

Japanese councillors' house burnt. Please inform press none of staff injured.'[1] A small temporary embassy office was quickly set up in the recently completed Imperial Hotel, which had been only slightly damaged. The consulate, off-compound on the seventh floor of a modern stone building owned by the Industrial Bank of Japan, was not damaged although the furniture was thrown about. Palairet cabled the ambassador 'Will you prefer to live at Imperial Hotel or shall I have a wooden bungalow built on embassy lawn. Imperial wedding has not yet been postponed but it probably will be.'

Julius Bradley, the Office of Works architect based at Shanghai, hastened to Tokyo, arriving on 18 September. The UK staff, after a fortnight of living outdoors in what had thankfully been temperate weather, had just moved into a large temporary wooden shelter, divided into cubicles by matting and curtains. About 100 Japanese servants and some homeless and hungry expatriate British residents were also encamped in the compound. Bradley found that only the rackets court and the recently completed attachés' offices remained intact: all the other buildings were split or ruined, falling chimneys having done much of the damage, and most of the perimeter wall had collapsed **(Fig. 9.1)**. Fortunately, the compound water well was undamaged. Bradley worked hard to get more huts built out of materials from the wrecked houses and the chancery offices were operating in the attachés' building by early October. The exposed strongroom in the ruined chancery building was surrounded by a barbed wire fence to deter thieves.

Palairet and Bradley soon leased three houses outside the compound. One, a relatively undamaged Mission House in Hirakawa-Cho, capable of taking six UK bachelors, was hired from the bishop and sufficiently repaired for occupation by 1 November; another, a little-damaged house in Tansumachi was hired for Palairet from the Russian naval attaché who was leaving Tokyo; and a third in Aoyama Omote-Cho was rented for the ambassador for three months, the hope being that the temporary shelter would have been vacated and converted into an interim residence by then. Bradley wrote to Richard Allison, the Office of Works chief architect in London, in early October that he felt

> totally unable to convey to you adequately an idea of the wholesale disorganisation which has resulted from the earthquake. All the resources of the country will be insufficient during the next few months to supply materials for the temporary buildings for the city of Yokohama and the many square miles of Tokyo which have been devastated and it is not reasonably to be expected that the requirements of the British Embassy will receive much consideration from the Japanese authorities in view of their own necessities.

9.1. Rear view of the Tokyo ambassador's residence, built by Robert Boyce in 1875, after the Great Kanto Earthquake of September 1923.

There was not much that London could do except ask questions and approve requests. Bradley wondered how quickly a beginning could be made on permanent replacement buildings: he suggested that a reputable firm such as Trollope and Colls, which was proposing to establish a branch in Tokyo, should be employed on a cost-plus basis for the rebuilding, for which he hazarded a rough estimate of £250,000-300,000. He thought the problems were severe enough to justify the Office of Works' director of works, Sir Frank Baines, visiting Tokyo but Baines declined. There was uncertainty in the Foreign Office whether families should return home or wives should accompany new appointees. The Admiralty complained to the Office of Works that the ambassador had 'grabbed' for one of his own staff the accommodation on which their naval attaché had his eye, which drew the curt offer 'to extend the present temporary accommodation, so as to form a cubicle or bedroom such as those provided for other members of the Embassy staff'. Other departments started sending in bids for temporary and permanent accommodation in Tokyo. Decisions were therefore needed quickly on whether to continue housing the attachés off-compound or to build new houses for them on-compound. Bradley took it upon himself to plan the future layout of the compound without knowing what buildings would be required, while London maintained that the attachés' accommodation could not be decided until Bradley's layout had been considered.

In mid-November 1923, the Office of Works recommended to the Treasury that an early start should be made on permanent reconstruction, not least so as to keep together the labour teams that had built the temporary buildings and were clearing up the demolition sites. The Treasury wanted answers to four questions. Could the British government be sure of priority of treatment in respect of labour and materials? The answer was unlikely. Would the Japanese government have any objections to the early commencement of reconstruction? None. Would there be any objection to employing Chinese labour? Yes, there would. And should the attachés remain off-compound? Yes, so as to prevent overcrowding: nobody queried whether housing more than one UK family per acre would really constitute overcrowding. London was not, however, prepared to be rushed into reconstruction.

Allison was content for Bradley to take the lead in re-planning the compound because he knew it so well, could phase new work around the temporary structures, and was close to the views of the ambassador and staff. But Allison thought that the 1870s Boyce designs of the destroyed buildings were commonplace and hoped to do better architecturally. Initially, he let W.J. Roberts, Bradley's junior in the Shanghai office, develop designs during the winter of 1923 for the two main buildings **(Fig. 9.2)**. Later on, Allison withdrew this design work from Shanghai and had it completed under his eye in London.

Hundreds of tremors in the months after the earthquake, and an especially severe shake on 15 January 1924 toppled most of the rest of the damaged buildings. With London dragging its feet on reconstruction, Bradley sought approval, quickly given, to take up an option that he had earlier and far-sightedly placed on the purchase of two steel Truscon huts, each 96 ft by 28 ft, that were on the high seas from America. He intended to erect one close to the south gate for chancery offices and the other on the residence lawn as a godown. By spring 1924, therefore, six months after the earthquake, some sense of order and operations had been achieved on the compound. It would take almost another five years to start the construction of permanent new buildings.

Bradley re-planned the compound along much the same lines as it was, siting many of the new buildings on the cleared and consolidated sites of the old ones. The only aspect of the rebuilding of the compound that was taken back to first principles was, for incontestably good reasons, the structural

9.2. An architect in the Shanghai office of the Office of Works, W.J. Roberts, proposed these two schemes for rebuilding within months of the earthquake. Top, for the ambassador's residence and, bottom, for the chancery, students' quarters and archivist's flat. Neither scheme was adopted but features of both were retained.

design. The Japanese government, which had decided quite quickly after the earthquake that the capital would remain at Tokyo, appointed a commission to investigate how to rebuild the city, and to explore the structural implications for new buildings. Ten months after the earthquake, with the temporary rebuilding of the city of Tokyo almost complete, the Japanese government plans for permanent rebuilding were behind schedule. Although Baines had declined to visit Tokyo, he took the lead in London in deciding how to incorporate seismic resistance in the design of the new buildings. He believed that each should, if possible, lie predominantly north-south because the record of earthquakes in Japan showed that the seismic movement was mainly along the east-west axis. He wanted the buildings to be of monolithic reinforced concrete construction, with flat roofs and without applied decorative features, sitting on integral reinforced concrete skeleton rafts not less than 4 feet deep, carried on friction piles 15-20 feet long. Baines sought the advice of the Office of Works consulting engineer, Dr Oscar Faber, who had wide experience of the East. Faber supported Baines' emerging conclusions and the proposal for reinforced concrete boxes sitting beside each other, with between four and twelve inches between them, so that the boxes could move independently in a shake.

The problem for the architects was that the engineers' north-south preference for the lie of the buildings conflicted with the unanimous preference of occupants for the main rooms of the houses to face south. This led to a more general argument between Baines and Allison about where to strike the balance between structural confidence and architectural freedom. Allison reacted to his boss in the time-honoured manner of affronted architects:

> Accepting … the advantages claimed by constructing strictly on the engineering lines laid down by you, I suggest that the gain would not sufficiently compensate the loss resulting by the sacrifice to a considerable extent of the convenient working and comfort of the buildings, the interest of architectural treatment and the general amenities of the Compound, to say nothing of considerable additional cost. …. It will be clear that I attach the greatest importance to the architectural aspect of the problem, while realising fully that special assistance from the Engineer is necessary in this particular case if successful results are to be achieved. In my view the aim should be reasonable compromise rather than the imposing of hard and fast engineering restrictions on the Architect.

Earle chimed in with a manuscript note:

> I do strongly agree with the CA [chief architect] that the design must be to some extent a compromise involving perhaps some extra risk. If the entire amenities of the house have to be sacrificed to obtain the best earthquake resisting building obtainable, it is I think going too far. We shall get no thanks and lots of abuse by the occupants for a generation or two. … I would sooner see a building that may partly collapse with amenities, than a shock resisting block with none.

Baines calmly set out his case:

> It remains to be seen whether reasonable structural conditions, to give reasonable safety to occupants, will affect adversely the architectural

amenities of a scheme. As a general principle, practical requirements to meet certain known conditions, dealt with faithfully architecturally should give the best results - for the architectural problem is the solving of the practical one. There must of course be some compromise and this has always been in mind. We should have little excuse in the event of our new buildings being subject to 'partial collapse' - with consequent risk of serious injury to occupants; and if the point was put, in some such form, to the future occupants they would inevitably press, I think, for safety within reasonable limits.

William Leitch, Earle's under-secretary, tried his administrative hand at bridging the remaining gap:

> The best course appears to be to authorise the Director of Works to proceed with the preparation of plans ... on the lines of the form of construction most likely to resist earthquake shocks, and to consider those plans from the point of view of the amenities desirable for such buildings, and the extent to which it may be possible, with safety, to modify them with a view to securing additional amenity.

Baines was asked to proceed with plans accordingly. Meanwhile, the ambassador commended Bradley's proposed compound layout to London, emphasising the need to limit the spread of fire by setting the houses well in from the boundaries and keeping them well apart from each other. He was prepared to provide an office and house for the commercial counsellor on-compound but still resisted houses for the three service attachés for fear of overcrowding. Allison, rather late in the day, thought the requirements should be more definitively stated: if overcrowding really was a problem, he suggested that some semi-detached houses might be a good idea. He also succeeded in requiring the commercial and chancery offices to share the same building. Allison's biggest problem was with Roberts' proposed design for the ambassador's residence. It had the entrance with a *porte cochère*, as had its predecessor, in the middle of the main, south, face of the residence, which meant that the main rooms jostled for position along the front of the house, on either side of the entrance hall, and the ballroom was pushed right to the back of the house. Roberts had retained this arrangement solely to preserve the private lawn, to the east of the former residence, which the ambassador regarded as sacrosanct because it was the nicest and coolest place to entertain in summer. Allison sketched out a solution with the drive and entrance to the east side of the house, thereby sacrificing the east lawn but enabling more of the principal rooms to face south and relate directly with a fine south lawn. He invited Roberts' and the ambassador's views on these suggestions. The ambassador understood all of Allison's arguments but still refused to lose the east lawn. Roberts, caught between his local diplomatic boss and his distant architectural one, inclined to the view of the former.

This design stand-off was only one of several reasons for the project slowing down in mid-1924: difficulties were foreseen in obtaining materials and labour, there were uncertainties about costings and methods of contracting, and the report of the Japanese Commission on methods of construction was still awaited. The ambassador, still Eliot, sought to break the impasse in a letter to the newly appointed First Commissioner at the Office of Works, Viscount Peel, in November 1924:

> I fear that the Office of Works is inclined to regard Ambassadors as importunate persons who are insatiable in their demands for houses and furniture. The delay in reconstructing the Embassy here is, however, a sufficiently important matter to claim your attention. Though it is considerably more than a year since the earthquake occurred not a single permanent building has been even commenced and all the residences and offices in the compound are strictly temporary constructions.

The Office of Works did, however, make a little progress. The First Commissioner approved the plans at the end of January 1925 and asked that the drawings be sent to Post for comment. Leitch was dubious: 'Apart from the delay involved in doing so, the department is being steadily forced into the view that too much consideration can easily be given to the views of individual Ministers, with resultant trouble and expense on change of occupancy'. The ambassador duly made his suggestions in May 1925, introducing them thus: 'I understand it is particularly desired that the modifications proposed may be kept within the narrowest possible limits and I have endeavoured to comply with this condition'. He marked each suggestion with an A or B to distinguish between items of the first importance, the great majority, and those which were merely desirable, just a few. Baines had, meanwhile, sent his chief quantity surveyor, Widdowson, to Tokyo. He estimated the buildings would cost London prices plus 30 per cent; he ruled out lump-sum tenders because the availability and cost of materials in Tokyo was so uncertain; and he concluded that there was no alternative to undertaking the work through a cost-plus contract. Ideally, a British contractor would be available with American or German, or even Japanese, contractors as alternatives: 'The latter proposal is, I think, impossible ... and I think it would be a great pity if the British Government had to go to an American or German firm for the building of the Embassy in Tokyo'.

Throughout the three years from 1925, while the reconstruction project was marking time, there was an incessant flow of suggestions and comments. The Treasury maintained that the inclusion of a ballroom and a squash court in the plans was 'open to question'. The Foreign Office was able to put its mind at rest and, in conceding, the Treasury adopted a rare resigned note '… one never knows with these big schemes, which always seem to cost far more than anyone expects at the outset'. The Japanese asked in July 1925 whether they might take a slice off the north end of the compound to enable the streets to be improved in that area. The ambassador, in mock-humble mode, '… so far as I am able to judge of a question that has a technical side', suggested how a satisfactory deal could be done, including squeezing a concession from the Japanese in Yokohama: his idea worked out well. Bradley noticed in December 1925 that Japanese consent should really be obtained before felling a large *hinoki* tree that was in the way of a new building. This tree was not only beautiful and revered in itself but was apparently one of many planted years ago by the Japanese Government every 3 *ri* apart (about seven-and-a-half miles) over an extensive area for the purposes of land measurement. Embassy staff successfully argued that it would be simpler to move the house than the historic tree. The Office of Works had built and maintained the former greenhouse at Tokyo, although it had consistently refused to have anything to do with greenhouses at consulates, but wanted to avoid providing a new one in Tokyo: 'In the case of an ardent gardener [greenhouses] would become a source of all kinds of fastidious demands, while under the care of an officer quite uninterested they would be liable to neglect.' Should the ballroom have a sprung floor? Earle opined that 'I think a spring floor a doubtful asset in a private house.'

The overall estimate in 1926 was still within the £300,000 hazarded by Bradley nearly two years previously, mainly because the exchange rate had been moving in sterling's favour. Even so, financial cutbacks were essential in that year and a moratorium was placed on the starts of all new permanent buildings. A dismayed new ambassador, Sir John Tilley, described the compound to Earle as 'a horrible wilderness of ruins and shanties …'. He feared having to spend his whole tour in the converted big wooden shelter that had been thrown up immediately after the earthquake **(Fig. 9.3)**. The Treasury was insisting on being sent comparative floor areas because it understood that the proposed embassy in Tokyo was going to be much larger than the concurrent proposal for Washington. Allison, who had been forcing Lutyens to reduce the cubic capacity of the Washington buildings, had no option but to try to reduce the Tokyo ones also, even though that might lead to more delay and new plans. Helpfully, Tilley did not think he needed quite so many reception rooms because

9.3. Exterior and interior views of the ambassador's temporary residence in Tokyo six months after the earthquake. It was occupied by three successive ambassadors over the next eight years.

a ball on a huge scale … is difficult to contemplate. Among the Japanese there is Baroness Nishi who comes to dances, very pretty but quite small, and I have seen Mrs Debuchi take a turn, but she is even smaller; there are perhaps half a dozen others; and in the colony there are two English girls whom we should ask to a grand ball, and Mrs Royle once found a typist at Yokohama who usually goes about in riding boots but does dance, and there is the *corps diplomatique*, but a ball room and drawing room would amply provide for them without the help of a library and morning room.

Allison achieved reductions of 10-20 per cent, bringing the total area down to about 64,000 square feet for 18 buildings (compared with about 48,000 square feet for 20 buildings pre-earthquake). Having got its pound of flesh, a Treasury official minuted, 'I think … that we should not be insensible to the desirability of somewhat imposing buildings … in a city now being rebuilt on a very considerable scale, and a country of such extreme prospective importance'.

Various justifications were rehearsed for further postponing the start of reconstruction. Neither the Americans, housed in one wing of the Imperial Hotel, nor the French, were further ahead. The temporary buildings were, conveniently, judged by Shanghai to be just serviceable for another ten years. Meanwhile, the residence plans, still reflecting Eliot's insistence on a south entrance, were sent to Tilley for comment. He thought them misguided: he claimed that the ballroom was in the wrong place, and the south side of the house should be kept for living rooms instead of being sacrificed to the hall and entrance, which ought to be on the east side. Tilley betrayed no sign of knowing that he was pushing at an open door or of directly disagreeing with his predecessor. Allison returned to his own earlier scheme, moved the entrance to the east and, in a way that may have been suggested by Lutyens' contemporaneous plan for Washington, brought the ballroom into the centre of the house. Working drawings were at last put in hand **(Fig. 9.4)**.

The intention by then was to build the chancery and boundary wall first, and then the residence. Earle answered Tilley's inevitable complaint about not building the residence first by explaining that the order was dictated both by the progress of the drawings of the complicated residence building, and by his staff wanting to learn by experience and not tackling the main building first. James Wynnes was posted to Tokyo as the Office of Works' resident architect and arrived in February 1928. His first task was to draw up and tender a lump-sum contract with a Japanese firm for the first phase of the work. The corresponding schedule of prices would then be applied to the construction of the residence and other buildings as soon as their working drawings were complete.

Allison sent Earle a drawing of the residence elevation in March 1928. Earle minuted Peel: 'Here is the elevation of the earthquake resisting Embassy building at Tokyo and in my opinion, considering the restrictions, quite a dignified design. I think we should send it to the Foreign Office to see as the Secretary of State may like to see it and either he or we could show it

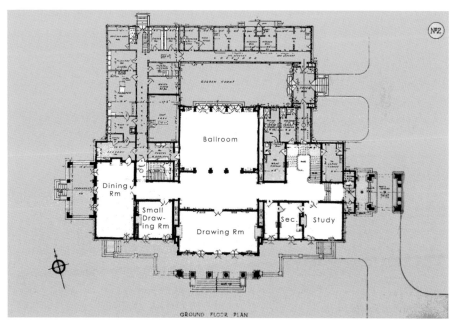

9.4. Ground-floor plan of the Tokyo residence, as finalised by Richard Allison in 1928 and as built in 1930. The main corridor runs from the entrance at the east side to the dining room at the west. Allison may have been influenced in this arrangement by Lutyens' concurrent proposals for Washington.

195

to Sir John Tilley who is now home on leave.' Peel drily replied: 'Certainly. Sir John Tilley may be interested to see the house of his successor.' Earle's assistant secretary, Eric de Normann, annotated that he did not think it necessary to send the elevation to the Foreign Office because 'they have seen the plans'.

The Japanese construction firm, Shimizu, won the first contract, to last 18 months from August 1928 to February 1930 and the offices were occupied at the end of April 1930 **(Fig. 9.5)**. Tilley said that he would prefer to move into the archivist's flat above the offices than remain in his timber shed. A second contract, for the residence, main entrance and servants' quarters was won by Kunoike Gumi Ltd and was to run from June 1929 to March 1931. Tilley left Tokyo in April 1931 and the next ambassador, Sir Francis Lindley, moved into the residence in September 1931 **(Fig. 9.6)**. He wrote to Earle a few days later about his delight with the house but how expensive it was going to be to live in, and he also had ' to heat and light a row of office buildings such as I have never seen at any other mission'. It was still some years before the rules were changed to relieve ambassadors' allowances of this expense. A third contract, for all the southern end of the compound, was to run from April 1930 to March 1932.

The sterling costs of building in Japan dropped steadily over the course

9.5. The chancery and junior staff quarters building in the Tokyo compound, completed in 1930. It faced the main compound entrance.

9.6. The ambassador's residence in Tokyo in 1964. The entrance with *porte-cochère* is on the right. Beyond the house is the 'village' of Japanese domestic staff quarters, and the garages.

of these contracts and the final overall estimated cost, excluding furniture, was down to £172,000, making the rebuilding of the Tokyo compound perhaps the most financially fortunate diplomatic building project of all time. Towards the end of the project, the Treasury went out of its usual way and wrote nicely to Earle that 'Their Lordships desire to record Their satisfaction at the way in which this important undertaking is being handled by your Department'. Earle noted in the margin 'amazing and gratifying'. Wynnes, the resident architect, received most of the credit, which infuriated Allison who pointed out, in an over-reaction on behalf of his London staff, that identical buildings would have been provided whoever had acted as resident architect. 'I hope the First Commissioner will be made aware of the true position in justice to Architects and Engineers at Headquarters who have worked enthusiastically as a team to get satisfactory results and whose efforts any success achieved will certainly be very largely due.' Bradley, now back in London, more realistically commented that 'Ambassadors always believe in flattering the man on the spot'.

Washington
The Washington project started with Montgomery hearing from Washington

197

in October 1923 that, as he explained to Earle, 'a very big price could be got for the present site and a new site could probably be got for a great deal less, so that a considerable proportion of the money obtained by the sale of the old one would be available towards building a new Embassy'.[2] This could be the key to solving what had become the problem of the Connecticut Avenue house. Although it was the social centre of diplomatic Washington and much admired by all who were entertained there, the case for moving to new premises in a less congested area had grown very strong. Temporary huts for offices proliferated in the garden, the noise of the double tramway meant speech was only practicable if the windows were closed, the bustle of commercial activity made the streets congested, and the proposed widening of Connecticut Avenue, which would require the demolition of the massive porch at the front of the house, was the last straw.

Earle was immediately attracted by the idea described by Montgomery, but understood that the ambassador, Sir Auckland Geddes, was not in favour of moving. Montgomery averred that 'the personal view of the Ambassador for the time being is not necessarily conclusive', especially as Geddes was about to leave Post. The next ambassador, Sir Esme Howard, asked for his considered view in April 1924, took a statesman-like line:

> I should like to state at once, before going further that, while I have tried to consider the whole question with the utmost impartiality, my own inclination would be strongly in favour of keeping the Embassy where it is in order to avoid the great personal inconvenience and extra trouble which the erection of a new Embassy and the move from one house to another will entail. I mention this to avoid misunderstanding if I seem, for public reasons, to incline to the other solution of the question.

Howard identified three possible sites and he showed these to Earle during Earle's first visit to America in October 1924. Together they selected an irregularly-shaped scrubby site, set back from the road, on high ground on the extension to Massachusetts Avenue. The site had two accesses, good views over the city and in summer was significantly cooler than the city. The Naval Observatory lay behind the site and, with a public park on one side, there was little likelihood of it becoming surrounded by development. Howard recalled ten years later:

> There was one feature of it that pleased me greatly. The ground was covered with low secondary scrub and as I pushed my way through this the first time I went to inspect the site I put up a covey of about a dozen quail. I remembered old stories which aged warriors told in my youth about their

having spoken to men who had shot snipe in Belgrave Square, and I then determined that the quail on the site of the new Embassy should be recorded for the future.[3]

The site was four-and-a-quarter acres and was being offered by Harry Wardman, a Yorkshireman who migrated to America as a young man and had become Washington's most successful property developer. An exchange deal was agreed: Wardman would give the Office of Works the Massachusetts Avenue site and $300,000 in exchange for the embassy site on Connecticut Avenue. This was a similar type of deal to that negotiated with Nai Lert in Bangkok three years previously, except that in Washington the cash sum was not payable by Wardman until the embassy had vacated the Connecticut Avenue site. An agreement was accordingly signed in May 1925 by the Commissioners of Works with Wardman and two associates, Thomas P. Bones and James D. Hobbs, who may have been the actual owners of the site that Wardman had so skilfully packaged and sold. The subsequent deed of April 1926 recorded the conveyance of Lot 40 in consideration of $10 and 'other good and valuable considerations', a form of words that generally signified a tax stratagem.

Earle contended that a British subject had to design the new embassy building at Washington, and he had the good fortune to be able to recommend Sir Edwin Lutyens as the obvious candidate. Lutyens had the previous year been the first British architect to be awarded the Gold Medal of the Institute of American Architects: Earle argued that the British government would be paying a fitting tribute by selecting the architect whom the host country had so honoured. Earle also had the confidence of knowing Lutyens quite well, not least because he and Lutyens' wife, Emily, were cousins. The Treasury was sticky about the appointment, having heard that Lutyens' reputation 'is that of an extremely extravagant architect who doesn't care what he lets his clients in for'. Earle prevailed, however, and Lutyens visited Washington in April 1925 to see the site on his way to New York to collect his medal. Howard later recalled that Lutyens

grasped at once the possibilities of the site for the house, garden and chancery. When I complained, because I could not see visions, that I thought it would be considered curious in Washington that the offices should be put facing the Avenue so as to hide the greater part of the Embassy House he replied: ' In England we don't like to put all our goods in the shop window,' and he certainly did not.[4]

Lutyens, having seized on his great design idea during that first visit, developed it on his homeward voyage, and the following month 'talked embassy' with his friend Harold Nicolson, whom he may have supposed might one day live in it as ambassador. Lutyens' commission was not formalised until June 1927 mainly because the Office of Works spent many months arguing internally about whether the competent Frederick H. Brooke, the embassy's retained local architect in Washington who was to be associated with Lutyens to oversee the job on site, should be commissioned direct by the Office of Works or by Lutyens as a sub-consultant. Allison, not quite trusting Lutyens' financial control, preferred the former, but Earle, supported by Baines, ruled for paying Lutyens the full six-per-cent fee and leaving him to settle terms with Brooke. Another reason for the delays was the sheer difficulty of communicating with Lutyens while he was spending so much of his time in New Delhi.

The awkward shape of the relatively small site forced Lutyens to adopt a radical solution **(Fig. 9.7)**. That the result was such a triumph, and the awkwardness turned to such advantage, was testament to his genius. In plan, the chancery offices were arranged on two storeys in a U, with the open side of its court facing north-east on to Massachusetts Avenue. The much larger residence, facing south-east over its garden and the city, lay behind

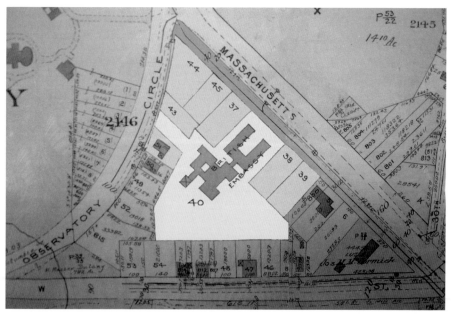

9.7. The site acquired in 1925 (Lot 40) on Massachusetts Avenue in Washington, with Edwin Lutyens' ingenious 1925 proposal overlaid. Lots 38 and 39 were acquired in 1930. Lots 37 and 43-45, acquired between 1941 and 1953, became the site of the new embassy offices, completed in 1960.

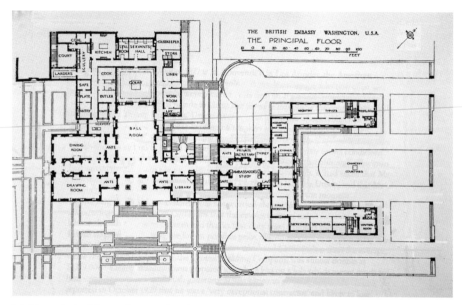

9.8. The principal floor of Lutyens' Washington embassy building. The main floor of the residence is at the same level as the first floor of the chancery building. The ambassador's study lies between the two and serves also as *porte-cochère* for entry to the residence at its basement level.

the chancery: except for its roof and chimneys, the residence was not visible from Massachusetts Avenue. A controlling axis of the buildings ran north-east to south-west through the centre of the chancery court, along the middle of the residence's main gallery, past the ballroom, between the dining and drawing rooms and, beyond the end of the house, up a straight flight of steps to where Lutyens proposed to put a small stone temple of peace on the far perimeter of the site.

Between the chancery and residence buildings, and lying on this same axis, was the ambassador's study, poised between his official and private domains **(Fig. 9.8)**.

A subsidiary cross-axis ran from the garden through the centre of the great south portico and then through the ballroom to a court surrounded by domestic and ancillary rooms. In section, the site ran gently uphill from Massachusetts Avenue. Lutyens controlled this slope by making the main floor of the residence level with the first floor of the offices **(Fig. 9.9)**. Access to the residence was by a level roadway around the outside of the offices bringing cars and visitors to alight beside the entrance at basement level beneath the ambassador's study **(Fig. 9.10)**. From this basement entrance, a wide staircase on either side ascended to the main corridor

9.9. Drawing by Cyril Farey, dated 1926, of Lutyens' whole architectural proposal from the south-east, viewable because Lots 38 and 39 were undeveloped.

without interrupting the vista along it in either direction. The exterior of the building clearly expresses its interior arrangement. Lutyens drew much from his admiration of Wren, and particularly the pleasant dignity of Chelsea Hospital with its great roofs and chimneys. But he also paid compliments to the host country, with reminders of Williamsburg and colonial traditions, especially with the south portico, only the second portico he designed for a major house. And everywhere are glimpses of Lutyens' personal and charming twists and trademarks.

Lutyens never needed to deviate from his original conception for the scheme but financial pressures from the Treasury, necessarily pressed on to him by Allison, forced him to make a succession of revisions to areas, specifications and minor arrangements. Lutyens, unused to be being so strictly controlled and despite Earle's cousinly 'Dear Ned' support, became disheartened but never gave up. That he liked Allison is clear from a short letter he wrote to him in 1933 upon hearing that he was shortly to retire, and which Allison stuck into his scrapbook,

> My dear Dame Alice,
> I am very sorry to see your hour has struck. I shall miss you: your constant patience and good will was ever my plan.
> Ever yours, E Lutyens

That Allison may have shared his sense of humour is suggested by two other notes he stuck into his scrapbook, both picked up while visiting mission houses in the 1920s. From Harold Nicholson in Constantinople: 'The Ambassador wishes me to tell you that you will be most welcome tomorrow (even if you have no frock coat) for the King's Birthday Garden Party'. And from William Clark, high commissioner, in Ottawa: 'We also hope you will be able to come in on Sunday evening to our quite informal supper at 8. Dinner jacket, of course.'[5]

With the main elements of the Washington design so sturdily and convincingly in place, the cuts and revisions were more tiresome and time-consuming than difficult to arrange. Many of them concerned planning details in the chancery and the domestic offices but, as the arrangements for both of these were rather like those for service wings in country houses, Lutyens had immense experience and unrivalled ingenuity in solving them. In the event, unnecessarily many cuts were made and some, including a garage, laundry and manservant's house, had to be re-instated after completion. Another late revision had a felicitous result. Lutyens met the need to increase space in the offices by adding second floor pavilions to the two chancery wings, thereby significantly improving the composition fronting Massachusetts Avenue **(Fig. 9.11)**.

The embassy proposals, for which the leading architectural draughtsman Cyril Farey drew two successive sets of presentation drawings, were widely discussed in Washington. The designs were shown to the American Fine Art

9.10 Exterior and interior of the ambassador's study in the Washington embassy. It linked the residence and the chancery physically, operationally and symbolically

9.11. Cyril Farey's drawing of the chancery from Massachusetts Avenue, with end-view of the residence roof behind. Lutyens later added a third floor to the ends of the chancery wings.

Commission in accordance with an offer that Earle had made to President Coolidge when Howard had taken him to see the President in 1924. It was assumed by the industry that Wardman would, somehow or other, win the construction contract. The American construction unions vociferously opposed even inviting Wardman to tender because he had a reputation as an anti-union contractor and as an employer of coloured labour. The British Trades Union Congress supported its American brothers by writing to the Foreign Secretary warning him off Wardman. The Office of Works agreed to put a fair wages clause into the contract and Wardman undertook, if he won the tender, to employ union labour at union rates but not on union conditions. Wardman, who also had his supporters as an Englishman who had done well, was determined to play a significant part in building the embassy of his home country in his adopted one. The Office of Works had no compelling reason to exclude him from the tender list and he was therefore among nine firms invited to tender in July 1927, while the ambassador continued to receive various union delegations threatening to boycott British goods if Wardman won the contract.

In the event, Wardman tendered lowest at $691,000, 3½ per cent lower than the next lowest and 35 per cent lower than the average of all the tenders. The Office of Works, as was its practice, invited Wardman to confirm or revise his bid, to which he responded with a still lower tender of $643,191.

Notwithstanding the evident risk, Wardman was awarded the contract in January 1928 and preliminary work started on site the following day. The Treasury gave its final approval to the latest scheme in May 1928 in the sum of £193,000. A commemorative cornerstone was laid by Howard on 3 June 1928, the King's birthday: sealed in it was a copper box containing plans of the embassy and two short and apposite documents, one signed by Howard and the other by Vincent Massey, the Canadian minister in Washington.

The 64 contract drawings that Lutyens' office sent to Brooke were a masterly set, and were matched by Brooke's exemplary performance of his duties. Lutyens visited Washington again, with Allison, in April 1927, and twice more during the construction period. The financial crises that followed the stock market crash of October 1929 struck Wardman hard and he lost possession of many of his properties. The Office of Works granted a six months' extension of time on account of late deliveries of the hand-finished facing bricks and of some detail drawings from Lutyens. But Wardman was struggling even to buy enough materials to keep the works going on site and had to be subsidised by the Office of Works to heat the building in order to dry it out. He had no prospect at that time of paying the $300,000 to the Office of Works when the embassy vacated Connecticut Avenue. No wonder that the project lost momentum. Earle went to Washington in spring 1930 to 'try and expedite' its completion, not least because the recently-arrived new ambassador, Sir Ronald Lindsay and his American wife, Elizabeth, were living in an hotel and keen to be out of it. Earle was able to ensure that Wardman kept going and that some momentum was sustained.

The offices were optimistically deemed ready enough for the staff to move into on 30 May 1930, and the Lindsays insisted on moving into the residence a week later, although it would not have been accepted from the contractor in normal circumstances. Elizabeth Lindsay, encouraged by Lutyens to keep a daily diary of things that were wrong, sent the first three weeks worth of her 'purple document' to Earle, detailing the miscellaneous uncompleted items and the remedial works that were noisily and dustily taking place all around her. To Lutyens she wrote that 'we are giddy with confusion, deafened by noise, poisoned by flies, exasperated by ineptitudes and overrun by rats'. The poor lady soon had a severe heart attack and was away from Washington for most of the next nine months. Lutyens sent an experienced and pragmatic architect, H.J. White, from his office to Washington for five weeks from early August to ensure that everything was set right.

The outturn cost of the building, excluding furnishings but including

9.12. The portico in the south front of the Washington residence.

post-contract minor additional buildings, was about £205,000. To add to the Lindsays' woes, nothing had survived in the budget for the garden to be laid out and planted to Lutyens' design and Earle was unable to allocate any more money to the project. He was put into touch, however, with 'a very patriotic Englishman resident in New York, and head of an important business, ... who on arrival in England called on me and asked how much money I required to make the garden.'[6] Earle thought not less than £7,000 and subsequently received a letter from his visitor, Samuel Agar Salvage, who had introduced viscose, later called rayon, into the United States, saying that he and several other British subjects in New York were prepared to provide £10,000. This sum would additionally enable a hard tennis court and a swimming pool to be built for the staff of the embassy. The garden works were therefore put in hand **(Fig. 9.12)**. The swimming pool was sited on the main building axis in the south-west corner of the garden, where Lutyens' small temple would have been if it had survived the cuts. A pergola was built on the way to the pool from the house and stones within it record the generosity of Salvage and his seven co-donors.[7]

The garden was changed in another way at this time. It came to Lindsay's notice that two plots (nos 38 and 39), comprising 40,000 sq. ft, adjacent to the south-east side of the chancery on Massachusetts Avenue, might be for sale for about £32,000. Earle was tempted. Lindsay told him 'The first thing I want to impress on you is to keep your project secret. Don't tell anyone you are in the market; especially any American'. In favour of purchase was improvement of the garden and protection of the security and privacy of the embassy from an unsuitable future development next door. Against purchase was the price, and the embarrassment of seeking to acquire now what could have been had at much less cost five years earlier. The greater irony, however, was that, had these plots been acquired earlier, the whole site would have been a much more sensible shape and Lutyens would never have needed to find such a clever solution. The Treasury, 'somewhat surprisingly' thought Earle, agreed to the purchase. The vendor was by then in a great rush to sell because she wanted the money to invest in the depressed stock exchange. The Treasury, again surprisingly, authorised the expenditure in advance of parliamentary approval of the Estimate. The Office of Works had no money to integrate the new land into the garden and it was Lord Lothian, Lindsay's successor in 1939, who paid privately for that to be done.

In March 1931, a recovered Lady Lindsay wrote to Earle to tell him

> how really beautiful this place is. I am more and more amazed at your foresight and imagination in having selected this particular site. ... The Embassy is extraordinarily beautiful, both inside and out. ... you have surpassed even yourself, and I shall never be content until you and Sir Edwin have seen this place in its finished form, and have realised the beauty of your joint accomplishment. ... If anyone ever says to you that anything is wrong here, bid them come and see for themselves, and talk to those of us who are fortunate enough to live in this house.

She wrote to Lutyens in similar terms on the same day. Earle sent Lady Lindsay's letter to Montgomery, saying

> I think you may be interested to see this letter that I received today from Elizabeth Lindsay whom I am glad to know has recovered sufficiently to return to her post. It is somewhat exaggerated in language as regards the part I played but it is a valuable document in the event of any possible criticism.

The permanent under-secretary, Sir Robert Vansittart, annotated 'All's well that ends well. (I suppose this is the end?).' It was.

10

Buildings 1930-1940

From St Petersburg to Moscow

On 31 August 1918 the Bolsheviks raided the embassy in St Petersburg, on the first floor of Prince Soltykoff's house, and held the staff for five weeks under stressful conditions in the Troubetskoi Bastion of the Fortress of St Peter and Paul. Among them was Cecil Mackie, a long-serving vice-consul, who wrote at the end of October, once back in London, to the Secretary of the Office of Works, Sir Lionel Earle, to report his return and to apologise for having been unable to submit the Post's accounts for the September quarter. He continued:

> On our liberation from the fortress we were all obliged to give a written undertaking that we would quit Russia by the first diplomatic train and before doing so I called at the Embassy and made an inspection of the building. I found the damage done by the raiders was not very great. Some of the doors of the reception rooms had been forced open and in most cases the locks had been hacked away with hatchets. … On the Chancery floor and Grand Staircase where all the firing took place a considerable number of shot marks were visible.[1]

The Bolshevik Antiquarian Committee apparently listed the British property left in the house, which was then sealed off and lay empty for six years, while the Office of Works continued to pay rent to the Soltykoffs until the expiry of the lease in December 1924, mainly to ensure that the furniture and belongings left in the building would be protected. The Soltykoff family, knowing that it would lose the house on the day that the British government ceased to lease a major part of it, tried in vain to persuade the Office of Works to buy the house, or at least to extend the lease for another year. Foreign Office minuting commented that 'If we could share his [Prince Soltykoff's] opinion that that Govt will collapse within the next 12 months we might consider his proposal'.[2] In July 1925, the Soviets agreed to a team entering the house to dispose of its contents and to return private property to its owners, although they had by then been compensated for their losses. The Foreign Office invited bids from nearby Posts for the furniture: Helsinki, with its newly bought residence to furnish, was a keen respondent. Oswald Rayner, a temporary clerk in the Foreign Office and F.J. Rutherford, from the supplies division of the Office of Works, were allowed into the house on 1 October 1925. It took them eight weeks to sort everything out. In all, £12,000 worth of goods were recovered, packed and dispatched. Earle congratulated the pair 'for the expedition and management of this odious duty under most trying circumstances'.[3]

Meanwhile, a new British mission was being established in Moscow, the capital of Russia again after 200 years. The British government formally recognised the Soviet Union in 1924 and Robert Hodgson, who had been in Moscow since 1919 as head of a commercial mission, was appointed chargé d'affaires in that year. He continued to live and work in the house on which he had taken a lease in 1921 at 46 Varovskaya (now Povarskaya): a solid, Art Nouveau, two-storey building, with its rooms arranged round a double-height hall. Diplomatic relations were severed in June 1927 when Britain accused Russia of espionage, and Hodgson was withdrawn. In his absence, British interests were looked after by the Norwegians, who renewed the lease on the so-called Hodgson House at London's request. Relations were resumed in December 1929, and Sir Esmond Ovey was appointed Britain's first ambassador to the Soviet Union. He moved into the Savoy Hotel in Moscow, where his diplomatic staff was already living and working, because the Hodgson house was full with commercial and consular staff. With over a dozen UK-based staff, Moscow was already a large embassy.

Ovey's first idea was to take over the Hodgson house as his residence and find another building for the staff, but in mid-January 1930 the Central Bureau for Assistance to Foreigners, BUROBIN, showed him a house at no. 14 on the Sofiskaya Quay that had belonged to the Charitonenko family, and had a magnificent view of the Kremlin across the river. Pavel Ivanovich Charitonenko had built up a large business growing and refining sugar beet and in 1879 could afford to buy this site and in 1891 to demolish the house that was on it and start to build his own. He employed V.G. Zalessky as architect for the house and other buildings and Fyodor Shekhtel for the main interiors. It had been an open secret that this house might be offered to the British embassy but Ovey, with an eye only on a chancery building, had not looked at it before. He told Earle, on the same day that he visited it, that he was 'very much struck with it', particularly as he thought the house and its side buildings were large enough to house the whole embassy, and that he might be able to move in within weeks.[4] He asked for an Office of Works representative to come and have a look as soon as possible and Hewlett Edwards inspected the house in February. He thought it would do well and embarked on rent negotiations with BUROBIN. The sticking point was clearly going to be the 200,000 roubles (about £20,000) compensation that BUROBIN was asking for re-housing the tenants about to be dispossessed. The Office of Works was concerned that this money would be entirely wasted if the embassy did not remain in Moscow for the long term. The figure also bore less resemblance to the realistic cost of re-housing tenants in Moscow than to the premium that the Soviet government had needed to pay on a house in Chesham Place in London.

The First Commissioner of the Office of Works, George Lansbury, told the Foreign Secretary, Arthur Henderson, that he was prepared to defend the proposed deal in the House of Commons because he thought that its terms were the best obtainable but he presumed that 'as the matter is really more political than anything else' Henderson would want to submit the case to Cabinet. The Cabinet on 5 March was 'unfavourably impressed' and wanted further information from the First Commissioner. A frustrated Ovey on 8 March reported two new developments from Moscow: a rumour that hotel prices were about to double, and a warning that an American concern with a large contract with the Soviet government was anxious to lease the Charitonenko house. The Foreign Office passed Ovey's telegram to the Prime Minister's office: Ramsay MacDonald merely annotated it 'I leave it to the F.O.'. Lord Stamfordham, the King's private secretary, told the Foreign Office 'that His Majesty The King did not consider the present arrangements for housing the Ambassador satisfactory or dignified, and that he hoped an improvement could be made'.[5] The Cabinet approved the case at its next meeting, and a twenty-year lease on the Charitonenko house, with a £20,000 initial premium, was signed by Ovey and BUROBIN in June 1930, to run from that August at £4,000 per annum **(Fig. 10.1)**. On the same day, the Office of Works signed a construction contract with Gasso, a German firm, for a £20,000 programme of ingoing works to enable the property to house chancery, other embassy offices, the ambassador and family, and his UK staff and their families. On the same day also, a new lease, for four years at £2,500 per annum, was signed for the Hodgson house,

10.1. 14 Sofiskaya Embankment in Moscow, opposite the Kremlin, designed by Vasily Zalessky for Pavel Charitonenko and completed in 1893. While a Soviet government guesthouse 1919-1930, guests included H.G. Wells, Arthur Ransome and Isadora Duncan. Leased from the Soviet authorities in 1930 and served as offices and residence until 2000.

to provide both working and living accommodation for the commercial counsellor and the consul-general and their staffs: there was only room for bachelors.

Pavel Charitonenko's two daughters, Princess Nathalie Gortchacoff and Helene Olive Charitonenko, both living in Paris, wrote in July to the Office of Works: 'Having been deprived temporarily of all our property and belongings in Russia and being therefore in an extremely difficult pecuniary situation we venture to apply to your sense of justice and beg you to consider our claim to a part of the rent'.[6] All the sisters received was a letter from the Foreign Office pointing out that the Soviet government, as the lessor, was entitled to the whole rent.

Ovey moved into the Charitonenko house just before Christmas 1930 and the rest of the embassy on 7 January 1931. The internal arrangements were far from ideal, and the services were unreliable. The ambassador lived mainly on the first floor but the dining room was on the ground floor and the kitchen in the basement **(Fig. 10.2)**. The main hallway served the residence above as well as being the chancery waiting room. Secretaries lived in the wing blocks, and the ground floor library was their mess. The counsellor, William Strang, lived in a disjointed set of rooms on the ground floor, facing the garden. He described the conditions to his counsellor colleague at the Foreign Office, Horace Seymour, a month after moving in:

I myself have settled in quite comfortably and have little to complain of, except that I still have no kitchen and that the curtains the Office of Works sent me were a couple of feet too short. With regard to the Secretaries, Greenway and Walton ingenuously believed the representative of the Office of Works when he told them that their wing was ready for occupation. They accordingly moved in and have regretted doing so ever since. The pipes are frozen and no water runs in their bathroom, the gas functions spasmodically, the geysers are ineffective, the heating stoves are inefficient and their bedrooms are so cold that, in really cold weather, even to sit in them in fur coats is a hardship. ... The consequence is that they are under-nourished and under-warmed. This cannot be good for their work and must constitute a further strain on already over-burdened nerves. ...

The clerical staff are even worse off. When the wind is in the north, the chancery is so cold that they need overcoats. So far as their living quarters

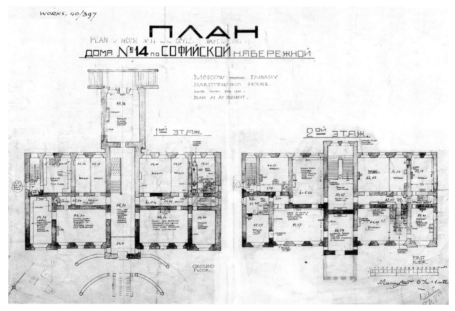

10.2. Russian drawing of ground and first floors of the Charitonenko mansion, marked up by Hewlett Edwards, Office of Works architect, on his first visit in 1930. Offices went into the ground floor, with ambassador's study in the 1911 rear extension: and residence into the first floor, with ballroom facing the Kremlin.

are concerned, if their heating functions slightly more efficiently, it does so more dangerously. This morning Vincent and Low are both down with poisoning from the fumes of the stove.[7]

After this shaky start, the Charitonenko buildings housed most of the embassy, through thick and thin, for the next 70 years.

The Dominions

The 1930s opened with the acquisition of the first British high commissioner's house in Ottawa and closed with his colleagues in South Africa and Australia being likewise accommodated. The origins of this additional responsibility for the Office of Works stretched back to when some colonies of settlement became dominions on their way to fully self-governing statehood. Canada became the first dominion with the confederation in 1867 of Ontario, Quebec, New Brunswick and Nova Scotia. An Imperial conference in 1907 strengthened the concept of dominion, and Australia, New Zealand and Newfoundland were designated dominions in that year. A Dominions section was also created within the Colonial Office and became a separate Dominions Office in 1925. The newly-created Union of South Africa became a dominion in 1910, and the Irish Free State in 1922. The dominions joined the Imperial War Cabinet during the First World War, signed the Treaty of Versailles and gained separate representation in the League of Nations. The Statute of Westminster in 1931 granted full self-government and self-determination to every dominion whose parliament voted to ratify the statute.

The British sovereign was head of state of each dominion, and represented in each by a governor-general: in the early days, most business was done between him and the Colonial Office. Canada appointed the first dominion high commissioner in London in 1880, a process that was preceded by long consideration of what to call the appointee. He could not be a resident minister because that would connote a more diplomatic role than was appropriate for the representative of a part of the empire. Other dominion high commissioners were appointed in London by New Zealand in 1905, Australia in 1910 and South Africa in 1911: they were not treated as diplomats, were not members of the diplomatic corps and had no dealings with the Foreign Office. Their lot may have been slightly improved during the 1920s when they were allowed to wear a diplomatic uniform on ceremonial occasions. By the mid-1920s, governors-general were having increasing difficulties in reconciling their dual roles of representing both the British sovereign and the British government. A 1926 conference decided that, if dominions so wished, the governors-general would represent the sovereign, just as ambassadors did in foreign countries, and Britain would send its own high commissioners to dominion capitals to represent the British government.

Britain subsequently appointed high commissioners to Canada in 1928, South Africa in 1930, Australia in 1931 and New Zealand in 1939. Responsibility for their accommodation was handed to the Office of Works by the Dominions Office in 1929, and the Vote called 'Diplomatic and Consular Services' was re-named 'Public Buildings Overseas' in the same year. In 1948, by which time the dominions were widely exchanging their own high commissioners with each other, Commonwealth prime ministers decided that their high commissioners should rank with ambassadors and have comparable diplomatic status, privileges and immunities. They could not decide, however, whether to call them ambassadors and so kicked that ball into the long grass – where it remains. To most intents and purposes, the two roles are nowadays similar. The term 'dominion', although it still has specific legal relevance in some parlances, fell out of general use as the Commonwealth developed, and particularly after the demise of the Dominions Office in 1947: 'realm' has since then been the preferred term.

Sir William Clark was the first British high commissioner to be appointed – at Ottawa in 1928. He had a wide civil service background and for the preceding ten years had headed the Department of Overseas Trade. He shared his thoughts about his future accommodation in Ottawa with the Dominions Office in early 1929:

> I have been looking into the question of a residence for the High Commissioner. It seemed desirable to avoid delay as the furnished house which I now occupy has only been taken, as you are aware, [for a few months] and I have had ample evidence of the difficulty of finding a suitable house on a temporary basis. Ottawa is a city where there are very few houses on even a moderately large scale. Owing to the shortage and the high cost of domestic servants, the tendency even for people who are comparatively wealthy, is to live in small houses and to do their entertaining at the Country Club and the Royal Ottawa Golf Club. You have informed me that entertaining on a lavish scale … would not be expected of the High Commissioner, but it is obviously necessary that he should be in a position to give dinner parties and other entertainments on a moderate scale in his own house.[8]

London agreed in principle that a search for a suitable house should be put in hand and a few possibilities arose, including a site on which a residence might be built. With no precedent for a high commissioner's house, its size and the status that it should project was not clear. The recently bought embassy house in Helsinki was suggested as a suitable analogue. In April, the inevitable debates about how large the dining room should be and whether there should be a ballroom were cut short by Clark telling London that a most promising house called Earnscliffe might soon be coming on to the market. It had once belonged to Sir John Macdonald, Canada's first Prime Minister, and stood on a fine site by the Ottawa River in the good suburb of Rockcliffe. It was possible that the (Canadian) Conservative party might want to buy it as its leader's residence, and Clark knew that three other foreign governments were looking for suitable houses. The chief architect of the Office of Works, Richard Allison, visited Ottawa in September 1929 and thought that Earnscliffe would be a satisfactory acquisition if it became available **(Fig. 10.3)**. It did: two months later, it was offered to Clark for $100,000 with the Canadian Prime Minister's assurance that the British government could not do better than buy this house. The Treasury was content, with two provisos: 'that the Dominions Office (1) will not make the acquisition of the new Residence the occasion for recommending improved salary or 'frais' for Clark [and] (2) will not support Clark in any demand for immediately improving the property beyond such reconditioning and

10.3. Earnscliffe, bought in Ottawa in 1930, Britain's first high commissioner's residence. Built in 1857: 'a sensible Scots-type family house, … built by Scots masons for a Scots emigrant who had done well for himself'. It has been extended over the years.

10.4. The upper floor of the stable block at Earnscliffe became the high commission offices in 1931 and chancery remained here, with various extensions, until well into the 1950s.

decoration as the Office of Works deem necessary'. At the same time, the Treasury confided to the Office of Works:

> As regards reconditioning Earnscliffe should we acquire it, I hope Allison will keep immediate expenditure down. I was a little alarmed at his figures and his reference to the new heating apparatus, etc. A house in Ottawa which has been in the occupation of well-to-do people is likely to be adequately heated even if the apparatus is not 1930 pattern.[9]

An additional financial and operational advantage of Earnscliffe was that the high commission office could be accommodated in the stable block that went with the house **(Fig. 10.4)**. The Post was authorised in January 1930 to offer $90,000 with flexibility to go up to $100,000 and agreement was reached. Essential refurbishment and ingoing works were put in hand, and Clark moved into Earnscliffe in October 1930.

Sir Herbert Stanley, previously the Governor of Ceylon, was appointed in 1931 to be Britain's first high commissioner in the Union of South Africa. He would also take over from the Governor-General the high commissioner role, and associated staff, for the native territories of Basutoland (later

Lesotho), Swaziland and the Bechuanaland Protectorate (later Botswana). The two roles, and the two halves of the new high commissioner's office, were respectively referred to as Representation and Administration.

The designers of the Union in 1910 had given South Africa three capitals to prevent any one province becoming too powerful. Hence, Cape Town (in Western Cape, former Cape Colony) became the legislative capital; Pretoria (in Gauteng, part of former Transvaal) became the administrative capital, and Bloemfontein (in Free State, former Orange Free State) the judicial capital. The high commissioner therefore needed a residence in both Cape Town, for the parliamentary sessions in the first half of each year, and Pretoria, for the other six months.

In Cape Town, Stanley took a lease from Lady Graaff on a house at Milnerton, to expire at the end of 1936. His successor, Sir William Clark from Ottawa, disliked the house but the Treasury was refusing to purchase an alternative, although lease expiry was approaching. Undaunted, Clark identified a chance of acquiring one of the best and latest houses in Cape Town: Silvertrees, on the Hen and Chickens Estate in the area now known as Bishopscourt. The house, which lay in five acres of well-landscaped grounds, was attractive, about five years old, of two storeys beneath a thatched roof, would need some enlargement. The Treasury agreed in January 1937 to buy the house and adapt it as appropriate within a total of £20,000. The architect of the house, Brian Mansergh, was commissioned to design and build the necessary extension, and the garden was made slightly less elaborate so as to be manageable by two men.

In Pretoria, Stanley was provided by the South African government with houses that it owned on an estate, called Bryntirion, that adjoined Government House. Out of the blue, in October 1937, and five days after his father's death, a Eugene Maggs wrote to Clark:

> It was the wish of my late father, Mr Charles Maggs, that his house 'Greystoke' with the four erven [plots] on which it stands, should be offered as a gift to his Majesty's Government in the United Kingdom.
> The house would be … available for occupation any time after 30 April 1938. There are no stipulations nor suggestions regarding the use to which the house should be put.
> My father wished as a South African, to express his gratitude for the United Kingdom's friendship towards his country: he hoped that his old home would be associated with the closest friendship between his Majesty's Government in the United Kingdom and his Majesty's Government in the Union of South Africa.[10]

Charles Maggs was born in London in 1863 and went to South Africa in 1880, where he made his fortune and became a director of many enterprises, including the National Bank. He had built Greystoke and landscaped its garden in 1911 on a site between Pretorius and Schoeman Streets, in the district immediately south of Bryntirion, at a cost of about £25,000, and lived in it for the rest of his life. At the time that the offer of its gift was made, Clark had only just settled into another new residence at 14 Bryntirion, which the South African government had enlarged for him and which he had no wish to leave. He therefore thought that the offer of Greystoke should be accepted and the building converted to offices. The Office of Works, however, did not relish abandoning its own laboriously prepared plans for a new office building in Bryntirion in favour of a conversion job at Greystoke. The Maggs offer was not therefore received with the delight that it deserved. Edward Muir, then a young principal in the Office of Works, minuted sourly in November 1937:

> In order to save us embarrassment, [Maggs] did not leave us the house in his will, but the high commissioner, with the help of the heirs, who are no doubt anxious to get this expensive property off their hands, has contrived to give the offer such wide publicity that it will undoubtedly be rather embarrassing for us to refuse. ...
> We have had experience in the past of costly white elephants presented to us by people who wanted to get rid of the liability for keeping them up. Lord Rosebery's villa at Posilipo [sic] was the worst case of this kind. ... We ought to be very chary of taking on properties which have not been examined by our own architects.[11]

Other, and worthier, considerations prevailed and the Maggs family was informed the following week that the offer was accepted. Vivian Rees-Poole, in association with the Public Works Department, was selected as architect for the conversion of Greystoke to offices. By way of commemorating the gift, the high commission suggested paying £80 for a stained-glass coat of arms designed by Rees-Poole but the Office of Works 'did not take to' this idea and suggested instead a bronze plaque, for which Muir proposed the wording: 'By the wish of Mr Charles Maggs, his executors presented this house to his Majesty's Government in the United Kingdom 1938'.[12] Clark properly wanted something longer and warmer and suggested what, with little subsequent alteration despite another attempt by Muir to shorten it, became the final handsome wording.[13] Greystoke was occupied in March 1939 and, with additions in the 1950s and 1990s, remains the high commission offices.

In 1931, Britain announced that it would be appointing a high commissioner to Australia, pending whose arrival Ernest Crutchley, then the British government representative for migration in Melbourne, would move to Canberra and establish a high commission there. The site for the capital of the newly-federated Commonwealth of Australia was chosen in 1908 and the land surrounding what became Canberra was constituted as the Australian Capital Territory in 1910. An international competition that attracted 137 entries for the design of the new city was won in 1911 by Walter Burley Griffin, a landscape architect from Chicago. Construction work on the new city started in 1913, but development was slow until the mid-1950s and the central Burley Griffin Lake was not dammed and filled until 1963. The first Parliament House was built in 1927, designed by J.S. Murdoch, a Scottish migrant who was architect of many of Canberra's early landmark buildings.

The first substantial permanent house in the city was also designed

10.5. Homewood, in Karori, Wellington, was bought as the high commissioner's residence in 1958. The original house on the site was remodelled and extended in 1904 by the architect Joshua Charlesworth. Homewood had for long been one of the centrepieces of Wellington's social and community life.

by Murdoch and built in the district called Acton in 1913 for Col. David Miller, the administrator of the Capital Territory. Called The Residency, the house was intermittently the base for the succession of administrators, committees and chairmen who wrestled with the development of Canberra through thin times. In the mid-1920s, it was re-named Canberra House but was not continuously occupied. Crutchley, therefore, had no difficulty in renting Canberra House in 1931 for his residence and he found office space in East Block, close to the then Parliament House. The Treasury, however, delayed appointing the first high commissioner for financial reasons and it was not until 1936 that the eventual appointee, Sir Geoffrey Whiskard, arrived in Canberra. He moved straight into Canberra House, which had been enlarged somewhat in the months since Crutchley had vacated it.

The first British high commissioner to New Zealand, Sir Harry Batterbee, who arrived in Wellington in 1939, had no such good fortune. One site that his staff inspected with a view to demolishing the existing house and building a replacement was called Homewood, in Karori, to the west of Wellington. But the gardens had recently been so splendidly laid out that the high commission staff, fearing that the property would be more of an upkeep liability than an asset to the British government, lost interest. Meanwhile, a six-month lease was taken on a recently completed modern house called Ranelagh at 1A Wesley Crescent, which was owned by Theo Kelly and designed by R.G. Talboys and Associates. Because Ranelagh was on the small side, despite a splendid recreation room and roof terrace on the second floor, a flat in the adjacent house, Airlie at 5 Clermont Terrace, was also leased for domestic staff accommodation. The lease on Ranelagh was extended several times during the Second World War to March 1944, when the Office of Works (recently subsumed in the new Ministry of Works) decided not to renew it again. Kelly sold the house and the new high commissioner who arrived in 1945, Patrick Duff, a former Secretary of the Office of Works, had ignominiously to move into the house that used to be leased by his official secretary. Fortunately, Ranelagh soon became available again for lease and Duff moved in, and it was bought in 1950. In 1958, Homewood, the house which was injudiciously spurned nearly 20 years earlier, was back on the market. The same mistake was not (quite) made twice **(Fig. 10.5)**.

Earnscliffe, Silvertrees, Canberra House and (though not acquired in the 1930s) Homewood were all significant and admired domestic buildings in their own right, well known to their host communities. They were, and they all remain, apt houses for their high commission roles.

Europe

The only significant mission house to be replaced in Europe during the 1930s was at Athens. The Dragatzani Street house, built in 1835, first leased about 1859 and bought in 1899, was overcrowded, much the worse for wear and in an area that was deteriorating. Earle recalled that 'The view from the study over the Acropolis was magnificent, but since the War, commercial buildings have developed in the shape of modified skyscrapers, and have consequently obliterated the principal charm of the residence'.[14] By 1927, the Treasury had authorised the search for a replacement and encouraged the Post, in the light of recent successes in South America, to look for sites as well as houses. A Greek architect, M. Kouremenos, offered to take over the Dragatzani Street building, re-house the legation temporarily, and build for it anew on a site satisfactory to the British government, all at no net cost to the Office of Works. He said that his financing would be provided by the Public Functionaries Fund. The Office of Works turned him down.

The exasperated minister, Percy Loraine, persuaded himself and his staff that the whole legation, including himself, could operate from a new suburb of Athens called Psychico, about seven kilometres from the centre,

10.6. The hall and ballroom of the Venizelos house in Athens, designed by Anastasios Metaxas, completed in 1932 and bought as the legation house in 1936. Chancery was well housed in the basement, in a panelled suite of rooms that was designed as Eleftherios Venizelos' library.

where land was cheap and the cost of buying it and building anew could be recovered from the sale of the Dragatzani Street house. Loraine produced a report signed by advocates of the scheme. The Office of Works was doubtful that this would work in practice, but found that the Foreign Office was prepared, on balance, to take the advice of the Post. Several contiguous sites, comprising about five acres, were bought in March 1929, shortly before Loraine was posted to Cairo. His successor, the Hon. Patrick Ramsay, thought that the new site was too far away from the city centre and produced a document signed by people who agreed with him: some of them, Earle later recalled, had also signed the first document. The Office of Works fell back on its solution of last resort, which was to reconstruct the Dragatzani house. By early 1936, the plans and the funds were ready; the clerks of works were on the point of leaving England; Sir Sydney Waterlow, the minister, had rented a house in Psychico into which to decant for the duration of the works, and the reconstruction contract was due to start on 1 May.

In mid-March, Eleftherios Venizelos, 'the maker of modern Greece', died in exile in Paris. Shortly afterwards, Waterlow was approached by Lady Crosfield, a close friend of Venizelos's second wife, Helena Schilizzi, who said that Schilizzi wished to offer to sell her Athens house at an attractive price to the British government for the use of the legation. In early April, Waterlow told London by telegram that 'Mme Venizelos is most anxious for sentimental reasons that house which she completely built four years ago should become His Majesty's Legation. House and land cost her £100,000 but she would sell to us for £50,000'.[15] Helena Schilizzi came of a wealthy eastern Mediterranean family but was born and spent much of her life in London where she married Venizelos in 1921. She bought the land for their new house in Athens, on the corner of Vasilissis Sophias Avenue and Loukiana Street, from the National Bank of Greece in 1928 and commissioned Anastasios Metaxas as her architect. Schilizzi rather wanted a small house where she and her husband could grow old together but was pressurised by her husband's friends and supporters into something much larger so that they could all meet there. The house, gently neo-classical, was completed in 1932. She never liked it much and had no requirement of it after her husband's death. She did, however, need a way of exporting some of her assets from Greece.

Waterlow was interested, and a visit to the house soon afterwards substantiated his enthusiasm. It was well located, in excellent condition, contained offices suitable for the chancery, including a large library on the lowest floor that had been planned for political meetings. A week later, Waterlow appealed direct to Sir Robert Vansittart, the permanent under-secretary at the Foreign Office, 'to use your influence to secure this unexpected windfall. All that is immediately required is to divert to Mme Venizelos the sum earmarked for reconstruction of the present legation'.[16] And the following day he reported 'King George [of the Hellenes] asks me to tell you he hopes that we shall accept Mme Venizelos's offer as the best solution to our problem', adding for good measure, 'I learned that the scheme of building music hall opposite the present legation will probably mature this year'.[17]

Howard Jones, a senior architect in the Office of Works, went to inspect the house the following week and the clerks of works' departures were postponed. At the end of April, Alec Hardinge, at Buckingham Palace, told Ormsby Gore, First Commissioner at the Office of Works, that he was hoping for favourable consideration. Patrick Duff, Secretary at the Office of Works, replied 'One has to be pretty careful in these matters, as our sad experience here is that it is not often that one can buy a ready-made house and, even at considerable expense, in adaptations, make it really satisfactory for the special purposes of a Legation and Chancery. However, we are going most carefully into this present proposition ...'.[18] At the beginning of May, Schilizzi adjusted her offer to £45,000, including £3,500 worth of fittings. Jones reckoned that the land alone was worth £30,000: although the running costs would be more than the present legation, he thought the house would provide the best chancery offices anywhere. The Treasury agreed to the purchase in early June, subject to parliamentary sanction. In normal circumstances, Schilizzi would be paid with drachmas obtained from the sale of the Dragatzani house, but she wanted payment in sterling in London, which was incompatible with Greek law. Duff asked Waterlow whether he thought 'that the Greek government would look with a benevolent eye on some means of getting over this difficulty?'. Waterlow told the chief clerk at the Foreign Office 'as to the sterling we have to pay, I refuse to believe that I can't square the Greeks'.[19] £45,000 was duly passed by the Office of Works to the Treasury Solicitor and the purchase was completed on 7 October 1936. Waterlow moved in immediately, followed by the chancery two months later. He reported that 'King George, the Crown Prince, Prince and Princess Nicholas of Greece, Princess Irene and Princess Katherine recently took tea in the new house and afterwards inspected it, in every corner, from the boiler room in the basement to the electric laundry on the top floor'[20] **(Fig. 10.6)**. The Dragatzani house was sold the following year. The English Preparatory School was granted use of the Psychico site as playing fields and it was finally sold in 1949.

10.7. The Kuwait agency house, designed in Delhi under the eye of Robert Tor Russell and completed in 1935, with offices on the ground floor and residence above. The dumbbell plan is fronted with a deep curved structure that provides an entrance carriageway below and veranda above.

Kuwait

While Waterlow was giving tea to royals in a smart purchased house in a European city, Harold Dickson was retiring after the recent completion of his long struggle to build a new agency house in Kuwait. Dickson was appointed agent in Kuwait in 1929 and, with his wife Violet and two small children, had no option but to move into the disintegrating 1870s building on the busy foreshore that had served as the agency since 1904 and was leased from the Sheikh. Within months, he was reporting '… as a result of recent heavy rains a large portion of the Agency spare room verandah collapsed last night … and room is now uninhabitable' and, two days later, 'the rest of spare room verandah collapsed last night. Agency now left with only one bedroom'.[21] The Dicksons put in hand such repairs as they could through a helpful Persian contractor while pressing the political department of the Government of India in Calcutta hard, through the resident in Bushire, for money for a new building.

Dickson briefed the Bushire residency engineer about how a new building might best be planned. He thought it particularly important to have a downstairs receiving room. 'The Sheikh calls usually twice every week throughout the year, and it is awkward as well as undesirable to have to take him and his entourage every time up to one's private apartments and hide away one's family in another part of the house, this is especially so as his visits usually last as long as an hour and a half'.[22] Verandas were used as living rooms during the summer, especially in the damp season. 'I know of

10.8. Part of the splendid deep and, relatively, cool veranda at the Kuwait residence in the 1960s.

no verandas in the Gulf less than 14 ft. in width, many are twice as broad'. Some drawings were sent from Bushire to Calcutta but the proposal became bogged down in related indecisions. In 1930, a mighty cloudburst further damaged and flooded the agency building and, thanks to a heated appeal by the resident at Bushire, officialdom in Calcutta and London at last took serious notice of Kuwait's plight. The Government of India and the Treasury each agreed to pay its 'moiety' of the costs of a new agency building.

With this reassurance, Dickson approached Sheikh Ahmed in 1931 for a site and was offered a 1.5-hectare plot next to the sea at the eastern end of the town. Dickson had the foresight to request, and Ahmed the generosity to grant, a guarantee that the beach in front of the new agency compound would in perpetuity be kept free of boats and fishing paraphernalia and would not be built upon. Delhi sent the Bushire assistant engineer to survey the site and to start on the design and Dickson was not slow to draw on his long experience in the Gulf in fully briefing him. But still nothing seemed to happen. Kuwait was evidently a low priority for the Public Works Department in Delhi that was responsible for designing government buildings. The resident at Bushire called on Robert Tor Russell, chief architect to the Government of India, when he visited Delhi in May 1931 and persuaded him to give the Kuwait project an effective push. Outline drawings, signed by Russell, were ready in August 1931. Although Dickson and local advisers were sceptical of some aspects of the design and specification, it was clear to them that Delhi was now in earnest and it might be imprudent to seek any but minor changes. The Treasury was concerned by an increased estimate but did not intervene. Construction started in mid-1932: good quality burnt bricks were sailed to the site from Amara, on the Euphrates above Basra; teak logs came from India and furniture for the reception rooms from Maples. The Dicksons moved into the almost completed building in February 1935 **(Fig. 10.7)**. There were the usual squabbles over the out-turn cost but the actual exceeding worked out at less than five per cent. The building turned out to be a considerable success, especially the huge curved first-floor terrace, and, thanks to Dickson's vigour and eagle eye, probably the best agency in the Gulf **(Fig. 10.8)**.

Dickson retired in 1936, when he and Violet went back to live as the Sheikh's tenants in the restored former agency building. He died in 1959 but Violet lived on in the house until evacuated to England, at the age of 94, when Iraq invaded Kuwait in 1990. The old agency building is now repaired and is called Dickson House, a cultural centre.

Far East

The 1930s saw two developer deals for new consulate-general buildings in Indonesia and Philippines, colonies respectively of Netherlands and the USA. Both consuls-general and their offices were in outmoded and crowded expatriate houses because there were none better to rent, and the Treasury was not in a financial position to buy sites and build at such Posts as Jakarta and Manila. But both cities had relatively sophisticated property expertise which the consuls-general had the initiative to exploit so as to yield much better accommodation at affordable rents. The basis of each agreement was that the developer would provide an acceptable site and build a house on it to an agreed plan and specification for an agreed rent and term of years. The agreement in Jakarta was drawn up in 1931 with a Dutch insurance company which would buy the prime site at no.1 Jalan Imam Bonjol, build on it a consul-general's house designed by the respected local architect J.FL. Blankenberg, and have it ready for occupation in 1932 for a term of 30 years. All aspects of the agreement were scrupulously carried out and the house, in a strong traditional Dutch colonial style with solid horizontal lines and tall tiled roofs, continued to be leased by the British government until 1981 **(Fig. 10.9)**. The building is now the Museum Perumusan.

In Manila, the consul-general, Arthur Blunt, was able in 1936 to call on the advice of James Wynnes, the Office of Works architect in Shanghai. Here the developer was Sing, Yee and Cuan Incorporated, and the outline design was prepared by Wynnes for a site on Santa Clara Street, in the district of

10.9. The consul-general's house in Jakarta, designed by J.F.L. Blankenberg and built in 1932 in a deal with a Dutch insurance company. The text of the proclamation of Indonesia's independence was hammered out here in the early hours of 17 August 1945 by the nationalist leaders.

Santa Ana, on the bank of the Pasig river. The house, completed in 1938, was innovative in appearance **(Fig. 10.10)**. It would probably have run into trouble if submitted to London for approval but, as part of a developer deal, the design did not need submitting. The plan was simple, with dining room, living room and study in line, facing the river behind a full-length veranda. The consul-general-but-one after Blunt, Wyatt Smith, who was never enamoured of the house, had the misfortune to be interned in it with his family for five months from January 1942. The house was destroyed by civilian looters soon after Smith was released and sent to Shanghai.

Unfinished business

Two large embassy residence projects at Rio de Janeiro and Ankara were started before the outbreak of the Second World War, and had to be suspended for its duration. The Rio saga reached back to the purchase of an embassy house at 71 Rua Real Grandeza in 1928, with the intention that the existing house would be demolished and another built in its place. But objections soon surfaced about the future suitability of the site. There was a suspicion in London that some members of the British community in Rio were joining the chorus in the hope that the Office of Works would instead buy one of the sites that they had to offer. The debate stalled while the Brazilians toyed with the idea of a diplomatic enclave in Rio and the great financial crisis then took its toll. By the time that both were over in 1935, a new ambassador, Sir Hugh Gurney, was asked to assess the position. He recommended against re-developing the Grandeza site, for reasons that the Office of Works found unconvincing, and the Secretary, Sir Patrick Duff, sent his own senior team of William Leitch, assistant secretary, and A.J. Pitcher, assistant chief architect, having induced all parties to agree to abide by his team's conclusions.

Leitch reported in October 1938, favouring the purchase of a different site at 360 Rua São Clemente, building on it a new residence and leasing space elsewhere for the offices. The new site, adjacent to one that the Americans had recently bought, was a long thin rectangle, about 80 metres wide, that ran for about 750 metres from the street frontage up the hillside behind, rising almost 400 metres. The site was relatively flat for the first 150 metres, and here stood a house that would be demolished and replaced. The vendor, the de Almeida e Silva family, wanted £30,000 and were prepared to accept a sterling cheque in London provided that the price in the contract was quoted in *milreis* at the official rate. The Treasury wondered whether the Foreign Office might 'be able to say whether we can obtain the benefit of the black market in some other way which did not offend the Brazilian Government'.[23] The outcome of that debate is unclear but the site

10.10. The consul-general's house in Manila, designed in outline by James Wynnes, Office of Works' architect based in Shanghai, and built by a developer for lease in 1938.

was bought in January 1939 and Pitcher concurrently produced an outline design for a residence on it.

Pitcher's design was roundly criticised by Gurney as fulfilling 'my worst forebodings and shows a sad lack of comprehension of the requirements of an embassy'.[24] In view of its internal resource pressures, the Office of Works had already decided that much of the architectural work would have to be done in Brazil. A respected local British architect, Robert Prentice, whom Leitch and Pitcher had met during their visit, was therefore commissioned to elaborate Pitcher's design, produce the working drawings and supervise the job on site. Prentice was a 55-year-old Scotsman, trained in Edinburgh and Paris, who had worked successfully in Rio since 1922. Gurney, who had been playing with plans of his own, was happy with the choice of Prentice. Pitcher sent his outline proposals to Prentice who, after consultation with Gurney, produced a revised plan, of which Gurney approved. Pitcher went along with the revisions in principle but by then war clouds hung heavily over the project and it was definitively postponed in October 1939.

Ankara was further advanced. The Office of Works' design for the residence was started on site in 1938 about 200 metres south-west of the First Building. Once it was wind- and weather-tight in 1941, the Office of Works reluctantly conceded that the interiors of the shell should be temporarily sub-divided into offices, stipulating that partitioning work must not damage the walls. For the rest of the war, to help cope with the much enlarged staff, the dining room contained the chancery, the drawing room two registries, the bedroom floor was mostly taken over by the military, the future lawn by Nissen huts and the future tennis court by a garage and maintenance unit.

11

Second World War and Aftermath 1940–1950

Wartime

Less than three weeks after war was declared in September 1939, Edward Bridges, then in the Offices of the War Cabinet, wrote to government Departments:

> At the moment, your Department, in common with others, is, I am sure, far more concerned with the steps to be taken to win the War than thinking about the record of the War. It may, indeed, seem a little incongruous to start thinking about the History of the War, but I suppose we must assume that in course of time an Official History of the War will be written.
> If no steps are taken now to make sure that the essential material for a History of the War is collected and preserved in convenient form, Departments will be put to a great deal of trouble later on. The object of this letter is, therefore, to suggest certain simple arrangements.[1]

The Foreign Office and the Office of Works had begun intermittent discussions in 1937 about air raid precautions at overseas Posts. They confined themselves to office premises, because staff were expected to take their own precautions in residential accommodation, and decided that protective measures should only be taken at European Posts, where the two key aims were to provide gasproof accommodation and to improve fire-fighting capacity. By the end of 1938, refuge shelters had been completed in the European offices and, at Foreign Office behest, in Tokyo. When war was

11.1. Wartime extensions to the Washington chancery building: a single floor filled most of the courtyard, and second-floor offices filled the gaps between the portico and the two pavilions. They were all removed after the large new offices building was completed in 1960.

imminent, diplomatic representation in enemy or occupied countries was withdrawn. If time and management were available, staff residential leases were terminated and furniture and possessions stored in the mission houses. Valuable plate and pictures were removed where practicable, notably the Paris collection to the chateau at Chambord. The keys to the mission houses were given to the appointed protecting power, which was the United States at most Posts until its entry into the war in December 1941, and afterwards Switzerland. Caretakers were retained or taken on at most Posts to look after the buildings as best they could. UK staff were initially interned at some Posts if they had not been able to leave in time: most of them were repatriated during the course of the war.

By March 1940, parts of the Office of Works had moved out of London: the secretariat that dealt with diplomatic and consular buildings was installed at the Palace Hotel in Rhyl in North Wales, and the Chief Engineer's Division was in the Marine Hydro also in Rhyl. It is an illusion to imagine that bureaucracy lessened in time of war: it just used smaller sheets of thinner paper. As the war progressed, Posts in Allied and neutral countries became increasingly crowded as staff from many branches of government were sent overseas to liaise, lobby, supply, procure, administer, propagandise and spy. Heads of mission and their families contracted into smaller and smaller residential quarters within the mission houses as they lost their dining and drawing rooms to offices: some moved out completely into rented flats. Temporary offices were built in courtyards or across lawns, and additional space was leased on *ad hoc* terms, with expenditure being authorised wherever works were in the direct interest of the national war effort. Washington, of course, attracted the largest number of new staff, several hundred of them. In early 1940, two hutments with 16 rooms were put up. By the end of 1940, a one-storey building of 19 rooms had been inserted into Lutyens' chancery courtyard and another floor built on top of parts of the chancery building **(Fig 11.1)**. In 1941, a three-storey block of 97 rooms was thrown up on a newly acquired adjacent plot (Lot 43 in Fig. 9.7); and another floor added in 1944 **(Fig. 11.2)**. Specialist aviation staff moved into Andrew Mellon's former residence on the corner of 18th Street

11.2. Lot 43, beside the Washington embassy's secondary access to Observatory Circle, was acquired in 1941 and these temporary offices quickly erected on it to cope with some of the wartime surge in embassy staff numbers. They were demolished in 1958.

and Massachusetts Avenue, and the press section into a nearby house leased from the widow of Harry Wardman.

When Moscow came under dire threat of German seizure in the autumn of 1941, the Soviet government instructed all diplomatic missions to evacuate the city for its fallback seat of government at Kuibyshev (now called Samara), on the Volga, about 500 miles south-east of Moscow. The entire diplomatic corps was given eight hours' notice to leave by train on 15 October 1941. It took nearly five days to reach Kuibyshev, where much of the Soviet government was already established. The 89 Britons were uncomfortably lodged at the barrack-like Pioneers' Palace, but the ambassador, Sir Stafford Cripps, was able to rent a bungalow a few days later to share with senior colleagues and to house makeshift offices. The mission remained in Kuibyshev for 18 months.[2]

The tide of war turned. On 13 September 1944, a British ambassador, Duff Cooper with his wife Diana, was back in Paris. He recorded in his diary that

> [we] went to the Arc de Triomphe where I had to lay a wreath on the grave of the Unknown Soldier, and then to the Berkeley Hotel, where we always used to stay, and which Freddie [Fane, comptroller of the Coopers' household] has requisitioned complete for us and the staff. There we had an excellent lunch, and then went round to the Embassy. The whole of the ground floor is choc-a-bloc with the furniture of thirty-two different households who stored it there when they had to leave Paris in 1940. This is gradually being removed. The rooms are in perfect condition. There is at present a lack of electricity and no water at all. I think we shall probably get into it in a few weeks.[3]

And they did – on 10 October 1944. On that same day, Cooper embarked on what became his major contribution to the house: 'Charlie Beistegui [friend, art collector and interior decorator] came round in the morning to discuss the possibility of turning my sitting room into a library'.[4] The Coopers were in Paris for three years, during which they used the fine old house to dazzling effect.

The embassy in Ankara was not slow, either, to make its mark. When the staff saw that the end of the war was imminent, they removed all the temporary partitions from the unfinished residence and on 9 May 1945, two days after the German surrender, held a series of events in the cavernous shell: a victory celebration service at 11.00, a cocktail party at 17.30, and a supper party and dance at 21.30. During the day over 1,000 guests came. Directly afterwards, nearly all the staff moved to Istanbul while the residence was finished, fitted-out and furnished, concurrently with the First Building being converted entirely to offices. William Silcock was the energetic clerk of works who supervised the contracts: £60,000 had been spent on the residence before work was halted in 1941, and now another £17,000 was spent on completing it. The ambassador and his staff returned from Istanbul and moved into the completed Ankara buildings in October 1945.

During the war, the Office of Works was enlarged from a central building agency into a full-scale Ministry of Works, charged with harnessing the building industry to the war effort. The commissioners were replaced by Ministers, whose brief extended to all the new civil and building works of government departments, repairing war damage to public buildings, controlling the building materials industries, and long-term planning for post-war physical reconstruction. The Ministry of Works, which it remained until 1962, emerged from the war with Duncan Sandys as Minister and Sir Percival Robinson as Permanent Secretary. The most senior professional officers were a director-general of works, Charles Mole, and a chief architect, Arthur Rutter. Eric de Normann, who had been on the Office of Works' administrative staff from 1920 until 1935, returned in 1943 as Deputy Secretary. Among his direct responsibilities was the Public Buildings Overseas Section, which included diplomatic and consular buildings, to the oversight of which he brought experience and continuity until his retirement in 1954. George Brown, who was Minister of Works for six months in 1951, thought highly of de Normann and recalled that it was 'quite easy to persuade oneself that he came over with the Conqueror and had been running the Office of Works ever since'.[5] De Normann soon re-established an overseas network with regional Works offices in Shanghai, Singapore, Cairo and Washington.

It took the Ministry of Works some months after the war ended to piece together all that had happened to its buildings overseas. Once a fairly full picture was available in November 1945, de Normann minuted 'On the whole I suppose that we are lucky that worse damage was not suffered'.[6] Deep frosts during the European winter of 1942 caused the most damage to many buildings. There were isolated reports of stolen furniture, broken seals, opened safes and missing silver. What emerged strongly, however, was how effectively, and often gallantly, and sometimes heroically, caretakers at Posts had looked after the buildings entrusted to them. Stories abounded of rooms found just as they were left before the war, and of smiling caretakers and local staff standing on the steps of mission houses in smart uniforms to greet the returning UK staff.

The greatest destruction of British buildings was in Berlin itself, where both the embassy house on Wilhelmstrasse and the consulate-general on

11.3. The site of the former embassy house in Berlin at 70 Wilhelmstrasse (see Fig. 5.6) in the foreground, with the remains of the Adlon Hotel and the damaged Brandenburg Gate beyond, in a 1950s photograph.

Tiergartenstrasse were destroyed during Allied bombing raids in late 1943. As the Swiss reported in a telegram from Berne in December 1943: 'Embassy almost completely destroyed by fire and high explosive bomb though gold and silver articles, certain valuable carpets and pictures and some items of furniture belonging to the former diplomatic staff, saved … . Caretaker and family unhurt, but have lost most of their possessions'[7] **(Fig. 11.3)**. The Budapest legation building on Verboczy Utca was destroyed by bombardment during the Russian recapture of the city, and the leased Branicki palace in Warsaw was completely destroyed by fire during the Uprising of autumn 1944. The former Vienna embassy building on Metternichgasse suffered an aerial bomb. Elsewhere in Europe, buildings at Belgrade, Bucharest, Helsinki, Riga and Sofia were slightly damaged by nearby blasts, and in Moscow the Sofiskaya buildings were hit by firebombs. In China, the Chungking consulate-general was considerably damaged by Japanese air attack during the Sino-Japanese War, Hankow consulate-general was destroyed by bombing in 1944 and several other Posts suffered minor damage or looting. In Bangkok, where some of the compound buildings were taken over by Japanese and Siamese authorities for hospital purposes, the north-east corner of the residence was rocked by a bomb but a Swiss presence deterred any subsequent looting. In Saigon, the consul-general's residence was destroyed by air attack in February 1945. The leased Manila residence was destroyed by looters.

British military personnel were generally the first to return to cities from which diplomatic missions had been withdrawn before or during the war, sometimes accompanied by a diplomat in a liaison capacity. These personnel used the mission buildings, if they had survived, for accommodation and messing. The military head was generally succeeded by a senior diplomat, who carried the title of Political Representative or High Commissioner. Once full diplomatic relations were restored upon signature of the relevant peace treaty, this diplomat generally became the ambassador.

The first priority for the Ministry of Works was to make the damaged buildings fit for re-occupation or, if necessary, to find alternative buildings. One source of alternative buildings was ex-German embassy properties. In London, the ex-German embassy at 7-9 Carlton House Terrace was taken over by the Foreign Office at the end of the war. In some formerly-occupied countries, Control Commissions or similar bodies were set up by the Allies to hold ex-German assets of all kinds in trust for the host government. Any Ally was permitted to negotiate with a Commission for the acquisition of ex-German property for its own diplomatic use, and the British government met various of its post-war diplomatic accommodation requirements by taking over ex-German buildings in this manner. The proprieties, of course, had to be strictly observed.

In Madrid, where the ambassador had been squeezed out of his house on Calle de Fernando el Santo by the expansion of chancery offices, thoughts turned in late 1944 to what to do once the war was over. Numerous permutations were examined before it was concluded in September 1945 that the offices should remain at Fernando el Santo and that the best proposition for the residence would be to acquire the former German residence at 3 Hermanos Becquer. The other three trustee powers were prepared to grant the British a one-year lease to run from 1 Jan 1946. An additional advantage of this house was that it was part-furnished, because 'The Germans were just filling it with brand new furniture throughout when the war came to an end. ... The house is full of a large number of excellent new upholstered chairs and sofas, very few of which have yet been covered, but for which there exists a lot of good artificial silk in a cupboard'.[8] But just before he moved in, the ambassador, Sir Victor Mallet, found that the house was less furnished than he expected because '... in the last few days the Czechoslovak Legation have put in a claim for all the Persian rugs and two of the large chandeliers...and the grand piano'.[9]

British hopes that it could buy the house, and perhaps also the former German offices, at the end of the lease were dashed when the co-trustees were not prepared to agree, so the lease was renewed annually for the next three years. In 1948, the trustees decided to auction both properties. The Ministry of Works, with Treasury approval to bid up to £130,000 for the residence only, feared that the Americans would trump it at auction. In the event, the Americans did not bid and a British offer of 8.5 million blocked pesetas (about £84,000 at the diplomatic rate of exchange) was successful in July 1949: the purchase was completed in April 1950 and 3 Hermanos Becquer remained the residence until it became unacceptably overlooked by adjacent developments in the 1970s.

In Copenhagen, the British Military Mission expropriated the row of three villas, at nos 36, 38 and 40 Kastelsvej, which had been the residence and offices of the German embassy. The British handed the villas over to the Danish government and took a lease on them in 1946. A comparable arrangement was reached in Berne: at the end of the war, the Swiss government took possession of the German embassy properties and in June 1946 agreed to lease them to the British government in exchange for Swiss use of the two British legation buildings on Thunstrasse. The British legation thereby became admirably housed in the former German residence at 32 Brunnadernrain and the nearby German office annex at 83 Willadingweg from 1946 until political pressure compelled the arrangements to be unwound in the mid-1950s.

In Vienna, a member of the Control Commission for Austria and minister-designate for the British legation in Vienna, William Mack, suggested in February 1945 that the house which the Office of Works had built at 6 Metternichgasse in 1875 and 'which we sold for a disgraceful song to the Nazis' in 1938, as de Normann expressed it, should be requisitioned as a suitable future residence. It was too early for London to take a view. The building had suffered damage, mainly from a bomb on the servants' wing at the rear, but the structural walls stood sound. It became the property of the Republic of Austria in 1948 and the Austrian government repaired the roofs. The Ministry of Works leased a temporary residence nearby at 12 Metternichgasse and various searches were carried out for a permanent alternative. Meanwhile, in the context of exploring the mechanics of a possible re-purchase of 6 Metternichgasse, the Ministry of Works argued that the 1938 transfer was a 'dispossession' within the meaning of a recent law and was advised that, in order to avoid the taking of evidence and further investigations, the Republic of Austria would agree to restitute the property provided that the purchase sum was returned. This affordable consideration tipped the balance in favour of regaining the former house. A settlement agreement was signed in October 1950 and the equivalent of £9,152 14s. 5d. paid back. Re-instatement works cost about £80,000 and the building resumed life as the British residence, after a 12 year interval, when Sir Harold Caccia took up occupation as ambassador in 1952.

The most far-reaching acquisition of former German property was in Italy and not directly the result of the Second World War. In the early hours of 31 October 1946, the embassy house in Rome was blown up by two suitcase bombs planted in its main entrance by members of Irgun, a Zionist paramilitary group **(Fig. 11.4)**. The Italian Security Police was soon recommending that the whole embassy should move to premises more easily protected than the temporary arrangements that had been put in hand. The

11.4. The embassy house, next to the Porta Pia in Rome, that was seriously damaged by terrorist bombs in 1946. The ruins were quickly shored up so that the road could be re-opened and stood like this until their demolition in 1952.

ambassador, Sir Noel Charles, and de Normann satisfied themselves that leasing the former German Embassy, the Villa Wolkonsky and its grounds, would provide the best means of meeting the requirement. After Rome was liberated in June 1944, the Wolkonsky estate was sequestrated, on the grounds that it had been used for non-diplomatic purposes (including interrogation and torture in the basement) and entrusted at the end of the war to the Allied Control Commission. Charles approached the Commission, which quickly agreed that Villa Wolkonsky should be made available to the British government, although it had only recently permitted its use by the Italian Ministry of the Treasury, who had started to move in. The Italian Red Cross also had about 100 men sleeping in the hutments in the villa's grounds. It was not therefore until January 1947 that the villa became vacant and most of the British embassy moved in: the residence into the 1890s main villa, chancery offices into Princess Zenaide Wolkonsky's 1830s villa, and other offices into the hutments and the former German minister's house **(Fig. 11.5)**. The Villa Wolkonsky suited the British embassy so well that the British government resolved later in 1947 to buy it. The purchase negotiations drifted on through the next few years, and were largely conducted through Washington. In the end, the British government agreed to pay £190,000 for Villa Wolkonsky and the deal was completed early in 1951, in parallel with a payment of £18,800 for the Villa Crispi for the consulate-general in Naples.

Foreign Office reports and reforms
The Diplomatic Service and the Foreign Office had been amalgamated in 1919, in the wake of the First World War, and created an enlarged Diplomatic Service. A further amalgamation, with the Consular Service, had been debated throughout the inter-war years, as both services grew larger and their functions increasingly overlapped, and the long-held social, educational and functional objections to a merger were subsiding. A majority of the members of a departmental committee, convened in 1938, came down in favour of a merger on the dual grounds that there should be a fusion of politics and commerce in foreign affairs and that the members of a Foreign Service should be representative of the whole nation. Anthony Eden, Foreign Secretary, published in 1943 a White Paper, 'Proposals for the Reform of the Foreign Service', that was to influence all post-war planning for British overseas representation and that cast the die for the merger. Implementation began in 1946: the Diplomatic Service thenceforth embraced all Foreign Office, diplomatic and consular staff. The extent to which the diplomatic and consular streams translated into two streams within the Foreign Office,

11.5. The 'new' Villa Wolkonsky in Rome, built in the 1890s by the Campanari family and enlarged in the 1920s by the German embassy. It was leased in 1947 from the Allied Control Commission for the British ambassador's residence and bought in 1951.

variously called A and B, administrative and executive, policy- and non-policy-capable, and other names, was debatable.

On overseas accommodation, Eden's White Paper resolved that

> the effective representation of this country abroad will ... involve the provision of adequate government buildings ... as well as adequate staffs, and it will be essential, after the war, to remember that economies on buildings and staffs are false economies if they result in impaired efficiency or in reduced security for confidential papers.

Besides the White Paper, two reports produced during the war helped to lay the foundations, however flimsily, for the post-war approach to building, leasing, maintaining and furnishing what could, at last, properly be called diplomatic accommodation overseas. The first was a summary by Viscount Davidson of the views that he formed about Britain's present and future representation during an official tour of South American Posts in 1942. The second was a 1944 summary of the findings of a Foreign Service Accommodation (Advisory) Committee.

Davidson was a considerable figure: an MP, former chairman of the

Conservative Party and the organiser of its central office. He had left politics in 1937 and devoted most of his attention to South America, where he owned large estates in Argentina. He was renowned for his attention to detail. He undertook his tour as an honorary adviser to the government on commercial relations with South America, and his recommendations for diplomatic buildings were sensible, well-informed and far-reaching.

Davidson foresaw the post-war expansion of overseas staff and realised that residential accommodation would need to be provided officially for all UK-staff at missions. He thought that residences and offices should henceforth be accommodated separately unless there were compelling security reasons for their sharing the same building. Offices should be leased because changing local conditions were likely to affect their suitability. They should be in the main business centre and well planned and equipped so as to work efficiently and impress visitors. Residences should be freehold, not too far from the city centre, designed as a dignified example of local traditional architecture, and have adequate space for both indoor and outdoor entertainment. The main reception rooms should be capable of carrying out their functions without disturbing the private quarters of the house. Adequate accommodation for guests must be included because Davidson thought it 'safe to assume that the trend of the future with the spread of democratic principles will be towards larger rather than smaller parties and more rather than fewer visitors in view of the development of air travel and the speeding up of transport generally after the war'.[10] He thought the furnishing and equipment of all residences should be the responsibility of the British government and that

> furnishings, pictures and decoration should be undertaken by an interior decorator who may be an architect, but not by an architect, pure and simple. … Everything from the linen to the linoleum, from the china to the clocks, from the cutlery to the cretonnes, from the pictures to the piano, should be British and the finest examples of modern craftsmanship. Flexibility should be the watchword and quality the rule. … The aim should be to avoid the stereotyped official style and to give play to the personal taste of the British representative and of his wife too while ensuring a high general standard.[11]

Davidson thought the Ministry of Works should plan the furnishing and equipping of premises as an important post-war function once it became possible to export goods from the UK, and should carry out inspections of Posts. Inspectors should be selected with care: 'If the local representatives of the Department are all of the same type as for example the insignificant little man in Buenos Aires, some other system is clearly required'.[12] Davidson sent his views and recommendations to Robinson at the Ministry of Works in July 1943, emphasising that he thought his principles applied well beyond South America.

In early 1943, the Permanent Under-Secretary at the Foreign Office, Sir Alexander Cadogan, wrote to the Permanent Secretary at the Ministry of Works, then Sir Geoffrey Whiskard, to report Eden's view that too many of the mission buildings overseas were inadequate and that 'at the end of the war, if not before, we shall have to review our accommodation abroad'. Three special considerations would need to be borne in mind: separation of confidential from public areas of offices; larger staff numbers, especially of subordinate grades; and the need to assume that heads of mission might have no private means and that their residences would therefore need to be equipped with 'china, glass, linen or plate as well as pictures and minor items of furniture'. Cadogan suggested that a standing committee should be established in London for the purpose of 'supervising the planning, decoration and equipment of Foreign Office buildings abroad.' Besides the obvious membership, Cadogan had in mind a representative 'of some artistic body like the Royal Fine Art Commission, of a retired diplomat of experience, judgment and good taste and of an interior decorator, who might be a woman and able to advise on the internal arrangements of the residences'.[13] This was the origin of the Foreign Service Accommodation (Advisory) Committee.

The Ministry of Works was affronted. All of these issues were already its responsibility and it had no intention of transferring any of them to a committee. It succeeded, however, both in inserting the parenthetic 'Advisory' into the committee's name, with a view to ensuring that no binding conclusions were reached, and in levering its own man, de Normann, into the chair. Three senior diplomats represented the Foreign Office; two senior diplomats' wives represented the running of big houses; a Royal Academician architect and the Director of the Victoria and Albert Museum represented the arts establishment; and the Ministry of Works fielded one of its former chief architects, Sir James West, and the two secretaries.

This committee put its name to a wordily innocuous report in March 1944 which accepted the main tenets proposed by Davidson. On the design of buildings, it considered using more 'outside' architects and insisted that the best local architectural advice should always be obtained but accepted that selection of an architect and how he should liaise with the Ministry would depend on the circumstances. 'The Architectural treatment of the building is for the Architect to determine but he should have regard to traditional English ideals whilst designing the building in harmony with its surroundings'. Residences should have private quarters for the head of mission and family, separate from the formal reception rooms, including a small dining room to seat, say, 12 persons. For the formal rooms, 'we suggest a large drawing room with parquet floor for dancing, in place of a ballroom, and a large dining room to seat up to 50, 40 or 30 according to the size of the Post'.[14] There should be up to nine bedrooms, three of them for official guests, with seven bathrooms; and, for embassies and large legations, servants' accommodation for up to ten permanent indoor servants. Gardens should be designed by the architect responsible for the house to ensure that they could be used for entertaining.

For offices, the Advisory Committee's report recommended that, wherever possible, all of a mission's staff, including the consulate, should be accommodated in the same office building for which a typical plan was suggested that included a large conference room, cellular offices in separate confidential and public areas, two or three spare rooms, a small cafeteria, and flats for a resident clerk and security officer or caretaker. Office furniture should be of good design and uniform appearance, with special attention being paid to the ambassador's study. The committee felt unable to lay down any uniform standards of accommodation for consular Posts because of their diversity. It thought that consulates in the capitals of foreign colonial territories and in the Near and Far East should be designed somewhat on the lines of small legations, but should come after them in priority terms.

The committee specified a handsome list of what it thought should be supplied by the Ministry of Works at public expense, though it decided not to press for the wider distribution and topping-up of plate for the time being. The committee was divided about whether air-conditioning was objectionable on grounds of health, but concluded that portable air-conditioning units should be provided at really hot Posts, and refrigerators should be supplied free of charge. The report specified a range of paint colours for walls and hoped that occupants would be restricted to them.

A few months after the committee's report was circulated, a commentary was compiled of views received. Some objected to a general rule that offices should be situated away from residences: they thought offices should be joined to the residence or, at the furthest, across the garden or road. A safe or strongroom would be required in the head of mission's own bedroom if the offices were separate from the residence because 'he will often be working on secret documents late at night'. There was a general preference for adapting houses rather than building them anew. Nine bedrooms might not be enough if an incumbent's family had a resident governess and a personal private secretary. There was general support for an Advisory Committee continuing in being, provided it had on it a 'woman of experience and taste. If real taste is allowed to direct operations, then there would be no objection to a large degree of uniformity'. The compiler of the commentary, however, gave the last word to a junior correspondent who thought that

> the whole of your report deals with accommodation to be used by the diplomatic and consular staff. What do you propose in respect of Branch B and C personnel (ie accountants, archivists, cypherers, shorthand-typists etc) who are even less able than diplomats to provide their own furniture? It is, I think, important (a) that their jobs should be made attractive by giving them good conditions, and (b) that in some countries they should not be forced into undesirable boarding houses.[15]

The Foreign Office created a Conference and Supply Department in 1945 and charged it additionally in 1948 with buildings, motor cars, food and other supplies for Posts overseas. This department naturally became the Foreign Office's main point of contact with the Ministry of Works. Its first head was Colonel G.R. Codrington, succeeded in 1952 by Brigadier Charles Steel. Steel was commissioned into the Royal Engineers in 1921, served in East Africa during the war, was taken prisoner in 1942, and served in the British Military Mission in Greece from 1945 to 1952. The name of his department was changed to Accommodation Department in 1965, and he remained at its head until 1967, providing the Foreign Office with some rare continuity in the post-war world.

Rio de Janeiro

The recommendations of the Foreign Service Accommodation (Advisory) Committee were first applied to the residence at Rio de Janeiro when design work for it resumed in 1944. The assumption was that Britain would be returning to South America in a big way, and especially to Brazil, the continent's largest country, with the longest established British embassy, and the most senior ambassador. The Foreign Office initially wanted to build new embassy offices in the garden instead of keeping them in town: 'far better to have the Chancery in the Embassy grounds. I cannot imagine that in these days of cars distance would render the work of the Commercial Section difficult if it was also moved to the new site'.[16] The Ministry of Works succeeded in contesting this but Howard Jones, one of its senior architects who had also been a secretary to the Committee, rather rashly told Robert Prentice, the appointed local architect, that, instead of amending the pre-war scheme, 'we would prefer to allow you complete freedom to design a scheme which will meet the points raised by the Committee'.[17] This left

11.6. The newly-completed ambassador's residence in Rio de Janeiro in 1950, designed by Robert Prentice. Perhaps the largest white elephant in the history of the British diplomatic estate. The podium was faced with marble and the building with stucco.

far too much leeway to Prentice and the ambassador, Sir Noel Charles, who was adamant that the British building should not be dwarfed by the huge new American construction next door.

The scheme grew steadily out of hand and was never effectively restrained by London **(Fig. 11.6)**. While a quiet formal exterior and Adamesque interiors were rationalised as recalling memories of past influence and close collaboration with Argentina, a British architectural correspondent wondered whether it would not be perceived instead as 'a sandhill where diplomatic ostriches may bury their heads against the present'.[18] The building was completed in 1950 to both fanfare and derision **(Fig. 11.7)**. The costs increased from a 1945 estimate of £200,000 to a post-1949 devaluation out-turn of just over £400,000. De Normann briefed his permanent secretary on the eve of his appearance before the enquiring Public Accounts Committee:

> It is a well-known fact that the South Americans and the people of Brazil in particular judge very much by external appearances. We purposely as

a matter of policy built this fine new Embassy and furnished it in order to impress the native and the reports [of ambassadors] go to show how successful we have been in furthering our diplomatic standing in Rio'.[19]

Further embarrassment was to come. Within only a few years, the idea of moving the capital from Rio to Brasilia was gaining currency. Sir Edward Muir, who became Permanent Secretary of the Ministry of Works in 1956, first saw the residence in 1960 and wondered:

> What can one say? Of its sort it is a most magnificent effort. It is not, of course, to everyone's taste and it is highly derivative both in style and decoration. But as a really sumptuous piece of showing the flag, I doubt whether we have ever done anything to equal it. Furthermore, enormous care was obviously taken over its furnishing and equipment. How we, the Treasury and the Foreign Office between us ever came to build a house of such fantastic size in the years immediately after the war is another question.[20]

To which the best answer is probably that there was at no time a properly agreed brief for the building **(Fig. 11.8)**. Ambassadors continued to use the

11.7. The reception room or ballroom of the Rio residence in 1950. The ceiling was based on one by Robert Adam in Wynn House in London; some of the furniture was original; the walls were shades of buff, pink and green, and the curtains were gold.

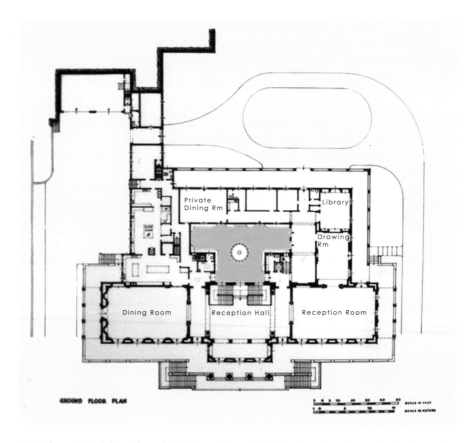

11.8. The principal floor plan of the Rio residence. The inclusion of a private suite for the ambassador and family, at the rear, was a desirable advance but its scale grew out of hand.

Rio 'white elephant' residence until the embassy moved to Brasilia in 1972. It was sold in 1975 to the Mayor of Rio for £2.2 million: it serves today as the Palácio da Cidade, and is maintained in excellent condition.

New demands

There was so much diplomatic accommodation work to be done in the late 1940s that the Conference and Supply Department of the Foreign Office and the Public Buildings Overseas Section of the Ministry of Works hardly knew on what to focus their attentions. There were three main kinds of demand. First, backlogs and damages caused by the war, finding alternatives to lost buildings, and completing those which were stalled. Second, changed accommodation requirements that flowed from global political changes, particularly the onset of the Cold War and the Partition of India. And third, new accommodation requirements concomitant with the increase in staff numbers overseas and the Eden reform programme that required them to be accommodated to better than pre-war standards.

While meeting these demands was high on the Foreign Office's agenda, it was much lower down the Ministry's. Eric de Normann, as a deputy secretary, worked hard to strengthen the old 'dips and cons' section but it faced the major obstacles of the Ministry's preference for not employing consultants, even though it was short of key professional and technical staff, and of shortage of currency and materials supply. Many of the priorities were cloudy because the reforms were being introduced, for neither the first nor last time, without much regard to their implications on accommodation budgets and programmes. The result was that large numbers of new staff were living overseas in hotels and hostels and working in temporary and substandard offices until something more satisfactory could be devised, funded and completed – a process that necessarily took years. Many of the requirements were also new to the Ministry, used to mission houses and fairly spartan consulates. Now, with the separation of offices from residences on the agenda, the post-war programme required four different types of accommodation: residences for heads of mission or Post, offices for all staff, residential accommodation for all staff, and communal staff facilities at Posts for amenity, social and sporting activities. And, added to the Ministry's responsibilities for purchase, lease and construction of buildings, were now added those for maintaining, furnishing and equipping them.

Some early post-war decisions concerned what to do about former embassy and legation houses, especially in Europe, that had been taken over by offices during the war. The options were to leave the offices in occupation and find another residence, revert to a residence and find other offices, or find a way of sharing the house, if large enough. Despite Davidson's and the Advisory Committee's recommendations, there was still opposition, especially in the upper echelons of the Foreign Office, to the policy of separating chancery from residence. De Normann remarked

> When we have pointed out [to the Foreign Office] that the Americans have of recent years adopted [such a] policy, the reply has been that American Ambassadors don't do any work anyway. ... I think the time has come when the Foreign Office will have to accept the position that the Head of Mission goes to his office like any Cabinet Minister.[21]

Practical pressures and the passage of time gradually wore down the old guard. The Hôtel de Rodes in Brussels remained as the offices and the residence moved into a leased house in Rue Ducale in 1945, which the Ministry bought two years later. The Fernando el Santo building in Madrid remained as offices and the residence moved into the former German residence in 1946. And likewise in Bucharest, where 24 Strada Jules Michelet remained the offices and the residence moved in 1947 into a leased house. Conversely, in Lisbon, the Rua san Francisco de Borja house was entirely regained by the residence, as the last of its offices moved into the Palacio de Porto Corvo in Rua de São Domingos, which had been bought as offices in 1940. Beyond Europe, the houses in Dakar and Montevideo were among those that reverted to sole residence use. Perhaps the neatest resolution was in Paris where offices were scattered in the residence at 39 rue du Faubourg Saint Honoré, in its two pavilions and in leased floors of nearby buildings. Discussions about acquiring the mansion next door to the residence to house all the offices in the one building came to a halt when war started. The owner, Jacques Pereire, played safe during the war by leasing his house at low charge to the Vichy Ministry of Youth. Within two weeks of his arrival as ambassador in September 1944, Duff Cooper re-opened those discussions and was authorised by London to ask the French authorities to requisition Pereire's house for the embassy's use. The French agreed, even though it apparently meant moving out 500 French officials, and said that the terms would be the same as the Free French were enjoying in London. The building was exceedingly dirty throughout, and numerous repairs were necessary. Given the scarcity of labour and materials in Paris, the Director of Labour in Rear Headquarters at Paris was persuaded to lay on a 'Section of Pioneers' (a gang drafted in from the army) to clear up of the building, which took the dozen or so men several months.

Pereire House was brought fully into use at the end of July 1945. After a year, it was proving sufficiently satisfactory to justify its purchase, restoration and adaptation to permanent offices. The ambassador suggested paying for the house in goods or military equipment but the Treasury, after due rumination, preferred normal financing. The sale was completed in August 1947 for £242,000, partly paid with francs held by the embassy's Information Department that could not be repatriated, and the expectation was that the intended works to it would cost another £50,000. The plans for these works were shown to the Foreign Secretary, Ernest Bevin, for final approval. He was 'not satisfied that the desired result can be achieved at all with the existing building and has expressed the provisional view that it be completely demolished and the ideal offices erected on the site'.[22] Failing that, he would want the adaptations significantly reduced. He was persuaded off demolition and a revised scheme was ready in December 1947, estimated at £65,000, to be carried out in stages over three years. This work was completed in 1951. The Pereire building, with some extension in 1967 and many internal re-arrangements over the years, remains the embassy offices next door to the residence.

The huge increase in the number of UK-based staff posted overseas substantially increased the need for office space at many Posts. In developed cities, much of it could be leased, most commonly from banks, insurance companies and trading houses. The post-war rise of multi-lateral diplomacy, and the consequent need for office space for UK delegations, was mainly confined to developed cities, for example, New York and Geneva for the United Nations. But there were many Posts where leasable office space was unavailable, unsuitable or unaffordable and mission offices had instead to be built on land that the British government already owned or could acquire for that purpose.

Before the war, almost all staff except heads of mission had to find and lease their own residential accommodation, for which they were paid rent allowances. It took some years to work out how best to provide this accommodation for the greater post-war number of staff, many of them young, quite a few single, and few with any experience of hunting for their own accommodation. If the city had a functioning rental market in domestic accommodation, the most common mechanism adopted was for the administration section at a Post to assist incoming staff to find suitable property, to negotiate the lease with the landlord in the name of the mission, and to pay the rent to the landlord direct: these properties were called Foreign Office hirings. The problem with this mechanism, as a Foreign Office inspection of Warsaw in 1948 concluded, was that not enough expertise went into the selection of units or the drafting of their leases. The Foreign Office told the Ministry of Works that 'it would be ideal if [the Ministry] were responsible for all buildings abroad used as offices or residences by Foreign Office personnel and we are keen to make progress in that direction whenever opportunity offers'.[23] Meanwhile, Warsaw offered a test case and the Ministry of Works seconded an estate surveyor to Warsaw for a few weeks to sort out all the leases and to bring them into the Ministry's own name. This arrangement suited all parties and was adopted worldwide over the next few years. The change meant that the Ministry of Works was responsible for almost every unit of accommodation: the few exceptions included premises at the smallest Posts, at temporary Posts and at honorary consulates: also at New York, where landlords were wary of leases signed in the name of a diplomatic mission.

Leasing worked reasonably enough provided that there was property available to lease. In Posts where there was not, the Ministry of Works could buy single or several houses, build a block of flats for U.K staff or, in the case of single, especially female, junior staff, acquire hostels with messing facilities. The larger staff numbers also led to new requirements for communal facilities: cafeterias, clubs, clinics, shops, tennis courts and swimming pools, bungalows for recreational leave and so on. These facilities were often fairly easily achievable in the compounds of the Middle and Far East but required a good deal of ingenuity to provide elsewhere.

Disposals and claims

All these requirements, and plenty of unexpected other demands, kept the still-called 'dips and cons' section of the Ministry of Works fully occupied until the end of the 1960s. There had always been some compensatory reducing requirements when, for example, various consulate buildings were no longer required. But disposal action itself was a rarity. 'The house and site seem to have disappeared' mourned a surveyor in London when trying to trace a consulate in Fernando Po. The Treasury, in acceding to a request for its permission in 1923 to sell to the Siamese government a disused building in Chiengrai, added somewhat plaintively to the Office of Works: 'I am to suggest that, when occasion offers, enquiry should be made as to the possibility of selling any other government property which is no longer required'.[24]

A more noticeable reduction in responsibilities eventually accrued from the consulates in China, where the disruptions of the civil war between the Nationalists and Communists in the late 1920s and the Japanese invasions in the 1930s caused the closure of many of the remaining consulates. An agreement of 1927 paved the way for what was called the rendition of extra-territoriality, and the concession areas at Hankow and Kiukiang were the first to be handed over to Chinese administration. Here and elsewhere, vacated buildings were variously disposed of: leased to tenants, handed over to the local or national authorities or requisitioned by them, damaged by war or riot beyond re-occupation, and a few sold. Some consulates that were re-opened after being ransacked had their strong rooms and safes smashed open and all their wiring, doorknobs and other fittings stripped out. The Office of Works kept a China Disturbances Account to which it charged remedial expenses in expectation of eventual compensation.

The formal end of extra-territoriality in China, and in consequence of the need for so many consulates, came in January 1943 with signature of the Treaty for the Relinquishment of Extra-territorial Rights in China, exactly one century after the ratification of the treaty of Nanking. Article 5 provided for the continuance of British occupation of legitimately acquired land and buildings by transferring their tenures to perpetual leaseholds, and granting full rights of disposal (other than to foreign governments and nationals). In 1949, the Communist armies defeated the Nationalists and took their capital at Nanking, Chiang Kai-shek retreated to Formosa (Taiwan), and the People's Republic was proclaimed on 1 October. The new regime soon required the registration of all foreign-held property, which caused a great deal of chasing after documents in Peking and London. It became clear how much miscellaneous consular property there was scattered across China: some of it was pretty well forgotten, even though the Ministry of Works was still paying the wages of caretakers at thirteen of the consulates, including at Changsha where only ruins remained. It was clearly sensible to comply with registering the properties so as to be able to dispose of them, even though registration meant that taxes became payable. Thanks, however, to meticulous past record-keeping in most consulates, and also in the Office of Works' office in Shanghai, and the efficiency of the Chinese bureaucratic machine, the property registration process was completed, except for the Peking compound, around 1950 with remarkably little pain.

When it came to disposals, the embassy in Peking in 1951 suggested dividing the consular properties into three categories. The first was property still in use, and well worth retaining: the Peking embassy compound, the Peitaiho summer retreat, Canton, Shanghai and Tientsin. The second was property not in use, or would soon cease to be in use, but was worth retaining in case it had some future use: Hankow, Mukden, Tsingtao, and Dairen. The third category, much the largest, was property unlikely ever to be used again: Amoy, Changsha (in ruins), Chefoo, Chengtu (which comprised only a site), Chungking, Foochow, Harbin, Ichang, Kunming (the lakeside site), Nanking, Newchwang (in ruins), Swatow, Tengyueh (in ruins), and Tsinanfu. Priority was to be given to disposing of those properties that were incurring the most continuing expenditure through taxes and caretakers' wages.

By working backwards from tax demands, the Ministry of Works calculated that its total holding in China might be worth about £3.5 million, even if sold to the Chinese authorities. The Changsha ruins were disposed of first, in 1952, for no capital benefit, the embassy note stating hopefully that the property 'may be utilised for some philanthropic or benevolent purpose in the public interest'.[25] When the Canton consulate closed in 1952, the Governor of Hong Kong persuaded London to hold on to the buildings and to sublet them. Three years later, however, the Counsellor and Consul-General in Peking, John Addis, told the Foreign Office that 'I doubt if we should ever need to open a consular establishment in Canton' and Canton went on the disposal list.[26] In 1955, the *chargé d'affaires* in Peking, Humphrey Trevelyan, re-affirmed to the Foreign Secretary, Anthony Eden, that he only wished to retain Peking (and Peitaiho), Shanghai and a house in Tientsin. In 1958, London agreed to pursue the sale of Chungking and Hankow next and despatched a Ministry of Works estate surveyor from Singapore, N.P. Lawrence, to inspect, value and negotiate the sales as best he could. As well as selling both premises, he managed to sell the site at Nanking which was acquired in 1937 when it looked as though it might remain as the capital.

Sir Eric Seal, a deputy secretary in the Ministry of Works, toured some of the residual China Posts with Charles Steel in late 1957. Seal took a nostalgic backward glance.

> The compound at Shanghai, with the possible exception of Bangkok, is the finest I have seen. In spite of the fact that most of the houses are empty and the office only a half or third used the compound is magnificently kept with trim lawns and plenty of flowers ... The No 1 house, now unoccupied, is a most impressive mansion. All the furnishings, including carpets and curtains, are being looked after most scrupulously by the Chinese caretaker ... The office block is a splendid one and contains not only what was the Supreme Court (now used for badminton) but also the judges' robing rooms and some of the wigs, amazingly well preserved.[27]

Except for Peking, compensation for all of the remaining properties in China, though for long in Chinese occupation, was finally paid in the early 1970s.

Claiming compensation for war damage, or for any other significant loss like the China consulates, was a necessary process but it took years, used up inordinate staff time, and generally produced rather little: indeed, most claims fell by the wayside for one reason or another. The claim for the legation building in Budapest that was destroyed in 1945 offers an example of the bureaucratic pain of a claim. The British military mission in Hungary alerted the Foreign Office Claims Department in 1947 that, if the British government wished to submit a claim for damages and restitution under Article 26 of the Peace Treaty, it would need to be made before 31 March 1950. The Ministry of Works suggested claiming £164,000 for replacement of the building and £15,000 for destroyed furnishings. Endless and spuriously accurate lists of the values of buildings, furniture, typewriters and minutiae were drawn up. The claim was submitted in May 1950 for about 6.4 million forints, amended in 1955 to about 8.5 million forints. After the overall claim with Hungary was settled in 1958, detailed claims could be made through the Foreign Compensation Commission, which insisted in 1959 that values should be presented in 1939 terms and expressed in pengoes, the currency that preceded the forint. In 1960, the Commission assessed the compensation due for the loss of the Budapest legation premises at £51,086, but pointed out that, as the money from the Hungarian government was insufficient, only a proportion would be payable, and over a period of years, because the Hungarian government's payments into the fund were based on the value of imports into the U.K. from Hungary. Ten far-from-equal instalments paid at roughly annual intervals over the next ten years totalled £12,464 19s. 8d. The Treasury agreed to abandon pursuit of the £38,000 balance of the claim in 1970, just about 25 years after the cause of the claim took place.

12

Cold War 1946–1983

Keeping going

Winston Churchill made his Iron Curtain speech – originally entitled 'The Sinews of Peace' – at Westminster College, Fulton, Missouri, in March 1946.

> It is my duty … to place before you certain facts about the present position in Europe. From Stettin in the Baltic to Trieste in the Adriatic an *iron curtain* has descended across the Continent. Behind that line lie all the capitals of the ancient states of Central and Eastern Europe. Warsaw, Berlin, Prague, Vienna, Budapest, Belgrade, Bucharest and Sofia, all these famous cities and the populations around them lie in what I must call the Soviet sphere, and all are subject in one form or another, not only to Soviet influence but to a very high and, in some cases, increasing measure of control from Moscow.

This speech signified the start of the 30-year Cold War. The temperature dropped sharply when Berlin was blockaded in 1948, and reached freezing point with the building of the Berlin wall in 1961 and the Cuban missile crisis in 1962. The thaw began when Mikhail Gorbachev became Soviet leader in 1985 and ended in 1990 with the re-unification of Germany and the withdrawal of the Red Army from Eastern Europe.

The British government maintained missions throughout the Cold War in all the Warsaw Pact capitals. Chancery, defence and related work occupied the most attention while many normal diplomatic contacts and social and cultural activities were moribund for decades. The accommodation priorities were necessarily mostly defensive: above all, in offices, to prevent physical intrusion into sensitive office zones and to minimise the scope for electronic eavesdropping, and, in housing, to provide staff with such comforts and communal facilities as practicable to counteract the oppressive environment and restricted social opportunities of their host city. East European governments set up variations of Diplomatic Services Bureaux within their foreign affairs ministries to provide diplomatic missions and their staff with offices and housing, to assist with provisions, local staff, transport and services, and to keep an eye on the diplomats' activities. The original Soviet body with these responsibilities, BUROBIN, allocated mansions for embassies to lease and insisted that all maintenance work on them should be undertaken by its own staff. For staff accommodation, it allocated flats for more senior staff and built dull blocks of small apartments for the rest, with all nationalities cheek by jowl. BUROBIN was succeeded in 1947 by the Administration for Service to the Diplomatic Corps, UPDK, but the role did not change: Romania had the ODCD, Bulgaria the BODK and so on. The Chinese and other Communist governments later copied these models.

These bureaux were, from the diplomats' perspective, bureaucratic, unimaginative, slow, expensive and inefficient. From a Communist government's perspective, of course, they provided unrivalled opportunities for watching diplomats and a formidable system of relatively polite control. Although they enjoyed manipulating the allocation of property between missions, the bureaux rarely used diplomatic accommodation, once allocated, as a direct political lever. In consequence, the idea of a 'political lease' had some force. Even if a tenant's right was insufficiently underwritten in an official lease document to satisfy an eagle-eyed Ministry of Works estate surveyor, it could generally be assumed that the right would be honoured, and that the hassle of trying to negotiate an amendment to the wording outweighed the risks of accepting it as it stood.

With the exception of the establishment of an embassy in East Berlin, upon the opening of diplomatic relations with the German Democratic Republic in 1973, no significant British embassy office in any Warsaw Pact capital was moved or substantially re-arranged or upgraded in the 40 years between 1950 and 1990. The risks of the technical security of alternative buildings being compromised were far worse than the inconveniences and inefficiencies of making do with the current buildings. Such building maintenance and technical work that had imperatively to be done in offices was undertaken by security-cleared personnel from the UK, much of it by Foreign Office and Ministry of Works technical staff. Many of the materials that they needed for this work were also sent from the UK under the same inspection-free arrangements that applied to diplomatic bags. There were only two developments at British ambassadors' residences during the Cold

War: the construction of a new residence in Warsaw during the early 1960s and the acquisition of an East Berlin residence in 1973. All new furniture, fabrics and domestic equipment for the Posts was imported from UK or Western Europe, and installed by visiting technical staff.

Moscow

The offices and residence remained throughout the Cold War in the former Charitonenko mansion on Sofiskaya Embankment (from 1964 called Morisa Thoreza Embankment, after a French Communist leader). There were, however, intermittent negotiations about moving elsewhere. These began in 1946 when the Russians were contemplating a scheme for laying out most of the island between the Moscow River and the canal as a memorial park and cultural centre, with the Charitonenko mansion, from which the British embassy would be ejected, as the focal point of this park. The Russians assured the embassy that they would make land available for a new building at one end of the island. This plan seemed to peter out but its existence alerted London to the insecurity of the embassy's tenure of the building it occupied. The Foreign Secretary, Ernest Bevin, visited Moscow in March 1947 with the UK Delegation to the Council of Foreign Ministers. Bevin thought that conditions in the Charitonenko house were below standard for his staff: he took matters into his own hands, telling the Foreign Office in a telegram that

> When I called on Generalissimo Stalin yesterday evening I said I wanted to ask him for a site on which to build a new British Embassy, offices and living accommodation for the staff. This indicated, I said, that we wished to remain permanently represented in Russia. Generalissimo Stalin said that he thought it would be possible to meet me.[1]

Five sites were offered for inspection over the following months but none was attractive enough to pursue. The ambassador was anyway recommending against building anew because the need for more office space was lessening, any new building would inevitably be poorly built, and the exchange rate was unfavourable. The hope was that the embassy could renew its lease on the Charitonenko house when the present term expired in June 1952. At the end of 1952, however, the embassy was told to leave within three months, surmising that the reason it was being told to go was that it caused offence by being so close to the Kremlin. Three premises were offered as alternatives but all were unsuitable. Lord Talbot of Malahide, a serving diplomat in the Foreign Office, was tasked in 1953 with finding a satisfactory way forward. He discovered that the Russians were again pursuing their town planning re-arrangement for the island. The Foreign Office and the Office of Works came close to acceding to a move but the Foreign Secretary, Sir Anthony Eden, made his 'greatest possible reluctance' known to his Russian opposite number, who agreed to look again at the Russian plans.[2] The result was a new five-year lease on the Charitonenko house which, with a five-year renewal, bought the embassy security of tenure until 1963. By then, the question of new sites for the British embassy in Moscow had become reciprocally linked with the Russians' requirement for new sites in London.

The first proposition, in the mid-1960s, was that the British could offer the St George's, Hanover Square, burial ground in London in exchange for a site on the edge of Moscow in the Lenin Hills: this was rejected by both sides. In 1965, the Russians were offered and accepted 1-7 Kensington Palace Gardens in London (as well as retaining no.13 which they already occupied) and in the following year the British were offered and accepted, subject to a few boundary extensions, a site on the Smolenskaya Embankment in Moscow. Some preliminary design work was done for both sites. The basis for a reciprocal deal evolved during the late 1960s to include second sites in each capital: at Kensington Barracks and on Vakhtangova Street. The Russians increased the pressure after 1969 by restricting subsequent leases on the Charitonenko mansion to ever-shorter terms. Political opposition to the deal grew in the early 1970s, culminating in 1976 when the publication of the Russians' plans for the Kensington Barracks site led to an outcry in London, especially about the way that its high and bleak perimeter walls entirely shut the embassy off from its neighbourhood. The British government therefore withdrew the Barracks site in 1978 and offered the return of the Vakhtangova site. The Russian invasion of Afghanistan at the end of 1979 put a stop to the negotiations.

Other Warsaw Pact capitals

The former legation house in Bucharest at 24 Strada Jules Michelet, bought in 1908, was no longer in a locality suitable for a residence when the mission returned after the Second World War. It was therefore given over entirely to offices and the British political representatives, successively Ian Le Rougetel and Adrian Holman, lived in a leased house until something better could be found. Le Rougetel decided that the requisitioned house belonging to Virgil Viorel Tilea at 15 Strada Emil Pangratti would suit well once the American mission had moved out. Built in the mid-1930s, it was well-planned and faced a National Park **(Fig. 12.1)**. Tilea, a prominent politician who had been Romanian minister in London and was an ardent supporter of King Carol before his enforced abdication in 1940, was now living in

12.1. The house at 15 Strada Emil Pangratti in Bucharest that Virgil Viorel Tilea built for himself shortly before his exile in England. He lost it in 1948 and the Ministry of Works leased it direct from the Romanian authorities until the early 1990s.

exile at Holton Place, Wheatley, in Oxfordshire. The Foreign Office asked him in September 1946 whether he would be prepared to lease his house in Bucharest once it was de-requisitioned. Tilea replied that he wanted to sell it instead – doubtless because the Romanian authorities were tightening their grip on private wealth. The Ministry of Works haggled him down to a price of £22,000 for the house and £8,000 for its contents, which the Treasury approved. Holman in Bucharest, increasingly agitated that all Tilea's property might be confiscated at any moment by the Romanian government, wanted quickly to sign a local contract that would permit him occupation immediately the Americans moved out in April 1947: 'It would be difficult for the Romanian government to turn us out when we were once in and far more difficult for us to get in if the Romanian authorities got possession first'.[3] Holman produced a list of what needed to be done to the house before he could occupy it, although he had earlier said that it was satisfactory.

The Assistant Treasury Solicitor in London was negotiating with Tilea in Oxfordshire but Tilea was not in touch with the rapidly changing politics and laws at home and had unrealistic hopes. To add to his sorrows, his wife, co-owner of the house, was living in Switzerland, which caused power of attorney problems until her death there in November 1947. When London, not for the first time, rejected Holman's wish for a quick local contract, he threw a tantrum and vowed to look for another house instead. At which point he received a communication from the Romanian government saying that he had 'full liberty to occupy the Tilea house.' Six weeks later came the amplification that 'I hasten to inform you … that from legal point of view there is no obstacle to the realisation of plan of the British legation as regards purchase of the Tilea house'.[4] Holman judged that the way was clear for him to move in, which he did in September 1947. His determination proved well -judged. Within months both the ministries of foreign affairs and finance were in the hands of the communists. Poor Tilea, with no cards left to play, offered the Ministry of Works a 25-year lease at a premium of £22,000, with options both for a further similar term and for purchase of the property at a nominal sum of £5 when the position was 'ripe' for him to register his title with the Romanian authorities. London declined and Tilea suspended negotiations in January 1948. He was stripped of his Romanian citizenship the following month.

London waited for the Romanians to raise the question of a lease. Instead, at the end of 1948, they wanted the Tilea house for a children's home and promised that 'another suitable residence' would be provided for Holman's successor. British intransigence in rejecting all alternative offers had the satisfactory result of automatically renewable annual leases for the next 40 years. From time to time efforts were made to buy the house but the Romanians declined them all.

The former legation house in Budapest, on Verboczy Utca and overlooking the Danube, was almost totally destroyed during the Soviet siege in 1945 and its ruins had been taken over by squatters by the time that the British military mission was established in Budapest. Within a couple of years, that mission acquired alternative premises for both the residence and the offices that outlasted the Cold War. For the residence, the mission leased for five years from August 1946 the house at 42 Lorántffy Zsuzsanna Utca, built in 1926 in the manner of a large French villa, in a good residential area of Buda **(Fig. 12.2)**. It was necessarily leased through the state-controlled diplomatic bureau but some rent was also paid to the landlord, Owen Tibor Scitovsky, an economist at Stanford University, via the British embassy in Washington. In 1952, the Hungarian government expropriated the property from Scitovsky and thenceforth the rent for the house was paid direct to the government but, with its agreement, a separate sum continued to be paid to

12.2. Drawing of the front elevation of the villa, built in 1926, at 42 Lorántffy Zsuzsanna Utca in Budapest for which the Ministry of Works part-exchanged the site of the destroyed former legation house on Verboczy Utca.

Scitovsky for the use of his furniture. Ten years later, Scitovsky discovered that the lower part of the garden, which comprised a separate plot called 38 Lorántffy Zsuzsanna Utca, had not been nationalised because it had no house on it, and was still in his own name. By then, the exchange of the ruined pre-war Verboczy Utca site for the Scitovsky villa had been agreed in principle and valuers were trying to decide the cash balance payable by the British government to acquire the freehold of Villa Scitovsky. In early 1965, the Ministry of Works paid about £65,000 to the Hungarian government for the house, and about £25,000 in dollars to Scitovsky and his mother Hanna (the actual owner) for their furniture and the part of the garden that they owned.

For offices in Budapest, the returning mission leased the former Hazai Bank building at 6 Harmincad Utca, in Pest, for 15 years from December 1947, from the First National Savings Bank Corporation of Budapest. The Hazai Bank commissioned the architect Károly Rainer in 1911 to design this building as its new headquarters. It is a five-storey block, plus basement and mezzanine, on an almost square plan with about 30-metre sides. The banking hall is almost central on the ground floor and rises through the mezzanine to a glass roof. The upper floors are therefore on a hollow square plan. The structure is a riveted steel frame, standing on the ferro-concrete bank vaults and supporting a ferro-concrete top floor, which originally housed the bank's filing department. Rainer revelled in getting every detail of the bank's planning correct and operationally up to date, and in introducing a range of charming flourishes. The building was completed in 1914. Hazai Bank occupied it with only minor alterations for the next 30 years. In early 1945, many citizens had taken shelter in its vaults during the Russian siege of Budapest, including bank employees, their families, and Jews under Raoul Wallenberg's Swedish protection. The building was damaged in the course of the fighting and parts of it caught fire on three occasions. Soviet troops reached it on 18 January and those sheltering in the building were able to leave. The bank never recovered from being systematically looted by the Soviets early in February, and was taken over by the First National Savings Bank Corporation, which leased the building to the British mission. It remains the embassy offices: the banking hall, for long occupied to great effect by the British Council, is an especially fine space.

The building that the Warsaw embassy left behind when it evacuated the city in September 1939 was a palace at 18/20 Nowy Swiat, leased from Count Branicki. Because Branicki had served notice that the lease would not be renewed beyond 1942, the Office of Works had just before the war bought from Counts Stefan Tarnowski and Benedict Tyszkiewicz a new site of 4,605 square meters on aleja Na Skarpie on which to build a new embassy. The Branicki palace was completely destroyed by fire during the Warsaw Uprising of autumn 1944. When the embassy returned after the war, it took temporary quarters on the first floor of the Hotel Polonia, at 39 aleja Jerozolimskie, until leasing in 1945 permanent office accommodation in the fine nineteenth-century palace at 1 aleja Róz. The first post-war residence was a modest leased suburban house at 10 ulitsa Narbutta. By the mid-1950s, a larger and better residence was required.

The Polish government in October 1945 expropriated the site that Britain had bought just before the war at aleja Na Skarpie so as to enlarge the adjoining public park. In 1960, it honourably settled this debt by granting a site of exactly the same area of 4,605 square meters at 5 ulitsa Bagatela rent-free for 80 years, with an option to extend for a further 20 years. A new residence, with an innovative plan, was designed in-house for this site by the Ministry of Works, advised by a succession of local architects. The Ministry's superintending architect, William Bryant, recorded a meeting he had with the head of the Polish State Building Organisation, CEKOP, who

12.3. The entrance front of the residence that the Ministry of Works completed in Warsaw in 1964. It had an innovative plan, designed in-house by John Kaye, and was the only new British diplomatic building to be constructed behind the Iron Curtain between 1950 and 1990.

had 'mentioned three [contracting] firms but recommended Enterprise for Industrial Construction No 1. He confirmed that it would be a waste of time to ask for competitive tenders as everything depended on the firm appointed to have the necessary suitable staff available at the time we wish to start building'.[5] Treasury approval was granted in March 1962 for £155,000 and construction proceeded: the final cost was £208,000. The ambassador, George Clutton, moved in during July 1964 **(Figs 12.3 & 12.4)**.

The relative success of this first diplomatic construction venture behind the Iron Curtain encouraged thoughts in London that the overcrowded and run-down offices at aleje Róz could be re-provided in a new building on a new site. The site selected, of about one hectare, was at the corner of Szwolezerow and Mysliewicka streets, in parkland not far from the city centre and in the right diplomatic area. Norman Isham, a senior architect in the Ministry of Works, designed a scheme of offices, four detached family houses, fourteen town houses, four flats and a large amenity centre, and gained planning consent for it in November 1971. On that strength, a 99-year lease of the site was agreed in 1972 at a fixed rent of about $20,000 per

12.4. Looking across the dining room into the main reception room on the first floor of the new Warsaw residence in 1964. A folding partition divided the two.

annum and the design developed in detail. Progress was, however, halted in 1975 by an absurd demand by the Polish authorities for an immediate lump sum payment in lieu of rents due over the entire term of the 99-year lease: it took four years of argument for the authorities to revoke this demand. The project went to tender in 1981 and prices, reflecting incipient political instability, came back impossibly high at over £15 million. The imposition of martial law in December 1981 put an end to the project and the site was given up a few years later.

Belgrade and Bonn
Yugoslavia, although not behind the Iron Curtain, had a property market with many Soviet characteristics. By 1950, the legation house built in Belgrade by the Office of Works in 1928, was thoroughly overcrowded with both residence and chancery. The adjacent site was therefore bought, for about £25,000, from the Serbian government, which had expropriated it for this purpose from its two owners. The Ministry of Works' intention was to build new offices on this site and return the original building to residence use alone. By 1953, however, this intention had been replaced by a preference for building a new residence in a more agreeable part of the city and converting the original building to offices alone. During President Tito's visit to Britain in 1953 the Foreign Secretary, Sir Anthony Eden, explained this accommodation dilemma in Belgrade and the Yugoslav

government responded during the following year with the offer of a site for a new residence. It comprised about 1.2 hectares at 1 Branca Djonovica and was accepted in 1955. R.P. Mills, a senior architect at the Ministry of Works, produced a serviceable but undistinguished outline design which was developed by the private architectural firm of Tripe and Wakeham. The residence was completed at a cost of about £180,000, and the ambassador took up occupation in 1959.

Bonn was a child of the Cold War. Although only a town, it became the capital of the Federal Republic of Germany in 1949 when West Germany was constituted from the three zones that had, since 1945, been under Allied occupation. At the same time, the role of British military governor changed to British high commissioner. The first high commissioners had their offices in Wahnerheide, an ex-Luftwaffe base and airfield, 16 kilometres north-east of Bonn. By 1950, this was too far out for efficient administration and for transacting business 'by calling the Germans to our presence'. The British mission urgently needed office and residence buildings into which to move so as to be able to vacate Wahnerheide. A freehold site of about 9,000 square meters was therefore bought in 1952 at 77 Friedrich Ebert Allee from Frau Gertrud Linden for £11,500. Offices, to austere standards, were quickly built here. The austerity was apparently explained by the construction costs being met direct by the Treasury, rather than chargeable to the Occupation Costs Budget, and a German desire for the building not to be so smart as to be unaffordable for commercial tenants after the diplomats had moved back to a re-established capital at Berlin.

The new offices, designed in-house by R.P. Mills in the Ministry of Works, turned out correspondingly mundane in plan and appearance. They were soon referred to as Britain's most unprepossessing embassy **(Fig. 12.5)**. The building comprised three storeys and a basement on an elongated L-shape plan, each floor with a spine corridor with cellular offices on both sides, and a large free-standing canteen hall nearby. A potential extension was site-planned that would turn the L into a U. The building was completed in late 1953 for approaching £150,000 and was so evidently too small that the extension was straightaway put in hand, with a corresponding enlargement of the canteen hall and completed in 1955, at a cost of a further £75,000.

The first high commissioners lived, while their offices were at Wahnerheide, in the requisitioned Schloss Röttgen, a large and isolated nearby mansion. Its owner was entitled to repossess it in 1953 and a search was accordingly started in 1952 for an alternative residence to lease in Bonn. Nothing suitable was found: Bonn was, after all, still no more than a town. Sir Ivone Kirkpatrick, the high commissioner, then learned that a requisitioned

12.5. The entrance to the embassy offices in Bonn, built quickly and cheaply by the Ministry of Works in two phases in 1952-5. The building served until the embassy's move back to Berlin was completed in 2000.

house at 39 Heisterbachstrasse in Bad Godesburg, a smart district in south Bonn on the west bank of the Rhine, might become available. It had been occupied until recently by the American high commissioner, General McCloy, and might be leasable once its owner, Frau Gertrud Strunck, regained possession. She decided, however, to sell rather than lease but was prepared to give the British government first refusal. The choice for the Ministry of Works was fairly stark: either buy Frau Strunck's house for about £35,000 for immediate occupation or build a new residence in the Bonn area that would cost more and take longer. Nor was there much room for negotiation because other missions and commercial interests were in the hunt for good residences. Given that the house was on the small side for its intended purpose, the Ministry of Works was keen to get the Foreign Office to make a long-term commitment to it. It succeeded only in eliciting the view that it would be unreasonable to seek to replace it within ten years and the observation that there was a vacant plot next door. The Treasury approved purchase of 39 Heisterbachstrasse at £30,000 plus £10,000 for ingoing works.

The house was de-requisitioned on 3 December 1952 and its purchase completed on the same day. It made a satisfactory residence: its small size was alleviated over the years by some re-arrangement and extension, and its lack of a garden was remedied for large occasions by overflowing into part of the adjacent vacant site to the north that belonged to the Diechman family. Nearly 20 years later, the Ministry of Works bought the adjacent site to the south from the Van Gülpen family for £427,000 with a view to building new offices there: it was also keen to build a penthouse residence on top and to sell 39 Heisterbachstrasse but made no headway with that argument. The office project petered out and the Van Gülpen site was disposed of in 1977. Berlin regained its status as the capital of a united Germany in 1990 and by 2000 almost all diplomatic missions had left Bonn and sold their buildings. The Cold War was well and truly over.

Peking

Britain recognised the People's Republic of China in January 1950 but the expected establishment of normal diplomatic relations did not follow, and the British mission that returned to Beijing from Nanking in February 1950 was headed by a chargé d'affaires and not an ambassador. The basis of British occupation of the old Liang compound was also now altered because, by the 1943 treaty that ended extra-territoriality in China, Britain had surrendered all the rights it had acquired to the compound under the 1901 Boxer Protocol and related agreements. Continued British occupation of the compound was clearly on sufferance, given that the treaty required the Chinese government to do no more than 'accord ... a continued right to use for official purposes the land which has been allocated ... on parts of which are located buildings' belonging to the British government. Within a month of the mission's return in 1950, the Chinese demanded to have back the unoccupied military compound and Britain unconditionally acceded. The only practical effect was that new tennis courts had be built in the former civil area. Two years later, the Chinese demanded the return of the recreation ground, used for an athletics field and extensive stabling, and this was likewise surrendered **(Fig. 12.6)**. Later in 1953, the House and Property Control Bureau of the People's Government of the Municipality asked the mission to complete a detailed questionnaire about the buildings on the remaining compound area. The mission politely obliged but jibbed at answering 'such intimate statistics' as details about the sizes of verandas and the material of which windows were made. In 1954, the mission was alerted to a proposal to build a large road across the compound and learned that its Russian embassy neighbour had plans to move which would leave the British as the only mission still in that part of the legation quarter. The embassy was anxious about how long it would be before it was finally evicted and directed to a new diplomatic enclave 2½ miles to the east, outside the city walls.

Another five years was the answer. In January 1959, at the start of the 99th year of British occupation of the compound, a diplomatic note demanded that all of the premises be vacated by 31 May 1959. London quickly realised that Britain did not have a leg to stand on: it had no deeds, had not paid any rent for 50 years, had not registered the property when requested to do so in 1950, and had had plenty of warning. The most that could be salvaged would be the offer of acceptable alternative accommodation and compensation for the buildings in the compound that were erected at British expense over the years. In March, London sent Tom Champkins and C.G. Libby, respectively senior architect and estate surveyor in the Ministry of Works, to report on the temporary alternative accommodation that the Chinese, in the shape of the Diplomatic Service Agency, were offering. For offices and residence, these were two recently completed two-storey buildings on adjacent 1½ acre sites, at 11 and 15 Kuang Hua Lu, Chien Kuo Men Wai, opposite the Albanian and Finnish missions. The Chinese were prepared to undertake the necessary ingoing works. Much later, it transpired that these buildings were designed by a Chinese architect who had been trained in Liverpool on a British Council scholarship.[6] For staff accommodation, Champkins and Libby were shown sufficient flats nearby, in newly constructed blocks of three to eight storeys, designed and built by the Chinese. The flats were more or less acceptable as temporary occupation.

Once Champkins and Libby reported that the terms of the Chinese offer of alternative accommodation were broadly acceptable, it became a scramble to complete the ingoings at the new buildings, arrange the actual move and clear out of the old compound, all before the end of May. Concurrently, too, the Chinese authorities were requisitioning the summer retreat at Peitaiho. Much of the burden fell on Richard Scott, the Ministry of Works' resident engineer in Peking. The end-May date slipped a few months, with Chinese agreement, but the new chancery was occupied on 8 September and the old compound vacated on 28 September 1959. Scott's diary recorded about that day:

> I handed over the British Compound to the Chinese Government at 10am. The Flag was hauled down by Wang (my head furniture coolie) and handed to me. I shook hands with Kuo at 11.15. FINISH. ...
> That day will always stay in my memory. No British Foreign Office staff were present. Everything was left entirely to me. I felt as though I were the only Englishman in China.

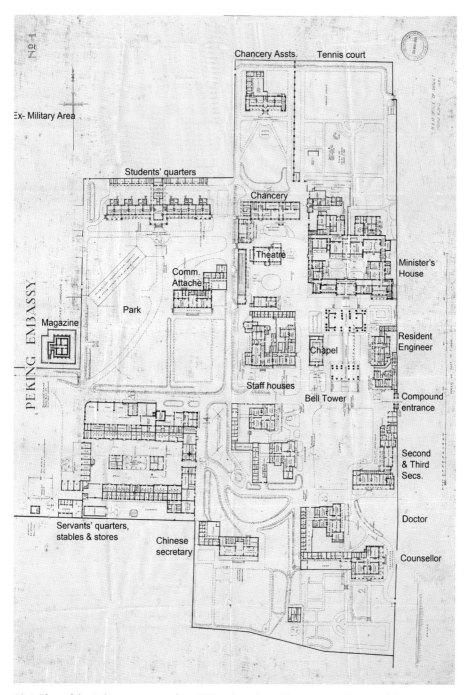

Labels on plan:

No 1

Ex- Military Area

Chancery Assts. Tennis court

Students' quarters

Chancery

Theatre

Comm. Attaché

Park

Magazine

PEKING EMBASSY

Minister's House

Resident Engineer

Chapel

Staff houses

Bell Tower

Compound entrance

Second & Third Secs.

Servants' quarters, stables & stores

Chinese secretary

Doctor

Counsellor

12.6. Plan of the Peking compound in 1951, when the military area and most of the recreation ground had just been given up (though the Magazine is still shown) and the compound's days were numbered.

I managed to re-furnish one room of my wonderful old house. My wife sent our cook and bearer with coffee and biscuits. I entertained some ten Chinese officials to a farewell ceremony before the closure. I was repeatedly asked why our Minister was not present. I made lots of impromptu and probably very feeble excuses. I was made to feel bitterly ashamed.[7]

The British government claimed £550,000 compensation based on the equivalent reinstatement of the buildings that it had lost on the old compound and the Chinese indicated as early as November 1959 their readiness to pay £250,000 based on their own assessment **(Fig. 12.7)**. The British, however, also wanted to link the compensation issue with an agreement on a future permanent site in Peking. Champkins and Libby had asked the Chinese to identify a site of about 12 acres. With the diplomatic enclave set out in blocks of two or three acres, the Chinese were shocked by the size of the apparent British requirement. They countered by demanding a comparable new site in London. The British saw the hopelessness of their case and accepted Chinese payment in local currency of £250,000 in mid-1961. That same year the Chinese government bought 31 Portland Place as its embassy building in London.

The Cultural Revolution in China began in 1966 but Britain did

12.7. The students' quarters in the Peking compound. This long narrow building was erected soon after the Boxer rebellion of 1900, on the seized site of the former Imperial Carriage Park as a westward extension of the original compound. The building housed twelve students, each with bed- and sitting-rooms, on two floors.

12.8. The building in a Peking diplomatic area into which the offices moved in 1959 upon surrender of the Liang compound. It was extensively damaged by rioters during the Cultural Revolution in 1967 and lay empty until the Chinese government undertook its restoration in 1971-2.

not come in for hostile attention until the following summer, when the mission office was broken into and a portrait of H.M. The Queen damaged. Disputes, mainly connected with the political situation in Hong Kong, escalated during August 1967 and an ultimatum was due to expire in the late evening of 22 August. Staff went to the office that day prepared for a siege, and were noisily harangued all afternoon. The crowds outside grew as the evening wore on, and the 23 British staff realised they would probably be there all night and began burning classified papers. Fifteen minutes after the ultimatum expired, a furious attack began, and the staff retreated into an inner sanctum. But even this proved unsafe, and some staff eventually pushed their way out of the building, being manhandled and assaulted as they went. The building was set alight and, in the middle of the night, the remaining staff were rescued by police and army and taken to safety. The building was a burnt-out shell by morning, and the residence was looted and empty. The police, however, had prevented the attackers from getting close to the apartment blocks.

After a spell of operating out of a flat, the mission office re-opened on the first floor of the residence. For three years the office building stood black, scarred and empty. The Cultural Revolution was strangled by Mao at the end of the 1960s and bilateral relations improved. In 1971, the Chinese government said that it would pay for repairing the office building and this work was completed the following year, when the residence reverted to the sole use of the head of mission **(Fig. 12.8)**. Full diplomatic relations were also resumed in 1972, and 22 years of a mission headed by a chargé d'affaires came to an end.

13

New Commonwealth 1947-1983

Background

While diplomatic accommodation languished in those parts of the world most affected by the Cold War, it burgeoned elsewhere with the emergence from colonisation of new independent countries. Of the almost-hundred countries that became independent in the 40 years between the end of the Second World War and 1985, about half were previously British colonies, protectorates, trust territories or other variation of dependency. Most of them were small islands, but the vast majority of the population was in the Indian sub-continent, central Africa and Malaysia. With the exceptions of Burma, Sudan and Somalia, all of the former British colonies joined the Commonwealth of Nations, so that almost all of the new British diplomatic representations in these countries were high commissions rather than embassies. The new accommodation required, ideally to be up and running by the time of each Independence Day, placed a huge project workload on the Ministry of Works in identifying, procuring and preparing suitable offices, residences and staff accommodation.

The first of the Independence Days was in 1947, when, 'at the stroke of the midnight hour' between 14 and 15 August, Pakistan was divided from India, both became independent, and both joined the Commonwealth. In the same year, in London, the Dominions Office combined with the India Office to form the Commonwealth Relations Office which, as decolonisation progressed, absorbed what was left of the Colonial Office in 1966 to become the Commonwealth Office. These Offices were therefore the Ministry of Works' client departments in respect of all the accommodation required for the new high commissions. The Foreign Office remained the client department in respect of accommodation required in any new country that was formerly the colony of another Power: for example, of upgrading the consulate-general's accommodation to legation and then embassy status at Saigon, in France's former colony of Vietnam. The Commonwealth Relations Office was inevitably less practised than the Foreign Office in getting its way on accommodation matters, and the Ministry of Works tended to accord it a slightly lower priority for attention.

It might have been expected that the British-built infrastructure of its dependencies would yield suitable accommodation for the incipient British high commissions. Most colonial governments, however, needed all their buildings for their successor national governments and were reticent about offering any of them up for Britain's use. Colonial governors were uncomfortable about Britain seeking a colony's help with such elementary house-keeping as procuring premises for a high commission, and were alive to the obvious presentational difficulty if Britain took over any building with too imperial an association. The simplest accommodation solution for a new high commission, though rarely available, was for a suitable War Office property to be transferred to the Ministry of Works rather than handed over to the new government: this applied, for example, in Banjul and Freetown in West Africa, and Kingston in Jamaica. Traditional British trading firms were also a source of land or buildings for sale or lease, particularly if they were anxious to offload some of their assets before independence. Sometimes, British officials already serving in colonial capitals, for example in Trade Commission or British Information Services offices, were able from their local knowledge to point the Ministry of Works towards promising accommodation possibilities.

Indian Sub-Continent
The independence of India required accommodating the future high commission in New Delhi and deputy high commissions in the three former Presidency cities of Calcutta, Bombay and Madras. The creation of Pakistan, an awkward marriage of two separate Muslim territories, required a high commission in Karachi, the capital of West Pakistan, and a deputy high commission in Dacca, the capital of East Pakistan. The Partition of India also entailed in 1948 the independence of Ceylon, requiring a high commission in Colombo, and of Burma (outside the Commonwealth) requiring an embassy in Rangoon. The need in the sub-continent was therefore for four

capital and four subsidiary Posts. The Ministry of Works did not treat these requirements, as it might have done, as a self-contained programme of works but as a set of discrete requirements, each of which had to find its place, and hold its priority, in the overall overseas programme.

In early 1946, the British government tasked W.D. Croft, an India Office official serving in the Office of the Cabinet Delegation in the Viceroy's House in New Delhi, with making recommendations for the provision of accommodation for the future high commission. Croft reported that all accommodation was exceedingly tight, most houses were already shared, and many senior people and their wives were living in hostels. He concluded that there was no alternative to dealing direct with the Government of India, which had requisitioned a great deal of property during the war. The Viceroy, Viscount Mountbatten, though keen to see the high commissioner installed as soon as possible, was not prepared to countenance pressure being put on any of the Indian princes for a de-requisitioned mansion.

For a residence for the future high commissioner, Croft proposed no. 2 King George Avenue, a well-sited but unexceptional two-storey official bungalow on a central circus with a large and fine garden. It had formerly been occupied by Sir G.S. Bajpai, secretary-general of the ministry of external affairs, and was now being shared by several senior Government of India officials. Croft thought 'this house is quite good enough to start with, and … it would be a very difficult matter to get anything else'.[1] For offices, Croft recommended no. 6 Albuquerque Road, a large new house, without any 'aggressive errors of taste', which had been requisitioned from the Khan of Badreshi as soon as he had built it and was being used as an army hostel for officers and their wives. Croft thought a three-year lease term would be negotiable provided that the house and the hutments in its garden were used intensively enough by the high commission not to create disparity with prevailing local practice. Despite the Commonwealth Relations Office's dismay that 2 King George Avenue was not prestigious enough, London quickly authorised negotiations to pursue both of Croft's proposals.

Croft had identified various works that would be necessary at the residence, including enlarging the drawing room, improving the staircase, and rearranging the bedrooms and bathrooms. Henry Medd, chief architect to the Government of India and formerly a long-serving member of Lutyens' office in Delhi, and Alexander Scott, the surviving partner in Sir Herbert Baker's firm, were both on hand to give advice. Adaptation work by the Public Works Department, estimated at about £6,600, started promptly and was optimistically intended to be completed in November 1946. The scope of work expanded, however, notably after the involvement of the

13.1. The garden front of the high commissioner's residence in New Delhi. Designed as a senior staff bungalow, probably in the office of Robert Tor Russell, chief architect to the Government of India, and built in the 1920s on the Viceregal estate, laid out by Lutyens.

first high commissioner, Terence Shone, who arrived in early November, and the work dragged on until the Shones finally took up occupation in April 1947. Richard Turner, the Ministry of Works' senior architect at Cairo, visited during this period to assess a looming 250 per cent overspend. He recommended, successfully, that the Ministry of Works should establish an office in New Delhi to bring better order to projects in the future. Arguments about responsibility for the residence overspend and whether stamp duty was payable on the lease transaction continued for years and delayed until 1954 signature of the ten-year lease that came into effect in 1946. The residence, however, proved a good long-term choice **(Fig. 13.1)**.

In contrast to the delays at the residence, the offices at 6 Albuquerque Road were operational in September 1946 and included a flat for the deputy high commissioner. But staff numbers in New Delhi, especially of junior and unmarried staff, shot up and 6 Albuquerque Road was soon overwhelmed. Two additional clusters of buildings were acquired, even though the market was scant and expensive. One was Eastern House on Mansingh Road, comprising five blocks that had been built by the Ministry of Information in 1944 and transferred to the Government of India in 1945 at a time, strangely, when no further British government use for them was envisaged. Eastern House was therefore leased for the high commission in 1947 to house the trade commission and information service offices, as well as flats for about 40 junior staff and a sick bay. The other cluster was at 16 and 17 Parliament Street. No.16, called Wenger's Flats, comprised 40 flats just suitable for higher and middle grade staff, and a perpetual lease on the block was bought in 1949 from the Sterling General Insurance Co. Ltd. No.17 was a large adjacent house suitable for communal messing, and was bought in 1949 from Sardarni Harnam Kaur. Unsurprisingly, none of these arrangements was popular with the British occupants but they had to suffice for the next ten years while a large new compound was being planned and built.

The Government of India first proposed in 1946 designating and developing a diplomatic colony, or enclave, for the permanent accommodation of diplomatic missions. By 1950, a large area at Chanakyapuri, just south of Government House (the former Viceroy's House), had been selected. Sites would be available to missions on perpetual leasehold terms with annual ground rent payable, and the Government of India would build all the infrastructure. General Sir Archibald Nye, who had succeeded Shone as high commissioner in 1948, argued to the Commonwealth Relations Office that, distasteful – even repugnant – as such an enclave would be for all diplomats and expensive for all governments, there was in practice no alternative to 'putting in our stake while we may'.[2] His arguments were accepted in London. In consequence, a site of just over 24 acres was acquired, with a capital premium payable of £156,650 plus a nominal annual ground rent, on which to develop offices for 115 UK-based and 200 locally engaged staff, and residential accommodation for the UK staff and their domestic servants. The address of the site was (and remains) Plot 3, Block 50C, Chanakyapuri, New Delhi.

The Indians proceeded rapidly with the infrastructure. Nye pressed for 16 junior flats to be ready by the end of 1952 but the Ministry of Works architects pointed out that some idea of a master plan was a pre-requisite to siting any such block. The Commonwealth Relations Office was only lukewarm in support: it 'sympathise[d] with the wishes of the Architects to do things properly by planning the site first. We should prefer it that way ourselves, other things being equal, but the time factor is a decisive objection'.[3] The Ministry of Works, unprepared to delegate the design work to its New Delhi office or to a local architect in India, and too stretched in London to undertake it, decided to employ an 'outside' or nominated architect. The choice fell on Herbert Rowse, who accepted the commission

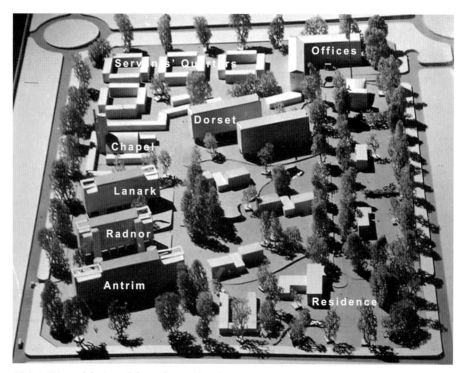

13.2. 1953 model, viewed from the north, of proposed development on the 24-acre compound at New Delhi. The residence was not built and nor was one of the two centre blocks. The other, Dorset, housed bed-sits for junior single staff and was demolished in the 1980s. A small hospital was built instead of the chapel.

at the end of February 1951. He was the architect of the Philharmonic Concert Hall in Liverpool and the British pavilion at the Empire Exhibition in Glasgow in 1938, besides much else. Rowse arrived in Delhi with his assistant, Donald Bradshaw, in early April but fell seriously ill with typhoid in early May, was in hospital for six weeks, and was back in England in mid-June with little accomplished. Expenditure cuts that autumn put the project into further delay, which led the high commission into turning part of the site into a cricket pitch and gave the Ministry of Works the opportunity to terminate Rowse's commission and undertake the work, when re-started, itself.

R.P. Mills, the Ministry of Works architect of the offices in Bonn and elsewhere, produced an overall compound plan and designs for the first few buildings, for which a model was ready by September 1953 **(Fig. 13.2)**. By and large, this was the scheme that came to be built. A north-south avenue connected the offices at one end with the residence at the other. Three houses for the most senior staff lay along the west side of the avenue and all the other staff accommodation, amenities and domestic staff quarters were relatively evenly spread out across the rest of the site to the east. This scheme, however, was criticised for both the layout and the small size of the flats, and numerous arguments were in train when Edward Muir, deputy secretary at the Ministry of Works, visited Delhi in November 1954 with Turner, by then assistant chief architect: 'We found that they were in a state of very great apprehension as a result of looking with an uninformed eye at the plans and layout which had been sent to them. ... Basically, the High Commissioner's [now Sir Alexander Clutterbuck] objection is to the whole concept of building a housing estate for the staff '.[4] Some of the apparently small arguments were evidently tips of cultural icebergs: the minutes, for example, of a meeting chaired by Muir during his visit recorded that

> The women present urged that single officers, even though provided with facilities for communal dining, should have somewhere where they could make tea or coffee and simple snacks. This was particularly important for women. The M[inistry] o[f] W[orks] representatives pointed out that this arrangement tended to result in uncleanliness. It was agreed, however, that this point should be sympathetically considered.[5]

There were no UK contractors working in India, nor Indian contractors who could be sufficiently relied upon, so the Ministry of Works opted to build the compound with a large directly employed labour force under its own supervision and to accept full financial responsibility. In early 1955, the final scheme was presented to Ministers, who professed to like it, and to the Royal Fine Art Commission, which was lukewarm but could be politely ignored. It judged that

> The layout of this scheme [is] unsatisfactory, both in siting of buildings and in landscaping, and it was not clear whether the site had been thoroughly surveyed [in respect of tree positions]. The architectural treatment was accepted, subject to improvement in detail.[6]

The compound was built in three phases. The first phase, 1955-7, included the boundary wall, roads and services infrastructure with plant house, 54 flats for middle and junior grade UK staff in three five-storey blocks, and sick bay, community centre, swimming pool and servants' quarters. The second phase, 1958-60, included all the offices, workshops and garages **(Fig. 13.3)**. The third phase, 1960-2, included the fourth block of flats and six houses for senior staff. The compound was to have included the residence but the renewal of the lease on 2 King George Drive in 1960, after skilful

13.3. The high commission offices at New Delhi, with hexagonal library in a reflecting pool. The Prime Minister, Harold Macmillan, laid the foundation stone in 1958, saying that the building would not be 'unworthy of the great mark which other great British architects have left in Delhi'.

lobbying by the high commissioner, Malcolm MacDonald, enabled the site at the compound earmarked for a new residence to be left as open space. Full occupation of the compound was achieved in 1962, 15 years after independence **(Fig. 13.4)**. Nos 16 and 17 Parliament Street were sold, and Eastern House handed back to the Indians.

The deputy high commissions in Calcutta, Bombay and Madras were all more easily and quickly suited. In each city, the offices were leased by the floor in commercial buildings, and in Calcutta the residence was also leased. In Bombay, the house that belonged to Muhammad Ali Jinnah, newly installed

13.4. The new compound at New Delhi at the time of its occupation in 1962.

as Prime Minister of Pakistan, was requisitioned by the Indian government and, respecting Jinnah's wish that it be let to a British tenant, was leased in 1948 to the Ministry of Works as the deputy high commissioner's residence. Jinnah's house, at 2 Mount Pleasant Road in Malabar Hill in South Bombay, was designed by the Bombay architect Claude Batley and lavishly built to Jinnah's own specifications in 1936 **(Fig. 13.5)**. It was too large for the deputy high commissioner alone and other UK staff were also housed in it until 1982, when the lease was given up. In Madras, Cottingley, in Nunqambakkam, an inner suburb, was leased in 1947 for seven years as the residence of the deputy high commissioner to southern India. A handsome two-storey bungalow built about 1912, Cottingley proved so satisfactory that the lease was renegotiated in 1949 to run until 1963. It was bought by the Ministry of Works in 1962, and remains the residence.

In Karachi, capital of West Pakistan, all the UK staff had to live in hotels and hostels for the first few years after 1947. A 15-acre compound at Clifton, called the Port Trust Estate, was bought in 1950. It had three good houses on it: Runnymede, formerly the chairman's house, became the residence; York Place, formerly the chief engineer's house, was converted into offices;

13.5. The circular terrace in the centre of the garden front of Jinnah's exceptional 1930's house, designed by Claude Batley, on Malabar Hill in Bombay. The building was unoccupied for many years after the lease to the British deputy high commission was given up in 1982.

13.6. The new high commissioner's residence at Colombo in the mid-1950s. The intention that it should be a trailblazer was never fulfilled. It is nowadays swathed in greenery and shaded by nearby planting,

and Acton House, formerly the traffic manager's, housed the senior trade commissioner. The intention was quickly to build a large hostel on some of the spare land. A meeting agreed that

> as the first stage, 20 single quarters of a sub-standard construction [defined as having only a twenty-year life] each combining one room and a bathroom, together with essential services and roads, should be provided to accommodate the staff now housed in hotels ... Feeding would be on a communal basis for both single and married staff, and separate messing accommodation would be provided.[7]

Several more stages were planned for later, but no development started on site before the Pakistan government's decision in the late 1950s to move the capital from Karachi to Islamabad in the north. Planning blight then befell the Karachi compound until the 1980s. In Dacca, capital of East Pakistan, all accommodation for the deputy high commission was leased until well after the country broke away from Pakistan in 1971 and became Bangladesh: Dacca was re-spelled Dhaka in 1982.

In Colombo, the Ceylon government was in 1948 persuaded to lease one of its scarce official houses, Four Furlongs, to the high commission as the residence, on condition that the British government would build a suitable new residence quickly. To its dismay and inconvenience, it had to wait six years for the return of Four Furlongs. The house that the Ministry of Works took so long to design and build was, in several ways, a first in the British diplomatic estate. It was conceived in 1950 as the prototype of residences for the East. It would be partially air-conditioned but the extent and cost of doing so, and the implications for the layout of the house, took time to thrash out. It was the first building that the Ministry built with directly employed labour, instead of employing a contractor, so as to keep capital costs down and ensure a reasonable standard of construction and finishes. And it was also one of the first of the Ministry's buildings overseas to be furnished in the so-called contemporary style, which also took time to agree. The resulting residence was occupied in 1954, and named Westminster House: it remains in use **(Figs 13.6 & 13.7)**.

Rangoon was the Post at which accommodation was most quickly and satisfactorily resolved because British commercial firms found themselves with more property assets than they needed for the uncertain times ahead and were glad to sell some of them to the British government. The Ministry of Works was able to buy a sound office block at 80 Strand Road, the main

13.7. The entrance hall of the Colombo residence in the mid-1950s. Its interior was intended as a showcase of British furniture design.

street, in 1948 and a green seven-acre compound with five large houses, called the Irrawaddy compound, in 1949. The vendors were, respectively, Graham Properties Company Ltd and Irrawaddy Flotilla Company Ltd, both of Glasgow **(Figs 13.8 & 13.9)**. Both properties remain in the estate, although they are unnecessarily substantial for today's dismal level of diplomacy with Burma.

Undivided India claims

The Partition of India produced a significant property conundrum. The Indian Political Service had for long mainly staffed, and the Government of India had chiefly funded, diplomatic and consular Posts in Nepal, Afghanistan, Persia and the Arab littoral of the Persian Gulf. Who now owned the property assets that used to belong to Undivided India, as the former British-ruled India was called in this context? Under international law, India clearly had the largest claim but Pakistan had an evident claim as a former part of Undivided India and Britain, too, had a claim as having, since at least 1900, paid a 'moiety', as it was always called, of the capital and running costs of these Posts. Britain had seen this conundrum approaching. On the day after Partition, the British high commissioner gave the secretary-general of

13.8. 80 Strand Road, Rangoon, bought in 1948 for embassy offices. Formerly known as Graham's Building, after the vendors, it was designed by J.G. Robinson and G.W. Mundy and built early in the twentieth century.

13.9. Belmont, the largest of the five houses on the Irrawaddy compound which was bought in Rangoon in 1949, became the ambassador's residence. Two other houses, Belwood and Belstone, became senior staff houses, and Belfield the Ladies Mess.

the Indian ministry of external affairs, Sir G.S. Bajpai, an *aide-mémoire* which began:

> His Majesty's Government in the United Kingdom are anxious to purchase certain of the diplomatic and consular buildings at places where there has hitherto been joint British and Indian representation by officers of the Indian Political Service, and where those buildings are partly or wholly the property of the Government of India as formerly constituted. The manner in which the buildings in question have been allocated between the successor Governments is not yet known, but His Majesty's Government believe that it may assist to a solution satisfactory to all parties if, as a basis for negotiation, their wishes are set out in one comprehensive statement.[8]

The statement proposed that, at Kathmandu, the 50 or so acres of the legation should be divided into two so as to give the British government the 'European-style residential buildings', and the remainder to India. At Kabul, it proposed that the British government should acquire all the legation buildings. In Persia, the British government wanted to acquire the whole of the consulate-general at Meshed but would sell portions back if India and/or Pakistan wished; it wanted to buy the Naidi property in Bushire, the consulate in Shiraz, and was prepared to retain the lease on Khorramshahr; but it had no interest in any of the other Persian consulates. The British government wanted to buy the political agency buildings at Bahrain, Kuwait and Muscat. The statement also proposed that purchases and transfers should be at agreed valuations on the basis of cost price, less depreciation, adjusted according to which party had contributed to the original costs of land purchase and constructions, and to subsequent upkeep.

The theory was clear: each of the three governments would declare what it wanted, properties would be valued and financial records consulted, negotiations would take place, and a master suspense account would record the financial balances of how much each government owed each other at the end of the exercise. That it did not work out at all like that was because the British government's assumption that it could deal direct with India and leave India to deal with Pakistan proved false. The British government therefore took 'palliative action … by a series of interim measures non-prejudicial to a final settlement', such as selling consulate properties in Persia that no government wanted and crediting the proceeds to a joint suspense account held by the embassy in Tehran. Legal advisers were called in to interpret arcane legal niceties. Both the Indian and British governments sent representatives to value the immovable and movable property in Persia and the Gulf, including buildings, furniture, office equipment, vehicles and boats: only property that was definitely to be sold escaped valuation. The whole exercise became submerged in its own bureaucracy, down to recording, for example, five padlocks at Bahrain, valued at 15 rupees, of which Britain's share was seven-eighths.[9]

A joint Indian and Pakistani *aide-mémoire* in 1963 revealed that they had settled some of their differences. It proposed that Kathmandu should stand as resolved between Britain and India in 1951, that Kabul and Meshed should go to Pakistan, the three Gulf Arab littoral Posts to India, and Britain should buy the other two governments out of Shiraz. Monies held in the joint Tehran suspense account should go in due course to India and Pakistan in the ratio of 82.5 per cent and 17.5 per cent. By this time, fifteen years after Partition, there was hardly anyone in London familiar with the saga and it took several years to research the issues and update the figures. In 1968, the British government approved a brief for the British side to use in an intended tripartite round of negotiations, and sent an *aide-mémoire* to the Indians and Pakistanis to the effect that it wanted to retain Bahrain, Kuwait and Muscat and would settle financially any rival claims to them.

The negotiations never took place. But by the early-1970s, the Indian and Pakistani governments had, in effect, reached their own accommodation with each other. Britain's case had been assisted in this respect by Arab sheikhs making it known that they would require properties to be returned to them rather than transferred by Britain to India or Pakistan. By the early-1970s, too, it was beginning for the first time to suit the Foreign Office to have a resolution because the Ministry of Works was unprepared to build on the Kuwait compound unless title to it was totally secure. In the event, the whole issue petered out and the suspense account was (presumably) at some point distributed. President Bhutto of Pakistan temporarily revived the issue when he asked the British Prime Minister, James Callaghan, in 1976 for the return both of the buildings that Pakistan still sought and of the Koh-I-Noor diamond.[10] He got nowhere with either. Pakistan, however, had the last laugh. The Foreign Office, imagining in the mid-1990s that it would have no further use for the compound in Kabul, handed it free of charge to Pakistan. When it sought to buy it back ten years later, the Pakistanis demanded an unrealistic price.

Africa
Sixteen British dependencies became independent in Sub-Saharan Africa in the twelve years from 1956, when Sudan became independent, to 1968, when Swaziland did so. Accommodation was therefore required at sixteen new capital Posts and for the three deputy high commissions in Nigeria's Eastern, Western and Northern Regions at, respectively, Enugu, Ibadan and Kaduna. Offices in the larger capital Posts were leased, in more or less adequate commercial buildings, many of them owned by British banks, until purpose-built new offices could be provided for them. The only Posts for which purpose-built offices were ready for occupation in time for, or very soon after, an Independence Day were the three last and smallest – in the former South Africa High Commission Territories at Gaborone in Botswana, Maseru in Lesotho and Mbabane in Swaziland during 1966-8. Kampala was the most fortunate larger Post because Uganda became independent in 1962 and the high commission moved into its new building the following year. At Dar es Salaam, the high commission moved into the leased top floors of the brand-new First Permanent Building Society building, later called Hifadhi House, in 1961. Lusaka and Lagos moved into new purpose-built buildings in the 1970s, Accra and Khartoum in the 1980s, and Nairobi in 1996. In smaller Posts, offices were more quickly converted from owned or leased houses.

Suitable residences to lease or buy were often problematic. The Ministry of Works therefore built new ones, to be ready as soon as achievable after the date of independence, at Accra in 1959, Khartoum and Lagos in 1961,

Freetown in 1965 and at the three small South African Posts concurrently with their offices in 1966-8. Suitable residences, or residences which could be adapted or extended to become suitable, were bought in Dar es Salaam in 1961, Nairobi in 1963, and Lusaka in 1966; and leased in Kampala in 1962, Blantyre in 1964, Banjul in 1965 and Mogadishu in 1968. Some of these were comfortable houses owned by the families of well-to-do expatriate traders or settlers. In some cases, like Dar es Salaam, the house was acquired in the expectation of being only a stopgap until a permanent residence could be built, at which time it would revert to the deputy high commissioner. In no cases did that actually happen: the stopgaps proved good enough, or extensible enough, to become permanent.

A considerable number of smaller houses was bought, and a few built, for senior members of UK staff: otherwise, leasing was the norm. The problem that was encountered more in Africa than elsewhere was the scarcity of safe and healthy living accommodation for young and junior, often single, UK staff. The Ministry of Works therefore fairly quickly developed designs for small and simple housing blocks of two to four storeys containing four to eight flats: these were built at Lagos, Accra and Freetown and were reasonably successful, not least because most were sited in conjunction with the amenity facilities.

Nigeria, with 40 per cent of the population of all the colonial territories that remained within the purview of the Colonial Office in 1952, presented the most complex accommodation problems in Africa. As early as 1956, four years before independence, the United Kingdom Trade Commissioner in Lagos wrote to Geoffrey Wilby, estate surveyor in the Ministry of Works:

> having seen the completely ridiculous position we were in in India, without accommodation for lack of somebody trying to plan a year or two ahead and the discomfort my colleagues and I suffered through living for long periods in hotel bedrooms, I am trying in the interests of my colleagues in the Board of Trade and you to help with some policy for the future.[11]

A senior Ministry of Works team, led by Richard Turner, assistant chief architect, visited Nigeria in August 1957 to consider possible sites for high commission offices and a residence in Lagos, and for deputy high commission premises in Enugu, Ibadan and Kaduna. The team's brief from the Treasury instructed it 'to enquire most carefully into the possibility of the Nigerian Government making houses available for H.M.G.'s use after Independence'.[12] The team looked at numerous possibilities, including such deals as swapping houses that were owned by the British government at the Tropical Testing Establishment in Port Harcourt for houses in Lagos. The colonial government turned down the team's suggestion that the chief secretary's house would make an excellent residence in Lagos for future high commissioners but later offered to release a comparable house and to present it as a gift. This offer was gradually reformulated, as successive houses were turned down as unsuitable, into the colonial government offering the combined sites of nos.6, 7 and 8 Marina Street, in Araromi. Here, the British government could demolish the three buildings and design its own residence, which the Public Works Department would build: the offer also included a £40,000 contribution to the building costs.

This was a hugely generous offer: Marina Street was the finest road in the city, and the site lay between it and the edge of the wide channel through which ocean-going vessels slid by on their way to Lagos port. No.6 was Flagstaff House, occupied by the general commanding the Nigerian military forces, and Nos.7 and 8 were occupied respectively by the directors of prisons and of inland waterways. The combined site of 1.36 hectares was large enough to accommodate an offices building as well, though it was intended to build only the residence before independence. The offer was accepted in 1958 and the new residence, designed by Lionel Brett, was completed in January 1961, just three months after independence.

13.10. Carcosa, built by Frank Swettenham in Kuala Lumpur in 1897. It was given to Britain by the Malaysian government in 1957 and was the high commissioner's residence until 1986, when it was exchanged for a new offices site in the centre of the city. It is now a boutique hotel.

Elsewhere

The Federation of Malaya, comprising the nine Malay States and the settlements of Malacca and Penang, gained independence and joined the Commonwealth in 1957. In 1963, Malaysia was created from the combination of the Federation, Singapore and Sabah and Sarawak. Singapore left Malaysia in 1965 and became independent on its own. Establishing high commissions in Kuala Lumpur and Singapore posed few difficulties because there had been strong British presences since the 1820s, and there were still British military bases. Offices were easily leased in both cities, and were replaced by new buildings in Singapore in 1973 and in Kuala Lumpur in 1989.

For the high commissioner's residence in Kuala Lumpur, the Malayans presented Britain with the best of all the (not very many) buildings that former dependencies gave Britain: the house called Carcosa **(Fig. 13.10)**. Frank Swettenham, who had played an important part in the creation of the original federation of four central Malay States which had accepted British protection, was appointed in 1896 the first resident-general of these States, to reside at Kuala Lumpur. For his official residence he selected a site on a hilltop in Damansara where, with A.C. Norman, the government architect, and C.E. Spooner, the Selangor state engineer, he built a splendid house in which he lived until the end of his appointment in 1901. Of the

13.11. Eden Hall, in Singapore, was built in 1904 by Ezekiel Manasseh on part of the large former Lady Hill estate. It was bought by the Ministry of Works in 1955 and later became the high commissioner's residence.

many speculated reasons for calling it Carcosa, a contraction of *cara casa*, 'dear house', is the least tortuous.

For the next 40 years, Carcosa was the official residence of the most senior British representative in Selangor. The Japanese occupied it during the Second World War as a senior army officers' mess, and the British military did likewise for a year afterwards. When civil government was re-introduced in 1946, chief secretaries took up occupation. In 1956, a year before independence, the chief minister of Malaya, Tunku Abdul Rahman, moved a resolution in the Federal Legislative Council to make a free gift of Carcosa to Britain as a token of goodwill. Although the resolution was passed unanimously, there was subsequent disquiet that the Rulers' Conference had not been consulted, and the Peninsular Malays Union opposed the gift. Nevertheless, the first British high commissioner, Geofroy Tory, moved into Carcosa in September 1957 and it served as an exceedingly accomplished residence for the next 25 years. Some senior Malays disliked its being on a higher hilltop than the Prime Minister's house and the Treasury disliked its size and the spaciousness of its grounds. When briefing the Ministry of Works on Lagos in 1958, it wrote 'You should not accept sites and houses which are uneconomic to maintain: the proposals should be re-examined with especial reference to the size of gardens: we do not want another Carcosa'.[13] It was returned to the Malaysian government in 1986 as part of an elaborate estate rationalisation exercise in Kuala Lumpur and replaced by a purpose-built new residence of more modern demeanour.

The Singapore residence, Eden Hall, was only slightly less agreeable than Carcosa and likewise had a strong history **(Fig. 13.11)**. It was bought freehold in 1955 for £55,000 as the residence of the Commissioner-General, then Britain's senior representative in Singapore: it subsequently devolved to the high commissioner. The vendor in 1955, Vivian Culienen Bath, insisted that a plaque should be installed at the foot of the flagpole with the inscription 'May the Union Jack fly here forever'. The sentiment echoed his stepfather who, in calling his house Eden Hall after Longfellow's *The Luck of Edenhall*, likened it to the goblet upon which the fate of the family depended.

14

Roles, Rules and Rations 1950-1970

Inside the Ministry of Works

The section of the Ministry of Works responsible for Public Building Overseas Services, which included staff working on diplomatic and consular buildings, was thoroughly over-stretched by the end of the 1940s, by which time the number of embassies, legations and high commissions had reached about 75. The Foreign Office was frustrated that its accommodation priorities were receiving less attention and money than it felt was their due. The Foreign Secretary, Ernest Bevin, wrote to the Chancellor of the Exchequer, Sir Stafford Cripps, in July 1949 'to ensure that in 1950/51 there is provided a sum necessary to make very real and appreciable advance and to achieve the first phase of a planned programme towards the completion of all our schemes throughout the world'.[1] Bevin amplified the scale of his thinking to the Minister of Works, Charles Key, emphasising that Foreign Office staffs overseas 'should be given the best conditions possible. This applies of course not only to the actual buildings, but also to the amenities appropriate to each locality, such as air-conditioning, cold storage, heating and so on'. Besides wanting the Ministry to provide fully-furnished accommodation for all staff overseas, Bevin wanted the plans for all building projects in the programme to be advanced so that each could proceed as soon as the funding for it looked possible rather than 'only then bringing the plans forward to the starting stage'. He pointed out that, of the 19 projects for which some funding had been allocated in that year, only six had actually begun work on site. These were as varied as new offices in Canton and Swatow, the conversion to offices of the Pereire house in Paris and of an apartment block bought under construction in Tel Aviv, the residence in Rio, and staff accommodation in Bahrain. Bevin told Key that 'both our staffs [should] keep their eyes fixed with determination on the object to be achieved, meeting all difficulties on the way simply as something to be got over'.[2]

Key, while welcoming Bevin's pressure on the Chancellor for more money, reminded him of the realities of life within the Ministry of Works. 'In the past we have provided accommodation for certain staff in compounds in Oriental countries and there are several schemes in being for the erection of staff quarters but we are a long way from accepting responsibility for providing fully furnished staff quarters all over the world'.[3] The reason that his Ministry was spending less than was allocated was that it was insufficiently resourced to accelerate, and certainly could not bring forward unfunded projects without delaying funded ones. It was subsequently agreed that points that 'merited careful investigation' included using more local architects, giving the Ministry's regional offices wider financial authority, and permitting Posts to purchase locally more of the furniture and equipment that they needed rather than wait six months for it to be supplied from the UK. The Foreign Office afterwards suggested that having its own qualified surveyor would relieve some of the pressure on the Ministry. Suspecting that it harboured ideas of setting up its own works organisation, the Minister of Works, by then the impulsive Richard Stokes, stamped firmly on this idea in 1950. He conceded, however, that his staff needed strengthening and wondered whether the Ministry's regional offices were really necessary for minor work.

> I should have thought that now that Embassies are becoming more and more useless, because everything has to be referred to Whitehall before any decision is taken, compared with the old days when Ambassadors really did take responsibility, this kind of maintenance job ought to devolve, except on major issues, on the Embassy staffs themselves. We might have to keep travelling inspectors and advisers but I cannot believe that would amount to over £200,000 a year.[4]

Travel restrictions being enforced by the Treasury put paid to this devolutionary idea. Meanwhile, the Ministry's architectural staff feared that their in-house monopoly of design work, as championed by the director-general of works, Charles Mole, might be coming under attack because de Normann, the deputy secretary, had suggested that an eminent Italian architect might be asked to design the new embassy for Rome. De Normann had in mind both 'the constant difficulties encountered in finding sufficient staff in this country to man adequately the Public Buildings Overseas Services with architectural staff, and … the fact that Italy alone amongst foreign countries might be regarded as having an architectural tradition greater than that of this country'.[5] The in-house professional staff, suspicious of this emollient, complained to the chief architect, Arthur Rutter. He minuted his senior colleagues:

> I have been made aware of a feeling of apprehension on the part of the staff
> … . It may be that [appointing a foreign architect] is the proper policy to
> pursue. It may be that in our present condition it would be difficult for us
> to undertake the work, but I do think that a clear statement of the reasons
> for the adoption of such a policy are very necessary unless the apprehension
> is to grow into discontent. … [Public Buildings Overseas] is a service into
> which we have in the past and should in the future draft men of first-class
> architectural attainment, but we shall fail to achieve any result likely to cause
> satisfaction to ourselves or to the [diplomatic] Service … if whenever a
> scheme of any importance is to be considered we proceed to entrust it to a
> foreign architect.[6]

Rutter's views epitomised the insularity of the in-house system. Like most building professionals in the Ministry, he had joined as an assistant or draughtsman, after some school training, and learned almost everything on the job. He had worked his way up a system in which few professionals entered or left mid-career, and in which there was little lateral movement, even within the Ministry. In this cocoon, insulated from external influences and ideas, in-house sections with assured workloads became complacent and even arrogant. Innovation was problematic, interference resented, and the need disdained to engage with the professional world outside. The Ministry hardly exposed its professional work to informed criticism and therefore was unable to measure its success realistically. Upon completion of an embassy building, it did no more throughout the 1950s and 1960s than issue an anodyne press release, drafted by an administrator from professionals' notes, which would be largely ignored.

On the other hand, the Ministry's in-house architects were thoroughly familiar with their client's requirements and operating systems, they produced a wide range of buildings which functioned as intended and lasted well, and they were deeply loyal to the Ministry. In the nature of the civil service, they had wider administrative and financial duties than most architects, so the design and supervision of their buildings was a smaller part of their jobs than it would be in the private sector, with the result that they deputed more to their assistants and draughtsmen.

The chief architect was credited with all the architectural work produced by the Ministry, and the rest of the team went unmentioned. Architects did not initial their drawings and they failed to preserve their sketch designs and most of their files, so it is impossible today fully to work out who actually designed what. The architects harboured deep suspicions about, in that uniquely parochial phrase, 'outside' architects, also referred to as consultant, private, independent, nominated or external architects. The more elevated private practices in London were occasionally referred to as 'Harley Street architects', a throwback to the 'art architects' of a century earlier and a precursor of the 'trophy architects' of half a century later. Ministers and senior officials were mostly ardent supporters of in-house working, not least because they were fed a steady diet of in-house advice, which included vivid reminders of the private sector's failings. The Ministry of Works' resolute insistence on doing practically everything in-house was undoubtedly one of the main reasons why it was never able to match the achievements of Britain's other major public architectural and construction bodies, and especially of the London County Council.

Eric Bedford succeeded Rutter as chief architect of the Ministry of Works in 1950, at the young age of 41. He had joined the Office of Works in his mid-twenties in 1936, having shown early promise by winning the Royal Institute of British Architects' Grissell Gold Medal in 1934 for the design of a railway terminal. His early years as chief architect were quite successful, notably his work on the 1953 Coronation decorations, for which the tubular steel arches in The Mall and the pavilion at the west end of Westminster Abbey were much commended, especially by Her Majesty The Queen. But Bedford slowly reverted to in-house type and never became a forward-looking force within the Ministry. His blunt and sometimes arrogant manner, combined with great shyness and dislike of speaking in public, did him no favours with his senior colleagues who clearly found his self-esteem irksome. Although Bedford was renowned for wielding a red pencil over his staff's work, none of these amended drawings seems to have survived. Bedford remained as chief architect until 1967, when the role was abolished and he became director of special architectural services in what was by then the Ministry of Public Building and Works for the last three years before his retirement.

R.H.M. Thompson, parliamentary secretary at the Ministry in 1962, was unusual in voicing scepticism about in-house working. In supporting a

Ministry drive for publicity and recruitment, he minuted that he had been

> steadily plugging the theme that here in the Ministry of Works we have the
> finest team of architects and engineers anywhere in the country, that we are
> building for the future, and that we are innovators and experimenters not
> afraid to utilise new techniques, new designs and new materials. If this is to
> be generally accepted and believed, which it deserves to be, it is important …
> that our professional officers play their full part in the extra-mural activities
> of their profession … . It is difficult to maintain that we are as good as we
> are unless the associated professions are familiar with the work, the articles,
> and the papers produced by our people.[7]

Bedford was typically defensive, pointing out that

> his division had a more restrictive contact with the profession as the emphasis
> in the Department's architectural work lay in teamwork. As the professional
> standing of the Department's architects depended, and at present thrived, on
> the quality of their work, he did not feel that increased personal publicity
> through professional associations and press was necessary.[8]

Specialist and professional staff had almost always been answerable to
generalist administrative staff in the Office of Works. After the Second
World War, when activities grew rapidly in extent and complexity, a more
formalised system was introduced to ensure uniformity of outlook, intention
and procedure. This system involved brigading each works group, in this
case Public Buildings Overseas Services, with a secretariat of civil service
administrative and executive officers, in this case Assistant Secretariat 15, or
AS15 for short. The two groups were headed respectively by an assistant
chief architect and an assistant secretary, each with a hierarchy of staff whose
members mainly liaised with the level-pegging member of the other group.
The secretariat's job was to brief and regulate the professionals and to screen
them from contact with the other involved government departments,
mainly the Foreign Office and the Treasury, by conducting most, if not all,
of the works group's correspondence and related conversations. The assistant
secretary was, almost by definition, an A-stream administrator with a good
mind, varied experiences and plenty of confidence. He was assisted by an
A-stream principal of like characteristics, and by executive officers, with
less sharp minds, fair shares of common sense and high tolerance of detail.
An assistant principal, a grade exclusively for a high-flyer in training, was
generally attached to AS15 because the role, with its overseas angle, was one
of the more probable in the Ministry to offer him or her useful experience

for the future. The likelihood was that few, if any, of the staff in the secretariat, apart from the assistant secretary and the principal, had ever been overseas, let alone visited an embassy.

Working through a secretariat was, as intended, a stifling system for the architects. They had no option but to put up with it but some did not hesitate to speak their own minds when opportunity arose. De Normann, the Ministry's deputy secretary and a generalist administrator *par excellence*, forlornly minuted AS15 in February 1953, after attending a discussion about Cairo with the Foreign Office, 'Once again I was struck by the fact that the Foreign Office always seem to be in a position to quote our own architects against the Department. ... Our architects have no business to give the Foreign Office advice at all. It should always be given to A.S.15'.[9] Antony Part, who became permanent secretary in 1963, recalled that on arrival he

> was appalled by the attitude of the Ministry of Works administrators towards the architects and their professional staff. These were regarded as a lower form of life: indeed, in much earlier years the architect concerned was not allowed to accompany an administrator to Buckingham Palace to advise on work there as he was not considered to be a gentleman.[10]

Although secretariat staff knew the Whitehall ropes better than architects and engineers, and certainly wrote better letters, the internal briefing and questioning processes took up inordinate amounts of time. The arrangements often brought out the worst in both sides and obstructed pursuit of the best solutions: the opposite of team-working. The architects, over-sensitive to being cross-questioned, tended to mount their high horses: the secretariat people, unable to make qualitative judgements, interested themselves in rules and figures. Of all the professions, the architects had the closest and most tedious contact with secretariat: their professional engineering and quantity surveying colleagues, with whom they kept up semi-cooperative and slightly bantering relationships, got off more lightly.

At the start of a project, which the secretariat generally and disconcertingly referred to as a 'case', the secretariat was responsible for agreeing the schedule of requirements, i.e. the accommodation to be provided, with the Foreign Office, which in turn agreed it with the Post. This schedule alone sufficed as the brief for an in-house architect because the background and objectives of the project were already well understood by him. For offices, schedules were drawn up by enumerating the roles and grades of staff and apportioning to them the *per capita* areas allowed for each grade. The main problem was that nobody could be sure what the future number and grade profile of staff at a Post would be, so that months could pass while AS15 sought unachievable certainty instead of accepting best informed guesses and planning for flexibility. Richard Turner, assistant chief architect, explained the problem to under-secretary Ken Newis in February 1960:

> I am convinced: (a) that our present approach is much too inflexible, (b) that we are forced to take far too much notice of the opinions of staff in post (and who will certainly not be there when the office is built), (c) that by approaching the problem from a much more practical viewpoint we could, in agreement with both the client and the Treasury, settle the majority of briefs within a matter of weeks and not years, as at present. Time and time again we are presented with allegedly urgent schemes and then ultimately we seem to be held up because the Post is strengthened by the addition of a clerical officer, a typist or the like.[11]

This prompted the principal in secretariat, Peter Jenkins, into trying out what he described as

> an experiment in the case of the new offices at Madrid. ... Once the requirement has been agreed with the Treasury an architect goes out to Madrid and discusses the requirement with the Post on the spot so as to get the full flavour of any special needs the particular Post may have. Once this has been done the Ministry ... then go ahead and erect the building without further reference to the Post. The only other references which are made would be to expert Sections such as the Telephone people or the Security people in London.[12]

It was absurd to suggest that any Post, the future user of the building, could be excluded from the process, and to suppose that a Post had nothing to offer in the way of local advice. Jenkins' idea was withdrawn. The secretariat's incomplete grasp of the architect's role was likewise revealed in a 1960 procedural note which included 'on the receipt of Treasury approval in principle AS15 instructs the Architects to proceed to sketch plan stage within the figures approved by the Treasury. ... If necessary an Architect should visit the Post [i.e. for the first time] and discuss the design of the building in the light of local circumstances'. The Fulton Report on the Civil Service, published in 1968, concluded that professionals and specialists in government departments were not given due responsibility or authority, and it strove for better integration of professional and administrative skills. The laborious dual hierarchy system was dismantled soon afterwards.

Space standards
As the office-building programme grew after the Second World War, both at home and overseas, it became necessary to codify space standards for

301

buildings so as to be able to specify requirements, keep costs under control and treat staff equitably. A Treasury report of 1944, published in 1947, called *Working Conditions in the Civil Service* showed the way. The introduction of standards, however, precipitated a flood of rules, procedures, manuals, scales, forms, entitlements, allowances, tolerances and guidelines. Secretariats took so readily to the formulation and application of standards, in themselves an important way of rationing resources, that considerations of flexibility and proportionality were forced to the margin, whence they could only be retrieved by seniority and perseverance.

The first space standards for government offices, expressed as square feet per head according to grade, were brought into effect for new buildings in the UK in 1955. The Foreign Office afterwards wrote to the Ministry of Works to say that the new standards were too small for diplomats overseas.

> [W]e are firmly of the opinion that, to do their job properly, it would be unreasonable to expect officers overseas who have representational duties to carry these out in offices of the size given to their counterparts in London – or even slightly larger than these offices. It is our conviction, based on many years of serving in foreign capitals (how pompous that sounds!) ['and is!' – a reader pencilled in the margin] that an officer is at a distinct disadvantage in dealing with his visitors (be they locals, visitors from the United Kingdom or his *chers collègues*) if he is put into a pokey office – and United Kingdom standards do result in pokey offices. It is not enough if the equipment supplied to him – desks, bookshelves, carpets etc – is on a scale superior to that issued to his counterparts in London; it is also the matter of sheer space, and the atmosphere of dignity that this automatically gives, which really counts.[13]

The Foreign Office got its way in 1961, when a superior scale for office sizes overseas was agreed. It ranged from, at the top, a Grade 1 ambassador having an office of 550 square feet through, in the middle, a first secretary having 200 square feet and, at the bottom, a typist having 60 square feet, with 40 square feet for each additional typist in the same room. Greater flexibility was granted to commercial sections of missions, because it was held that they most needed to impress their visitors, and an architectural design tolerance of 5 per cent was permitted for the whole building. More strategically, the ratio of usable office (net) area to total (gross) area – i.e. including circulation areas, service spaces and so on – was not to be less than 70 per cent. This high figure was not always achievable. When the Lord Privy Seal, Edward Heath, heard about this ratio in March 1961, he argued for doing battle with the Treasury because he looked with favour on new buildings he had seen in Germany, with large halls and plenty of marble. The

Minister of Works, John Hope, thought Heath had a point but he himself 'had no desire to see the Department burst into Teutonic vulgarity'.[14]

Space standards for residential accommodation overseas were naturally more contentious than for offices. Heads' of mission residences were particularly difficult because interest in them was so senior and so acute, and there was no analogue among senior public officials at home with such large-scale entertaining responsibilities: top Services brass, for example, entertained in their messes rather than their houses. The first area prescriptions after the Second World War for new residences (which no longer included space for chancery) were derived from the expected maxima of cocktail guests (allowing about 10 square feet each) and formal dinner guests. For senior ambassadors, the allowance was for 250 cocktail guests and 30 formal dinner guests. The number of diners was, in practice, the key number that determined the size of a residence because the maximum number of guests who could be seated at a long straight table at a formal dinner in a rectangular dining room effectively determined the size of the other reception rooms and many other aspects of the whole residence. Some ambassadors related their own dignity and popularity to the formal dining capacity of their residences, so the longer the table the better. When an architect suggested to the war-time ambassador at Rio de Janeiro that a U-shaped dining table for the new residence would be a more efficient use of space, Sir Noel Charles riposted that the idea 'smacks too much of a Chamber of Commerce celebration'.[15] Under pressure from the Treasury during the 1960s, new ways of setting space guidelines for senior staff were painfully agreed and haltingly introduced. By 1968, the gross area of a new residence for a grade 1 ambassador was set at 14,640 square feet.

Space standards for staff residential accommodation were easier than for residences because they were less entertainment-led and there were plenty of analogues in the Services' married officer quarter scales. Early post-War prescriptions were based on cocktail and dinner guest numbers down to second secretary level, the lowest of the so-called representational (i.e. officially entertaining) grades, at which the numbers were 80 and 8 respectively. Junior staff, also called non-representational staff, were to have a lounge, a dining room to seat six (the two might be combined), one to three bedrooms depending on family size and one bathroom. These prescriptions were gradually codified and revised, such that by 1970 the standards were 2,800 square feet for counsellors, 1,650 square feet for second secretaries, 1,200 square feet for married non-representational staff and 550 square feet for singles, all with a variation of plus or minus 10 pr cent 'on account of job requirements or the particular circumstances of the Post'.

There was an obvious need for some system of space standards for staff residential accommodation: even under rent allowance systems by which staff were free to find and rent their own accommodation, space standards were necessary to enable the allowances to be set. They were, nevertheless, always and inevitably a prickly subject: they were intended as norms – neither maxima nor minima, and certainly not entitlements. But their administration became a time-consuming nightmare because they were too inflexible a tool to apply to the myriad of different circumstances. The space standards related mainly to the grade of occupant, and insufficiently to family size and circumstances. They were applied inflexibly all over the world, and made no distinction between city centres and outer suburb locations. They were developed for application to the design of new buildings but they came to be applied to property that was for purchase or lease, for which purposes their room sizes were too specific, especially for parts of the world that built their accommodation differently from the British and gave proportionately more space to reception rooms and less to bedrooms. A range of permissible flexibilities came into use, especially when rent ceilings were introduced as a complementary means of control, but they failed to damp down many of the arguments. Space standards did, however, achieve one sort of equilibrium: peripatetic diplomats found them inadequate; home civil servants serving at Posts and used to the size of their own homes found them broadly acceptable; and most visitors and observers found them unnecessarily generous.

Air-conditioning
After floor-space, air-conditioning was the commodity which had the greatest and most expensive impact on diplomatic accommodation overseas. It therefore required the full standards and rationing treatment. It was invented in America in 1902 by Willis Carrier, who later spearheaded its development through the Carrier Corporation. The installation of air-conditioning boomed after the Second World War in urban office and residential buildings in developed cities with hot summers. The first air-conditioning units in the diplomatic estate were installed by the military during the Second World War in the legations at Jedda and Baghdad. As wartime facilities closed down, the Gulf political officers benefited from the transfer of the surplus air-conditioning units. Soon, requests for air-conditioning units were arriving from all over the world, most deservedly for windowless cipher rooms with heat-producing equipment in the tropics.

The Treasury chaired a meeting in November 1949 to assess the necessity of air-conditioning and establish a policy for its provision. The problem was to measure intolerability when so many factors affected it, like temperature, humidity, seasonal duration, day and night variation and exposure to breezes, quite apart from the differences between human beings. The meeting proposed that lists be drawn up of category A Posts, where full air-conditioning would be provided in new buildings, and category B Posts, where partial air-conditioning would be considered on receipt of inspectors' and medical reports. Air-conditioning would not necessarily be provided immediately in existing buildings, even in category A Posts. The Ministry of Works pointed out, with reference to the design work that it was doing on the new residence for Colombo, that the capital cost of providing air-conditioning in a new building was largely offset by its enabling smaller rooms with lower ceiling heights, but running costs, of course, were much higher.

The Ministry's first measure of intolerability was to consider each case on its merits in the light of the Post's monthly position above or below a curve that it attributed to a Dr Brunt. It abandoned this methodology in the mid-1960s in favour of the US Weather Bureau's Temperature and Humidity Index, THI, also known as the Discomfort Index. Scores were drawn up and Posts placed accordingly in four categories. At category I Posts, scoring over 75 points, offices, living and dining rooms and permanently occupied bedrooms would qualify for air-conditioning (and the bedrooms of visiting schoolchildren would also qualify if the score exceeded 100). Aden had the highest THI score of 198 but Karachi at 122 was a more typical example of a category I Post. At category II Posts, Tel Aviv for example, offices and permanently occupied bedrooms would qualify; in category III, only offices; and in category IV, less than 25 points, there would be no entitlement to air-conditioning except in rooms, excluding kitchens, that contained heat-producing equipment.

The Ministry rationed out an annual bulk financial provision to what it assessed as the most deserving cases, but Treasury agreement was required in almost every instance. For new buildings, there were various options: to air-condition fully, partially, install trunking so as to air-condition later, or provide units in selected rooms only. Decisions could take months, if not years, of argument with secretariat and the Treasury and played havoc with project programmes. There were, however, some valuable trade-offs besides the cost savings that lower ceilings and smaller areas afforded new buildings. The largest trade-off was that summer residences became unnecessary and were either phased out or compromises struck. At Tehran, for example, the Ministry agreed to continue maintaining the summer residence at Gulhak in the cooler foothills in return for not air-conditioning the Ferdowsi residence in the centre of the city. The Treasury was said to have authorised a new launch to be kept at Tarabya in the 1950s under a gentleman's agreement whereby ambassadors in Ankara would not press for more than a cottage as their summer residence on the Bosphorus.

The THI categorisation sufficed, more or less, until 1980. By then, in many cities, commercial offices and well-to-do homes were all air-conditioned. Posts needed to offer the same level of comfort in order to tempt Americans and Japanese, in particular, to come to work or to dinner. More flexibility had been introduced to cope with Posts with just a few horrendously hot months that were otherwise in a low-ish category: after all, it was pointed out, central heating was based on the coldest months. And, with dropping numbers of domestic staff and more diplomats' spouses spending more time in kitchens, air-conditioning was authorised for some kitchens for use during the preparation of food but not – the approval optimistically made clear – while the ovens were on.

Fridges, freezers and domestic equipment
Panama City was the first legation house to be equipped with a mechanical refrigerator upon its completion in 1926, Santiago the first embassy in 1929, and Ottawa the first high commission in 1930: all these were supplied form the United States. The Office of Works agreed in 1930 to supply mechanical refrigerators to consular Posts in the Far East provided that the consul paid 7.5 per cent per annum of the capital outlay, and for all the costs of running the machine. The demand for refrigerators in residences, where they could greatly ease the logistics of entertaining, did not take long to gather force. The Office of Works tried to prioritise and ration according to the funds available but there were other problems: unless maintenance was scrupulously carried out gas fridges sometimes caught fire when the flue was dirty, and water-cooled fridges required a clean water supply. Requests for second fridges were not far behind. William Leitch, in the Ministry of Works, wrote in 1935 to Sir Harry Batterbee, in the Dominions Office, that the high commissioner in Pretoria, Sir William Clark, was asking for a second refrigerator, about which

> our general policy ... is to supply machines that should meet the normal needs of the household ... [not] on the basis of maximum demand ... we do not supply refrigerators for the cooling of bottles or drinks; this we expect to be done by means of ice blocks manufactured in the refrigerator or bought for the purpose. We said at the time [of supplying Clark's previous Post, Ottawa, with a second fridge] that the case of Ottawa was unique, and was not to be brought up against us elsewhere, and we cannot agree to treat Pretoria in the same exceptional manner ... and I hope that you have no

intention of asking us to treat High Commissioners more favourably than we treat Ministers.[16]

The Treasury decided against adjusting the 7.5 per cent annual charge in August 1939, vainly 'hoping that this official supply won't spread to temperate countries even if the blandishments of Mr Therm [the character in a current advertising campaign to sell more gas] do succeed in popularising their widespread use here'. The arguments about supply trickled on through the war. A frustrated Office of Works engineer, tucked away in Rhyl, who administered the supply of all mechanical and electrical items, recorded in 1941 that he had 'received a reply ... from which it appears that the present is not a suitable time to consider standardisation of refrigerators'.[17] The Shanghai office kept meticulous track, as always, of what machines of which type and capacity were in use where, because charging for them depended on accurate records. De Normann's 1944 Advisory Committee foresaw that refrigerators would soon be required at temperate Posts. When their provision and running costs in due course became a charge to public funds, Richard Turner, then senior architect in Cairo, worried that fridges were being used 'as room coolers, servants sitting by the open doors'. In 1956, Robert Marshall, the principal in AS15, wishing to slow down the Foreign Office's impatience to supply all staff with fridges, pleaded that only four of his fifteen staff had one at home.

Scales of entitlement were, naturally, introduced in 1960. For each grade of staff, there were differently specified permitted cubic footages of refrigerator space for temperate and tropical climes. The tropical standard for a Grade 1 ambassador was 20 cubic feet and for a single junior officer, 8 cu.ft. The Treasury twice refused to increase this scale during the 1970s but relented in 1980, when the cubic footage nearly doubled for most staff in tropical zones, which meant supplying them with two refrigerators each. The whole bureaucratic rigmarole was gone through again with freezers a few years later. Tel Aviv got the first freezer in May 1952 because it was recognised that it had to import so many of its basic foodstuffs. Meanwhile the ambassador in Jedda was storing his food in the freezer of his American colleague. Ministry of Works engineers turned down a request for a freezer at Canton on the grounds that food to be stored must be best quality and perfectly fresh, which he doubted was the case in Canton. Although the appearance of fridges with freezer compartments complicated life for the rule-makers, it was settled that five or six freezers per year would be sent to the most highly prioritised Posts. Marshall minuted 'I am not disposed to increase the rate of supply: we must give this equipment proper trial before we begin to supply in quantity'.[18] The 1960 standards allowed provision of freezers to heads of mission and some other senior staff, and for communal use in certain circumstances. In 1980, it was accepted that, where there was a poor local food supply, a 10 cubic feet freezer would be supplied to all staff.

Somebody asked whether washing machines would be next. They were, followed for residences by cookers, driers, dishwashers, irons, radios, televisions, pianos, fans, smoke-alarms, fire-extinguishers, floor-polishers, light fittings, wardrobe heaters, garbage-disposal units, water-filters and lawn-mowers. The Ministry of Works also supplied domestic equipment to all heads of mission in proportion to the capacity of the residence for entertainment, including glassware, china, cutlery, crockery, linen and kitchen equipment. This marked the end of incumbents needing to use any of their personal furniture and belongings, and hence of the Foreign Office needing to call upon the discretion it enjoyed from the Treasury to allow heads of mission to transport up to 10½ tons of their possessions to Posts (down from the 17 tons that Sir Horace Rumbold had taken to Berlin in 1928). It also marked the beginning of an era when a new head of mission could entertain at full-scale on arrival, without waiting for his heavy baggage. Staff benefited also from many of these dispensations. In the end, nearly everybody was supplied with enough of nearly everything they needed and this form of rationing ceased.

Cost-effectiveness

The purchase, design and construction of new offices and residences had for a century before 1950 been the central themes and activities of the development of the diplomatic estate. As the numbers of Posts and staff grew after the Second World War, and as new tasks were laid upon the Foreign Office and other departments represented overseas, parallel estate programmes of selling, leasing, maintaining and furnishing properties became of much increased importance and occupied a markedly greater proportion of the total available funding, especially during financial crises when capital expenditure was most heavily hit. This evolving programme structure both enabled and encouraged better comparisons to be made, and discrepancies identified, in the effectiveness of various types of expenditure and relating the conclusions to different parts of the world and to future expenditure allocations between programmes.

The Select Committee on Estimates recommended in 1954 that there was a better financial case for buying than leasing property in the United States. The Ministry of Works followed this up with the purchase of houses for the consuls-general at Cleveland, Los Angeles, New York and San

Francisco between 1954 and 1958, and conducted a series of comparable internal exercises in Paris, Washington and Ottawa in the late 1950s. The first formal examination of the question started in 1959 in response to a proposal by the Chancellor of the Exchequer, Derek Heathcoat-Amory, who was concerned by the high costs of renting property overseas. The report of an inter-departmental working party on the Cost of Accommodation Overseas surveyed staff residential accommodation in 20 widely different Posts that together accounted for about 40 per cent of the current total £1.35 million residential rent bill. The study looked at the financial implications of buying or building, to a standard that reflected the best currently rented, for 50 per cent of the UK-based staff complement in each grade, assuming a 5.5 per cent interest rate. It concluded that there was scope for savings of between 30 and 50 per cent on middle grade and junior staff housing in many of the capitals examined, and that small blocks of flats would be a good solution in some cities. The study recommended that a £1.5 million programme of buying and building, spread over five years, would be a worthwhile investment, and should by its end produce annual savings of £160,000 per annum. This sum for investment in 'economic' purchases was to be additional to the normal programme of 'operational need' purchases. The Chancellor approved the report in early 1960, and its implementation funded various of the staff residential acquisitions, whether by purchase or the construction of small blocks of flats, during the first half of the 1960s.

Vienna Convention on Diplomatic Relations, 1961
Although the basic rules regulating diplomatic relations between states had been stable for over 200 years, the 1961 Vienna Convention on Diplomatic Relations, signed on 18 April 1961 and ratified by the UK on 1 September 1964, became the cornerstone of modern international relations. It was drawn up under the United Nations framework for the codification and progressive development of international law, and it now has 187 parties. A strong reason for its success has been the effectiveness of reciprocity as a sanction against non-compliance. The Convention included fundamental rules for diplomatic accommodation. The 'premises of the mission' are the land and buildings used for the purposes of the mission, in effect the offices, and the residence of the head of mission, but not of his staff (Article 1). The receiving state shall facilitate or assist the sending state in obtaining such premises (Article 21). The premises of the mission shall be inviolable, they may not be entered by officers of the receiving state except with the consent of the head of mission, and the receiving state is under a special duty to take reasonable steps to protect the premises of the mission (Article 22).

The sending state and the head of mission shall be exempt from all dues and taxes in respect of the premises of the mission, unless they represent payment for specific services rendered (Article 23): thus, missions are not exempt from that portion of local property tax that relates to such services as refuse collection and street lighting that benefit the mission.

A misunderstanding has lingered that land and buildings occupied by the mission legally constitute a detached part of the sovereign territory of the sending state or, like former concession areas, are extra-territorial. They are neither: they derive their inviolability solely from the terms of the Convention. The mooted compulsory purchase by the receiving state of mission land or buildings for road-widening works provides an example of the kind of conundrum that arises. The sending state can argue that such works infringe the inviolability of its mission's premises but it has to accept that the land it occupies is subject to the laws of the host country. Negotiation, co-operation and compensation provide the only answer.

Ministry of Public Building and Works, 1962, and Plowden Report, 1963
In 1962, the Prime Minister, Harold Macmillan, announced the merger of the Ministry of Works, which had only ever undertaken civil works, with the Works Departments of the three Armed Services to create the Ministry of Public Building and Works (which lasted less than ten years and continues to be referred to here as the Ministry of Works). Geoffrey Rippon was the first Minister and Antony Part the first permanent secretary who together had to make this multiple marriage work. Sir Donald Gibson, who had been the architect to the War Department since 1958, became Director General of Research and Development in the new ministry and, from 1967 when Bedford's chief architect role was abolished, its undisputed professional head as Controller-General. Richard Turner carried on as director of works (overseas) with an expanded remit. Otherwise, the merger impacted little on the teams involved with diplomatic and consular works.

Also in 1962, Macmillan appointed a committee under the chairmanship of Lord Plowden 'To review the purpose, structure and operation of the services responsible for representing the interests of the United Kingdom Government overseas, ... and to make recommendations having regard to changes in political, social and economic circumstances in this country and overseas'. Plowden presented a lucid report, mostly written by Donald Tebbit, the Foreign Office secretary to Plowden's committee (and later a chief clerk), in December 1963. It found no major deficiencies but proposed a wide range of rationalisations and adjustments to increase efficiency. Its ultimate aim was to amalgamate the Foreign Office and the Commonwealth Relations

Office into a single Foreign Office but its recommendations stopped short of that step lest it 'be misinterpreted as implying a loss of interest in the Commonwealth partnership'. Plowden instead recommended keeping the two departments separate but combining their personnel (and that of the trade commission service) into a united diplomatic service, administered by a combined Diplomatic Service Administration Office.

Ten of the 603 paragraphs in the Plowden Report dealt with accommodation overseas. The committee, building on the 1959 findings about the cost-effectiveness of purchasing, recommended that the government should own a far higher proportion of the living and working accommodation that it required overseas, and specifically thought that 'it should be the aim to own at least two-thirds of the residential accommodation required for staff abroad'.[19] It wanted the Ministry of Works to be more flexible in its arrangements for maintaining and furnishing accommodation overseas, though it recognised that much would depend on well-trained and efficient administration officers at Posts.

The Plowden Report was generally accepted and implemented, undisturbed by Harold Wilson's Labour government coming to power in October 1964. Wilson gradually took the steps that Plowden had envisaged: in 1966 he merged the Colonial Office into the Commonwealth Relations Office to create the Commonwealth Office, and in 1968 combined that with the Foreign Office to create the Foreign and Commonwealth Office (henceforth referred to here as the FCO). The new Labour government's Chief Secretary to the Treasury, John (always known as Jack) Diamond, formerly a chartered accountant at the head of his own firm, was convinced that the costs that the government was incurring overseas were too high. In 1966, he set in hand a thorough review of the diplomatic service's post-Plowden standards of accommodation and in September of that year visited the Posts at Accra, Rome, New Delhi, Singapore, Bangkok and Vientiane, accompanied by the Foreign Office's chief inspector and a senior Treasury official. Diamond considered

> that the traditional diplomatic style of entertainment, and the standards of accommodation provided to support it, involve costs out of proportion to the value obtained. I recommend that these should be revised; and that, with the exception of heads of missions and, where appropriate, one or two other officers, entertainment should be put on the basis of justified specific purposes only.
>
> It follows that accommodation standards should no longer allow for the present lavish reception and dining areas and guest-suites; and I recommend that the far more modest standards used by our armed forces abroad should

be taken as a basis.

The extraordinarily high cost of all home-based staff abroad drives home the need to apply the severest standards in considering the value of any function performed.[20]

His more detailed paragraphs and appendices were harder-hitting, and reflected the worsening financial crisis that resulted in the devaluation of sterling in late 1967. Subsequent discussions between departments on accommodation space standards and entertainment allowances dragged on through most of 1967 and 1968 without reaching agreement. Planning work on future residence and staff accommodation schemes ground almost to a halt for want of knowing what size they should be. The slowdown suited Diamond's purpose, and he supplemented it in 1966 by calling halts to the two largest projects then in hand, at Rome and Brasilia. Projects that did proceed were designed and built in accordance with the prevailing semi-official view of the ongoing discussions. Diamond's obduracy eventually forced the Diplomatic Service Administration Office, advised and assisted by the Ministry, to propose in 1968 a more rigorous, and more codified, set of residential area standards. In February 1970, the Treasury, eschewing 'any further discussion of detail', pared these areas down a little more and instructed their adoption for all new accommodation. But, by then, the peak of the requirements for new residential accommodation had passed.

15

In-house Production Line 1950–1970

In-house process

The in-house team of architects in the Public Buildings Overseas Services section of the Ministry of Works designed well over 20 offices and nearly 20 residences between 1950 and 1965, almost all of which were completed before 1970. In addition, it was responsible for other planning and building works all over the world, including a range of staff accommodation blocks, and for innumerable feasibility studies. This was a prodigious output, especially considering the trials of the approvals process and the additional load of using directly employed construction labour in cities where no reliable local contractor was available nor British contractor could be induced to build at affordable cost.

Eric Bedford was the Ministry's chief architect for all but the last three years of this period. Although he was credited ex-officio with many of the buildings, just as he was with the Post Office Tower in London in 1965, the only overseas building designs in which he appears to have been closely involved were the offices in Washington and the residences in Warsaw and Mexico City. Answering to Bedford on overseas buildings was Richard Turner, assistant chief architect and, from 1960, director of overseas works, and William Bryant, the superintending architect who succeeded Turner as assistant chief architect in 1960. For most of the period there were five or six senior architects in the section, each with a small team of architects and assistant architects and access to a large and flourishing drawing office. The senior architects who retired during the 1950s were Douglas Alexander,

Kenneth Judd and Reginald Mills; during the middle of the period the senior architects were John Kaye, Tom Champkins, Charles Kidby, James Truscott and Ralph Adams; and, by the end of the period, Tony Exley, Peter Wheeler, Gordon Hindle and Ron Adams had replaced retiring colleagues.

The design approach to office projects was somewhat mechanistic: the architect dissected the long-debated schedule of requirements and re-assimilated it as cellular offices on either side of a central corridor in a concrete-framed rectangular block. Offices to which the public would have access went on the ground and lower floors, confidential offices and the ambassador's suite above them, and secure offices and registries at the top. By juggling these constituents around, and relating them to the site and permitted maximum building height, the length and height of a block would emerge. There was a need for a few large rooms, like the ambassador's office and a conference room, and these could generally be included without the loss of too many internal columns. Sometimes, one or two small flats with a separate entrance were required for a UK security guard or communications technician and his wife, and these could be made to fit into the office grid quite well. Basements were common for plant rooms and storage.

The block was carefully positioned on the site in relation to boundaries, entrances, orientation and levels. There was always some accommodation, typically a clubroom garages, workshops or local staff quarters, that for one reason or another could not be fitted into the main block. This invariably resulted in a building tail, usually of one floor but sometimes two, that was sited at an angle to the main block and, if long enough, used to enclose, for example, an adjacent service yard.

After the architect had arrived in this way at basic siting and sizing decisions for the block, his scheme went to the drawing office where dimensioned plans and sections were drawn up with a grid, wall thicknesses, and window and door openings: elevations came later, though the draughtsman might produce a block axonometric drawing of the buildings. The intended use of rooms in the confidential areas of offices was never identified on the drawings: rooms were numbered and a key to their uses was kept separately. The scheme was then shown to the in-house structural and mechanical/electrical engineers, and the quantity surveyors, all of whom had close familiarity with the genre. The objective at this stage was to ensure that there were no potential problems that could not be ironed out in the usual manners, like thickening the slabs, enlarging the plant rooms, providing more ducts and reducing the specification. Cost analysis and estimating for overseas buildings were relatively undeveloped arts in the 1950s: the technique generally adopted for an overseas project was to estimate it at UK rates and then add or subtract a percentage to reflect building costs in the relevant city.

The building plans were then handed to the secretariat which sent them to the Foreign Office with such support and questions as it thought relevant, and the Foreign Office sent them to the Post with its own views and questions. There followed a tedious sequence of exchanges about distances between this and that office, changing requirements and mistaken assumptions. Occasionally, schemes were presented to the Post by the architect, and this could stanch the flow of minor points, but travel was at a premium and the secretariat preferred to control the arguments through correspondence. The architects responded to the conclusions of this checking process by making changes to the plans that they liked or could accept, and by arguing to the secretariat why other changes would be impossible, too late or too expensive. Projects often lost momentum that was hard to recover at this stage in an over-subscribed programme. If disagreements could not be resolved at this level, they were escalated to ambassador, permanent secretary or even minister levels in the hope, usually forlorn, that a clear-cut decision might result.

Washington offices, 1951-60
The requirements for a new office building in Washington were laboriously hammered out in London during the early 1950s, once three more pieces of contiguous land had been acquired to form a good large site just to the north of Lutyens' building. Numerous government departments that had fiefdoms dispersed about Washington in rented offices and temporary buildings needed to be consulted about re-housing them in a single new building. Bedford, Bryant and Alexander between them produced a sketch design that was presented to the Royal Fine Art Commission for consideration in October 1954. Customarily, neither the architect nor the client was permitted to attend the commissioners' deliberations, though Bedford sometimes had a discussion with the Technical Committee, which met beforehand. Among the commissioners who first saw the Washington proposal were John Betjeman, Lionel Brett, Frederick Gibberd, William Holford, Geoffrey Jellicoe, Henry Moore and J.M. Richards. The formal minutes of their meeting were blunt: 'The proposed addition of an office block, in a modified Lutyens manner, was considered unsatisfactory. A good contemporary design would be preferable'.[1] Bedford minuted within the Ministry 'At the Technical Sub-Committee I thought I was leading by 4 to 2 in favour of the general approach to the problem... . I do not think we should be dismayed ... since we have at least drawn the fire of the

Commission and that is mainly the point of an early approach'.[2] The Foreign Office was by now asking for even more accommodation and Bedford was anyway forced into some replanning. The Commission saw the scheme for the second time in February 1955 but to no greater effect: the minutes recorded 'A revised design for the office block was considered below the required standard, and the employment of an independent architect should be recommended'.[3] The Commission's chairman, Lord Crawford, wrote to the Minister of Works, Nigel Birch,

> The first design tried to echo the Lutyens building, by repeating certain of its features. We said this was not, in our view, a good idea. A model has now been prepared for a more or less 'modern' alternative, neither better nor worse than hundreds of other buildings, and completely undistinguished. ... We do not think it nearly good enough for so important a purpose and site. ... Should not a real effort be made to produce something really first class? It would need an outside architect to do this: as it was done in the case of Lutyens, do you think it would be possible to do the same today?[4]

The record of Birch's subsequent talk with Crawford included Birch saying that

> he would feel more inclined to consider an outside architect if a British architect with the genius of Lutyens was living today. ... Lord Crawford

15.1. 1955 model of Bedford's Washington office proposals on Massachusetts Avenue, with the Lutyens buildings to the south, and a circular conference hall, later called the rotunda, close to the junction with Observatory Circle. The plan was a large hollow square on four, five and six floors.

said that the Commission had no prejudice of any kind against the MoW's architects doing the work; ... it was simply that ... if this was the best the MoW could do, an outside architect might be approached.[5]

Crawford put it more succinctly in a personal letter to Birch a few days later: 'we thought what was submitted was awful and that those who produced it were not likely to produce anything tolerable'.[6] Around the same time, the ambassador, Sir Roger Makins, wrote to the chief clerk, Roderic Barclay, doubting that the Royal Fine Art Commissioners were the best people to judge sentiment in Washington. Barclay replied that he was 'sorry to say that the Ministry of Works seem to have got themselves into rather a tangle about the whole project. ... In the circumstances we can encourage and exhort but there is a limit beyond which we cannot press them'.[7] By April 1955, the costs had escalated and the architects were instructed to bring them down to below £1.0 million. There was clear scope for pruning, given, for example, that the fiefdoms had ratchetted their storage requirements alone up to about 28,000 square feet, more than 20 per cent of the building's total area. Birch was content in August 1955 for Bedford to submit revised proposals to the Royal Fine Art Commission, which subsequently thought that the 'revised design was considered acceptable in its general lines, but further consideration should be given to the treatment of the roof structures and other points of detail'.[8] The Ministry chose to regard these remarks as the Commission's endorsement and had no further contact with it about the Washington project **(Fig. 15.1)**.

Bedford took the scheme to Washington in April 1956, primarily to show it to the ambassador, who told the Foreign Secretary, Selwyn Lloyd, that the plans 'looked too much like a modern factory to fit well into that part of Washington'.[9] At that time the scheme comprised 122,500 square feet, housed 549 desk users, excluding 'sub-clerical staff such as messengers', and provided 235 car paces, including 20 under cover for official cars, all still within the £1.0 million cap. A year's delay was then imposed on the project for wider financial reasons. In March 1957, the new permanent secretary at the Ministry of Works, Edward Muir, went to Washington to show the scheme to the various semi-official bodies there and to pave the way for construction. Muir thought that the Zoning Commission in Washington had been favourably impressed, but the ambassador, by now Sir Harold Caccia, 'gained the strong impression that none of them wished to go on record as formally agreeing to the scheme'.[10] A couple of days later, Caccia met the National Capital Planning Committee and learned that it would prefer a more residential scale and feel. None of these Washington bodies was sure of its own powers, nobody much liked the scheme, but nobody actually stood in its way. So it slipped through, just, thanks to the deft handling of ambassadors, who did not like it much either but sorely needed it. The local building regulations were changed not long afterwards to eliminate the kind of ambiguities that had let the scheme through. It became apparent later in 1957 that the building would be four feet higher than was now permissible. Bedford therefore moved the roof-top canteen into the basement and the ambassador told the National Capital Planning Committee that the top floor was being removed. The canteen, however, soon had to find its way back to the roof and Bryant instead reduced the floor-to-ceiling heights throughout the building sufficiently to reduce its total height to the new limit.

H.M. The Queen laid a foundation stone during her state visit in 1957, and construction started in 1958 by John McShain, Washington's pre-eminent contractor (and racehorse owner), at a contract figure of $3.3 million with a contract period of 600 consecutive days. Selwyn Lloyd, by then Chancellor of the Exchequer, opened the building in September 1960. It remains in full use, though its appearance has never satisfied anyone, and internally, except for the rotunda, it is rather oppressive and dull **(Fig. 15.2)**.

15.2. Interior of the 62-foot diameter Washington rotunda at night in the 1960s. The single-piece, white satin curtain, with its design in black of Shakespearean characters, was electrically drawn and passed behind the free-standing columns.

On the other hand, it was strongly built, effectively serviced, and has proved operationally fairly efficient.

Offices designed in-house, 1950-70

Washington, though easily the largest, was not the first office scheme to be built after the Second World War: that was Bonn, completed in 1953. Also completed in that year was Canberra, designed by a Sydney firm of architects, E.A. & T.M. Scott, commissioned by Alexander on a visit in 1949. The main purpose of that visit was to select sites for both new offices and residence because the leased office space was too small and the Australian National University wanted Canberra House back. The chosen new office site, of 0.8 hectare, was at Yarralumla Section 43, within the area designated for diplomatic buildings on Commonwealth Avenue, the main roadway between Parliament Hill to the south and the commercial centre to the north. Scott completed here in 1952 a two-storey rectangular block parallel and close to the avenue. Due to the fall of the site, it was three storeys at the rear. Scott allowed for an extension at right angles to the avenue to house the service attachés who were expected eventually to be transferred from Melbourne: this was duly built in 1960.

After Canberra came an in-house three-storey block in Cairo in 1956, with a double-banked centre corridor on each floor. The building was curved in plan in response to the curved site perimeter behind and to avoid the prior demolition of an existing chancery offices building. Curved buildings had been proposed by consultants in two previous planning studies for compounds – at Baghdad by Wilson and Mason in 1947 and Kathmandu by Tripe and Wakeham in 1951 – but Cairo was the only one to be built **(Fig. 15.3)**. Its design progress was delayed for a year by a debate about whether or not it should be air-conditioned: the outcome was that it should be designed and built for the later insertion of air-conditioning plant and trunking. The ambassador at the time, Humphrey Trevelyan, recalled that the building was

> designed soon after the Festival of Britain, with every wall flaunting a different colour and ostentatious reproductions of the royal arms picked out in white on the front of the ambassador's desk, [and] was known locally as 'by South Bank out of Great West Road'. The decorations were reluctantly modified on my protest.[11]

The Suez crisis occurred within months of the building's completion and it lay almost empty for the next few years, after which it proved much too large. Also completed in 1956 were buildings for the political agencies in

15.3. The embassy offices in Cairo. Completed in 1956, soon after a 25-metre strip along the Nile frontage of the compound was surrendered for construction of the Corniche road and shortly before the Suez débâcle caused a four-year breach in diplomatic relations.

Bahrain and Abu Dhabi, both with offices on the ground floor and residence above, both by Bryant and both built with directly employed labour under the supervision of Ministry site staff, with all ordering, supply and cost control functions exercised by Ministry staff in London. This manner of organising construction, pioneered on the Colombo residence, was proving remarkably successful and also economical, partly perhaps as a result of the heavy London management overheads not being included in the costings. It helped greatly that the Ministry's preferred kind of modernism, involving reinforced concrete frames and slabs and blockwork infilling, was so readily achievable in the conditions of then-undeveloped cities teeming with unskilled labour.

Fifteen straight rectangular blocks of various heights, all with central straight corridors serving mainly cellular offices on both sides, were completed during the 1960s, five of the earlier ones with directly employed labour. Although they all shared substantially similar office layouts, their site arrangements were widely different. The structural frame was exposed on most of their exteriors, but cladding and spandrel finishes varied between granite, travertine or available local stone or brick and, if none available, imported vitreous mosaic. The first of the 15 was in the New Delhi compound, a five-storey block by Judd built contemporaneously with Washington: it had a subsidiary wing at right angles to it, and a separate hexagonal library with a covered connection. It is unclear whether the idea for this separate little building derived from or suggested the rotunda at Washington. Two rather similar four-storey offices by Truscott were completed at Saigon and Jakarta in 1962 **(Fig. 15.4)**. The Jakarta building was severely damaged by fire during riots the following year: rebuilding it to the same design, at Indonesian expense and again by directly employed labour, started in 1967 and was completed during 1968.

Ottawa, after Washington and New Delhi the largest new office building with a gross floor area of about 60,000 square feet over nine floors, designed by Bryant, was completed in 1964 on Elgin Street **(Fig. 15.5)**. It housed 220 staff, many of them in the British Pensions and National Insurance Office that served Canadian military veterans. External facings were in various

15.4. Saigon offices, completed in 1962. The site was formerly occupied by the consular residence, completed by the Office of Works in 1932 and destroyed by bombing in 1945.

15.5. Ottawa offices, completed in 1964. The building brought together six sections of the high commission that had been in different leased offices since soon after the war.

polished Canadian granites, and the building was fully air-conditioned and double-glazed. The internal finishes, in the idiom of the day and in the words of the press release, were

> generally simple, with plastered walls in light colourings blending with grey steel furniture, suspended acoustic tile ceilings, and linoleum floors. Natural maple wood has been used for doorframes and windowsills. Walls around the elevators are paneled in attractive melamine laminate, while the entrance-hall walls are faced in polished Blue Pearl granite … The High Commissioner's Office is paneled in Rio rose-wood, from Brazil, and has a teak and ebony floor. Door furniture and other fittings are in silver-bronze; the furniture is of rose-wood, the desk-top of pale-grey leather; the carpet is claret-coloured, the curtains in muted-gold, and the chairs are upholstered in olive-green leather, or black and olive tweed.[12]

In Europe, Berne was built by Searle in 1964, a four-storey block on the site of the former legation house. Oslo, of three storeys, was built by Bryant in 1966 along Thomas Heftyesgate, the northern perimeter of the legation site that had been bought in 1906. At Athens, where four contiguous lots behind the building bought from Venizelos' widow in 1936 were tortuously acquired in 1950, Kaye built a five-storey block in 1968. And, in the same year, Truscott completed at The Hague a four-storey extension behind the 400-year-old house that had recently been acquired at 10 Lange Voorhout. This was the most troubled of all the post-war office contracts: the face of the old building, which was to have been preserved, fell down; the Ministry's drawings were found to be inadequate; Dutch building costs escalated and sterling devalued; the contractor stopped work to ensure that his claim would be taken seriously; and the press had a heyday. The result was that the Treasury's approved cost of £348,000 was exceeded by over £120,000. The other 1960s straight blocks included Tehran and Colombo, four and six storeys respectively by Kidby in 1966; Buenos Aires, five storeys by Truscott in 1968; an extension by Kidby in 1967 to a five storey block in Tel Aviv, bought when under construction as apartments and re-planned and extended as offices; and smaller buildings at Gaborone in 1967 and Mbabane in 1968 **(Fig. 15.6)**.

15.6. The main elevations of four 1960s office buildings designed in-house. Clockwise from top left: Colombo high commission (completed 1966) on a site transferred in 1961 from the War Office; Oslo embassy (1966) in the grounds of the residence, bought in 1906; Buenos Aires embassy (1968) in the grounds of an intended residence bought in 1938; Berne embassy (1964), on the site of the former legation house, bought in 1913.

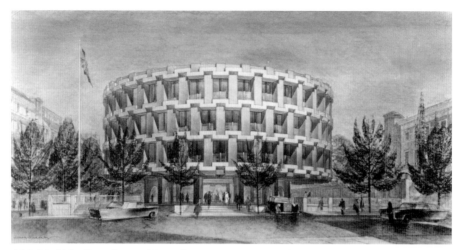

15.7. Madrid offices, designed by William Bryant and completed in 1966. This drawing, by William Suddaby, was exhibited at the Royal Academy in 1961. A welcome departure from the succession of straight blocks but an awkward building to manage and protect.

The first move by the Ministry's in-house architects to a more sophisticated architectural massing than a straight block came with Bryant's proposals for Madrid, where it was decided in the early 1960s to demolish the now-decrepit buildings at 16 Calle de Fernando el Santo and build anew on the, not very large, almost square site. Bryant proposed a hollow drum of three floors, supported on sturdy columns and massive radial beams that cantilevered the outer face of the building out to the edge of the site, above an open ground floor that was chiefly used for staff car parking. Muir visited Madrid in May 1961 to take final decisions with the ambassador. He concluded,

> and I repeat I did give a great deal of thought to this matter on the spot – I have come away quite satisfied that the right thing to do is to go ahead and build the rotunda. ... I see no reason at all why we should not get a great deal of credit for it ... the only minor criticism that I heard of the rotunda was from some rather dim character in the Information Section who will no doubt have been posted elsewhere long before it is finished.[13]

Muir was unperturbed that the Spanish press was already calling it 'the bullring'. Internally, the continuous circular corridor lay closer to the inner, open court than to the outside edge of the building so that it served small and ancillary rooms on the inner side and all the main offices on the outer. The elevational treatment was much more vigorous and assured than customary for the in-house architects, and may have owed something to Spence's concurrent planning for Rome, and possibly also to the circular American embassy in Dublin, designed by John M. Johansen and completed in 1964. Work started on the Madrid site in January 1965, with Helma-Laing S.A. as contractor, and was opened by the ambassador in October 1966: the total cost was £425,000 **(Fig. 15.7)**. After Madrid, a few of the office plan forms loosened somewhat, in some cases to integrate residential units into the same scheme. Thus the Jerusalem offices, which Kidby completed in 1967, incorporated a new residence for the consul-general. At Stockholm, Bryant arranged three floors of offices around two internal courts in 1967, with a mainly open ground floor, as in Madrid, and with an ungainly terrace of staff duplex flats above one full length of offices **(Fig. 15.8)**.

All of these offices remain in use except Bonn, Madrid and Colombo, which were all sold in the 2000s: Bonn because the embassy returned to Berlin, and the other two primarily for reasons of physical security.

Separate residences
The argument that started in the 1920s about separating offices and residences from each other had not been entirely won by the mid-1950s, despite endorsement in the Advisory Committee report of 1944. Unsurprisingly, the last redoubt of the dual occupancy of mission houses was a few senior

15.8. Stockholm offices, designed by William Bryant and completed in 1967. A first, and un-repeated, attempt to provide flats above the offices.

ambassadors. When the new Washington offices were being designed in the 1950s, the ambassador still expected to remain in his Lutyens study and to have a tunnel to the new building in case he should want to visit it. In the event, cost pressures won. It was cheaper to include an office for the ambassador in the new building than to build a tunnel from his study in the residence: he therefore had to walk 50 metres in the open air from home to office, where was provided a backdoor for his personal use. That was the symbolic end of the argument: thenceforth, new residences were separate from offices and vice-versa.

The advent of mono-purpose residences had several consequences. A gradual change of nomenclature was a minor one of them. For example, pre-war, the embassy house, where the ambassador lived and his chancery worked, was generally referred to as the 'embassy' (the previous meaning of which as 'the ambassador and his entourage' having long been obscure). Post-war, the term 'residence' came to apply to the house in which the ambassador lived, and 'embassy' to the building in which the ambassador's office, chancery and other offices were accommodated – often also called the 'offices'. There were occasional later ambassadorial initiatives to have the residence again referred to as the embassy but none lasted beyond the initiator's incumbency. Legations were unaffected by this change of nomenclature because they were all upgraded to embassies during the 1950s, though the term minister lingered on to describe the second-in-command at the largest Posts (including high commissions).

Three other changes, all more managerially significant than nomenclature, flowed from the advent of mono-purpose residences. First, with the great increase in staff numbers at Posts and hence in the size of the offices, residences were no longer the predominant buildings at most Posts, although many remained the most historical. Second, as chanceries, other offices and junior resident staff moved out of mission houses, many of them suddenly became much larger than necessary for residences. And third, as only the head of Post and family lived in the residence, no other senior member of UK-staff was any longer directly involved in its arrangement and management. This loss of wider Post involvement in residences opened the way for more individualistic and transient enthusiasms to flourish on the part of incumbents. The system of allocating a valuable publicly-owned and furnished residence, for a few years at a time, to a senior individual or family incurred many personal, social and financial ramifications for the smooth management of the operation. The scope for altercations was endless. Those between incumbent, predecessor and successor were best summed up by Diana Cooper's biographer – 'no new broom sweeps cleaner than that of an incoming ambassador'.[14] Heads of mission could be nervous about what successors would think of their decisions about a residence. Ambassadors, it was always said, had only two timescales for building or maintenance works: 'this must be finished before I leave' and 'not in my time': a variant, if a works project was the right thing to do but would be dusty or noisy, was 'don't you dare start on this until after I've gone'. There were constant points of friction between the subjective, committed, short-term outlook of an incumbent and the more dispassionate, long-term and specialist outlook of the involved estate managers and other bureaucrats with responsibilities for keeping costs down and property assets well husbanded.

It is not surprising that a head of Post could become so absorbed in his residence. It was his theatre of operations, the stage on which the effectiveness of much of his performance would be judged, enjoyed and remembered. The arrangement worked best, of course, when an assured incumbent made a fine house work hard and made a wide range of visitors think the better of Britain for it. A fine house with a difficult incumbent was usually less successful than a difficult house with an assured incumbent. This truism was often overlooked in endless preoccupations with small matters which the Ministry of Works could not escape. Humphrey Trevelyan, definitely of the assured school, captured some of the relationship with the Ministry of Works and its successors, with whom

All ambassadors have a running battle... . This provides a salutary counter-irritant, which absorbs all the surplus emotion of the ambassador generated by his political and personal problems. The ambassador protests that the new furniture makes his drawing-room look like the front parlour of a brothel, that his office would be more suitable for a couturier in Buenos Aires, that the chairs for the staff flats, received after a two and a half year delay, collapse when the occupants sit on them.

There is however another side to the picture. The post of the ministry's local supervisor is well in the danger zone: its occupant is a long-suffering man. The new ambassador's wife inevitably has tastes different from her predecessor's. The Nasmyths and the reproduction regency chairs go back into the store-room and are replaced by the latest productions of Messrs Heal and the Marlborough Gallery. With the next incumbent the process is reversed. The much harried supervisor consoles himself by having the best furnished flat in the embassy.[15]

Dick Scott, the maintenance engineer at Peking in the late 1950s, and the author of the only publicly available diary of his daily doings, found his own way to manage his side of this awkward relationship. The diary started with the address that he received from a lady who called out to him at 7.30 on his first morning, as he stood on the veranda of the engineer's house in the compound, 'We hate the Ministry of Works here!'. But he was a patient and gifted man and before long he was reading the lesson in chapel on Sundays, before returning to the enormous task of dismantling the boilers. Among many ups and downs, he related

> That afternoon the Minister sent for me and gave me a lesson in diplomacy. He told me that when the Minister said he would "be grateful if" what it really meant was that I was to "ruddy" well do as I was told. I then suggested that he would probably resent interference from the Chinese Government in the running of the Chancery or ministerial affairs and therefore it was but natural that I should object to similar occurrences in my domain. The Minister however was adamant and very stern so I was obliged reluctantly to give way. ... I felt very very sore over the whole proceeding. As I was about to leave his office, however, the Minister smiled happily at me and asked me to his house that evening to sing Schubert. All was well![16]

John Kaye, a senior architect, perhaps strayed further than he might have done when informing a colleague officially about the action he was taking in response to a request by Sir John Clutton at Warsaw 'for a second lavatory basin in the master bathroom as he thinks that if the next ambassador has a wife they will need one. I am refusing this ... although I appreciate the Americans do it, I can never imagine one of our ambassadors liking the idea of washing in tandem'.[17]

Residences designed in-house, 1950-70
The 1940s residences at Ankara and Rio de Janeiro were the last to reflect the scale and ambience of the nineteenth century European noblemen's houses that had served diplomats so well. They had huge rooms, wide stairs, roughly symmetrical plans and rigorously symmetrical elevations. Post-Second World War designs were to be differently conceived: smaller, plainer, planned more freely and cheaper to run. The main role of a residence, and the main criterion by which its effectiveness was judged, was to be a machine for entertaining on both large and small scales. Besides having enough space, the demands of this role included satisfactory car-parking and drop-off, easy but discreet access to cloakrooms, an entrance hall large enough for some milling about, fluid flow to, and between, the reception rooms, and easy access to a terrace and garden. Serving staff needed to move freely and relatively unobserved between the reception rooms and servery areas, and to the main bedrooms. By and large, if these requirements could be met by the

design, the bedrooms and, in larger new residences, the ambassador's private quarters could all be relatively simply fitted into place.

Canberra was the first residence new residence to be designed and built after the war. Alexander selected the site on the ridge of a hill in Deakin during his visit in 1949. It was a condition of the commissioning of the same Sydney practice as designed the offices in Canberra that the outline plan for the residence should be produced by the Ministry of Works. Alexander produced this himself: he sketched out a long, thin, low-key, two-storey building along the top of the ridge. The new Conservative Minister of Works in 1951, David Eccles, was robust in resisting suggestions from the high commissioner, Sir Stephen Holmes, for changes to the plans, minuting de Normann 'I agree you should take a firm line. Whatever we said we would do for Sir S. Holmes he would think of something more ... a year's trial should be accepted as good sense'.[18] And Eccles was unperturbed when a former high commissioner in Canberra, Sir Ronald Cross, complained that the house would lack a proper sense of tradition and dignity. The Holmeses occupied it in October 1953, and succeeded in annoying London by not inviting the architect to the house-warming party **(Fig. 15.9)**.

15.9. Entrance front of the Canberra residence. The building was sketch-planned by Alexander and developed by E.A.& T.M. Scott of Sydney, and completed in 1953. The main reception space is opposite the entrance hall with dining and drawing rooms on either side, all overlooking the terrace and garden.

The furniture, furnishings and colours were provocatively and rather self-consciously modern. The front door was painted bright primrose, the dark brown carpets were 'scattered with lime green and yellow stars', the legs of the chairs stuck out at an angle, and a modernist occasional table had won a prize in the recent Festival of Britain **(Fig. 15.10)**. Lady Holmes, the high commissioner's wife, was quoted in the press just before she left for Australia that, although the Ministry of Works had told her that Australians liked Regency furniture, she had chosen modern furniture because she wanted them to see modern British design. Lord Carrington, the second occupant of the house, perhaps unaware of Lady Holmes' admission, later wrote that 'the interior looked like a bad parody of a tourist-class lounge in a P&O liner'. Otherwise, he thought the house was 'well laid out and convenient'.[19]

The second post-war residence, Colombo, was occupied in March 1954. The plan was an L-shape, with a double-height hall occupying the corner, and drawing room and dining rooms along the limbs. Colombo was designed to be 'in the contemporary style' and as a showcase of British furniture. The Ministry of Works, however, had few ideas about contemporary furniture and therefore turned to the Council of Industrial Design to suggest firms who might be invited to offer designs and prices. Pieces were chosen, including

15.10. Reception space in the Canberra residence in 1953 with its original furnishings and furniture.

by Eccles, on design rather than price criteria, and most of the reception room furniture was designed by Dennis Lennon and made by the Scottish Furniture Manufacturers. The walls in the reception areas were in 'shades of grey, and the ceilings in primrose and china blue with certain elements picked out in white.' This provided, the Ministry's press notice went on to say, 'a light, cool background of colour and surface for the brightly coloured curtains, fabrics and the specially designed furniture'.[20] Eccles had asked the high commissioner, Cecil Syers, to send him his impressions after moving in. Syers wrote:

> Let me say at once – 'Westminster House' is a success. It is a charming, gracious house and a house in which it is very easy to live with comfort of body and spirit. ... We can sincerely congratulate you ... on a dignified house, representative of British architectural, constructional and decorative genius, of which you may be justly proud. ... Indeed it is fascinating to see [visitors] come through the glass doors from the front hall and stand amazed by the size and splendour of the scene before them. ... even the critics must grudgingly admit that Britain has shown herself still a pioneer.... I am completely, and my wife well on the way to being, converted to the air conditioning about which we were doubtful at first.
> P.S. This letter has been seen and approved by higher authority, i.e. my wife![21]

It was not until 1959 that the next in-house residence was completed at Accra. The Royal Fine Art Commission had been lukewarm. It said in October 1956 that the design 'should be simplified to give it greater dignity' but a revised design 'was not considered an improvement. A more distinguished architectural treatment was required.' The third offering, in February 1957, fared better and 'was considered an improvement, and a more developed version would be seen in due course', but it never was.[22] The built design was a straightforward rectangular two-storey building with a reasonably tidy plan, except for a single-storey kitchen protruding at one end, with an elegantly composed exterior **(Fig. 15.11)**.

The in-house design for Belgrade, contemporaneous with Accra, and equally frowned upon by the Royal Fine Art Commission, was detailed and developed by Tripe and Wakeham, an unexciting but reliable commercial practice widely used by the Ministry at home. The main part of the plan was a long thin rectangle, with two storeys, with the main entrance at one end, and a service wing out to one side. It was an improvised and dull plan and the house had few admirers. The Belgrade residence manual, drafted by a departing ambassador in 1977 for the benefit of his successor, said this about the interior of the house:

15.11. Garden front of high commissioner's residence in Accra, completed in 1959. The reception rooms are in line along the garden front, with the kitchen sticking out at the end.

The original décor was strictly Festival of Britain and the main reception room was designed much more as a cinema than a drawing room. The Queen's State Visit in 1972 fortunately allowed a complete transformation. … Anyone who wants to revert to contemporary furniture … could presumably do so, but anyone who strips the wallpaper and plaster from the dining room and goes back to the original open stone work will find that they have reverted to something looking exactly like the dining area of a Yugoslav Youth Hostel.[23]

15.12. Garden front of the efficient but small Vientiane residence, completed in 1960.

A residence in Vientiane was completed in 1960 to much the same successful plan as Accra but somewhat reduced in scale **(Fig. 15.12)**. To the Foreign Office's abiding annoyance, it was this residence that Jack Diamond, when chief secretary to the Treasury in the mid-1960s, commended as the model for new residences elsewhere. The residence in Khartoum, completed in 1961, was altogether a more sophisticated building, with a three-storey rectangular framed structure that presented an unfenestrated elevation to the street on its entrance side and balconies on the other three sides overlooking the garden **(Fig. 15.13)**. Only the entrance hall, cloakrooms and a staircase were on the ground floor: the rest of it was an open terrace that flowed into the swimming pool area and garden.

In the early-1960s, the in-house architectural team, stimulated by some younger blood and perhaps stung by the Royal Fine Art Commission's repeated strictures, began to give more thought to the design of residences. The Warsaw residence, designed by John Kaye under Bedford's eye, and completed in 1964, was the first in which a more imaginative form of spatial planning than rooms-off-corridors was explored. Kaye's design was for a three-storey building on a rectangular plan, with the, by now, usual one-storey kitchen and service excrescence. The building's central element was a

15.13. Khartoum residence, completed in 1961, on a site bought for the purpose in 1958. A site adjoining the end of the garden was bought in 1963 for a block of staff flats but new offices were instead completed on it in 1985.

333

double-height first floor which produced a handsome reception hall but also an uncomfortably tall dining room and drawing room next to it. The private sitting room, dining room and study were on the ground floor, giving on to the garden terrace, and all of the bedrooms were the equivalent of three floors above, on the top floor. Externally, the tall first floor was given heavy emphasis by projection on all sides and being clad in dark grey polished granite, in which was etched an enormous coat of arms above the entrance.

In May 1963, the ambassador, Clutton, sent a personal appeal by telegram to London:

> New residence was topped off today. Polish workers threaten to hoist black flag unless stood drinks by architect. Rightly point out that drinks on Ambassador are not the same thing. Would be most grateful if, for the sake of Bedford's and the Ministry's good name and flow of smoke up chimney in upward and not downward direction, previous decisions can be reversed and authority given for supply of such well earned refreshment as charge on Ministry's account.[24]

The Ministry was unmoved but the Foreign Office put the issue to the Treasury as a point of principle that the building owner and not the intended occupant should pay for such customary ceremonies. The response was graceful: expenditure could be charged to the job if it involved primarily the people who had contributed to its realisation. It was agreed in principle that the Warsaw residence should be furnished in a modern idiom under Bedford's eye: his conception was to make the reception area, which faced north, bright and light, and the dining room, which faced south, rich and glowing, and that in general there should be a contrast between the simple strong lines of the furniture and the colourful warmth of the fabrics.

A new residence in Mexico City was required because the offices had in 1950 squeezed the residence out of the former legation house in Cuauhtemoc Colony and ambassadors had been in leased houses since then. A steeply sloping new site was bought in 1960 in Tacubaya and John Kaye produced designs for a new residence almost concurrently with Warsaw. Again, the representational floor, though this time level with the entrance and of only single height, separated the private quarters on the floor below, permitted by the steep fall of the site, from a line of bedrooms on the floor above that gave on to an enormous roof terrace **(Fig. 15.14)**. A circular stair, with a lift up its middle, connected the three floors. Like Warsaw, too, it had dark granite cladding on its entrance side, with a large engraved coat of arms. The residence was completed in 1966: it is a rather clumsily articulated building but a successful residence in use.

Other planning activities, 1950-70

A good deal of attention during this period was devoted to the compounds, especially those that provided ready-made and cost-free new sites for buildings. Although there is no precise definition, a compound in the British diplomatic estate has several characteristics: it exceeds several hectares in extent, it has controlled access, and it contains the offices and at least one other accommodation type, whether residence, staff accommodation, or amenities and ancillaries. The archetypal compounds were, and remain, Bangkok, New Delhi, Tehran (Ferdowsi) and Tokyo: all large rectangles of land, procured in one piece (albeit on perpetual leases in two cases), built to a plan, and with all four types of accommodation. The two largest compounds, at Addis Ababa and Tehran (Gulhak), are distinctly non-rectangular: Gulhak was acquired in pieces, and both were haphazardly, but only lightly, developed over longish periods. Abu Dhabi, Ankara, Cairo, Dubai, Kathmandu and Seoul are all compounds by virtue of their size and mix of uses. The Irrawaddy compound in Rangoon, which does not house the offices, was the only one bought fully developed, while Karachi was bought half-developed. Large houses acquired with generous gardens or grounds in which other uses have been inserted, like Kingston and Oslo, barely qualify as compounds.

The production of feasibility studies for the future development of existing compounds or the initial layout of projected acquisitions was a continuing process, especially in the Middle East where the Cairo compound, the

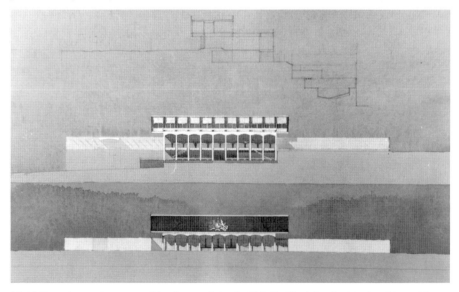

15.14. Drawing, perhaps one of the few surviving by Eric Bedford, for the Mexico City residence, completed in 1966. At top, section through the steep site; at middle, the garden front; at bottom, the entrance front.

Tigris site in Baghdad and both Tehran compounds were examined for their capacity to take large staff hostels. None progressed beyond the feasibility stage, not least because hostels proved a relatively short-lived requirement. Three large and vacant areas of land were also under consideration for development as compounds in the Middle East in the late 1940s and early 1950s: the West Bank site in Baghdad, the Abu Roumaneh site in Damascus, and a 40-acre site just north of Jedda. None of these, either, progressed beyond outline layouts by British consultancy firms with local connections.

The appointment of these firms was one of several concessions that the Ministry of Works made to private sector architects during this period. Local architects on term commissions had for long been retained at several Posts so that architectural attention could be given to buildings more quickly and perhaps, depending on local circumstances, more expertly than by visitors from London or one of the regional offices. In several instances, like Prentice in Rio de Janeiro and Scott in Canberra, the Ministry of Works commissioned a local architectural office of substance to execute schemes under its close eye. The in-house architects were relatively at ease with consultants of this kind because, with their distance from London and their unarguably greater local expertise, they were no threat to the in-house team's professional hegemony. Likewise, the in-house architects worked well with senior members of colonial Public Works Departments, with whom they had natural professional public service and bureaucratic affinities.

By the end of the 1950s, the Ministry's in-house architects were sure that they were doing difficult overseas projects well, that they had earned the right to continue monopolising them, and that any suggestion that any of them should be handed to consultants would undermine their position. They were able to encourage their masters in the Ministry to believe that outside architects would take too long to learn the ropes, that the in-house teams would not have time to teach them or correct their mistakes, and, anyway, outside architects had a bad reputation for gilding their projects and over-spending. There was doubtless some truth in the last contention: although in-house projects also overspent, their architects had more ways of burying or spreading the costs. Senior in-house architects probably feared, too, that eminent external architects would find ways of feeding ambassadors and Ministers with unwelcome professional ideas. These alarms beset architects much more than their other building professional colleagues because the structural engineers had for years been farming out their reinforcement bending schedules to consultants, and the quantity surveyors their bills of quantities, and neither was disconcerted by consultants in the same way as architects.

The underlying reason, however, for the in-house architects' difficulty in working with consultants was that they lacked both confidence in dealing with respected and successful private architects and experience in controlling, and of getting the best out of, their consultants. Briefs and briefing procedures hardly existed in the in-house life: schedules of accommodation were all that were needed because everyone was familiar with the requirements that the buildings were to meet. In other words, the in-house architects had little idea how to behave as clients, and there was nobody to teach them. The Ministry learned the hard way.

16

Lagos, Rome and Brasilia
1957–1970

Royal Fine Art Commission

The Royal Fine Art Commission was the main advocate during the 1950s for loosening the Ministry of Works' in-house architectural grip on the design of diplomatic offices and residences. The Commission was created in 1924 as a body of informed opinion to which major questions of taste could be submitted. Sir Lionel Earle, as Secretary of the Office of Works, had felt the need for such a body when embroiled in the choice and siting of war memorials in London in the early 1920s and proposed that it be modelled on the American Commission of Fine Arts, which was founded in 1910. The new Commission had no executive powers but it quickly acquired considerable cultural authority and its observations were taken seriously by architects and clients alike. Its relationship with the Ministry of Works was obviously difficult and the Ministry thought it was in danger of exceeding its remit. In 1950, Eric de Normann, deputy secretary at the Ministry of Works, refused the Commission's request for a list of the Ministry's forthcoming schemes.

A compromise was worked out in 1952 and the scheme for new embassy offices at Washington was the first overseas diplomatic project to be submitted to the Commission in 1954, followed by schemes for New Delhi, Belgrade and Accra. The Commissioners were not impressed by any of these schemes and came to doubt whether the Ministry's in-house architectural team was capable of doing credit to Britain abroad. This was the first time that the design of Britain's new diplomatic buildings was institutionally ascribed an

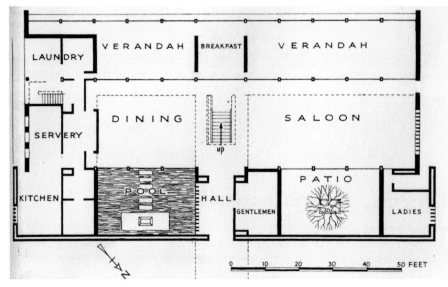

16.1. Ground-floor plan of the high commissioner's residence at Lagos, designed by Lionel Brett in 1958 and completed in 1961. A bold idea but unworkable for a head-of-mission residence at the time. The Ministry of Works added a separate hexagonal private sitting room to the right.

important role in representing and promoting Britain. The Commission wanted the Ministry to appoint a selection of top-flight private architects to design a few buildings with more considerations in mind than mere operational necessity. The chairman, Lord Crawford, brought pressure gently and privately on successive Ministers of Works but to no avail until 1957, when Hugh Molson lent a receptive ear.

The three projects at Lagos, Rome and Brasilia were the result: the first major diplomatic buildings to be commissioned from private architects in the UK since Edwin Lutyens was appointed for Washington 30 years before. The short and sharp Lagos residence episode came first. Rome and Brasilia were long-running sagas throughout the 1960s, both interrupted by Britain's dire economic straits which culminated in the devaluation of sterling in 1967. There was one great difference: Sir Basil Spence's Rome offices were eventually built but Peter and Alison Smithson's Brasilia scheme was abandoned.

Lagos residence, 1958-61
The first project selected for this high-profile non-Ministry design trial was the new residence that would be required for the British high commissioner in Lagos after the independence of Nigeria on 1 October 1960. A splendid

site for it had already been acquired. Lionel Brett, a rising establishment architect, a Royal Fine Art Commissioner and grandson of a former Secretary of the Office of Works, was accordingly commissioned in mid-1958. Molson was pressed in the House of Commons to say why he had selected Brett, especially since the roofs had recently blown off 50 houses he had designed in Hatfield (an accusation from which he was later exonerated). Molson could say no more than that his decision was taken after consultation with his advisers. There was not time to organise a competition 'even if I had been satisfied that one was desirable.' He went on

> I am not in favour of competitions as a method of appointing architects for schemes of this type. In the course of the last hundred years my Department has organised competitions of this kind on a number of occasions, and in not a single case has the winning design in a competition for a major government building been carried out.[1]

The Royal Institute of British Architects publicly disagreed with this approach. Brett, nevertheless, was clearly under pressure to find a modern

16.2. Looking down the main double-height volume of the Lagos residence in 1961, with the reception area at front and the dining area beyond the stair.

architectural solution to the diplomatic residence design problem. He spent several days in Lagos in June 1958 staying with the deputy governor-general, Ralph Grey, and his wife. They, and the governor-general himself, briefed Brett on their perceptions of how a residence would need to work in a post-colonial country. Brett alighted on the idea of a single major double-height volume to which all other rooms would be subservient. He laid this space down the centre of a rectangular plan, with only a stair and bridge dividing it into what were called the dining room and reception (or saloon) **(Figs 16.1 & 16.2)**. His fellow Royal Fine Art Commissioners, in the minutes of their October 1958 meeting, recorded that Brett's proposals 'were commended … as an individual and imaginative design'.[2] Brett also proposed, as he recalled in his autobiography,

> that every item in my long creamy-white house, from the teaspoons to the carpets, should be the best that British designers could produce; Edward Bawden should design the Royal Arms, black mosaic on white, over the entrance, Reg Butler make the courtyard bronze, Jo Pattrick master-mind the interior. The Ministry, keen to turn over a new leaf, offered apparently unlimited resources; it was my first experience of sloppy Government financial control, and after the rigours of New Town housing it was a shock.[3]

Architecturally, Brett's was a rational and enterprising plan, and it was approved by the Commonwealth Relations Office. The side-lined Ministry of Works in-house architects withheld their counsel, although they must have suspected that the design was too domineering to stand a chance of suiting a succession of incumbents. The building was well under construction

16.3. Entrance front of the Lagos residence, seen from Marina Street. A cantilevered bedroom provides the *porte-cochère*, and the site for a Royal coat of arms by Edward Bawden.

16.4. The lagoon side of the Lagos residence, with the private sitting room tacked on at left. A line of bedrooms lies above the full-length veranda.

when Viscount Antony Head was appointed the first high commissioner. A former army officer and Conservative minister of defence, he was married to Dorothea, an accomplished portrait painter and the daughter of the ninth Earl of Shaftesbury. They were a very different couple from the senior colonial service couples who had briefed Brett on what they envisaged would be the requirements. Lady Head intensely disliked the 'sort of concrete Design Centre' that was being built and she was in a position to affect the outcome. Brett's commission was terminated by the Ministry, the in-house architects took a grim satisfaction in finishing off the building, furnishing it more in sympathy with Lady Head's Regency preferences, and adding a separate hexagonal pavilion as a properly private sitting room. The building was occupied in January 1961, missing Independence Day by four months **(Figs 16.3 & 16.4)**.

The Minister, John Hope, rammed the lesson home when he reported to Sir Edward Muir, permanent secretary of the Ministry of Works, after a visit to West Africa in 1961, that the buildings which we erect overseas should, in general, be designed in the office rather than by outside architects. I appreciate that there will always be a few buildings for which, for very special reasons, we must choose the most suitable man from the entire British architectural field. The offices in Rome … are an example and the embassy … in Brasilia is another. Apart from special cases of this sort, however, I am convinced that the experience which our architects acquire by specialising on diplomatic buildings throughout the world gives them a long 'start' over an outside architect.[4]

A piece in *The Guardian*, titled 'Undesirable Residence', was scathing about the result, and particularly about its failure to do justice to the magnificence of the site. It concluded 'Humorists with a nautical upbringing simply call it "The Heads"'.[5] Manuscript annotations on the Colonial Office file include 'I agree with every word of this! It is a lamentable building'.[6] Sir David Hunt, deputy high commissioner under Lord Head and high commissioner 1967-9, wrote more thoughtfully in 1975 that

> I myself was rather taken with the appearance. … It was when I came to live in it that I realized its functional shortcomings. Essentially it was one huge room, looking like the arrival hall of a Scandinavian airport. Carried away by enthusiasm for open-plan living and despising any idea of ambassadorial discretion the architect had arranged for all the bedroom doors to open onto this main room; … if the High Commissioner was in his study he could not leave it unobserved. … Nevertheless, with the sliding windows opened onto the lagoon and the steady breeze blowing through, it was a pleasant enough place.[7]

Other high commissioners put up with the house with equally mixed feelings but its life was cut short after 15 years when the land was compulsorily re-acquired by the Nigerian authorities to make way for the Victoria Island ring road, and Brett's unfortunate house was demolished. The residence moved to a more ordinary house that was enlarged for the purpose, and remained there until the move to Abuja in the 1990s.

Rome offices, 1958-71

Muir suggested to his Minister, Molson, in 1957 that an entirely new design for the Porta Pia site in Rome should be commissioned from an eminent private architect. After two false starts in the decade since the embassy was bombed in 1946, one involving an in-house scheme and the other a commercial deal, it was time to try another tack. Molson, already critical of his in-house architects' design for the residence in Belgrade and before

Brett's Lagos commission misfired, readily agreed. Basil Spence was an easy and obvious choice of architect in 1958: Coventry Cathedral was nearing completion, he was the current president of the Royal Institute of British Architects and, at 52, was becoming Britain's most famous living architect. No announcement about his selection was made at the time but Spence was evidently advising the Ministry privately during 1959 and 1960 while the accommodation requirements were being thrashed out with the Treasury. By the time that he was formally commissioned in November 1960, Spence was well on his way to finalising his design concept for the embassy: drawings dated December 1960 show all of the main characteristics of the completed building in place **(Fig. 16.5)**.

Spence took the Rome commission extremely seriously, determined to honour the challenge of designing for his country next door to Michelangelo. He involved both his son John and his son-in-law, Anthony Blee, closely in the project. His concept was a hollow square plan on two storeys, raised up on 16 sturdy concrete posts. This had the combined effects of increasing the apparent mass and monumentality of the building, reflecting a traditional palazzo form, yet letting garden and water flow through beneath the

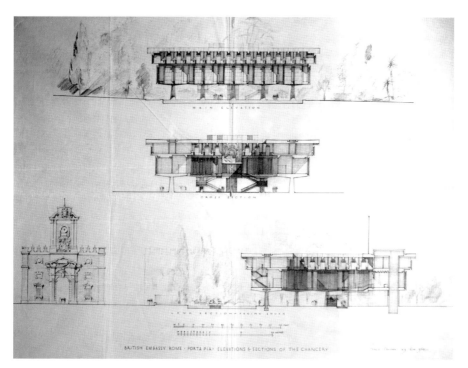

16.5. Drawing by Basil Spence for the embassy offices in Rome dated 29 December 1960, just a month after the public announcement of his commission.

building. He took his main horizontal levels directly from the Porta Pia so as to match its height and scale, and he found different elevational rhythms for his two floors to reflect their interior workings. The whole was to be clothed in travertine. A block of 14 staff flats on the eastern half of the site was more loosely planned on three floors above a floor of common services.

The original brief was for a maximum net internal area of 23,000 sq. ft, excluding garages but including 1,000 square feet for design flexibility, to be achieved within a cost limit of £250,000. This cost limit never had much chance of coping with Spence, and the soaring costs of labour and materials in Rome quickly drove up the estimates. Ove Arup and Partners were commissioned as structural consultants, with Edmund Happold as their project officer; the Ministry's own engineers were responsible for the mechanical and electrical works; and Reynolds and Young were the quantity surveyors. Professor Luigi Nervi was appointed as Spence's Italian architectural consultant, not least to add gravitas to dealings with the local authorities. The Ministry authorised Spence in May 1962 to present the design to his fellow Royal Fine Art Commissioners and they were 'pleased to see this scheme and had no comment to make on it. They wished it every success'.[8]

With that reassurance, Spence presented his design in September 1962 to

16.6. Overhead view of the model for Spence's proposed embassy offices at Rome. Michelangelo's Porta Pia is at top left and the intended siting for a block of 14 staff flats is at right.

a joint meeting of two key committees of the Rome *comune* (municipality) and five distinguished architects invited by the *comune* as town planning experts. As things stood at that time, the Porta Pia site was designated in the draft 1962 *piano regolatore* (town plan) as a special area where nothing could be either demolished or erected. Italia Nostra, a powerful conservation body, wanted to turn the site into public open space. Spence therefore needed to persuade the *comune*, a notoriously riven and fractious body, to change the site's designation to *edilizia speciale* (special building zone) to render the scheme even theoretically permissible. The meeting was make-or-break for the project and Spence rose magnificently to precisely the kind of occasion for which he had been appointed. He won the day by illustrating how essentially respectful his design was to the city of Rome. Descriptions vary about the width of the winning margin. One version is that he was given a standing ovation. John Burgess, a Ministry official accompanying Spence at the meeting, more staidly thought that the scheme was 'generally admired'. An embassy official, later briefed about the committees' private discussion after the British team had left the room, said 'evidently, it was by no means plain sailing'.[9] In any event, a ratification process, culminating in signature by the President of the Republic, was set in train and two years later Spence's building became legally buildable – provided that it started on site by mid-1967 **(Figs 16.6 & 16.7)**.

Spence was authorised to start on the working drawings in July 1963, for which purpose he opened an office in Rome in a flat at Via Guilia 163. The estimates continued their upward march, fuelled by rising costs, space additions, and changed methods of construction to £950,000 in 1964. Periodically, Spence went back to the drawing board to see what more could be cut back but he was ever shorter of options. The squash court, swimming pool and floodlighting all went: the Rome authorities' request for the original stable block to remain led to a saving, but it looked as though the block of staff flats would be the next victim. There was then a hiatus of three years while financial crises caused the suspension of building programmes across the whole of government. The chief secretary to the Treasury, Jack Diamond, proposed in 1965 that a halt be called to the Rome project with a view to looking at it again in two years' time with a cap on it then of £1 million. Spence was appalled, and threatened to resign. His spirits had not been lifted, either, by meeting at a dinner George Brown, then Secretary of State for Economic Affairs. Referring to the embassy design, Brown had said 'Throw it away! – we don't want that sort of thing'.[10]

Muir, shortly to retire, wrote to his Minister, by now Charles Pannell, in January 1965 in impassioned terms unusual for a permanent secretary:

16.7. View from the north-east of Spence's model for the Rome offices. The flats in the foreground were omitted from the project for cost reasons, and that half of the site has remained undeveloped.

> I think that to draw back now from this splendid scheme – and I mean splendid – would be a tragedy. We quite deliberately appointed Sir Basil Spence as our architect knowing perfectly well that he was not the man to give us a cheap job. We did it precisely because a cheap job was not what we wanted on what everyone who has seen it must agree is one of the most superb sites in Rome - perhaps the most superb City in Europe. If we are to use this site, and I am sure we ought to, we must put a building on it which is worthy of the site, let alone worthy of ourselves - and I think we still have some reputation in the world. ... You will see that I am personally very deeply committed to this scheme: of course, I am – I have been closely concerned with it from its inception and I have visited Rome on a number of occasions in order to do what I could to push it forward. I think that when we have Sir Basil's proposals for amending the scheme we ought to go into battle with the Chief Secretary with all guns firing - and I think that if we do we shall win. If we lie down under the Chief Secretary's tentative two-year delay the scheme is dead.[11]

A team of senior officials was dispatched to Rome to assess whether to cancel the project. Its recommendation to proceed as planned prompted an intensive new round of lobbying. The issue almost went to Cabinet in September 1965 but Diamond relented, provided that no more than £100,000 was spent on the project in the forthcoming 1966-7 financial year. This meant not starting on site until autumn 1966. Just before then, and after the tenders had been issued, Diamond found himself with no financial leeway left and he demanded deferment of the project for an indefinite period. The Minister of Works, by then Reginald Prentice, told the House of Commons that 'it had been decided to defer the two large projects for new embassies at Rome and Brasilia'.[12] The tenders were withdrawn, and another review was put in hand. It came to the same conclusion that building the offices was the best economic answer for the embassy in Rome but it found that the economic case for building the block of 14 flats was no longer convincing. This block was therefore taken out of the scheme, which meant that there would be room to build a new residence on the eastern half of the site at a future date. This idea had been anathema to a succession of ambassadors, content with living in the Villa Wolkonsky, but was favoured by the current incumbent, Sir Evelyn Shuckburgh. During the hiatus, the internal layout of Spence's building, which had never delighted either the embassy or departments in London, was somewhat re-arranged, mainly to meet changing security requirements. As a result, the Foreign Office told the Ministry that it was 'satisfied that what we have now produced is, by and large, the best we can do with the Spence building itself. Short of scrapping the whole thing and starting again we cannot eliminate [its deficiencies] completely'.[13] London dared not be more radical for fear of Spence exploding and the *comune* reneging.

The Treasury finally gave approval for the project to proceed in July 1967, with a cost limit of £850,000, on the express conditions that the Villa Wolkonsky estate would be sold upon completion of the office building and that the ambassador would move into a leased residence. Tenders for the office contract were invited in October 1967. Laing declined and Taylor Woodrow wanted to work with an unsuitable Italian partner with the result that the three returned tenders were all from Italian firms. Despite devaluation of the pound during the tender period, the tender of Impresa Castelli came in lowest at only a little over £850,000. It was accepted on 28 February 1968 and a token start was made on site the next day to conform with the building licence which was to expire two days later and had already been significantly extended. Spence wrote to the Ministry 'As you know, I had a feeling that I might not live to see this building'.[14] But he did: it was completed in June 1971, about ten months later than planned, at a cost of £890,000. Julian Amery, the eighth Minister of Works to have held office since Spence was commissioned 12 years previously, performed an inauguration ceremony on 20 September 1971.

The building opened to much fanfare and some admiring architectural reviews but it somehow struck a slightly false note: admirable and skilful in many ways but a little *passé* for the modern embassy of a country about to join the European Economic Community. Shuckburgh, the ambassador who had worked closely with Spence during 1966-9, captured some of this ambiguity in *The Architectural Review*.

> Sir Basil never did conceive that he was designing a mere office block, even when this would seem to have been the commission given to him. He took a bolder view and assumed that since he had been invited by the British Government to design an official building on one of the most prestigious sites in Europe, if not in the world, then presumably something beautiful and splendid was expected of him. ... So he went ahead and designed a building of the greatest distinction, ingenious, imaginative, self-contained and worthy of the situation in which it stands. In short, he assumed that a chancery building designed by himself should carry the full prestige of an embassy.[15]

Spence's success in presenting a fairly small office building as a major monument on an illustrious site deserved applause. Spence set his heart on his initial conception and proved strong enough to force it through to completion. Without him, there would never have been embassy offices on the Porta Pia site, and the Ministry had ample reason to be grateful to him. Nevertheless, as embassy offices (which it remains) the building has always been rather a disappointment, largely because it could never be operated in the way that Spence envisaged: the dignified and ceremonial arrival route was hardly used because of security risks; the grand staircase was closed for most of the time, forcing staff and visitors into the single inadequate lift in one corner; the offices on the so-called *piano nobile* were awkwardly shaped for working in; and the furniture that Spence had bullied the Ministry into being allowed to design was disliked.

Spence infuriated many of the Ministry staff over the years by being over-bearing, fussy and difficult to work with. There had therefore been little enthusiasm for appointing him, when the opportunity arose in 1967, as the architect for the residence that might be built on the eastern part of the Porta Pia site in lieu of the abandoned block of staff flats. In the event, no progress was made on this project because no agreement could be reached on the size that the residence should be. Spence, aware that a residence was in the offing but that funding it would be difficult for the Ministry, took it upon himself to explore alternative ways of funding, including an unconvincing scheme that he outlined to Shuckburgh over a lunch in November 1968. As Shuckburgh recorded it, Spence was in touch with a developer who he thought might be very interested in purchasing the Wolkonsky site with a view to constructing a large (30-storey) block of offices where the present villa stands and utilising the remainder of the property partly as a car park and partly as gardens which could be made available to the Comune for public use. He said that this firm would be likely to be willing to pay a very large sum indeed, so that HM Government would not only cover the full cost of the Chancery and the residence but would be able to return a substantial sum to the taxpayer. All this clearly is thought of by Spence as a means of facilitating and speeding up a decision to build a residence and to entrust its design to himself.[16]

In a later variant, the developer would put up a new residence at Porta Pia for £100,000 in return for an option on Villa Wolkonsky. Spence's preparedness to go to such lengths to capture a design job did him no credit in the eyes of the civil servants, who were waiting for him to be 'quite clear of the site' before deciding who the architect of the new residence should be. Shuckburgh maintained that Spence should at least be used as an adviser. In mid-1970, soon after Diamond ceased to be chief secretary, the Treasury authorised a planning start on a residence of not more than 8,500 square feet at an estimated cost of £180,000. The director of Estate Management Overseas, Francis Walley, was left with 'the ticklish job of letting Sir Basil know that we do not wish to commission him to execute the work, but would be happy to work out a method of associating him with the work'. Walley subsequently recorded

> I ... had a very bad reception. He wished to design the residence himself and was not willing to be associated with it in any other way. He obviously felt very keenly about it and said this action was tantamount to dismissal. He said among other things that should he not be given the commission he would be forced to take it to the highest level and mentioned the Prime Minister and Foreign Secretary. I said I would report how strongly he felt to the Secretary.[17]

The Ministry buckled and Spence was asked in January 1971 whether he would be willing to undertake the design and execution of a smallish residence on a tight budget. His acceptance was not a surprise: he had apparently told the Foreign Secretary that he would be prepared to waive his fee in order to keep costs down. Spence subsequently produced an atrium design for a relatively modest residence. The Foreign Office then decided that the status of the ambassador at Rome should be upgraded, which would necessitate a larger residence. Spence was confident that his concept was right enough, and the site large enough, to cope with a larger residence and still retain the proportions which he thought vital: he said he was prepared to stake his professional reputation on producing a really good house. But the Minister, Amery, was by then having second thoughts about selling Villa Wolkonsky and instructed Spence that he should do no further work on the scheme until he had received a revised brief. On leaving this meeting, Spence mournfully (but not quite accurately, as it turned out) mentioned that this might well be his last job. A revised brief was never issued to Spence or to anyone else. Amery told the Foreign Secretary that the Porta Pia site was simply not big enough to take the kind of residence needed in Rome. The eastern half of the site remains unoccupied.

Brasilia, 1959-68

The proposal to move the capital of Brazil from Rio de Janeiro on the coast to the central plateau inland dated from the nineteenth century but it was not until 1955 that a parliamentary commission selected the specific site for the future capital, which was to be called Brasilia. The competition for the 'pilot' plan was won in 1957 by Senhor Lúcio Costa, who became the principal urban planner: Oscar Niemeyer was appointed principal architect and Roberto Burle Marx the landscape architect. The city's infrastructure and main civic buildings were built in the late 1950s, and the city was inaugurated as the capital in April 1960. Two years earlier, the British government, with deep misgivings because the enormous Rio residence had only been in use for eight years, selected a 2.75-hectare freehold site for its future embassy offices and residence at Plot Number 8, Avenida das Nações, close to the lake and next to the Australians. This site was granted by deed of gift in 1960. Residential accommodation for the 30 or so UK staff likely to move to Brasilia was expected to be leased in the market.

The Foreign Office and the Ministry of Works in 1959 began drawing up schedules of requirements for the accommodation to be built. By then, the development of Brasilia was creating a lot of excitement around the architectural world, as the Brazilians talked up their hopes for the future diplomatic buildings to represent each country's past, its contemporary tendencies, and how it saw its future. William Holford, who had been a member of the competition jury for the Brasilia pilot plan, told Muir that both Costa and Niemeyer hoped that the range of new embassy buildings overlooking the lake would be 'the best of their kind in the world' and designed by the 'most interesting architects' in their respective countries. The case for an architectural competition for the British embassy buildings was unanswerable, even for the Ministry of Works. The problem, however, was that it had never written a proper brief for an overseas building, let alone for a competition, and was uncertain how to go about it.

After consultation with Holford, who succeeded Spence in 1960 as President of the Royal Institute of British Architects, Eric Bedford, the ministry's chief architect, reluctantly proposed in 1961 a two-stage open competition, but without first stage entrants being required, and certainly not paid, to visit the site. The competition would be run in accordance with the regulations of the Royal Institute of British Architects and Bedford expected it to take 17 months. The Ministry's legal advisers, completely unfamiliar with architectural competitions but presumably anxious to help, commented that

> the competition conditions are being drafted by administrators and architects and not as an exercise of legal skill. To a lawyer the result is a hodge-podge of contractual matter and a variety of matter not of a contractual character, it being impossible to separate one from the other. What the legal consequences of it all is going to be no lawyer could possibly say.[18]

Bedford was keen to ensure that 'the Ministry is not in any way committed to going ahead with the implementation of the winning design'.[19] The Treasury agreed the draft competition conditions in October 1961, but without a commitment to air-condition the buildings and baulking at the prospect of paying for any of the competitors to visit Brasilia. The Ministry then decided to fall back on a limited competition. Holford and Bedford drew up a short-list of six practices: Casson and Conder, Denys Lasdun, Robert Mathew Johnson Marshall, Powell and Moya, Peter Smithson, and Yorke Rosenberg and Mardell. Assessors also needed to be appointed and paid: Holford and Bedford were obvious assessors and they recommended that the third should be Costa. The competitions code of the RIBA apparently laid down that the 'combined fee for the assessors cannot be less than 1/5th of 1% of the estimated cost of the job plus 25 guineas'.

Two years later, the Ministry was considering abandoning any form of competition and making a direct appointment instead, in which case Bedford advised selecting Lasdun. The Minister, Geoffrey Rippon, decided in favour of such a direct architectural appointment during his visit to Brasilia in early 1964 and interviewed Lasdun on return. Lasdun said he was honoured to be asked but declined because he had too many other projects already. Ten days later, Muir and Bedford interviewed Peter Smithson: he and his wife, Alison, were establishing themselves as leaders of the modern movement in Britain, and were at the time working on the modernist but unalarming Economist Building on St James's in London. Smithson, who personified the kind of architectural rhetoric that was emanating from Brazil about what embassies there should strive to achieve, was very interested in the project. Muir recorded:

> He is obviously not an extremist but a man of firm ideas who will not brook much interference with what he wants to do. This is all to the good from our point of view. ... Mr Smithson blenched slightly at the idea of incorporating the Piper pictures [from Rio] in the new house. ... I think we ought to appoint him.[20]

The Foreign Secretary, Rab Butler, had no objection, though he had never heard of Smithson, and added 'I presume that ... you will not necessarily have to accept his design if you or I do not like it.'[21] Rippon offered Smithson the commission at the end of February 1964: in accepting, he said that he could not start for a month or two and he wanted Alison to be involved with the project. They started work in April 1964 with a brief specifying in total 37,000 square feet, a cost of about £320,000 at UK prices (roughly £450,000 at Brazilian prices), and an expectation that a construction contract would be let in March 1966, two years thence. Ove Arup and Partners were appointed as structural engineer, the Ministry's own mechanical and electrical engineers were detailed to the job, and James Nisbet and Partners was the quantity surveyor.

The Smithsons visited Brasilia in the autumn and showed Muir and Bedford their emerging ideas in October 1964. Their concept was one long, thin, straight building, about 150 metres in length, running close to one side of the rectangular site for almost its entire length. The narrow strip of site between the building and the boundary was the entrance side, and the wider strip the garden side. The number of floors varied between two and four as the building went along, 'riding the landscape' as they later put it. The residence and the offices were at either end and they met near the middle, where they shared a large entrance hall and both had access to a reception hall above. The building was divided lengthwise into six slightly unequal bays, separated by five concrete service and stair stacks. Between these stacks ran pre-stressed longitudinal concrete beams, necessarily quite deep because they were spanning up to 25 metres, which enabled the external walls to be extensively glazed beneath wide overhangs. The external finish was exposed concrete tinted red in correspondence with the surrounding earth and hills **(Fig. 16.8)**.

The Ministry was a little surprised to see a single building rather than two separate ones but did not object in principle to the proposal, even though it foresaw some potential security problems. The Smithsons argued

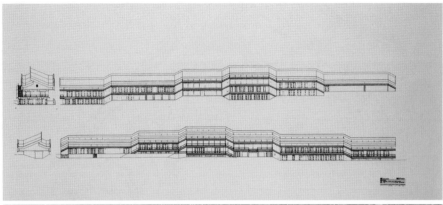

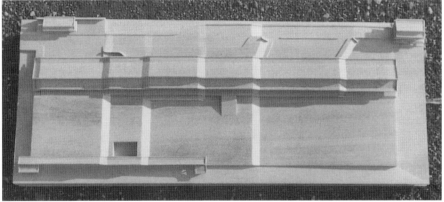

16.8. The Smithsons' 1965 proposal for Brasilia: elevations (and sections) above and plan-view of model below. They later described it as a 'squashed crocodile' of red-tinted exposed concrete 'riding the landscape'. The offices were to be to the left, and the residence to the right, off shared entrance and reception halls in the middle.

that a unified building was more appropriate to the site and had the advantage of avoiding the impression that there was another building close by. The Ministry was much more concerned that the proposed area was far in excess of the stipulated 37,000 square feet, which would have serious cost implications. The Smithsons successfully argued that some excess of the brief was justified, and the permitted figure was increased to 43,000 square feet with the cost limit raised proportionately. Three months later, however, the Smithsons' revised proposals only brought the area down to 49,000 square feet and the costs to £947,000 at UK prices.

Despite the clear difficulty that the structure of the scheme was incapable of being sufficiently scaled down to meet the real requirements, the Smithsons refused to let go of their concept, and the Ministry unwisely stopped short of insisting. A third version, in June 1965, brought the area down to 45,500 square feet and the cost to £681,000. The two floor segments that were occupied by the private quarters and bedrooms of the residence were conceived, to a greater degree than any other of the floor-segments, as concrete shelves on which 'curved interior partitions form rooms as freely as if they were decorative containers on a shelf'.[22] The room layouts, with their sinuous corridors and spaces around the 'jars' could be flexibly re-ordered during the life of the building **(Fig. 16.9)**. These were attractive ideas but hopelessly unlikely to survive an onslaught from future occupants and their spouses. Nevertheless, the third version was accepted in principle in November 1965 by the Minister of Works, Charles Pannell, and the Foreign Secretary, Michael Stewart, but with significant misgivings about its affordability and the necessity of overseas payments. The Royal Fine Art Commission, asked for its views, said that it was 'much interested in the scheme and thought it should be warmly commended.' in January 1966.[23] NOVACAP, the planning authority for Brasilia, also welcomed the design.

By this time, the Smithsons had started on the working drawings, entirely on their own initiative and at their own risk, to try to catch up with the original programme. They presented the scheme again to ministers, this time including the chief secretary to the Treasury, Jack Diamond, in March 1966. Diamond, looking to call a halt to excessive expenditure just as he was doing on Spence's concurrent Rome scheme, insisted on a deferment until an ongoing review of standards of diplomatic service accommodation was completed. The Smithsons were aghast. Alison expressed her disappointment in unexpected terms to the Minister, Pannell, a week or so later:

> Our anguish is not altogether unlinked to the political/economic scene for we receive a great many enquiries as to how the Embassy is going, mainly from laymen and foreigners; and when they learn it is stalled the reaction at present is on the average that as a country we are becoming just like a South American State. It is very hurtful to be tarred with this sort of reaction; also since there is more truth in it than one can bear to face: for what is meant by this aphorism is of course a state in a wobbly economic condition, drained, and thereby dominated, by the military.[24]

A fourth version succeeded in bringing the estimate down to £581,000 but, although accepted by the Treasury at official level, it was rejected in August 1967 by Diamond, who said that there ought to be a completely fresh start unless the scheme could be reduced to below the originally briefed area and cost limit. Diamond explained the following month to a new Minister

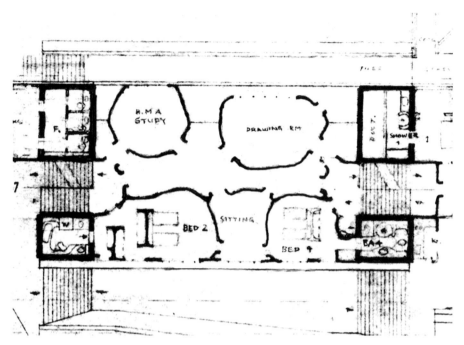

16.9. Sketch plan of part of the residence in the Smithsons' proposal for Brasilia. The intended plastic treatment of floor layouts is evident: rooms were conceived as 'decorative containers on a shelf'.

of Works, Robert Mellish, that 'One major cause of trouble on this scheme has been that the Smithsons designed a building far in excess of what your Ministry or the Diplomatic Service considers necessary, and I could not accept that the Exchequer should bear the result of that'.[25] Diamond's proposal was tantamount to a total rejection of the Smithsons' scheme but still they pleaded for the opportunity to try once more to cut it back. Meanwhile, as prolific lecturers and writers in the architectural arena, with a significant following of young modernists, the Smithsons were lobbying their friends and contacts hard. They chose to describe their scheme in public as 'more than a building, it's a working climatological, cultural and technological test bed … It'll be a cultural bomb'. *The Times* published a letter from a Stephen Gardener, concluding 'Let's hope that it comes off and does not go off: and that it is, by the way, also an Embassy'.[26]

The fifth version, produced in October 1967, appeared to fit the bill until it was realised that important areas and costs had been omitted. The Smithsons said that they were not prepared to develop the scheme further

without a fresh commissioning letter, a public statement to the effect that
their scheme had been accepted in principle, and a new date for a start on
site. The Minister refused, and they carried on.

At the end of 1967, three external considerations affecting the future
of the project were being weighed. First, the Brazilian Ministry of Foreign
Affairs was far behind with its own plans to move from Rio to Brasilia and so
the urgency for the British embassy to have a new building ready was much
reduced. Second, the Foreign Office's security requirements were changing
and any design that unified offices and residence in one building was ruled
unacceptable. And third, the recent devaluation of the pound caused the
cost of the Smithsons' scheme to rise completely out of reach. There was
therefore a strong case for aborting the Smithsons' current design and an
excellent excuse for terminating their commission, two decisions that were
reached at the end of November 1967. The Smithsons argued for putting
their commission on hold but Mellish would not agree. In March 1968,
Baron Kennet, formerly Wayland Young, wrote in manuscript to Mellish:

> I hear rumours around the architectural undergrowth that you may be going
> to fire the Smithsons from the Brasilia Embassy project. I hope this is either
> exaggerated, or else that there is some very good and defensible reason for it.
> Delay, of course, is an economic necessity but, unless they have blotted their
> copybook in some way, dismissal would, I think, cause a good deal of outcry
> among the intelligentsia, and perhaps in the architectural press.[27]

Mellish signed the termination letter to the Smithsons in April 1968 and told
the House of Commons in June that there would be a two-year deferment
of the Brasilia embassy project and that the decision about future architects
for it would be taken later. There was a good deal of public interest in the
fate of the Smithsons' scheme, some of it doubtless stirred up by themselves.
A *Times* leader supporting the Smithsons entitled 'Wanted: an Embassy' was
published in June 1968 and concluded that 'the impetus that a brilliantly
designed embassy would give to Britain's architectural image abroad is badly
needed'.[28] This was followed by *The Architectural Review* devoting its own
editorial to the case in August.

> As a result of what has been done by the Minister, Britain's architectural
> reputation in Brazil is at a low ebb, and this applies to Britain's official
> architectural reputation elsewhere in the world. At long last work has just
> begun on Sir Basil Spence's very prominent Embassy building in Rome, but
> elsewhere, especially where the designs have been made by the Ministry's
> own architects, the results are dismal and depressing. The situation can only

be retrieved by commissioning and completing buildings of the quality of the Smithsons' for Brasilia.[29]

This judgement had to be taken on trust because, at the Smithsons' request, the Ministry had agreed to transfer copyright in the drawings from the Crown to the Smithsons, who then refused to let them be published for another seven years. A Foreign Office minister, Fred Mulley, consented to Peter Smithson calling on him in summer 1968 to describe his criticisms of the Ministry of Works, how badly he had been treated, and why he thought the Foreign Office should take charge of its own building programme. The Smithsons eventually published their plans, with an article, in the *Architectural Review* for 1975. It offered some clues to how their self-obsession may have distracted them from paying sufficient attention to their client's practical requirements.

> Even after all the time that has passed it is still painful to write about past lost hopes. To design an Embassy for his country is the most flattering commission an architect can be offered, especially in a city he admires…
>
> What were we then to offer in Brasilia as an idealisation – a representation of our own dream for a more egalitarian society with more varied and more spontaneous social forms? The parade-ground perfection of Niemeyer's main buildings set against that void-with-horizon-behind is so spectacular that it needs to be matched by a very intense form if any counter intention is to be felt. The low-lying 'squashed crocodile' form of our project in some way arises out of a wish to be heard for a moment, and in that moment to give a glimpse of another social formulation via the quiet shifting imagery of the facades and the internal arrangements they represent. …
>
> We were dealing with an architecturally literate audience, understanding the need for architecture as continental people do – an audience whose elite could appreciate the fine subtleties and edge of any architectural performance, and an international architectural elite – for Scharoun was down the road, Le Corbusier up the road, Niemeyer in town, Lucio Costa near to hand and, as Costa said, the Brasilia School of Architecture 2000 miles away from other styles….
>
> Michelangelo was never so messed about by his Pope.[30]

The following year, Peter Smithson wrote to the ambassador in Brasilia, Derek Dodson,

> We still hope to be able to build 'our' Embassy in some form, somehow, someday, as Basil Spence finally built 'his' in Rome. … we designed a very polemical building, capable, we thought, of representing the special flavour

of this country in contrast to that of France or Germany or the countries of Eastern Europe. We still think this is an important idea – one worth struggling to bring about.

Do you think you could bring this issue once more into public debate now that the political climate in England seems to be on the point of unfreezing?[31]

The answer was no: not least because the Property Services Agency had already decided, two years earlier, that it would design the future Brasilia embassy in-house.

17

Internals and Externals

Background to furnishings

The Office of Works first became responsible for furnishing its overseas properties in the late 1860s when it began to supply domestic and office furniture, including safes, to consulates in the Far East. The necessary items were requisitioned by its Shanghai office and sent to Posts from London. A major increase in this responsibility came in the 1870s when the Office of Works was required to fund the furnishing of the State rooms of mission houses. Here, the selection of items and fabrics was mainly made by incumbents and their wives, after which the Office of Works procured the goods and sent them to Posts. In 1900, Robert Boyce pointed out that good-enough furniture for the Far East consulates was being made in Shanghai and Hong Kong and need no longer be sent from UK, adding that 'excellent curtain stuff and carpets are now both made in China and Japan'. A reader with a red pencil annotated in the margin 'yes, but where *taste* comes in better to send from home'.[1] From 1914, all salaried consular Posts were furnished at public expense and, from the 1920s, most mission houses. The Office of Works also supplied furniture to other Posts at a charge to incumbents of 7.5 per cent of its value per annum. After the Second World War, and in accordance with the Advisory Committee report of 1944, all the rooms in all head of Post residences were to be officially furnished. This practice was extended during the 1950s to all staff accommodation, whether bought, built or leased on unfurnished terms.

After the Second World War, the Ministry of Works established its own Supplies Division to manage the design, procurement and provision of furniture, materials, equipment and fuel for all government accommodation within the UK. Within this division was created a section to handle the requirements of the overseas estate, including the domestic equipment required by head of mission residences, such as cutlery, china, glass, silver and linen. Any equipment, however, that required electricity, like table lamps and irons, was specified and procured by the electrical and mechanical engineers responsible for the buildings. There was a gap inside the Ministry of Works between the architects for the buildings and the suppliers of the furnishings that was never effectively filled by what might have been the pursuit of interior design. This gap was cultural, as well as a managerial: most of the architects were professionally trained while most of the furnishings staff in the supplies division had a technical background. The Ministry made little attempt to bring these two groups of staff together into a meaningful collaboration on building interiors.

This was particularly unfortunate after the Second World War in respect of the reception rooms of major residences where a third involved party, the head of mission and spouse, obviously had an important interest. The Ministry had for long been able to rely on the aesthetic judgements of incumbents and the skills and craftsmanship of suppliers to do justice to the traditional requirements of State rooms. As succeeding generations of incumbents became less assured in their views and experience, and suppliers with the necessary skills became rarer and more expensive, the interior design gap became wider and deeper. The Ministry had no skilled in-house interior designers or decorators to fill the gap and practically no knowledge about how to find and brief them in the private sector. In 1962, the first draft, later amended, of an answer to a Parliamentary Question vainly sought to paper over the gap:

> The fully qualified architects responsible for designing and maintaining our embassies abroad are also responsible for interior decoration. They act in conjunction with a team of furnishing experts, who hold no certificates of qualifications but have a wide range of experience. Their continuing activities in this field keep them abreast of modern trends in design and décor so that organised refresher courses are considered to be unnecessary. In an otherwise all male staff two women are employed in an advisory capacity; both hold the Diploma of Decoration at the London University and are consulted mainly on colour schemes.[2]

The Taste Committee
The Ministry of Works' lack of assurance in this field led to endless arguments and dismay. The most authoritative attempt to breathe fresh air into the

debate started soon after the Lagos residence furnishing débâcle in 1960. The Minister of Works, John Hope, wrote to the Foreign Secretary, Selwyn Lloyd that 'I am getting together a small Committee to advise ... on matters of taste and decoration, and have already roped in Sybil Eccles [wife of the former Minister of Works] for a start'.[3] Hope intended to call it the Advisory Committee on Matters of Taste, if that was not thought too precious – which it was. It was instead called the Advisory Committee on Decoration and Furnishing but was nevertheless dubbed the Taste Committee by officials, who saw little likelihood of it doing anything useful. There would be no public announcement of its formation and it would advise privately. The Committee was chaired by John Hope and its membership, besides Lady Eccles, comprised Paul Reilly (Director of the Council of Industrial Design), Lady Frances Balfour (a senior Foreign Office wife), the Hon. James Smith, and, from the Ministry, Sir Edward Muir (permanent secretary), Eric Bedford (chief architect) and Harold Glover (Director of Supplies).

The first meeting was in December 1960. Hope said that he wanted the committee to confine itself to the interiors of overseas residences: it would not be asked to advise on their elevations or design. He was recorded in the minutes as having

> the highest regard for the abilities and good taste of the Ministry's own staff concerned with decoration and furnishing. He felt, nevertheless, that in order to give the taxpayer a further assurance that his money was being spent wisely, it would be right for the Minister of Works to be advised on these matters by a group of people representing informed outside information in the same sort of way as a distinguished committee advised him in the selection of pictures for public buildings. The Committee would be asked to advise on problems of design involving both modern and traditional styles. It would be open to the Committee to suggest the use of an outside designer in appropriate cases.[4]

Despite these intentions, the committee was soon diverted into the less demanding tasks of updating the ranges of china, cutlery, plate and glass that were issued to residences. The Warsaw residence was the only new project to be discussed in the first couple of years, and Bedford and Glover ensured that there would be no ground-breaking outcome nor significant encroachment on in-house hegemony. At the committee's instigation, however, some of the furniture was designed by Robin Day and Robert Heritage; and a large set of silverware, intended for adoption as well at other new residences, was commissioned from David Mellor. It was never much liked in Warsaw, where the forks were found uncomfortable to use, with the result that the set spent much of the next 30 years in a Croydon basement and was never duplicated for any other Post.

Frances Balfour was the first to bale out of the Taste Committee, after about half a dozen meetings: she wrote to Hope 'I have not got the necessary experience or knowledge of modern design and, quite frankly, I do not find "contemporary" furniture suitable in any way for Embassy Reception Rooms'.[5] Geoffrey Rippon succeeded Hope as Minister in July 1962 and waited six months to chair his first meeting, the committee's tenth. In November 1963 the Foreign Service Wives Organisation was setting up a sub-committee of its own to channel the views and complaints which, 'of course as we know too well', in Muir's phrase, were always being made by its members about the Ministry's furnishing and equipping of diplomatic houses. Another meeting in 1964, 18 months after the last, broadly approved Bedford's proposals for the Mexico City residence. He had waited until there was almost no time left to show the design to the committee. Meanwhile, the ambassador's wife, Mabel Cheetham, who had a New York qualification in interior design, had complained that insufficient Mexican materials and craftsmanship were being incorporated into the Ministry's intended building. Bedford's rather awkward explanation was that

> Usually … a local architect who equally knows the position regarding the availability of materials and local practices, and who does not wish to impose his own design ideas is the combination - this is what has happened in Mexico City. By this means the policy of the department of introducing something of the British outlook in design, and accordingly their way of life, is brought into the solution and becomes part of Mexico without, of course, ignoring those small items of local flavour which are thought to be desirable.[6]

By 1965 the value of the committee was in doubt. Members complained, reasonably enough, that the Ministry officials bulldozed their views through by claiming that the machine had moved too far forward to change direction more than marginally. The Foreign Office thought that the committee was psychologically a good thing and that, if the Ministry disbanded the committee, it would need one of its own. At a meeting in December 1965 with the Minister, by then Charles Pannell, and the Secretary, by then Antony Part, Bedford said he would prefer to see the committee abolished because it lowered the morale of the department: better to have expert interior designers in the office than rely on an outside committee. Part said that he did not think the Ministry had shown itself very expert in the embassy furnishing field: he nevertheless wanted to keep furnishing matters with the controller of supplies rather than bring them under the chief architect. The Taste Committee drifted on with a changed membership and rare meetings for another few years.

The only other outside expertise commissioned during this period was the appointment in 1959 of Sir James Mann, Keeper of the Wallace Collection, to keep a curatorial eye – or 'to curb the less happy caprices of successive tenants' – on the valuable chattels in the Paris residence, which he visited annually. He was succeeded in 1964 by Sir Trenchard Cox, Director of the Victoria and Albert Museum. Howell Leadbeater, who succeeded Glover as Controller of Supplies, later stood the role down. Its next incarnation was not until 1980 when the Foreign Secretary, Lord Carrington, appointed John Cornforth, a scholar of English interiors, as an historic buildings adviser to ensure that the reception rooms of the more historically important residences were expertly maintained and presented. He held this appointment almost until his untimely death in 2004. Cornforth, although he ruffled some feathers, had an unerring sense of the feel of a room and how to dress and use it to best effect. He thought of F.J. Eckersburg's lovely Norwegian landscapes painted on the walls of the Oval Room in the Oslo residence as 'a relief in lonely moments at receptions'. He came to realise that

> Official residences are peculiarly difficult to bring alive, and tend to go dead with unnerving speed: the introduction of 20th century pictures can be a real shot in the arm for them. … Of course, it is no use forcing [one] in because it may just sit about looking for its ticket home. And large angular abstracts tend to be unsuitably self-conscious in embassy rooms. … Such points are picked up abroad, where, rather surprisingly, visitors to embassies often look unusually hard at the rooms in which they are received, directing questioning eyes at unfamiliar styles and objects. They see the presentation of a house and the choice of pictures as a compliment (or otherwise) to the host country.[7]

Fine furnishings and chattels

The best interior created in any residence since the Second World War was probably Duff Cooper's library at Paris. He offered to give the embassy sufficient of his own books to form the nucleus of a good library if the Ministry of Works would pay for re-arranging his sitting room as a study and library to house the collection. The Ministry accepted the offer, little imagining either the cost or the success that would result. The project started conventionally with the long-standing local architect, M. Chatenay, producing a design and an acceptable cost estimate. But the Coopers quickly decided to seek a more imaginative design from their friend Charles de Beistegui and to commission Georges Geoffroy and Christian Bérard, both decorators, to undertake the work. Sourcing the materials was difficult at the end of the war and the eventual cost was more than double Cooper's first guess of £1,000, but the attractiveness of the result quelled all misgivings **(Fig.**

17.1. The Duff Cooper library in the Paris residence. The inscription, installed by Sir Glawyn Jebb while ambassador in the 1950s, reads (in translation) 'Duff Cooper … dedicated this place to the silent friendship of books so that readers might be numbered among his friends. Hail, friend, and read'.

17.1). Cooper's library was greatly appreciated by successive ambassadors for the next 20 years. In 1965, an incoming ambassador's wife, Lady Rachel Reilly, known for her enthusiasm for unsuitable modern paintings, wanted to repaint the library's tortoiseshell colouring, painstakingly based on a St Petersburg decoration, with three tones of pale grey. The Ministry explained the position carelessly and late to the widowed Diana Cooper, then 73, who complained vigorously to Muir, Sir Trenchard Cox and *The Times* to get 'this less happy caprice' overturned – in which endeavour, she characteristically succeeded. One of her own contributions to the Paris house, also executed by Christian Bérard, was to decorate her bathroom in the manner of a Napoleonic military campaign tent. No successor has seen fit to alter the concept.

One of the few other dramatic interior design initiatives in the second half of the twentieth century was in the Washington residence in the early 1980s when the ambassador's wife, Lady Mary Henderson, was given free rein to invite different British interior designers each to redecorate a major room. It was called 'Lutyens 1982: A British Embassy Showcase' because it was conceived to project the best of British interior design (as well as to persuade London to spend some overdue money on the house). Thus David Hicks overhauled the library, David Mlinaric the drawing room, and so on. John Stefanidis arranged Lutyens' ballroom 'as a series of after-dinner sitting rooms connected by a Tabriz carpet that was designed for Queen Victoria's reception at the opening of the Great Exhibition in the Crystal Palace'.[8] Some parts of the Showcase did not last long because they were insufferable to succeeding ambassadors. It was never evident that the exercise paid dividends, either, for the British interior design industry, and it was not repeated elsewhere.

In this respect, the Showcase was no different from numerous prior and subsequent attempts to incorporate British building products in new British embassy buildings or to provide British contractors with an opportunity to demonstrate the cost-effectiveness of their skills in overseas markets. The harsh fact was that sentiment about Britishness and the optimism of British exporters and contractors were at odds with the competitive contracting process. The question of using British materials in the new Washington office building, for example, cropped up in mid-1957 when the embassy pressed the Ministry of Works to ensure that as much material as possible was of British manufacture. The issue was kicked into touch by an agreement that contractors would be encouraged at the tendering stage to use British materials, but when the harder questions of guaranteeing delivery times and seeking waivers from import duties came into focus, it was decided to leave the decisions to US contractors. The result was that British materials were confined to items like balustrades and light fittings. In the 1980s, some more substantial materials, like Welsh roofing slate, were incorporated in new office buildings at Kuala Lumpur and Wellington, but such initiatives required great managerial perseverance and British industry was not rewarded with follow-up orders. As the Treasury accurately saw it in 1966:

> On the … possibility – that of using important buildings abroad as show-pieces for British products and materials and so helping to create local demand which should help exports – it seems legitimate to wonder whether, if special arrangements were needed to ensure that these products were bought, this would indicate that they were not competitive and would therefore be unlikely to sell locally whether they were shown or not. … If a British contractor cannot win your [construction] contract in 'open' competition is he likely to do better in tendering for buildings for other clients?[9]

With the exception of the furniture bought from Pauline Borghese with the Paris house in 1814, the best collection of furniture in the diplomatic estate was probably at Warsaw. It now comprises 21 pieces of early nineteenth-century French furniture, including writing tables, cabinets and commodes. The Zamoyski family commissioned some of this furniture in Paris, as well as a suite of settees and chairs, and imported it into Poland for the Zamoyski palace at Kozlowka, near Lublin in south-east Poland. The family then supplemented the pieces with identical ones commissioned from Polish craftsmen. Kozlowka was occupied by the Germans during the Second World War. After their retreat in 1944, Countess Zamoyski (the count was in a concentration camp) succeeded in transporting the furniture to Warsaw where her cousin managed to store it in a warehouse in the Praga district. Amazingly, the warehouse survived the destructions of the Uprising which laid waste to 80 per cent of the city. The British embassy hired the furniture from the Zamoyski family in 1945, 'when it was impossible to obtain anything else', as the most effective way of furnishing its newly-leased offices and residence.[10] In 1953, the Ministry of Works bought the 71 items that it was hiring, about half of them in good condition, for £1,500. The Taste Committee decided in 1962 that the new Warsaw residence should be furnished in a contemporary manner with the result that in 1964 all of the Zamoyski furniture ended up in the embassy offices at 1 Aleje Róz. After a few years, some of the best pieces found their way into the new residence but it was plain that better arrangements should be made for the bulk of the Zamoyski furniture, not least because the settees and chairs were mostly now in very poor condition, and some had been lost. A long debate in the early 1970s about how to arrange, and afford, repairs and recoverings revealed how culturally prized the furniture had become and that none of it would be allowed to leave Poland, least of all to be sold. A neat arrangement was then worked out. The British government would donate the soft pieces of furniture, in their deteriorated condition, to the newly rebuilt Royal Castle and its craftsmen would restore them for display. In exchange, the Royal Castle craftsmen would restore the hard pieces that would remain with the embassy. HRH Princess Alexandra accordingly presented 14 of the best soft pieces to the Polish National Museum at a ceremony at the Royal Castle in October 1974. They remain there, and restored hard pieces remain in the Warsaw residence.

Curiously enough, the most famous set of silver in missions overseas, known as the Beresford Hope silver, is also at Warsaw. Harold Thomas Beresford Hope, died in Athens in 1917 at the age of 35, while serving there as a secretary in the British legation. In his will, he bequeathed to the First Commissioner of the Office of Works an extensive service of silver, directing that it be held in trust for use in a future British mission in Poland once an independent Polish state was re-established. The bequest included a complete dinner service for 25, including 100 plates, 14 dish covers, 8 entrée dishes and covers, 6 gilt wine coolers, a fine George III 1811 dolphin centre piece, and candelabras. The Office of Works deposited the silver at Coutts and Co. When the Polish state was restored in 1919, it offered the service, then worth at least £2,000, to the ambassador, Sir Horace Rumbold. Rumbold accepted it but suggested a delay of a month or two in view of the threat of rioting in Warsaw. When that was past in 1921, his successor, Sir William Max-Muller, wrote to the Foreign Secretary, Earl Curzon, for the service. Curzon annotated in manuscript 'by all means let him have it. It is a very small affair'.[11] HMS *Castor*, about to pay a visit, took the silver to Danzig, whence Max-Muller collected it and put it to good use in his legation. George V's royal cipher was engraved on the pieces to signify the legation's ownership. The plate originally belonged to Marshal Viscount Beresford and was acquired after his campaigns in Argentina and Portugal during the Napoleonic Wars. It passed down through the family to the childless Harold. His sister, Irene Law, asked to explain the background to the bequest, wrote that Harold

> had looked forward to using the plate at a Legation himself had he lived, and, of course, risen sufficiently in the Diplomatic Service. He was extremely

anxious that a suitable and dignified use should be made of it, and that it should not be scattered among relatives who would not be in a position to display it to proper advantage. ... He selected Poland because he took a keen personal interest in that country, had travelled there privately, and hoped to see it an independent nation. My brother ... explained all these reasons to me at the time of making [his will]. There is no other history attached to the plate.[12]

This straightforward account has never been a match for imaginative alternative reasons for the bequest. The best known is that it was in atonement for the death of a Polish lady with whom Beresford Hope was having an affair in Berlin who shot herself in front of him upon learning that he had gone to the Palais de Danse with another lady.

The embassy left the silver in the strong room when it evacuated Warsaw in September 1939. When it returned, the strong room was empty and there was little that could be done. A few months later, Aliki Russell, the wife of the first secretary, John Russell, was casting her eye over some stalls selling old iron when she spotted a domed metallic object which turned out to be, beneath a coating of smoke and dirt, a silver dish cover. On closer inspection, it revealed George V's royal cipher. Mrs Russell, who had apparently never heard about the embassy's lost silver, unearthed and bought a dozen similar objects before she turned for home. The Russells then set to work in earnest. They discovered that the whole collection had at one time been in the possession of a couple called Laszewski, who lived in one wing of the former embassy on Nowy Swiat, and they had disposed of it gradually to different dealers. The Russells ran the Laszewskis to earth in a suburb of Gdansk and, after a private settlement failed, the embassy handed the matter over to the Polish government in July 1946. The Laszewskis were arrested and made a partial confession, and a few more items turned up. The following year, some more pieces were apparently on offer and Russell alerted London that they could be obtained by payment of a high ransom, but London let the opportunity pass. The embassy then concluded that nothing further could be done to recover more of the plate.[13]

Ten years later, however, two ice buckets turned up at the London antique dealers fair, and a pair of candelabra and a large venison dish were discovered in an antique dealer's shop in New York. This brought to 26 the number of pieces recovered from the 176 stolen. They were loaned first to the Victoria and Albert Museum and then, in 1962, to the Polish National Museum until the new residence in Warsaw opened in 1964. There the Beresford Hope silver remains and is used on formal occasions.

Responsibility for the silver and plate at Posts was transferred from the Foreign Office to the Office of Works in 1905, an event which may have prompted the ambassador in St Petersburg to propose, unsuccessfully, that he should gild his plate because that would 'not necessitate my having here an English underbutler whose sole duty is to look after the plate, and it takes him all his time to keep it in really good order'.[14] The Office issued new plate as normal equipment to embassy houses that had none, and re-issued to Posts that had lost theirs from fire, theft and war. Old plate from a Post that had been downgraded to legation status could be transferred to a new embassy, or, as in the case of Vienna's plate in 1921, divided between two new embassies, Brussels and Rio de Janeiro. A few large chandeliers were likewise re-allocated between Posts if one ballroom became suddenly much more important than another.

Artworks and emblems

Until the First World War, the walls of mission houses were mainly hung with pictures that belonged to incumbents. The exceptions included copies of State portraits, a few loans from the national galleries, and various gifts that had been made to missions. With the prevalence of professional heads of mission, less likely than their predecessors to own sufficient pictures of appropriate quality, a distinct problem of bare walls was looming by the 1930s. The Treasury and the Office of Works had instituted arrangements in 1899, formalised in 1907, to buy original paintings for ministers' rooms in London within an annual allocation of £300. This arrangement was extended in 1935, through a specific additional grant of £250 per annum, to head of mission residences overseas. The first significant painting to be bought with this grant was Count Alfred d'Orsay's 1845 portrait of Wellington, which was sent to hang in Paris (where it remains). In 1946, the Ministry of Works appointed a part-time curator of its picture collection, who reported to a Picture Committee, and the grant for overseas locations was increased to £1,000 in 1948. At the same time it was accepted by the Treasury that some pictures could be bought that were 'useful rather as wall decoration than as examples of pictorial art'.[15] The Picture Committee soon agreed that some of its funds should be spent on acquiring modern works of art, and in 1949 embarked on its first commissioning project. This was for five oil paintings from John Piper to fill the panels in the private dining room of the new residence in Rio de Janeiro. They were street scenes in the Georgian spa towns of Bath, Brighton and Cheltenham – highly successful paintings, of which four now hang in the Washington residence.

The Ministry's collection gathered strength, size and variety during

17.2. Sundial, by Ian Hamilton Finlay, commissioned in 1979 for the forecourt of the Bonn residence by what was then the Department of the Environment's Picture Collection.

the 1950s and 1960s. In the 1970s, while part of the Department of the Environment, its annual grant increased to £100,000, and the acquisition of modern paintings outstripped historical works. The first full-time curator was appointed in 1976, succeeded two years later by Dr Wendy Baron, who served for almost 20 years. During her tenure careful attention was given to 'placing particular items where they work hardest for their living, whether as diplomatic tools, as history or as samples of British achievement'.[16] The arrangements were not without their internal tensions between curatorial propriety and the display of paintings in crowded, hot and humid rooms, and between the relevance of subject to setting and an incumbent's preparedness to live with the result. The Collection embarked on site-specific commissions towards the end of the 1970s, especially for sculptures in mission grounds. The first of these was *Sundial* by Ian Hamilton Finlay opposite the front entrance to the residence in Bonn followed, in the mid-1980s, by *Arch Stones* by John Maine at Canberra and *Richmond Oak* by Kenneth Armitage at Brasilia **(Fig. 17.2)**.

The Collection was renamed the Government Art Collection in 1981, soon after its transfer to a predecessor of the present Department for Culture, Media and Sport. By the mid-1980s, the FCO was prepared to pool some of its funds with the Collection's so as jointly to commission both internal and external works for all major new buildings. This initiative was later strengthened by a 'Percent for Art' movement that sought to persuade public bodies to spend one per cent of a project's budget on incorporating public art. The FCO considered that half a per cent was more appropriate and worked on that basis, with striking results, until the end of the century.

The most famous statue in the diplomatic estate is that of Winston Churchill in Washington. Like many well-intentioned projects, it had fraught beginnings. The idea of a statue was first presented to the embassy in early 1963 by the Washington Branch of the English-Speaking Union with a view to siting it on the corner of Massachusetts Avenue and Observatory Circle. Muir thought it 'a highly embarrassing proposal' and the Minister of Works, Geoffrey Rippon, tried to persuade the Foreign Secretary, Sir Alec Douglas-Home, that, although the idea was a fine one, there was no reason to offer embassy land for it. He feared being sucked into consideration of the fitness of the future statue and, in any event, thought it should be nearer to the centre of Washington where it would more neatly reciprocate that of Roosevelt in Grosvenor Square in London. Douglas-Home was unimpressed by these arguments. Rippon tried again along the lines of it being 'inappropriate for a statue erected by American public subscription … to be sited on Embassy land', and was again rebuffed.[17]

The English-Speaking Union held a small, but squabblesome, competition for the design of the statue, won by the head of the sculpture department at the Cleveland Institute of Art in Ohio, William McVey. Muir told Rippon in October 1963 that he and Bedford were 'horrified by this obscene object'.

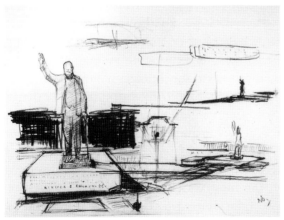

17.3. William McVey's winning proposal for a statue of Winston Churchill in Washington, sketched by Eric Bedford in 1963 while seeking to persuade the English-Speaking Union to accept a simpler setting than it envisaged.

17.4. Roman Halter's inventive 1979 flat filigree design for updating the royal coat of arms, widely used at diplomatic buildings during the next 30 years.

Bedford was dispatched the following month to assess whether the British government should accept on its land 'an ugly statue which would spoil our Embassy'. McVey, however, won Bedford's confidence, and Bedford in turn won the English–Speaking Union committee's agreement to a simpler setting on a revised site, which later moved again to its present position on the wide grass verge between the residence garden and Massachusetts Avenue **(Fig. 17.3)**. The statue was unveiled by the US Secretary of State, Dean Rusk, on 9 April 1966, the third anniversary of the granting to Churchill of Honorary Citizenship.

New representations of the royal coat of arms for official buildings were designed after the Second World War when cast metal versions were no longer available as stock items. Reynolds Stone, an engraver, designed the huge 18 feet tall and 25 feet wide coat of arms incised in 1960 into the external brickwork at the top of the stair in the Washington offices. The sculptor James Woodford was commissioned by the Ministry of Works for a new design of the royal coat of arms in 1962, and this was used for the large, nine-foot-square version that was incised in polished Canadian granite, picked out in gold leaf, in the entrance hall to the Ottawa offices in 1964. Woodford was also responsible for the two large bronzes of lion and unicorn on the gateposts to the Ferdowsi compound in Tehran, and for the design of a new consular shield. Richard Quinnell, an innovative blacksmith, made the coats of arms for the offices at Rome and Khartoum, and the residence at Caracas. It was Roman Halter, however, a Polish Holocaust survivor and, in the 1970s, an architect with his own private practice in London and Cambridge, who has left the most widespread mark at the entrances to diplomatic buildings. In 1979, he showed to Garter King of Arms, Sir

Colin Cole, a drawing showing how he would recommend modernising the royal coat of arms into a flat filigree design to be cast either in bronze or aluminium. Garter King accordingly appointed him 'Designer and Maker of Armorials' and his design has been used at about 50 overseas diplomatic buildings since then **(Fig. 17.4)**. As his title implied, he was also responsible for their production, placement and site fixing. He made castings in seven sizes up to 2.5 metres in height, including for Moscow and Berlin in the late 1990s.[18]

Grounds and gardens
The Office of Works distanced itself for as long as it could from anything to do with grounds and gardens because their upkeep had always been the responsibility of incumbents. Gradually, however, it was forced into accepting the costs of the basic maintenance of grounds that were clearly out of proportion to the buildings, at first at Posts like Tehran and Constantinople and later at Addis Ababa. The Public Buildings Overseas Services section of the Ministry, if it required advice, obtained it from the Bailiff of the Royal Parks, another of the Ministry's internal fiefdoms like Supplies Division. The Office of Works had for long been able, and unembarrassed enough, to complete the construction of new buildings and to pronounce them ready for occupation without having made any financial, design or practical preparations for their external surroundings. This happened most pronouncedly at Washington in 1930 when a generous group of British donors came to the rescue and completed the garden. It happened, too, at properties like Oslo and Ottawa which were bought with extensive grounds without consideration of the gardeners' wages that would fall to incumbents.

It was only in the aftermath of the Plowden Report in 1964 that provision for the upkeep of the gardens of heads of mission residences was transferred from *frais* to, as the Foreign Office circular put it, public funds. The grounds of the compounds were then still being run rather like army camps, with grounds maintenance officers managing the mowing and minimising everything else. Even in the early 1980s, the kerbstones of the compound roads in New Delhi were alternately painted white and black. Occasionally, horticulturally inclined heads of mission would seek the advice of the head of the local botanic gardens about what trees to plant or the identification of what was already growing. The gradual transfer of financial responsibility for residence gardens was accompanied, of course, by some the same panoply of regulations as applied to the furnishings. How much grass had to be cut and how often, for example, how thoroughly it should be watered, and whether to buy gardening equipment from the UK or locally all had to be prescribed or agreed. One Ministry official minuted another in 1952: 'we must have a good case before we fund even a trivial amount of dollars. The power mower, I agree, must be bought locally, but we should send the hand mower from this country'.[19] The ambassador in Warsaw in 1963, Sir George Clutton, in the context of planning the garden for the new residence, thought that

> the bulbs would be a legitimate charge on the head of mission here, but that the water plants, which are of a much more permanent nature, should be a charge on the Ministry of Works. Would you agree to this? Incidentally the pool will have to be stocked with goldfish. Are goldfish a charge on the Ministry of Works and do they remain on this establishment?[20]

Generally speaking, however, gardens were rarely as contentious as houses or furnishings because their entertainment role was less and their timescales tended to protect them from the attentions of the impatient.

18

Reforms and Upheavals
1968-1983

The Duncan Report, 1969

The devaluation of sterling in 1967, followed by the announcement of the withdrawal of British forces from East of Suez, forced the Foreign Secretary, Michael Stewart, to embark on another major review of the FCO, even though it was only five years since Plowden had reported. Stewart invited Sir Val Duncan, chairman of Rio Tinto Zinc, in August 1968 to review urgently 'the functions and scale of the British representational effort overseas' in the light of the difficult circumstances facing Britain. In other words, to find savings overseas, and fast. Duncan's two fellow committee members were Sir Frank Roberts, recently retired as ambassador at Bonn, and Andrew Shonfield, then of the Royal Institute of International Affairs. Soon after they started work, and as Plowden in 1963 had foreseen as desirable, the merger was announced of the Foreign Office and the Commonwealth Office to become the Foreign and Commonwealth Office (henceforth FCO).

Duncan reported in July 1969. His committee recommended strengthening and streamlining the FCO's operations, particularly in economic, commercial and managerial affairs. It thought that, for maximum benefit, the FCO should divide the world into an inner 'Area of Concentration' and an 'Outer Area' of lesser concentration, should maintain fewer Posts abroad and should divide them into 'Comprehensive' and 'Selective' missions, according to the kind and range of skills needing to be deployed. This approach was received with considerable caution in view of its inherent lack of flexibility to cope with changing demands. The last chapter of the Duncan report was devoted to accommodation. The committee approved of providing 'modern and well-equipped [office] buildings in the right locations' and heartily supported Plowden's target of owning two-thirds of staff residential units. In contrast to Jack Diamond, still chief secretary to the Treasury, it did not think that the scale of entertaining was extravagant and it affirmed that 'adequate accommodation must continue to be provided for the purpose' although noting that forms and customs of entertainment were changing. The Committee pointed out that agreement on residential accommodation standards was urgently required and preferred guidelines to strict definitions. Duncan's big overseas accommodation idea, however, was to set up a Crown corporation, to be known as the Overseas Diplomatic Estate Board, to own and manage all the accommodation on more commercial lines with a view to yielding significant savings.

The idea of some sort of finance corporation holding and administering the overseas estate was quite topical. As recently as December 1968, Diamond himself had considered a proposal that the Ministry should borrow overseas on mortgage to pay for diplomatic buildings but concluded that it would be damaging to the government's credit rating to be taking powers in Parliament to borrow money in this way. Duncan was nevertheless enthusiastic about finding a new financial way forward having had, according to Roberts, his enthusiasm fired by the ambassador in Tehran, Denis Wright, telling him that the embassy there was totally unsuitable and worth something like £6 million. The Banque Lambert had also told Duncan that it would be delighted to lend the proposed Board as much money as it could possibly need. The Duncan committee therefore asked the Treasury to prepare a draft paper on the concept and structure of a Crown corporation. Three months later, Roberts observed that 'the Treasury have had a series of second thoughts' and were now likely to 'throw as much cold water as they dare on the idea'. The Duncan committee stuck to its guns in its report and a study group was set up after its publication to examine all aspects of the proposal. In submitting an interim report on the proposed Board, Roberts commented in September 1969:

> The Treasury, on one pretext or another, are clearly out to delay and if possible wreck this recommendation. A more agreeable feature, however, is that they seem prepared to pay as the price some reform of the existing system. ... The Civil Service Department on the other hand seem rather attached to the idea, probably, I think, because they see in it a pilot project for hiving off and for experimenting in management techniques.[1]

The study group continued to meet and write papers throughout 1970 but the Conservatives' return to power in June that year, and Diamond's departure, made no difference to the Treasury's stance on the Estate Board idea, which was not finally killed off until November 1971. A written answer in the House of Commons summarised the reasons for its death. It would have less room for manoeuvre than the Duncan Committee assumed; it would have to remain accountable to Parliament, and to conform to the rules governing public expenditure, and its field for commercial decision would be limited by the need to retain or acquire particular properties for political, prestige or security reasons. The Board could never operate as a competitive commercial enterprise as was intended, for it would be a monopoly supplier to a single tied customer, the FCO; it would cost more than the present departmental arrangements for managing the diplomatic estate and a lengthy and expensive valuation of the diplomatic estate would have to be made before it could be transferred to the Board. Finally, the Board might not be entitled to the immunities and privileges enjoyed by British government departments and overseas missions. There was, however, a silver lining because

> practical measures are being taken to permit more flexible and more effective management of the Overseas Estate. First, Her Majesty's Government will establish a comprehensive and more stable programme for the acquisition or building of property over a 10-year period amounting to some £5 million a year. Secondly, wider financial delegations have been made to the Department of the Environment so that decisions on purchasing and building can be taken much more quickly.[2]

The intended £50 million property acquisition programme was regarded by the FCO and the Ministry of Works as a far better idea than the Estate Board. Unfortunately, the test discount rate – the cost of money to be used in discounted cash flow comparisons between capital and running cost options – touched 13 per cent in the early 1970s, with the result that few purchase propositions survived the comparison. By the end of the ten-year period, only a smallish proportion of the £50 million had been spent.

Property Services Agency, 1972
The new Conservative administration under Edward Heath in October 1970 gathered together, within a huge new Department of the Environment, the Ministries of Public Building and Works, Housing and Local Government, and Transport. Eight months later, Heath appointed Timothy Sainsbury, a director of the supermarket chain J. Sainsbury Ltd, assisted by H.J. Cruickshank, deputy chairman of Bovis, a major construction group,

to study and make recommendations on the exercise of the property management function in Government taking account of the type and distribution of departmental holdings of land and buildings and the particular constraints which apply to Government activity in this field, with a view to ensuring that holdings are put to the best use and that their total extent is kept to a minimum.

Sainsbury produced a preliminary appreciation three months later and his full report in spring 1972. The result, which the Prime Minister announced in a written answer to a Parliamentary Question in May 1972, was the establishment of a departmental agency, to be called the Property Services Agency (henceforth PSA). It would start operations on 1 September 1972 to provide government departments with property management, building construction and maintenance services – that is, the core role of the old Ministry of Works. To ensure the best possible use of resources, the Directorate of Lands and Accommodation from the Ministry of Defence was also incorporated. The PSA would be a 'hived off' accountable unit within the Department of the Environment, with its own trading fund, and headed by a chief executive of permanent secretary status, reporting directly to the Secretary of State for the Environment. The old Public Buildings Overseas Services section re-surfaced within the PSA as the Directorate of Estate Management Overseas (henceforth DEMOS). To help make its mark, the PSA had the curious idea of adopting brown ink on buff paper for all of its publicity and correspondence.

Early in his deliberations, Sainsbury became interested in the particular issues that affected the diplomatic estate overseas, and his proposal to write a separate short report on DEMOS, to be read in conjunction with his wider report on government property management, was accepted. The FCO saw this as an opportunity to test its latent case for managing its own estate: a briefing for the chief clerk prior to a call on him by Sainsbury in November 1971 adumbrated that 'the ideal might well be FCO total responsibility for administering the estate with the … professionals seconded to us. This would allow us to engage in direct negotiations with the Treasury. We are far from this ideal and there are several important reasons why it probably will never be attained'.[3] Sainsbury submitted his short report 'Government Property Management: the Overseas Estate' in March 1972, pointing out that

the tendency for … DEMOS to overemphasise their responsibilities for the costs of the service they provide has led them to assume the role of questioning the needs of their clients, in this case the FCO. As a direct consequence of this the client Departments have not become sufficiently involved themselves in considering the property costs of their policies. Responsibility for policy must necessarily, in my view, carry with it responsibility for considering the costs of that policy, and the ways in which these costs might be varied.[4]

The clear attribution of costs was one of Sainsbury's tenets. He had written, in some frustration, about this to the Treasury in January 1972:

We appear to be no further forward in continuing to keep two enormously expensive sites in Rome ... . This seems to be another example of the formula no attribution equals inaction. If the Ambassador in Post is prepared to put up with the inconveniences of being separated from his office in time and distance, and if the FCO are prepared to accept the high costs of the upkeep of both the building and grounds of the Villa Wolkonsky, then that Department has no incentive to change the situation. Equally the DOE has no incentive. Indeed it could be argued that since the planning and property problems are so complex and, whatever solution is adopted is likely to give rise to some criticism either in Rome or London, inaction is safer than action.[5]

To assist a more widespread understanding of costs, Sainsbury pressed for properties to be properly valued and for the financial relationship between the two departments to be changed from the present 'allied service', under which the PSA met the costs incurred by the requirements of the FCO, to a 'repayment service' whereby the FCO would reimburse the PSA for the work that it carried out on its behalf. The chief clerk was satisfied with Sainsbury's proposals as a stepping stone to a wider objective:

For the first time in the history of the Service, we have now got a decent sum of money, £5 million a year, over a sensible time scale, 10 years, to meet our office and residential accommodation needs overseas. What we now need is a proper organisation for managing the estate and towards this Mr Sainsbury's report points the way. I hope, therefore, the Secretary of State will endorse the general ideas in Mr Sainsbury's report and leave it to officials initially to fight it out in Whitehall: there will be a fight.[6]

The Foreign Secretary, Sir Alec Douglas-Home, agreed: 'Yes this is better. Do not let us use our new freedom to scrap too many of our spacious buildings. Many of them have the "style" which seems so elusive now'.[7] To test the repayment service idea, the FCO, PSA and the Treasury commissioned a review by Eric Stretton, an under secretary in the PSA. He concluded that the overseas diplomatic estate was the only area of PSA activity in which repayment services might be introduced. The PSA, put on the defensive by this awkward conclusion, proposed instead that the FCO and the PSA should experiment with some co-location of their staff so as to improve their inter-departmental communications. The FCO was torn. On one hand, it was tempted to fight for repayment services where it could call the shots, believing it would be more robust and effective than the PSA in argument with the Treasury and Parliamentary Expenditure Committees. It looked forward, for example, to the day when

> The FCO would be able to choose the kind and location of buildings for Embassy Residences, offices or staff houses which meet their operational and representational requirements in the country concerned. Subject to professional advice from the PSA, the FCO could be sure of being able to back its own judgment of its needs without the risks of argument and delay or even long term frustration by another Department.[8]

On the other hand, the FCO knew that some of its own recent and rapid changes of mind caused by wildly different views from successive ambassadors counted against its reputation for sound estate judgement. After weighing the balance, the FCO told the PSA that it would continue with allied services and would take up its offer to co-locate some staff, provided that the PSA's service improved to the point of becoming satisfactory. This would require the PSA to concentrate less on 'under-utilised' properties, and similar 'defensive' work, and more on much-needed future projects. The permanent under-secretary at the FCO, Sir Thomas Brimelow, made the point to the PSA's chief executive, Robert Cox:

> I hope you will not mind my saying that it sometimes seems to us that PSA attach less weight to our operational requirements than to considerations of estate management, when the two are in conflict. To take a current example, I am surprised it has been thought necessary to devote so much time to studying the possibilities of developing the Tokyo compound beyond the point which we, as client Department, have already indicated is acceptable to us.[9]

The co-location of a dozen or so FCO staff from its Accommodation Services Department with DEMOS in Croydon took effect in the mid-1970s. It did not solve any of the major problems but it did lead to better mutual understandings. The PSA learned more about FCO staff's personal and family concerns, duties and comforts abroad, often in really difficult circumstances, which estate experts should take more into account when assessing the suitability of property. And FCO staff came better to understand that the taxpayers' land and buildings had a value that needed to be husbanded in an informed and long-term way rather than damaged by the short-term subjective outlooks of transient occupants.

Sainsbury's short 1972 report on the overseas estate, besides raising the valuation and attribution questions, recommended an overall review of residences of heads of mission because he thought that some of the large and expensive 'classical' houses in Europe were not necessary for the satisfactory practice of modern diplomacy. He wanted the requirements to be defined and the suitability of the houses for meeting them to be assessed. The Director of DEMOS, Bertie Roberts, and the FCO's head of Accommodation and Services Department, David Crawford, reported accordingly in February 1973. They said nothing new or striking. Although heads of mission 'and their wives' found the increasing scarcity of servants burdensome, Ministers continued to require residences to 'be equipped to entertain on a large scale when necessary and to accommodate senior British visitors as house guests.' They pointed out, citing recent proposals to dispose of the residences at Copenhagen and Madrid, that moving an ambassador from a grand house in the centre of a city to a modern residence in the suburbs could harm the British government's interests by implying that the host government had become less important to Britain. But they also recognised that the PSA had a duty to ensure that property was put to the most economic use, and in their opinion some residences did occupy sites that were 'ripe for more intensive development and with high market values' whose disposal would release a capital gain and produce savings in running costs.

The residences review covered all 126 heads of Post residences in the estate at that time. It accepted that about half of the dozen or so residences that fell into a 'larger, older' category should be retained for political reasons despite economic arguments that could point the other way. It concluded that nearly 50 residences required active consideration, of which about a half were to be kept under review. Although the review was, rather mechanically, updated each year until 1982, it was never an effective instrument for forcing real issues into the open. In 1977, the chief clerk in the FCO, Curtis Keeble, was prompted by renewed interest in 'larger, older' residences to send a questionnaire to all ambassadors who lived in what he called the 'elderly' residences. They overwhelmingly thought that the houses worked well for their missions. Keeble submitted his survey findings to Ministers, commenting

I find the strength and unanimity of their feeling about the value of these houses surprising. Significant though their replies are, they must be judged against three other factors: the image of Britain which Ministers consider right for today, the willingness of younger members of the Service and their wives to run these houses in the future, and their ability to find the necessary domestic staff, and the cost of maintaining the present houses and the balance of financial advantage in changing them.[10]

One of the FCO Ministers, Goronwy Roberts, summarised to the Foreign Secretary, David Owen,

one objective in [a forthcoming] discussion should be to gain control of the diplomatic estate from the PSA and to establish clearly what we want of it; it is impossible to generalise about the style needed in various countries. I strongly support the views expressed by our Ambassador in Algiers, viz that if our diplomats live abroad as they live at home, we shall project neither Britain nor anything else.[11]

Central Policy Review Staff Report, 1977
Meanwhile, in January 1976, the Foreign Secretary, James Callaghan, tasked the Central Policy Review Staff with yet another major review of overseas representation, the third in 15 years. The terms of reference were

To review the nature and extent of our overseas interests and requirements and in the light of that review to make recommendations on the most suitable, effective and economic means of representing and promoting those interests both at home and overseas. The review will embrace all aspects of the work of overseas representation … whether these tasks are performed by members of her Majesty's Diplomatic Service, by members of the Home Civil Service, by members of the Armed Forces or by other agencies financially supported by Her Majesty's Government.[12]

The review, led by the head of the Review staff, Sir Kenneth Berrill, produced a large report in July 1977. Through a hint of intellectual bemusement, it betrayed some detachment from the practicalities of the world. Its main conclusion was that the British government was spending too much effort on many issues which did not justify the skill and dedication devoted to them, and its main recommendations dealt with which of these activities should be scaled down, and how. On accommodation, the review leaned more to the PSA's economic arguments than to the FCO's representational ones. The reviewers recognised

that reconciling operational, financial, estate management and on occasion environmental considerations is no easy matter. We nonetheless believe that the PSA has attached too much importance to good relations with the FCO as an end in itself and that the price paid for this has been waste of public money and lost or deferred opportunities to realize assets. Estate management considerations have not always been given their proper weight.[13]

The 14 accommodation recommendations (of 280 in all) included PSA assuming full responsibility for all accommodation at Posts, while granting greater delegation to Posts and making more use of rent allowance hirings. The target of owning two-thirds of accommodation overseas should be abandoned, and the £50 million programme ended. Residential accommodation standards should be revised downwards, not least to reflect the effect of another main recommendation to halve the FCO's annual expenditure on entertainment. Housing for staff should broadly reflect standards they would expect to enjoy in the UK (which begat the dismissive FCO expression 'Bromley Man'). Proposals should be drawn up to make a start on disposing of historic buildings; the personal taste of heads of mission should not influence the design of new buildings; there should be regular efficiency audits of PSA's estate management; and a few FCO staff should be seconded to the PSA.

The whole review incurred the deep hostility of the FCO, which put enormous effort in the next few years into opposing, neutralising or side-stepping the most unpalatable recommendations. Sir Andrew Stark, who had just left Copenhagen with a view to retiring, was instead retained to marshal the counter-attack. On accommodation, despite the recommendation that the PSA should have the prime responsibility for the diplomatic estate, the FCO returned to its latent idea of gaining control for itself. It could hardly expect to win but may have thought that attack was the best form of defence in the circumstances. The Foreign Secretary, David Owen, wrote to the Environment Secretary, Peter Shore, in March 1978.

> The accommodation needs of the Diplomatic Service overseas are peculiar in nature, and we need to find a means of meeting them which will ensure that such funds as are available are utilised according to our own operational priorities in meeting the tasks which Ministers place upon the Service. It is not a matter of the total amount of money available but of the assessment of priorities. Indeed it might be that, if we were able to work out a more generally acceptable arrangement, we could give up the £50 million building programme and also consider to what extent revenue represented by sales of surplus property could be used to finance some of the expenditure on new buildings. ... I should like to propose that officials from

385

our two Departments, perhaps with Treasury help should consider how an arrangement along these lines might be most efficiently achieved.[14]

FCO officials were minuting internally about conversations they had had with other government departments. One wrote 'It is a subjective point, but I feel that [the Treasury's] whole attitude ... is that [the FCO is] more likely than the PSA to be extravagant, and that the present double check should not be abandoned'. Another, 'In short, the PSA is preparing to argue that we already get everything we want under the allied service system, so why should there be any change? As I see it, the more we pin our argument to case histories, the more difficult we will find it to withstand reasonable assurances of future cooperation'.[15] Sure enough, as Shore replied to Owen in April 1978:

> I am far from convinced that any such change is either necessary or desirable. The Diplomatic Estate is of course an important backcloth for the efficient functioning of the diplomatic service. We must ensure that it fully reflects your operational requirements and on this your people do have in practice the final say on operational priorities. But the management of the Estate is a matter of considerable skill and complexity. It is a highly valuable asset ... so good and efficient estate management is an important factor. ... I would much prefer therefore to instruct our officials to concentrate on extending and deepening the close co-operation which already exists and to advise us on how the working methods between the two Departments can be still further improved so that management policies are fully responsive to operational and other requirements.[16]

The FCO talked with the chief secretary to the Treasury, Joel Barnett, who spotted some useful leverage. As he summarised it to the Foreign Secretary:

> I am not at all clear what purpose a change in the arrangement of the kind you describe would serve. However, you mentioned in your letter that you can go along with most of the recommendations in the CPRS review, and I think that we can most usefully consider your idea when we have seen in full what is the FCO response to the other recommendations about accommodation. ... As I understand it, PSA officials, who are in the lead on this part of the report, are waiting for FCO's considered views on a number of the individual items, and Treasury officials are ready to take part in discussing them.[17]

This put the FCO on the defensive. It had been delaying decisions about reducing entertainment expenditure, which was delaying decisions about how much reduction to accept in accommodation scales, which obviously now had to be agreed before the Treasury would begin to consider the FCO's case for greater control of the estate. Owen annotated a related minute 'We are not likely to win', and the issue faded.

FCO gains control

A year later, in May 1979, Margaret Thatcher led the Conservatives to power. In October 1980, Douglas Hurd and Geoffrey Finsberg, Ministers respectively in the FCO and the Department of the Environment, set up a 'Joint Review of Diplomatic Estate Management'. Its terms of reference were couched entirely in the context of the status quo:

> Granted the present framework of Vote accountability, Ministerial responsibility and Treasury delegations and ground rules, and the desirability of close and efficient liaison, to review the organisation and procedures of [the FCO's] Accommodation and Services Department, [and PSA's] Division of Estate Management Overseas, ... their inter-relationships and their several procedural relationships with Diplomatic Posts; to recommend improved practices within those organisations and procedures, ...[18]

The group, chaired by James Adams of the FCO, comprised seven other officials from the FCO and the PSA (but none a professional officer), and two members from the private sector. One was Idris Pearce, a partner in the major surveying firm of Richard Ellis, a member of the PSA's advisory board, and a property adviser to the Conservative party: he was later President of the Royal Institute of Chartered Surveyors and knighted. The other non-official member was Harry Smith, who had just retired from a senior management role in Barclays Bank International. Adams and his group produced a cautious report about procedural changes and outlined 48 recommendations for the refinement of current processes. Pearce and Smith contributed a section of their own entitled 'The View from the Private Sector'. Their argument culminated in one sentence in paragraph 9.14, an underlined portion of which said '... the whole of the diplomatic estate should pass from PSA to FCO control ...'. The concluding section of the final report sought to suffocate this idea because it

> suggests a major change in departments' role and Vote responsibility. The official members of the Group, noting that this change lies outside the Group's terms of reference, have not felt able to comment. They have rather concentrated on the development of proposals for decentralisation which are compatible with the present Vote arrangements. Though Departments will wish to consider the pace of change, the general trend is thus agreed.[19]

By officials, but not with the influential minority private sector view. This hot potato was passed to the politicians. Hurd, who had been a career diplomat for 15 years, and his Secretary of State, Lord Carrington, a former high commissioner in Canberra, both supported the radical change proposed by Pearce and Smith. It may have been slightly less welcome to Finsberg and his Secretary of State, Michael Heseltine, but it was in tune with the time and its being the brainchild of a trusted property adviser to the Conservative party diminished political opposition to it. Vote Transfer, the Treasury's technical term for transferring a spending responsibility from one department to another, was therefore agreed during 1982, to take effect on 1 April 1983. Practically all of the rest of the steering group report was rendered inapplicable.

The FCO thus became the first major government department to wrest control of the property that it occupied from the centralised government property department that had managed it for well over 100 years. Though it was no part of Pearce's and Smith's intention to begin the dismantlement of PSA, the FCO's departure from its grasp heralded the PSA's disintegration in the privatising climate of the Thatcher government. Other government departments gained increasing control of their estates during the 1980s and what was left of the PSA in 1990 was split into Property Holdings, which remained within government, and PSA Services, which was progressively commercialised before being sold a few years later. Property Holdings staggered on for a while and the rump of its responsibilities was reformulated in 1996 into the Property Advisers to the Civil Estate. This was absorbed into the Office of Government Commerce in 2000 and soon afterwards ceased to exist. Thus ended, without anyone really noticing, more than 500 years of the role of an Office of Works.

In-house coup de grâce
The 15 years between Sir Val Duncan's idea in 1968 of an Overseas Diplomatic Estate Board and, at the opposite end of the managerial spectrum, the actuality in 1983 of Vote Transfer to the Foreign Office was a period for the diplomatic estate of both policy uncertainty and financial stringency. The government's financial difficulties culminated in a halt to most capital investment during 1975, an International Monetary Fund loan in September 1976, and the Chancellor of the Exchequer imposing a 12-month moratorium on all new construction projects a few months later. These were the years, too, which saw the change from in-house supremacy to significant reliance on private practice, especially in the architectural field.

The Ministry of Works' experience of the three commissions with high-profile private architects for Lagos, Rome and Brasilia during the 1960s had not been a great success. This did not mean, at the beginning of the 1970s, that the in-house architects would again have things all their own way because two new factors came into play. One was the gradual run-down of all in-house staff as a result of the stringency measures and the other a frontal attack on the design quality of the diplomatic office buildings overseas that the Ministry had produced in-house since the war. The attack was led by J.M. Richards, editor of *The Architectural Review* from 1937 until 1971, architectural correspondent of *The Times* from 1947 until 1971, and the most influential architectural commentator in Britain. He was, besides, a Royal Fine Art Commissioner for many years from 1951 and had therefore seen at close hand the Ministry's resistance to change its in-house ways and to improve its architecture so as better to represent Britain overseas.

Sir Donald Gibson, the Ministry's controller-general, was stung by an editorial in *The Architectural Review* in August 1968 which described the Ministry's output of diplomatic offices as 'dismal and depressing'.[20] To an offer by Gibson to show him a sample of current Ministry work, Richards replied:

> my criticism of the Ministry's work overseas was solely confined to the work done for Foreign Office use … . I do feel strongly … about the poor standard of the work for embassies. I should be delighted to have a talk with you some time, as you suggest, and see the work you are doing. If you able to show me embassy work that is better than the work I know, I shall, of course, be delighted, although surprised.[21]

Gibson showed Richards 34 widely different projects in November 1968 and thought that he had recovered some ground. Three years later, however, and after Gibson and Bedford had retired and he was about to retire, Richards delivered the *coup de grâce* in *The Architectural Review* in September 1971. In the same issue that carried a lavish spread about Spence's recently completed offices in Rome was a starkly contrasting article entitled 'DEMO'S Dismal Record'. It was a survey, with unflattering little black-and-white snapshots and illegibly small floor plans, of 22 diplomatic office buildings designed in-house, beginning with Bonn in 1953 and ending with Islamabad in 1971. There were references to 'uncertain clienthood', 'inexcusably pedestrian designs' and an 'indictment of bureaucratic banality'. Much of the text itself was unsparing:

> Embassy buildings are the best permanent opportunity of presenting a country's image abroad and, while the ambassador's residence is only visited

by a select few, the chancery building is accessible to everyone. It will be apparent that none of the 22 chancery buildings illustrated here … measures up to this symbolic role. Though functionally never less than adequate, none is architecturally distinguished, and none would qualify for inclusion in an anthology of the best British buildings of the last 20 years.

The reasons for this failure are plain. … the fact that Ministry architects are civil servants, that advancement comes through seniority and that dismissal is virtually impossible will continue to discourage the best architects from going there. The Directorate of Estate Management Overseas … has the added disadvantage of serving the Foreign and Commonwealth office, where old-fashioned attitudes to matters of design remain deeply ingrained …

[Competitions] … would give our best designers a chance of showing the world that some of us do care about good architecture, even if our Establishment remains philistine and unable to see in a chancery building anything more than an office block.[22]

Two years later, in 1973, came the publication of an internal Department of the Environment inquiry into the 'Promotion of High Standards of Architectural Design', by Sir Robert Matthew, a former chief architect to the London County Council and now an eminent private practitioner, and William Skillington, a deputy secretary in the department. This report led to the appointment of Dan Lacey, a respected former county architect, as the director-general of design in the PSA as an indirect successor to Bedford who had retired three year earlier. Lacey established a high-profile in-house Design Office at the centre of PSA to demonstrate by example how to achieve higher design standards throughout the organisation. To the same end, he established a Design Panel to advise on major projects across PSA and to hold 'crits' with design teams. Lacey also kept a close eye on the selection procedures for the increasing number of architectural practices that were being commissioned by the PSA, both as another means of improving design quality and as a result of the government's run-down of in-house staff.

The Design Office never took on an embassy project but Lacey encouraged DEMOS to set up its own mini-design office under Alfred Coutts, a superintending architect, to design new embassy buildings that could no longer be delayed for Brasilia. Lacey's decision that Brasilia should be designed in-house drew a mournful letter in 1976 from Sir Hugh Casson, then president of the Royal Academy. Lobbied by Peter Smithson, Casson wrote to the Secretary of State for the Environment, Peter Shore, in November 1976:

It seems sad that our Embassies overseas, which should be regarded from the prestige point of view at least as seriously as the Ambassadors cars [which were mostly Rolls-Royces], are not even made subject to competition, or given to acknowledged heads of the profession, (as was done with Basil Spence at Rome). This is particularly the case in Brasilia ... I am of course not suggesting that the work should be returned to the Smithsons. We are all reconciled to the fact that this is not possible. ... I think it is regrettable that the policy seems to have been reversed [and] embassies in the more important countries are treated as no more important than Telephone Exchanges in provincial British cities.[23]

By then, Lacey and others had moved the PSA sufficiently forward on the design front for Shore to be able to dismiss this lament as outdated and to reassure Casson and others that projects already in the pipeline would prove the point. The PSA was trying to improve the architectural standard of diplomatic buildings in several ways. One was by appointing new in-house architects to DEMOS with track records of designing good new buildings (working drawings were by then nearly all being done by consultants): thus Adrian Bell, Kenneth Campbell, Alfred Coutts, John Hopewell, Norman Isham and John Watts found themselves working on diplomatic buildings. Another way was by ensuring that commissioned architects were thoughtfully selected, with a match between their professional strengths and the challenge of each project, and that they were properly briefed and controlled. Thus were practices like Powell and Moya, Robert Matthew Johnson-Marshall, Trevor Dannatt, and John Harris commissioned: humane and refreshing practices with dependable records. The PSA never went so far as to organise a design competition for any diplomatic building. The third way that the PSA improved performance was by introducing more effective in-house project management arrangements.

1970s projects
The new high commission offices building in Islamabad in 1971, designed in-house by Gordon Hindle and Tony Exley, although appearing in 'Dismal Record' as the latest of that line, was in some ways also a turning point in having a more innovative plan. The site was at the top of a low hill, off which nearly a million cubic feet of earth and stone were excavated and carried away by donkey. The building comprises a central four-storey rectangular block containing reception, waiting area, a small cinema and library on its lower levels and classified offices above. On either side of the central block, and slightly separate from it, lie two narrow three-storey blocks of unclassified offices, the gap being bridged once at each floor level **(Fig. 18.1)**. The offices extended to about 27,500 square feet of net area for

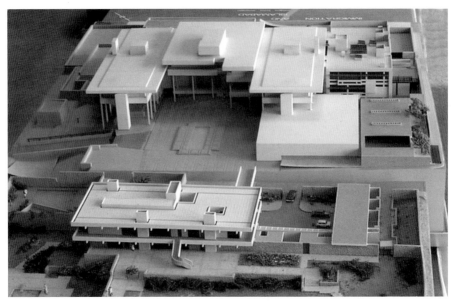

18.1. Block models of the high commission buildings at Islamabad. Above: offices completed in 1971 in white, and an immigration, visa and consular wing designed by Anwar Said with Thompstone, Wintersgill and Faulkner, completed in 1993, at right. Below: residence completed in 1976.

about 150 UK and local staff. The structure is a reinforced concrete frame, with concrete block infilling and partitioning, with anodised aluminium curtain walling and glazing, finished with plentiful use of local marble and stone externally and internally. Tripe and Wakeham were associated architects for the project and responsible for the production drawings and site supervision. On the furnishings side, the high commissioner's desk and meeting table were made of Indian laurel by Heals of London, and the chairs were QEII design by Race Furniture. The tables in the entrance hall were, as the Department of the Environment press notice had it, 'of unusual design in lightweight concrete with tops in matt black plastic laminate'.[24]

The first consultant to be commissioned for a major diplomatic building since the Smithsons in 1964 was Robert Matthew Johnson-Marshall and Partners in 1969, soon after Gibson had sought to persuade Richards that the Ministry would pay more attention to design. The practice was commissioned for new offices in the north end of the Bangkok compound, between Wireless Road and the great pond that acts as a holding tank during monsoon rains. The building was a three-storey hollow square plan with an open ground floor on the pond side, and an adjacent two-storey building for storage and ancillary functions, a separation of activities with a long in-house history. The building, completed in 1973, proved thoroughly satisfactory: efficient in its planning and quietly assured in its appearance, though the elegant external vertical bronze sun louvres lost some of their adjustability as the years went by. Occupation of the new offices enabled a programme to start of converting the large 1920s former staff houses in the compound back to UK staff residential use, though this time with two or four flats in each. The Bangkok office building was a success in another way: it demonstrated to the in-house sceptics of private practice, scarred by the bullying of Spence and wearied by the obsessions of the Smithsons, that it was possible to work constructively and harmoniously with consultants.

Concurrent with Bangkok were new offices at Singapore, on a large green site on Tanglin Circus which the Singapore government granted to the British government as part of wider arrangements for the withdrawal of British forces. This building, designed by the in-house architect Kenneth Campbell, was another significant break from the 'Dismal Record'. Campbell separated more fully than had been done elsewhere the high commission's private from its public areas. The former he put into a three-storey block of mainly cellular offices, with two parallel corridors down the centre of

18.2. High commission offices completed in 1973 in Singapore, with private offices in the left building and public areas in the right. Beyond, the British Council built a classroom block to comparable design in 1988. It was a condition of the land grant that the areas in front should remain as landscape.

each floor and small service and ancillary rooms between them. On the same podium, he put the public areas in a separate open-plan, one-storey building with a space frame roof and a continuous curtain wall of grey tinted glass, with a large car-park beneath. The entire exterior was clad with off-white glazed ceramic mosaic. The whole composition was light, bright, well considered in manner and detail, good to work in, and skilfully related to the topography and landscape of the site **(Fig. 18.2)**.

In the slipstream of their highly successful British pavilion at the 1970 Expo in Osaka (where they had nothing to do with the feeble displays within), Powell and Moya were commissioned in the early 1970s for two successive diplomatic building schemes. Events conspired against both. The first was in 1972 for new offices in Bonn. The early 1950s offices on Friedrich Ebert Allee had become seriously overcrowded by the mid-1960s. Building a further extension to them was possible but the erection of the Berlin Wall in 1961 had suggested that Bonn might remain the capital of West Germany for longer than was earlier imagined, or even permanently. This realisation prompted the question of whether a better long-term site and building should be sought for the embassy offices. Four possible sites

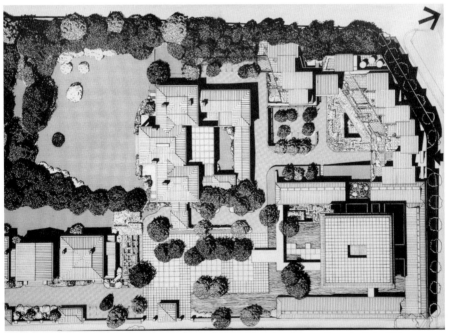

18.3. Plan of sketch design by Powell and Moya in 1974 for the north end of the Tokyo compound. The plan envisaged moving the formal compound entrance northwards to almost opposite the residence *porte-cochère*. A proposed five-storey square chancery building is at bottom right.

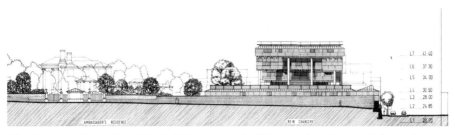

18.4. Section of Powell and Moya's 1974 proposals for Tokyo, with residence at left and chancery block at right. A new staff and service entrance was intended at the north end, to feed into a car-park at sub-basement level.

had been identified, and in 1970 the choice fell on the site immediately to the south of the residence on the Rhine in Bad Godesberg, called the Van Gülpen site after its vendors. This 1.5-hectare site was bought in March 1971 for £427,000, once Norman Isham, a PSA senior architect, had obtained a planning consent in principle to build embassy offices on it. Powell and Moya were commissioned in 1972 to take the scheme forward. Philip Powell spent a good deal of time on the project over the next 18 months. His proposal was characteristically civilised, with a four-storey chancery block rising through an agreeably laid out arrangement of lower buildings with corridors and courts facing the Rhine at the top of a landscaped bank.[25] The PSA was keen to replace the adjacent residence with a penthouse flat and a dedicated garden area at the offices but was unable to win the argument against an aghast FCO. By the end of 1973, however, it became apparent that the time and expense required for the development of this site was disproportionate to the ease of extending the current offices, and Powell and Moya's scheme was set aside. The Van Gülpen site was sold in 1977, by which time there was no need, either, for a new extension at the Friedrich Ebert Allee offices.

Powell and Moya were commissioned again in 1974 to design a scheme for all that part of the Tokyo compound that lay north of the residence. The brief was for about 6,000 square meters of office and ancillary accommodation, 35 flats for locally employed staff, and underground car parking for 60 cars. Their solution was a five-storey square block, with its floors stepping a little outwards as it rose, surrounded on three sides by one or two floors of ancillary accommodation. The staff flats behind were stacked up to four floors in a dogtooth plan, served by access balconies, above two floors of car-parking, workshops and storage. The elegant sketch design held much promise but the project was abandoned in the 1976 moratorium and never resurrected on the same scale **(Figs 18.3 & 18.4)**.

In Kingston, Jamaica, new offices were completed in 1976 in the 12-acre grounds of Trafalgar House, the residence. Designed in-house by Frank Cooper, the building was of two office storeys on a square plan, slightly raised above ground level by a semi-basement floor of car parking. The upper floor oversailed the lower on all sides, and had an internal garden terrace. It was a rigidly planned and constructed building, as befitted Jamaica's need for earthquake-resistant structures. Another in-house designed office building was completed in Lagos in 1977. The pre-independence intention in Lagos was that high commission offices would later be built on the same Marina site as the residence. That plan, however, changed soon afterwards and a site that had been reclaimed from mangrove swamp at Plot 5, Ahmodu Bello Road (several times since re-named) on Victoria Island was instead leased for 99 years from 1963. Here Alan Wild designed a slightly meandering one-storey building through which rose a square block of two more storeys. The ground's loadbearing capacity was low, so the foundations for the central part were piled, the single storey parts rested on a reinforced concrete raft, and all the cladding was made of glass reinforced plastic panels to save weight: they were moulded in Britain, many of them with projecting fins for shading the windows. The resultant appearance was hardly satisfactory **(Fig. 18.5)**.

Five residences were built during this period. Caracas, in 1973, was

18.5. Entrance front of the Lagos high commission offices, completed in 1977. Glass-reinforced plastic was used for cladding panels to save weight on the swampy ground.

18.6. Garden elevation of the residence in Caracas, completed in 1973. The Islamabad residence of 1976 shared much of the same planning, including reception areas on the first floor and bedrooms below.

essentially a linear plan with the reception rooms and a large terrace on the upper of two floors **(Fig. 18.6)**. Islamabad, designed in-house by Adrian Bell and completed in 1976 as the fourth phase of the development plan for the high commission in the new capital, was also linear with its reception rooms on the upper floor to maximise its views. Pretoria, in 1976, was an L-shaped plan with a swollen knuckle containing, again on the first floor, the reception rooms with circular stair from the foyer below. It was designed by David Wager in the London office of the South African practice, Gluckman, de Beer, Margoles and Partners. Manila, in 1981, was designed by Kenneth Campbell with a wide V-shaped plan with drawing room and a double-height dining room on the ground floor at the centre. A neat new residence in the Abu Dhabi compound was completed in 1981 by John R. Harris and Partners.

A depleted programme of new construction was not the only hallmark of the 1970s. Estate policy uncertainties, institutional distrust between the FCO and the PSA, particularly in respect of the future of major European residences, and ambassadorial inconsistencies all played their part in a great deal of effort achieving rather little. The combination of distrust and inconsistency led to false starts in both Madrid and Copenhagen on the question of whether or not to replace a large and elderly residence with an easier and cheaper-to-run smaller and newer one. In Madrid, there was a danger in 1969 that the residence at Hermanos Becquer would be unacceptably overlooked by a threatened adjacent development. A site in the excellent residential district of Puerta de Hierro was therefore bought in

397

1970 on which to build a new residence in expectation of selling Hermanos Becquer for a considerable sum. In 1971, however, a preservation order was served on it which greatly reduced the price that it would fetch upon sale and therefore called into question one of the reasons for moving. Ministers therefore decided that it should be retained after all and the new site at Puerta de Hierro sold, an event that was not achieved until 1977. Soon after that sale, and as construction of the new 12-storey Banco Coca building progressed next door to Hermanos Becquer, the ambassador concluded that retention of the residence was, after all, untenable. Another site in Puerta de Hierro, this time with a house already on it in Avenida de Miraflores, was therefore bought in 1978 for occupation, after ingoing works, in 1980. It was a two-storey house, some 30 years old, in the manner of a comfortable country villa, set in a well laid out, good-sized garden with a private swimming pool. It was occupied in 1980 and the former residence at Hermanos Becquer sold shortly thereafter.

In Copenhagen, an alternative to the much-loved old residence on Bredgade had been sought since 1963, when an ambassador first decided that it was no longer viable as a residence and the Ministry became nervous about the expensive refurbishment that it would require if retained. In 1967 a promising site at 2 Bernstorffslund Alle in Charlottenlund was bought with a view to demolishing the house on it and building anew. The Minister of Works, Robert Mellish, was asked in Parliament whether he would agree that 'selling the present Embassy, which is beautiful … and replacing it with a suburban building which will stand a 50-50 chance of being pretty ugly thanks to modern architects, is very false economy indeed?'. Mellish replied that 'All the expert advice is that we should sell it and buy a new property, and build a new Embassy which will be a credit to Britain – and I believe that there are good architects available to do that'.[26] The ambassador, Oliver Wright, applauded the move when he wrote to the FCO in August 1967:

> The purchase of the site for the new Residence brings us to the end of Round Two of the medium weight contest of the decade: Round One being the original decision to sell Bredgade. Seconds out for Round Three: an early decision to demolish this winter the house at present on the site. It needs to be done. It won't cost much. …
>
> Where, O where, is the Jack Cotton of Whitehall, the Charles Clore of Westminster? Why do only Government Departments do everything the hard way, the unprofitable way, making the minimum use of valuable assets? With all the property HMG own in the world, we could put our balance of payments right and increase our overseas assets into the bargain by proper estate management. How long, O Lord, how long?[27]

A very long time indeed, it would seem. Only 15 months later, Wright wrote again to the FCO:

> After a little over two years at this post, I am becoming, month by month, more convinced that the decision in principle to sell the Embassy in Bredgade and build a new Residence in the suburbs is wrong and that I was wrong to endorse that decision … after much thought, I must recommend that the idea of moving be reversed or allowed quietly to drop. … The longer I live in it [Bredgade], the less I can imagine how I or anyone else could ever have thought of giving it up … I realise that I am open to the accusation of inconsistency of judgment. But I would rather admit that I was hasty in judgment two years ago than bear the blame for all time that I allowed this lovely Embassy to be alienated from British ownership during my tour of duty here.[28]

The reversal was accepted and ambassadors remained at Bredgade for another ten years while the estimated cost of refurbishing it rose to £250,000. Meanwhile, the house on Bernstorfflund Alle lay dormant. When the whole question was revisited in 1978, the decision was again reached in principle to move. This time there was a satisfactory alternative residence available: Bernstorffshoj, at 6 Ved Slotshaven in Gentofte. Prince Axel, and his Swedish bride, Princess Margaretha, were given this property as their wedding present in 1919. The original house burned down and they built the present house in 1937. Princess Margaretha continued to live in it after the death of her husband in 1964 and died there in 1977. Bernstorffshoj had been identified in 1967, when Bernstorfflund Alle was bought, as a preferable residence if ever the princess was to leave it, and now she had. The PSA bought it in 1978 and returned it to good condition after its years of neglect. It was ready, after a scramble, for the ambassador, Dame Anne Warburton, to occupy just in time for the State Visit of Queen Elizabeth II in May 1979. Bernstorfflund Alle and Bredgade were both sold soon afterwards.

As a result of all the uncertainties and difficulties that had afflicted the diplomatic estate during the 1970s, it moved into the control of the FCO in 1983 with a light workload but a heavy backlog of overdue decisions.

19

Diplomats in Control
1983–2000

Vote Transfer and Overseas Estate Department

On 1 April 1983 the FCO became responsible for the management of the entire overseas diplomatic estate for the first time since the Treasury removed that responsibility from the Foreign Office over a century earlier. The Foreign Secretary, Francis Pym (succeeded after the General Election in June that year by Geoffrey Howe), was made a 'corporation sole' by Order in Council so that he and his successors could acquire and hold title to property abroad.[1] The minister of state was Douglas Hurd (succeeded by Malcolm Rifkind), the permanent under-secretary Sir Antony Acland, and chief clerk Derek Day. The FCO already had a dozen or so of its staff co-located with the PSA's Directorate of Estate Management Overseas in Apollo House in Croydon, and, a few months before Vote Transfer, it appointed Roger Carrick, then a counsellor in Washington, to be the head of the new combined department called the Overseas Estate Department (henceforth OED). The FCO took on loan 150 or so PSA professional, technical and executive staff working on the estate, about 40 of them serving at Posts as technical works officers, clerks of works and maintenance supervisors. The author of this book was fortunate to be selected as the leader of this brigade and became the deputy head of OED. He succeeded Carrick two years after Vote Transfer and served as head until 1997, when he retired and became an estate adviser to the FCO. He therefore played a central role in the development of the estate during the remainder of the period of this history. Carrick went on to a more illustrious career: from Croydon to

Chicago as consul-general, to Jakarta as ambassador and to Canberra as high commissioner, where he became Sir Roger.

At the time of Vote Transfer, the estate comprised 4,067 properties in 132 countries. 263 of them (about 7 per cent) were offices, 150 (about 4 per cent) were head of Post residences, 3,491 (85 per cent) were staff residential units, ranging from one-bedroom flats to counsellors' houses, and 163 (4 per cent) were ancillary buildings like garages. sixty per cent of the residences were owned and about 35 per cent of each of the other types of accommodation. Of the 2,250 or so leased units of staff accommodation, about 600 were leased for more than nine years: almost all of the rest were rented locally by Posts for their UK staff within area guidelines and rent ceilings set by London.

The PSA was doubtful that the FCO would have the right institutional attitude towards its new estate responsibilities. It feared that expedience, short-termism and subjective sentiment, rather than long-term value for money, would become the dominant factors. These forebodings were balanced, of course, by the FCO's contention that PSA staff were more interested in estate management principles than addressing the official priorities of the occupants of its properties. The Public Accounts Committee, familiar with the two departments' inability to agree about estate matters during the 1970s, decided to make its own enquiries. Just three weeks before Vote Transfer, it took evidence from Acland and the chief executive of the PSA, Montague Alfred, on the basis of a somewhat wary memorandum by the Comptroller and Auditor General, the government's chief spending watchdog who reported to the committee. Dale Campbell-Savours MP opened his questioning with characteristic verve: 'Is it not fair to say that we have had 10 years riddled with obstruction by the Foreign Office to PSA and other recommendations to cut down the size of the … estate overseas?'[2] Acland told the committee that he was 'ruthlessly determined to run the diplomatic estate cost effectively and efficiently.' In publishing its findings, the committee drew specific attention to overlarge residences at Singapore and Vienna, and the deputy high commissioner's house, Hamilton House, in Nairobi. More generally, the committee was

> concerned that FCO's reluctance to act on PSA's proposals … reflects undue emphasis on considerations of prestige or tradition and not enough on meeting contemporary diplomatic needs economically. In particular, we question the need to maintain in the 1980s a lavish style of personal accommodation which appears to have outlived its time. We therefore urge FCO to adopt a radical change in attitudes giving a new and positive emphasis to considerations of cost-effectiveness.[3]

The FCO took most of this to heart. OED published a paper on its future management of the estate in early November 1983. The third part, on policy prescriptions, began:

> The management of the Estate should be constantly influenced by the concept of the Estate as a tool of British diplomacy: this is its primary function. But if the Estate as a tool is to be effective in the longer term in providing the right support for British diplomatic activity it needs honing and sharpening. The policy prescriptions that follow are aimed at achieving this.[4]

The prescriptions included estate rationalisation; asset recycling; greater devolution of estate responsibilities to Posts (all in accordance with the government's 1982 Financial Management Initiative); flexibility in the design and application of accommodation standards; and making the best practicable use of historic houses. The rationalisation requirements imposed a heavy programme of work on OED. It had spare capacity for this, however, because the committed major project programme was small after the stultified 1970s. In 1983, the only projects on site were Khartoum offices (designed by John Watts) and the Brasilia offices and residence (both by Alfred Coutts), and the only ones in pre-contract stages were Accra offices (also by John Watts) and the offices, residence and 35 UK staff houses for Riyadh (by Trevor Dannat and Partners). Nevertheless, a re-structuring of OED for its new and heavier responsibilities soon became necessary. The PSA's Directorate of Estate Management Overseas had been structured with four essentially mono-functional groups, dealing with policy, estate surveying, maintenance and major works, each covering the whole world. By 1985, OED had re-arranged this matrix into three multi-functional groups (plus the major works group) each covering a geographical region so as to enable both closer multi-disciplinary working and greater familiarity of staff with smaller regions of the world.

Estate rationalisation and asset recycling
The first of the two main tasks for OED was to map out estate strategies for 50 or so Posts, where some rationalisation was clearly both desirable and possible, to replace the mechanistic and ineffectual Town Surveys of the 1970s. The second was to persuade the Treasury to agree to some mechanism by which the money raised from sales could be retained by the FCO to fund a rationalisation programme. In long-held Treasury theory, sales proceeds that had been predicted in Estimates could be added to the Vote as 'appropriations in aid' and spent in the same year as they were raised. This

enabled the Treasury to reduce the underlying Vote but, perversely, it did nothing to increase the funds available for investment. If the sales proceeds came in later, or the sale realised less, than was predicted, an overspend might even be incurred, which was still more perverse. Sales proceeds, on the other hand, that had not been predicted in Estimates, or were in excess of a prediction, went straight to the Exchequer as 'Consolidated Fund Extra Receipts' and could in no way benefit the investment programme. There was therefore almost nothing for a department to gain by selling an asset. The Treasury had occasionally in the past granted the PSA one-off exemptions from this regime in the UK estate but had not recently been prepared to do so.

The FCO set about trying to persuade the Treasury that it should be permitted to recycle all estate sales proceeds into a rationalisation account that would fund the provision of more economical replacement properties. This account would be separate from the normal Vote arrangements for operationally necessary projects that had no capacity to save running costs. In addition, there was every reason to include in an asset recycling agreement an end-year flexibility provision that would permit some proceeds, if not spent during the same financial year as they were received, to be carried over to the next year in a manner that the Treasury's annual accounting had forbidden since 1866.

The FCO's drive for rationalisation and asset recycling first and pre-eminently came together in Kuala Lumpur. The estate components here were the high commissioner's residence, Carcosa, that the Malaysian government had given to Britain in 1957 but was now keen to have back; leased offices on two floors of a nearby block; and unnecessarily many freehold staff houses, including two potentially surplus small housing compounds on Jalan Ampang and Jalan Ritchie. Crucially, too, there was an imaginative and pragmatic high commissioner, David Gillmore, who was later to become the permanent under-secretary. It did not take many months to work out a rationalisation strategy, assisted by healthily increasing land prices, that would exchange Carcosa for a good central site on which to build new offices and a few staff houses; provide a new residence by building on the site of one of the larger existing houses; and sell one of the under-used staff housing compounds to raise enough money to fund this programme of work. When complete, the other housing compound could be sold and its proceeds in turn invested in pump priming a rationalisation programme in another city. In the event, many of the Kuala Lumpur proceeds funded a cost-effective purchase programme of apartments in New York.

The Public Accounts Committee returned, as it promised it would, to

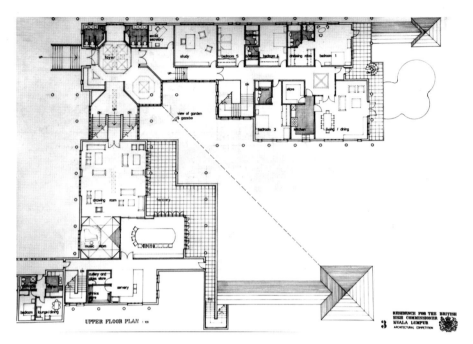

19.1. Upper floor plan of the Kuala Lumpur residence, 1986 competition-winning design by Brian Clouston and Partners and Kumpulan Akitek. Entrance at top left, with private wing ahead and reception rooms to the right. A clear distinction is made between public and private areas. North is to the left.

the FCO's overseas estate in March 1985, almost exactly two years after Vote Transfer. It was not satisfied about various issues related to overscale accommodation, although some of its earlier prescriptions had been effected. But the FCO had a good story to tell on rationalisation, and Kuala Lumpur in particular, and a deal with the Treasury on asset recycling was by then in sight. The committee, in effect, waved the FCO on its way, and did not specifically look at the estate again for another ten years. The asset recycling agreement was signed with the Treasury later in 1985. It covered the ensuing ten years and its main terms were that: the first £1 million of receipts each year would be returned to the Treasury (as a sort of tithe); the balance of receipts would be available for the FCO to spend on rationalisation projects; 'windfall' receipts (if any) would be surrendered unless agreed otherwise; up to £5 million could be carried forward to the following year; and a target was set for reducing estate running costs by £4-6 million a year ten years thence. The 1985 agreement looked more complicated than that, of course, and included provisions for exceptions and annual reviews, as well as relating

19.2. Competition elevations of the Kuala Lumpur residence. Top: garden front, as viewed from the Royal Selangor golf course. Below: private wing facing the garden.

the arrangements to conventional Estimates procedures, but it provided the FCO with the necessary financial freedom to move ahead.

In consequence, OED and Gillmore, and from 1986 his successor Nicholas Spreckley, implemented the entire Kuala Lumpur estate strategy over the next five years. The FCO was criticised by some for giving up Carcosa but the overall deal was easy to defend. The offices, amenities and housing for the new site acquired on Jalan Ampang in exchange for Carcosa were designed by OED architects John Bateman and David Pennington, and taken forward by Raglan Squire and Partners as executive architects, and built by Taylor Woodrow International. The 11-acre housing compound at Jalan Ritchie was sold. The site selected for the new residence was 27 Langgak Golf and the house on it, formerly occupied by the defence attaché, was demolished. OED organised an architectural competition for its replacement, which was won by Brian Clouston and Partners with Kumpulan Akitek, and the new residence was built by Bovis with Yeoh Tiong Lay **(Figs 19.1 & 19.2)**. Carcosa was handed back at the end of Gillmore's tour in 1986 and Spreckley moved into what was formerly the deputy high commissioner's house at 5 Jalan Syers until the new residence, the design of which he hated, was ready for him to move into in 1989.

The Public Accounts Committee pressed the FCO in 1983 for decisions to be made about the future of the large and under-used residence and garden at Vienna, one of the problems that the FCO and the PSA had for long failed to resolve. The residence was very expensive to run, the offices were in old and overcrowded leased premises, and there was plenty of room to build new ones in the residence garden. This garden was so large for two reasons: part of it had been the site of the stable block that was damaged by a bomb during the war and afterwards demolished, and another part, furthest from the house and formerly called 27 and 29 Salesianergasse, had been bought as a bombsite in 1950 'to preserve the amenities of the embassy'. This was an old and useful metaphor that meant 'enlarging the garden' to an ambassador and 'providing a future building site' to a Ministry estate surveyor. The ambassador, Michael Alexander, recently arrived from no.10 Downing Street as Mrs Thatcher's overseas policy private secretary (and formerly an Olympic fencing silver medallist) argued with exceptional vigour the case, such as it was, for keeping the whole garden intact. Carrick, though, was a formidable proponent of the estate's need to change: he was sceptical of

19.3. Embassy offices in Vienna, completed in 1988, on the site at the end of the residence garden where stood two buildings which were bombed during the Second World War. The new building was designed to house all three British ambassadors at Vienna. The Anglican church, Christ Church, is almost opposite.

much that his works professionals told him, and could give them a hard time with his questions but, once he had reached his conclusions, he was able to argue them with a clarity and force that PSA had never mastered. Acland, who was determined that important estate decisions should be taken in London, supported OED's case for rationalisation in Vienna and secured the Foreign Secretary's endorsement.

New offices, sketch-designed by OED architect Stephen Quinlan, with Dr Sepp Frank as executive architect and Ed Ast as contractor, were accordingly completed and occupied in late 1988 **(Fig. 19.3)**. Some of the surplus space on the ground floor of the residence was integrated into the scheme as consular offices. Although the whole site was then being more efficiently used, there remained a great deal of under-used space in the residence itself. OED explored the option of creating a large and self-contained apartment for the bilateral ambassador and his family on the second floor, enabling the grand rooms on the first floor to be available for official entertaining also by the two multi-lateral ambassadors to international organisations in Vienna. All three ambassadors fiercely resisted this proposal and it was dropped.

The vigour with which Alexander fought his corner in Vienna was almost matched by that of the ambassador in The Hague, Philip Mansfield, who objected to OED's proposal to move from the historic embassy house at 12 Westeinde which had been leased since 1861. Under the terms of the lease, full repairing liability rested with the tenant and the massive old building was slowly and expensively subsiding. Mansfield maintained that tougher negotiations with the Jesuit Fathers, the landlord, would elicit sufficient concessions to justify retention of the building, but OED found an acceptable and affordable alternative house on Plein 1813 which would provide a good long-term residence with many fewer risks attaching. Mansfield wrote sadly to the Foreign Secretary in 1984:

> I have the honour to report that on 11 October I held a Farewell Ball at the Residence to mark the end of 123 years during which the British Ambassador to the Netherlands has lived and worked at 12 Westeinde. Her Royal Highness The Princess Anne graciously attended the Ball as did Princess Margriet of the Netherlands and her husband … [It] unfortunately clashed with the last day of the 1984 Budget Debate when votes are taken at the end, traditionally late at night. Nevertheless at 1 a.m. the Prime Minister and his colleagues arrived in evening dress with their wives in euphoric mood. They were clearly determined to add their mark to this end of an era. … [O]ne figure will not appear in the balance sheet when the soundness of the decision [to replace the residence] comes to be reviewed; the immense

benefit to Her Majesty's Government of a well designed Residence which has been admired and loved by the Dutch for 123 years.[5]

One piece of estate rationalisation worked out disappointingly. OED built a fine car-park for official cars and vans beneath the lawn of the Paris offices on the rue du Faubourg St Honoré so as to be able to sell the overly valuable embassy garage on Rue Lesueur. An ingenious arrangement, designed by Olivier Nodé-Langlois, OED's retained architect in Paris, took cars underground from Avenue Gabriel all the way to the basement of the offices. The new garage worked well for a few years while OED laboured to sell the old one but it became largely redundant when the embassy decided to outsource its fleet of cars in the 1990s. This was a salutary illustration of the need, when more space appears to be the answer to an accommodation problem, to exhaust the managerial options before resorting to the builders.

Two of the tenets of rationalisation were that surplus, under-used or under-performing sites or properties should be either sold or developed, and that more intensive use should be made of compound land where practicable. Many projects flowed from this principle. In Dhaka, OED built a residence, designed in outline by John Hopewell, and offices, designed by Norman and Dawbarn, on a large undeveloped plot that the PSA had bought in 1978 in the diplomatic enclave at Baridhara. In Lilongwe, the relatively new capital of Malawi, OED built offices on a plot acquired for

19.4. Offices at the north end of the Tokyo compound, completed in 1988, to house commercial, consular, information and scientific sections of the embassy, and a multi-purpose hall. Designed by Kenneth Campbell, with Fukuwatari and Associates as executive architects.

the purpose in 1975, on which only amenity facilities had so far been built. In Lusaka, ten houses and an amenities building designed by OED architect Francess Easmon were built on a large vacant plot, and in Kinshasa Michael Pugsley, another OED architect, designed offices and several staff houses on the Raquette site that had lain vacant since 1931. Next to the residence in Helsinki was a site that the PSA had bought in 1972 and, rather disgracefully, cleared of its fine villa and then failed to develop: here OED built offices, designed by Stephen Quinlan. He and John Hopewell were also responsible for inserting new consular offices into the courtyard of the Paris embassy stable block in rue d'Anjou that was bought with the residence in 1814.

Better use of the compounds by inserting new buildings and saving off-compound rents was likewise pursued. New commercial and consular buildings in the Tokyo and Kuwait compounds, designed by Kenneth Campbell and Percy Thomas Partnership respectively, both worked well **(Fig. 19.4)**. In New Delhi, the cleared site of the 1950s hospital, replaced by a clinic elsewhere on the compound, was developed with 12 houses in a pleasant courtyard by the eminent Indian architect, Raj Rewal (and are now called Nightingale Court). In Rome, the old villa that Giovanni Azzuri had built in the 1830s for Princess Wolkonsky, and which had housed the chancery offices from 1946 until 1971, was converted to seven staff flats of varying sizes, and the house in which the pre-1946 German minister lived was refurbished for the head of chancery. Houses and flats for UK staff were also inserted into the compounds at Addis Ababa, Dubai and Kingston.

Several residential schemes for compounds foundered, however, at sketch plan stage because of different perceptions of what would constitute that old bugbear – overcrowding. Senior diplomats were not prepared to consider compound density in terms of bed-spaces per acre. Their perception of a desirable density was still generally conditioned by direct experience of Posts where and when space was not at a premium. Some of them had also been provoked into their doubts about whether these British oases could survive the architect's pencil and the accountant's calculator by several absurdly over-developed proposals by the PSA in the 1970s. In the 1980s, OED proposed two successive schemes, by Percy Thomas Partnership and Francess Easmon, for about 25 flats and houses in the 12-acre Tokyo compound, but both were abandoned. The first, inexcusably, was found incapable of meeting the seismic codes and the second, although it stacked up economically, simply incurred more ambassadorial wrath about over-crowding than OED, with too many other commitments, was able to confront at the time. Two schemes for different sites in the compound at Cairo also came to nothing: a six-storey staff block, designed by Seifert International, on the site of the old building near the centre of the compound that had become a rose garden, and a low office and staff flat building to replace the ballroom, designed by Jeremy Dixon in 1988. A design by Kenneth Campbell for about 20 staff houses in terraces on the adjacent site to Spence's offices in Rome and one by John Bateman for a dozen or so houses at the bottom of the lower compound in Ankara both had also to be abandoned when planning negotiations with the local authorities broke down for zoning reasons.

Another rationalisation idea – co-location with other organisations – had never made much headway, and OED's success was also limited. The basic concept of co-location was that a single British building in a city, generically referred to as Britannia House, should house, besides the diplomatic mission and other government departments, such non-governmental bodies as the British chamber of commerce, British Council, British Airways and such British companies as were interested. The idea, first mooted for New York and widely toyed with elsewhere, never blossomed beyond truncated versions in Brussels and São Paulo because, when it came down to negotiating commitments, commercial imperatives outweighed British sentiments. Co-location with one or two European Union partners fared somewhat better, in Almaty, Quito, Reyjavik and, eventually, Dar es Salaam, but there were fears that the advantages of sharing common spaces and services somewhat bluntened partners' commercial competitive edges. Co-location with Commonwealth partners was another possibility but hardly took off because it required commitments that were at odds with each mission's need for flexibility. A Europa house idea in Geneva failed for similar reasons.

Operational programmes
The rationalisation programme thus embraced all estate activities that were undertaken for 'economic' reasons, including disposal of properties, purchases, making more intensive use of existing assets, and investing in 'spend to save' schemes. The programme was funded by recycled monies yielded by the disposals. The ten-year target set by the Treasury in 1985 for reducing estate running costs was comfortably achieved. Operational programmes, funded by Voted monies, continued to embrace estate activities undertaken for reasons of 'need'. These included accommodation in new countries or capitals, works required by new policy priorities like security enhancements and visa regimes, and all activities imposed on estate managers by the sheer passage of time like lease renewals and liabilities, maintenance, refurbishments and re-furnishing. Many projects, of course, contained elements of both rationalisation and operational programmes but

were ascribed to one or the other.

The requirements for projects therefore arose for different reasons, were supported or opposed by different people, came into view at different speeds, and competed intensely for insufficient funds. It was difficult to assess priorities with so many parameters at work and whether to include or exclude a project within one of the programmes was sometimes a matter of harsh judgement. Given the delays, obstructions, reversals and other real-world factors bound to be encountered on many projects, over-committing the total programme at the start of a financial year by up to about 40 per cent was the only way of ensuring that a year's allocation of valuable funds, even with some end-year flexibility, would assuredly be spent where it was most needed

The three largest projects of the period, all operational, were driven by shifts of the world's geo-political tectonic plates. Britain required a new consulate-general in Hong Kong to be ready by 1997, when the territory became a Special Administrative Region of China. The end of the Cold War presented the opportunity, after 40 years of intermittent and fruitless negotiations, to build a new embassy in Moscow. And the re-unification of Germany, and the designation of Berlin as again its capital, required a new embassy building in Berlin. These three projects ended the twentieth century (and are the subject of the last chapter of this history).

The largest source of new countries was the break-up of the former Soviet Union in December 1991, after which Britain required some form of representation in 14 more capital cities. The most satisfactory result from the diplomatic accommodation point of view was in Latvia where Britain was first represented at Riga in 1921. Ten years later, the legation moved into a house at 5 Jura Alunana, in the Petrograd suburb, which the Office of Works had bought from Peter Bornholdt. This house was designed in neo-classical style by Heinrich Karl Scheel in 1876, to which the Office of Works added a small three-storey in-fill office building on the Andreja Pumpura frontage. The legation withdrew in 1940 when the USSR absorbed the Baltic States. The building survived the war relatively undamaged, and was occupied throughout the Soviet era by various Soviet authorities. British claims, first for its return and later for compensation, all came to nothing. The new Latvian government honourably returned the house to Britain in 1991, and OED commissioned the architects Jestico and Whiles for its careful refurbishment and re-arrangement. The mission re-occupied its building in 1995.

Riga was the exception. The usual procedure for the new Posts in the former Soviet Union was for a first secretary to go and live in an hotel and communicate with London via a satellite dish that folded out of a suitcase which he propped on the window sill. This accommodation stage would be followed by leasing a few flats for the several (or more) years that it took while a permanent solution, often including new construction, was identified and put into effect. Thus were the new Posts like Almaty, Ashgabat, Baku, Kiev, Tashkent, Tbilisi and Yerevan established. In the new Russia itself, Posts were opened in Ekaterinberg and St Petersburg, where a handsome villa, previously occupied by a Soviet music school, was leased and converted for offices with flats above. Much the same processes later applied to Posts in the new capitals that emerged from the former Yugoslavia, including Ljubljana, Sarajevo, Skopje and Zagreb.

The embassy buildings for the new capital at Brasilia were completed and occupied in 1984. The scheme for new buildings at Riyadh, which the Saudi authorities had designated as the new administrative capital of the Kingdom, was not far behind. Britain's compound of 1.5 hectares in the diplomatic quarter was planned to house the offices, residence and all of the amenities – multi-purpose hall, club room, swimming pool, and squash and tennis courts. The Saudis wanted members of the diplomatic missions to mix freely with each other and to this end forbade the development

19.5. Embassy offices at Riyadh, designed by Trevor Dannatt and completed in 1985: the exterior is faced with beige Riyadh limestone. Behind are a club, hall and squash court, service buildings and a tennis court and swimming pool.

19.6. The garden front of the residence at Riyadh, which stands in the centre of a strip of land at the back of the offices compound. The large central drawing room is behind the bay window, with the dining room to the right.

of single-nation residential compounds. The 35 houses for UK staff were therefore built in seven separate groups. Each house had a small internal courtyard open to the sky for cooling effect. Trevor Dannatt designed the compound buildings and the residence and his partner, Colin Dollimore, took the design lead on the housing (**Figs. 19.5 & 19.6**). Dannatt was amused that ambassadors preferred to have their desks across a corner of their office, so he sought to harness this waywardness architecturally by angling the corner of the building on that floor. The inadvertent result was to advertise to the whole world exactly where the ambassador was sitting. Laing Wimpey Alireza won the construction contract in competition in 1983 and the embassy took up occupation in September 1985. The total project cost was about £20 million.

The only other major new capital city undergoing its most active phase of development during this period was Abuja, close to the geographical centre of Nigeria, which was designated as the new federal capital in 1976. Abuja was slow, however, to gain momentum. The FCO accepted in 1990 the two sites allocated for offices and residence on 99-year lease terms. The Nigerian authorities then announced, with no warning, that its ministry of external affairs would be moving to Abuja that autumn. The FCO had neither time nor money to develop the sites and the emphasis moved entirely to acquiring leased accommodation. The high commission in Lagos at first leased a suite in the Hilton Hotel as a temporary liaison office staffed by a locally-engaged British wife. Over the next five years, OED managed to secure, through a succession of complicated lease and development deals, sufficient offices, a residence and 25 or so staff houses to cope with the gradual move of staff from Lagos, culminating in 1997 with the Post becoming fully operational, the high commissioner taking up permanent residence, and Lagos reverting to a consulate-general with a high commissioner's *pied-à-terre*.

Other new capital cities were theoretically designated, like Dodoma in Tanzania and Yamassoukro in Côte d'Ivoire, but never succeeded in enticing their ministries of external affairs to move to them, so the diplomats stayed

19.7. The embassy buildings on the Muscat waterfront, about 1970. The 1860s agency building is to the left of the flagstaff, with its later first-floor terrace facing Fort Jalali. The building to its right, bought in 1901, housed the surgeon, several clerks and the telegraph office. The photograph was taken from Fort Mirani.

put in Dar es Salaam and Abidjan. Most senior British diplomats had a horror of designated diplomatic enclaves and the FCO was adept at keeping out of them. Muscat was a case in point. While the Malaysians had made it plain and public in Kuala Lumpur that they wanted Britain out of Carcosa, the Sultan of Oman, Qaboos bin Said, was much more discreet about easing the British embassy out of the magnificent site that the former agency had occupied on the waterfront of a small bay in old Muscat, overlooked by two Portuguese forts, since about 1860 **(Fig. 19.7)**. The Foreign Secretary, Hurd, recalled that

> [the Sultan's] ministers for several years told me that His Majesty wanted to demolish our embassy to extend his already huge residence. I feigned forgetfulness and enlisted Margaret Thatcher on my side, having learned by now that whatever her misgivings about the Foreign Office, she always wanted to keep our traditional embassy buildings in their ancient splendour. The Sultan promised her to let us stay in possession until the year 2000, but alas the hints from his ministers soon recurred. The Sultan offered to finance for us a new modern office, and a big new ambassador's house on a rock above the Al-Bustani Hotel. There came a point when it was politic to yield to this generosity, and the Sultan fulfilled his promise meticulously.[6]

19.8. Model of the new residence at Al Rawdah, on a rocky promontory south of Old Muscat. The public reception rooms are in the long limb of the L-plan, private quarters and guest rooms in the short, with a shaded terrace between.

19.9. Interior of the entrance hall in the residence at Muscat, where the public and private areas of the house meet.

Indeed he did. There were still sites available in 1991 in the designated diplomatic area at Al Khuwair, on the seafront a few miles to the west of old Muscat, but that would be a poor place for a residence. After various negotiations, the Omanis offered two separate sites, plus £10 million to fund new buildings on them, in exchange for the present compound. Several background considerations prompted ready acceptance of this offer. The present compound would be difficult to protect in the event of an increased violent threat. The terms of the British government's tenure of it reached back into Undivided India claims that had never been definitively resolved: it could therefore be doubted whether the FCO had a clear enough title ever to sell the site on its own account. And, finally, the FCO thought (wrongly, as it turned out) that the Sultan was going to preserve the old agency building.

The new office site in Muscat, for which OED arranged a design competition in 1992 that was won by YRM Architects and Planners, was just outside and to the east of the diplomatic area, which enabled the new embassy to have a slightly different personality from the new embassies within the area. The Foreign Secretary, still Hurd, opened the offices in March 1995. The new residence site was on a rocky promontory to the south

417

19.10. The embassy offices at Dublin, completed in 1995, on a site that was bought from the Royal Dublin Society in a mature residential area. Designed by Allies and Morrison, who won the architectural competition for the building.

of Muscat, at Al Rawdah, on the way to Al Bustan. OED architect Andrew Slater produced a most successful design, based on an idea by Andrew Sebire, a valued architectural adviser to OED who had also been a member of the assessment panel for the office competition. The residence was brought to fruition by local executive architects, Huckle Tweddell Partnership **(Figs 19.8 & 19.9)**.

The replacement of outdated office premises by new buildings was a significant proportion of OED's workload. Some of these projects were inescapable, like the need for new accommodation upon expiry of an unrenewable or unsatisfactory lease, or the need, for physical security reasons, to move out of an unsafe local environment or building. These two factors often worked in tandem. Thus were new free-standing offices built in Amman, Bridgetown, Dhaka, Dublin, Nairobi, Port of Spain and Wellington, bought in Lisbon, and leased, with extensive ingoings, in Havana, Sofia and Tunis **(Figs 19.10 & 19.11)**. A review of security in the FCO, undertaken in 1985 by Anthony Blake-Pauley, paid particular attention to its overseas buildings and made proposals for relocating some and strengthening the defences of others in respect of site perimeters, gates and barriers, and glazing. Clive Newey, the senior structural engineer in OED, undertook several tours with a security colleague to specify such works, during the first of which he designed the simple but strong vehicle barrier that bears his name and the fencing specification that became known as Delhi railings.

Physical security was one of the two operational considerations that sent projects well up the priority list. The other was the introduction of visa regimes which required prospective visitors to the UK from designated countries to obtain a visa to enter Britain, for which they could apply at their nearest British embassy, high commission or consulate. Visa regimes were usually introduced with only a few months notice, which gave OED and other affected departments and Posts little time to ready the necessary waiting rooms, interview cubicles with their security screens and microphones, and back-office accommodation. In most Posts, the sequence adopted was quickly to extend the existing facilities with a temporary building to last until a more permanent arrangement could be leased or built: some of the superseded temporary buildings were then retained for other uses. The difficulty for the specifiers of the visa accommodation requirements was estimating the likely numbers of applicants: both under- and over-provision in different Posts was an inevitable consequence. There was early discussion

19.11. Model of the high commission offices on Nairobi Hill, designed by Cullum and Night-ingale, completed in 1997. Main entrance in the centre, approached from above, with high commission offices to one side and British Development Division to the other. Amenities and two staff houses in the foreground.

about centralising visa operations in regional centres but local transport and postal conditions worked against centralisation (which was better suited to passport issuing). Later, the outsourcing of parts of the visa–issuing process to travel agents and other private contractors took much of the accommodation load off Posts, with the result that some of them ended up with expensive surplus space: the Paris car-park lesson had not been learned.

The first new visa regimes were introduced in Africa and the Indian sub-continent in the mid-1980s. The most problematic accommodation was in Lagos, where a fully fitted-out leased building on Awolowo Road was closed down by the authorities after only a few days of operations because they judged that it was too close to the presidential palace (the result of a local breakdown in communications). In the second wave of provision at posts, new free-standing permanent immigration buildings were built in the compounds at New Delhi and Karachi; large extensions to the high commission offices were built at Dhaka, Islamabad and Lagos; and a huge visa operation was installed in leased offices in downtown Mumbai. Visa regimes for Turkey and the Maghreb were introduced in 1989. At Istanbul, the 1870 stable block at Pera House was converted to visa offices: this turned into a complicated contract because much of the building subsided during the works.

The refurbishment of buildings that were worth retaining but needed upgrading and updating was a significant programme in itself. It included extensive office refurbishment works at Budapest, Prague and Warsaw, all starved of attention during the Cold War, as well as at Canberra, Ottawa and Seoul. Major refurbishments were also undertaken at many residences, including Athens, Cairo, Hanoi, Oslo, Paris, Rome and Sofia. Apart from Dhaka, Kuala Lumpur, Muscat and Riyadh the only significant new residence to be built during this period was at Jakarta, designed by Denton Corker Marshall, a major Australian practice (which Stephen Quinlan had recently joined as their London partner). With the exception of Muscat, the new residences were all disliked in varying measure by their first occupants but, with judicious modification or refurnishing, they seem to have won over most successors.

Periodic FCO savings exercises involved the closure of a few Posts. If there was a functioning property market, any freehold houses or offices could be quite quickly sold. Some could be retained as *pieds-à-terre* for visiting diplomats, and this could usefully overlap, as Hamerton House did in Zanzibar, for example, with being a staff recreational retreat. If there was reason to suppose that there might be a later re-opening, it was wiser to lease out the vacated properties than to dispose of them.

Architectural competitions

There were in the early 1980s still some advantages to be gained from sketch planning schemes in-house before transferring all subsequent stages to consultants, preferably to UK practices with local offices or affiliations. This was particularly the case with new office buildings because the complicated operational and security parameters were second nature to in-house staff and unknown territory to consultants. Vienna, Helsinki and Kuala Lumpur offices were therefore sketch designed in-house before consultants were commissioned to take them through to completion. The pressure, however, to outsource more work to the private sector and to run down in-house design teams mounted during the 1980s and OED soon realised that it needed to be able to commission consultants at the design outset of every project.

Brasilia had come close, but there had never been a design competition for an overseas diplomatic project. The Lilongwe offices had been a minor and low-key design selection exercise between three invited practices.[7] The new residence in Kuala Lumpur presented exactly the right opportunity for a proper design competition. New design ideas were genuinely welcomed by the FCO, the in-house architects no longer resented the idea, and a competition would signify a marked change of course from PSA to FCO stewardship. The prevailing rules for architectural competitions, published and regulated by the Royal Institute of British Architects, were still over-prescriptive and, worst of all from a client's point of view, gave more leverage to architects on the deciding jury or panel than to the client. OED felt unable to recommend such an arrangement to the FCO and turned to John Partridge for advice: he was a member of an *ad hoc* advisory panel that the Minister, Lady Young, had set up for the estate, a founding partner of the leading firm of Howell Killick Partridge and Amis, and a deeply trusted colleague.[8] Partridge said, in effect, that OED should do want it wanted and, if there was any problem, he would help square the RIBA: there never was.

Writing the design brief brought into focus the question that had occurred so rarely in the history of the estate: whether to give guidance about how a new British building should look overseas and whether any style preference or influence should be indicated. The conclusion was that these decisions were better left to the architects and the assessors than tightly defined in the brief. For Kuala Lumpur, seven UK practices with some experience of Malaysia were invited to submit designs anonymously.[9] The design brief contented itself with saying that the residence was an important theatre of operations for the high commissioner. It should therefore be noteworthy; something rather special architecturally so that it can stand as a show-piece for Britain demonstrating the best in architecture and design; elegant without exaggerated pomp and circumstance. Guests from the host country should enjoy being at the Residence and when appropriate be given something of a sense of occasion At the same time the house should be welcoming and comfortable, as well as secure both for the High Commissioner and his family and for guests and official visitors.[10]

The Kuala Lumpur residence was the first of six similar design selection exercises organised and developed by OED over the next ten years. It was followed by the Moscow residence, and offices for Nairobi, Dublin, Muscat and Hong Kong.[11] The need of a new residence in Moscow vanished with the onset of *perestroika*, but all of the other five winning schemes were built without significant departure from the submitted proposal. The design prescriptions echoed the Kuala Lumpur brief: in Nairobi, the buildings 'should represent the best in British Architecture and Design; sit comfortably within their surroundings: be welcoming but provide security; and have dignity without pomposity'. In Dublin, the dignity was to be 'restrained'. In Muscat, the building must avoid 'the pompous and [be] without pastiche … must respond with manners and excellence …'. The Hong Kong brief wanted the building to be 'fine in appearance and welcoming in its public aspects; [and] identifiably British, if possible'. Invited competitions came to an end when the European Community's Service Directive came into effect and consultants' selection processes were bureaucratised. Berlin offices was the first competition for which expressions of interest were advertised under the new rules, followed, before 2000, by offices in Dar es Salaam and Doha. In recognition of OED's reputation for consistently building good designs, the Royal Institute of British Architects awarded its Client of the Year accolade to the FCO in 2001.

The cavalcade of managerial change
The years up to 2000 were productive ones for OED, and many parts of the estate were made to work better and more efficiently in support of Britain's diplomatic effort. OED, which accounted for about one quarter of the diplomatic service Vote, established a recognised place for itself in the life of the FCO, and few rued the demise of the PSA. They were also years of unrelenting managerial changes throughout government.
Concepts of 'accountable management' and 'management by objectives' had gained currency across government in the 1960s, and the PSA, for example, had been 'hived off' in 1972 as an executive agency in response to them. Changes quickened, however, during the Thatcher era as ministers

realised how little control they exercised over programme expenditure because of lack of information, direction and accountability. An Efficiency Unit was established under Sir Derek Rayner in 1979 to scrutinise specific programmes and to require changes that the Unit identified. The 'Financial Management Initiative', launched in 1982 by a White Paper called 'Efficiency and Effectiveness', was designed to inform departments about the real costs of their operations and to promote better management, not least through devolving financial responsibilities. Sir Robin Ibbs succeeded Rayner in 1983 and published the 'Next Steps' report in 1988 which encouraged the formation of free-standing agencies, under chief executives, to execute as much of the non-policy work of government departments as possible. Peter Kemp was appointed the government's Next Steps project manager, tasked with overseeing the creation of new agencies. For work that was less suitable for 'agencification', a system of 'market testing' was conceived under which the cost and effectiveness of an in-house activity was subjected to competition and, if the private sector could perform it more economically, the activity would be 'contracted out'. A blizzard of jargon swept through departments: target setting, performance measurement, risk assessment, stakeholders, partnerships, benchmarking, business process re-engineering, best practice and much else minted by a burgeoning management consultancy industry that could not believe its luck.

In 1992, the government introduced the 'Private Finance Initiative', a procurement system whereby the private sector funded, designed, built and operated public infrastructure in return for decades of government-guaranteed revenue payments. The overt justification was the common supposition that the private sector would perform these functions so much more efficiently than the public sector as to justify the greater costs. The great convenience of the Initiative for the Treasury was that the accounting rules did not then require the expenditure to be included in the public sector borrowing requirement, nor the new infrastructure capitalised as public assets in departmental accounts. The Treasury conducted a 'Fundamental Expenditure Review' on itself in 1994, and then required all other departments to conduct similar reviews to help them achieve better 'value for money'. In 1995, a White Paper announced the government's intention to introduce 'resource accounting and budgeting', based on private sector accruals principles, to replace traditional Vote accounting so as to be able to balance the totality of resources consumed against outputs and outcomes. The New Labour government, soon after gaining office in 1997, launched a Comprehensive Spending Review to impress its own stamp on all these proceedings.

Although most of these reforms were primarily devised for the big spending departments, the Treasury was insistent that small and policy departments like the FCO should follow the same prescriptions. The FCO, in consequence, devolved various financial responsibilities to its geographical 'commands' or directorates, and they in turn to their Posts. It replaced its Inspectorate with a Management Review Staff which offered advice when requested, which was often not when it was most required. It established a central procurement directorate which knew a great deal about purchasing goods and services but rather little about property and construction procurement.

OED was a clear candidate for constant attention: it could be made to work as an agency; it 'owned' valuable assets; was a cost centre; and many of its staff worked on both sides of the division between 'client' and 'service provider', between which the management theory of the day required 'clear blue water'. The FCO saw only disadvantage in agencification of the overseas estate so soon after wresting it from an inefficient agency, the PSA. The Foreign Secretary, Geoffrey Howe, averted an Efficiency Scrutiny of the estate in 1984 when he complained to the Prime Minister, Margaret Thatcher, in the context of garnering her support for an asset recycling agreement, that OED was 'in danger of being scrutinised into the ground. They need to be allowed to get on with the real job ...'.[12] OED proposed various activities for market-testing and subsequent contracting out, like furniture procurement and the supply of clerks of works and maintenance supervisers. It restructured itself to put 'clear blue water' between its client and service provider functions, regulated by a matrix of 'service level agreements'. It had difficulty in persuading Posts, in this brave new world, that they remained tenants of OED, as landlord on behalf of the secretary of state, subject to an older kind of 'service level agreement' called an internal lease. Posts were more attracted by the management consultant's version that turned the relationship upside down, regarding Posts as the clients and OED as the service provider.

Preparations for the introduction of resource accounting and budgeting had a great impact on the work of OED. Regular valuation of each property in the estate, long resisted as being an expensive practice yielding little practical benefit compared to obtaining specific valuations when required, became imperative. Valuations for 'existing use' and 'open market' values were commissioned for every freehold and long leasehold property in the estate to help identify latent value and provide the basis for the capital charging that the new accounting arrangements required. OED was unable to avoid undertaking a project through Private Finance

Initiative procedures. It explored a range of possibilities, even including new offices and staff accommodation in Moscow, before alighting upon the new embassy in Berlin as the project for which the Initiative might have the fewest disadvantages.

The twentieth century thus ended for OED with a continuing responsibility for undertaking a solid design and construction programme against the background swirl of unprecedented managerial change.

20

Hong Kong, Moscow and Berlin 1986-2000

A new consulate-general building in Hong Kong and new embassy buildings in Moscow and Berlin, all large projects by diplomatic building standards, were running concurrently during the mid-1990s. Each resulted from a massive geo-political shift. Although the Moscow building saga started in 1946, the project only took off with the arrival of *perestroika* in the Soviet Union in 1989; Hong Kong started with the Joint Declaration of 1984; and Berlin started with the re-unification of Germany in 1990. Hong Kong was the first of the completed buildings to open in 1997, with the other two following in 2000.

Hong Kong
The Sino-British Joint Declaration on the Question of Hong Kong, which the Prime Minister, Margaret Thatcher, signed in Beijing in December 1984, provided for the transfer of British sovereignty over Hong Kong to China in 1997. For 50 years afterwards, Hong Kong would be a Special Administrative region of China. Section XI of Annex I of the Declaration provided that 'The United Kingdom may establish a Consulate-General in the Hong Kong Special Administrative Region'. The negotiators of the subsequent Defence Lands Agreement on the transfer of Ministry of Defence sites to China did not take that opportunity, as history might have suggested, of earmarking a site for the future British consulate-general. OED and the FCO's Hong Kong Department therefore began to address the choice of a site in 1986.

427

The consulate-general would embrace the activities of four British bodies: the long-established British Trade Commission, the Joint Liaison Group (which was negotiating the details of transfer and would be phased out in due course), the passport/immigration functions then being carried out by the Immigration Department of the Hong Kong Government, and the British Council. There was a strong case for a single building to house all of these activities to help boost confidence in Britain's future role in Hong Kong. The governor, Sir David Wilson, thought the building should have 'dignity without prominence': the Prime Minister wanted Britain to have a 'prestigious building'. There was no doubt that the consulate-general should be in, or close to, the Central district of Hong Kong.

There were several accommodation options for the FCO: to lease the requisite space in an existing or forthcoming building, to buy a suitable building, to find a development partner who would fund a new building in return for future rent, and to acquire a site and build on it with Voted funds. An early preference, more wishful thinking than realistic even though long favoured by the House of Commons' Foreign Affairs Committee, was to acquire the Prince of Wales Building in HMS *Tamar*. The two principal British commercial land developers in Hong Kong, Swire and Hong Kong Land, were both keen to attract the consulate-general to one of their own present or projected buildings and lobbied extensively to this end. All of the commercial options, however, proved impossibly more expensive than the development of a site that either belonged to the Hong Kong Government or was part of the Ministry of Defence estate that was reverting to China. The acquiescence of the Chinese government, however, would be necessary in either of these instances.

Francis Maude, the FCO minister of state, pushed the governor hard for a Hong Kong government site and the choice narrowed to two: Beconsfield House in Central, and Colvin House, formerly the NAAFI site within the

20.1. Terry Farrell's 1992 competition-winning proposal for the Hong Kong consulate-general, represented here as a straight block rather than curved round the quadrant site. From left: UK staff flats, consulate-general (with passport, visa and consular sections in the bulge), shared entrance court, and British Council.

20.2. View of the consulate-general in Hong Kong from the east: the British Council is hidden by the curvature of the buildings. The Conrad Hotel, above Pacific Place, is at the right

old Victoria Barracks which lay just to the east of Central towards Wanchai. Colvin House gradually won the argument because it was more easily accessible, especially for the large number of students who would be attending the British Council's English language teaching operation. It was just up the hill from Pacific Place, then under development by Swire, which was likely to become the hinge of urban development between Central and Wanchai, and close to the new Law Courts building. There were two nice incidental touches as well: the new civic gardens through the old Victoria Barracks afforded a pleasant walk into Central, and the consulate-general would stand at the corner of Supreme Court Road with Justice Drive. The Hong Kong government transferred the site cost-free to the British government by a Private Treaty Grant in April 1993, and specified a maximum 19,000 square meters of total gross floor area.

OED selected Swire Property Projects Ltd as project managers, not least because of the symbiosis between the two developments of Pacific Place and the consulate-general, and in 1992 arranged a limited architectural design competition for the consulate-general building between six firms with experience of building in Hong Kong.[1] The required accommodation amounted to about 12,000 square meters, of which about 20 per cent was for consular, passport and immigration functions, 25 per cent for other consulate-general offices, 42 per cent for the British Council (including

20.3. Interior of one of the public waiting areas in the Hong Kong consulate-general building.

about 30 classrooms), and 13 per cent for staff accommodation (nine flats for UK staff). The main difficulty in formulating the brief was deciding how much space to give the Passport Section, given that there was expected to be a huge initial uptake and then a quieter period until renewals became necessary. Assessment of the competition entries was unusually straightforward. Most of them offered variations of Hong Kong's normal manner of arranging a slab block on a site. Only Terry Farrell proposed a radically different approach: his concept of building around the curved lower perimeter of the site, thereby finding an urban as well as an architectural solution, brought numerous other advantages of identity, access, economy, landscape, privacy and environment. The Farrell design was selected **(Fig. 20.1)**.

OED's project manager, Stephen Whittle, and the British Council's architectural adviser, Malcolm Reading, worked well with the Swire and Farrell teams through all of the subsequent design development and construction stages. The tender for the site formation contract was won by Gammon and for the main contract by John Laing International in conjunction with Hip Hing Construction. The Foreign Secretary, Malcolm Rifkind, performed the topping-out ceremony in January 1996, and the building was formally opened by HRH The Princess Royal on 30 January 1997, five months before Hong Kong's reversion to Chinese sovereignty. A facilities management contract, the first to be negotiated by OED, was in place with Colliers Jardine at the time of the consulate-general taking up occupation. The building's outturn cost was about £30 million. **(Figs 20.2 & 20.3)**

Moscow

At the same time as the consulate-general in Hong Kong was being completed, the embassy buildings in Moscow were starting on site after nearly 15 years of negotiations and preparations. In 1982, the FCO indicated to the Soviet Ministry of Foreign Affairs that it was prepared to re-open negotiations, stalled since the Soviet invasion of Afghanistan in 1979, on the long-running issue of alternative premises for the British embassy in Moscow. By then, Soviet leases from the Crown Estate Commission were running out for the several premises that the Soviet Union was occupying in Kensington Palace Gardens in London. It looked as though there might be scope for reciprocal arrangements by which each country, even in the chill of the Cold War, could assist the other in re-housing its embassy. Two sites were now available in Moscow: no. 10 Smolenskaya Embankment, of 0.9 hectare, on the river almost opposite the Ukrainia hotel, for new offices and staff accommodation; and a site on Voyevodina Street, of about 0.5 hectare, next to Spasopeskovskaya Square and the American residence, for a new residence. The FCO appointed Sir Curtis Keeble, a former chief clerk and recently retired as ambassador in Moscow, as its chief negotiator for new embassies in Moscow and London.

Keeble, while not conceding that the British were prepared to vacate the old Charitonenko mansion on Sofiskaya Embankment (by then called Morisa Thoreza Embankment), inched negotiations forward on the structure of agreements that would be necessary to regulate reciprocal arrangements. These needed to be for the long-term exchange of sites in London and Moscow and the construction on them of new embassy buildings whose security would not be so compromised that they were unoccupiable (a fate that had recently befallen the Americans). Keeble, advised by OED and an FCO assistant legal adviser, Jeremy Hill, envisaged three agreements: an umbrella Sites Exchange Agreement that would outline the arrangements for reciprocity and step-by-step concurrence in both cities, a Lease Agreement to control site terms, and a Building Agreement to control design and construction matters.

Nine rounds of stodgy negotiations took up the next four years. The British team was several times bounced by its Moscow hosts into delaying the initialling of an agreed draft until the VIP departure lounge of Moscow airport, only to find that by then it contained subtler changes than typing errors. Nevertheless, a Sites Exchange Agreement was eventually signed in Moscow in March 1987 by Foreign Ministers Geoffrey Howe and Eduard Shevardnadze. Conditionality was at its heart: neither side would vacate its present buildings until the construction of new ones was completed in both cities.

Meanwhile, OED had begun work on schedules of accommodation and outline designs for the future British embassy buildings in Moscow. The intention was that the design for the Voyevodina residence should be commissioned from a consultant architect and for the offices building on the Smolenskaya site, with its numerous security implications, from an OED in-house architect, and Kenneth Campbell was appointed to this role. An early outline design of his worked well and looked good. It ranged residential accommodation for about 30 UK staff on eight or so floors along the river front of the site, with a corridor behind, running parallel to the river, that also gave access, on its other side, to a hall, office block and ancillaries. The appearance was somewhat crystalline to help the building to hold its own between the large sombre Soviet blocks on either side **(Fig. 20.4)**.

In early 1986, the FCO convened a Moscow design panel to advise on all design and presentation aspects of the project. The Duke of Gloucester, himself an architect, was its chairman and among its members were John Partridge and Andrew Sebire, both highly regarded consultant architects, and several senior commercial advisers and officials, including the chief clerk, Sir Mark Russell, and the ambassador in Moscow, Sir Bryan Cartledge.[2] The duke and most of the panel paid a familiarisation visit to Moscow

20.4. Earliest sketch by Kenneth Campbell in 1985 for new embassy offices and staff accommodation on the Smolenskaya Embankment in Moscow.

later in 1986. On return, the panel turned its attention to some pressing architectural issues. As the project became more real, interested departments began paying more attention to how the building should be and the brief had in consequence changed since design work started. With Campbell soon to retire, and in-house resources no longer available to sustain design work on such a large project, the panel was keen to bring a major private sector architectural firm into play as soon as practicable. It proposed that OED should discuss the project and a possible commission with four major London practices with slightly different professional track records: Norman Foster, Philip Dowson of Arup Associates, Chapman Taylor, and Ahrends Burton and Koralek. OED met the principals in their offices and Keeble then chaired a fuller interview with each. Foster pulled out because he was too busy, Dowson was evidently wary and Chapman Taylor appeared more interested in the business than the problem. Ahrends Burton and Koralek seemed ideal from the FCO's viewpoint: supportive, rationalist, humane, and young enough to last through what might prove to be an unusually lengthy commission. They were accordingly appointed.

For the selection of a design, as distinct from an architect, for the residence on the Voyevodina site, the panel decided that a two-stage open competition should be held. The Treasury agreed that the guideline area of 880 square meters for this most senior grade of residence should be increased to 1,200 square meters. Expressions of interest in response to advertisements in the architectural press in March 1988 were received from 112 architects, 14 of whom were interviewed by John Partridge and others in June and reduced to eight.[3] OED took these short-listed practices to Moscow to show them the site, see the present residence in operation and discuss future requirements with the ambassador. Their eight schemes, of great variety and distinction, were submitted in October 1988. OED showed all of them to the Moscow planners, who pronounced none of them unsuitable.

The Duke of Gloucester chaired the assessment panel that comprised the chief clerk, the ambassador, John Partridge, and Andrew Sebire, with OED as secretary. After a wide debate, it came down to a choice between Julian Bicknell's skilfully arranged, beautifully drawn, neo-classical proposal and Allies and Morrison's inventive, elegant and modernist one. At the end, the two senior diplomats outlined the virtues of the Bicknell scheme and the two respected architects those of the Allies and Morrison scheme. The Duke, torn between the establishment and his profession, had doubtless seen this coming. OED's view was two-fold: competitions should ultimately be decided by the client, provided that he was well-informed, and not by architects, however eminent; and, given that the FCO would probably find a way of not building what it did not like, it made greater managerial sense to opt for the scheme more likely to be built. The Duke did a masterly summing-up, and left it until the end to plump for Bicknell **(Fig. 20.5)**.

The winner was announced at an exhibition of all eight schemes in the newly refurbished Durbar Court in the FCO in November 1988. The previous evening, Margaret Thatcher stepped across Downing Street to have a look. On being shown the Allies and Morrison scheme as the runner-up, she said 'Is that it?' with such disdain as to eliminate the point of further explanation. On reaching the Bicknell scheme, she said 'Ah, that's better, I like that' and spent a few minutes on its detail. There were a few brickbats in the architectural press about the selection but the assessors' report had pre-empted them. It said, in part,

> No single scheme could unanimously be acclaimed as outstanding and the winner was chosen by a majority decision.
>
> The winning design … offers an excellent internal plan, with a wide range of options for official and private functions. It is sensitive in both scale and appearance to a part of Moscow which has preserved its character amid widespread and traumatic architectural change during this century. The site planning has been handled very simply with the principal façade looking southward straight onto the square. … In stylistic terms the choice of this design will be controversial, but the majority view is that it will serve British interests in Moscow more effectively than any of the others submitted.[4]

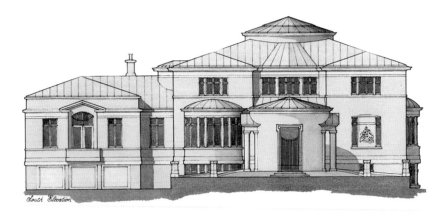

20.5. The front elevation, facing Spasopeskovskaya Square, of Julian Bicknell's 1988 design for a new residence in Moscow. Essentially a villa, the main house is formal and symmetrical, with a central hall, on the right the private suite, on the left drawing and dining rooms with a large reception room beyond them.

20.6. Model of Ahrends Burton and Koralek's ultra-high security Moscow embassy design, 1990. Viewed from the east, with entrance forecourt in front and the river beyond. The need for this scheme was overtaken by the thawing of the Cold War.

The project was never executed. Margaret Thatcher and President Mikhail Gorbachev agreed in principle in Moscow in June 1990 that the ambassadors should remain in their present houses in both London and Moscow. That was confirmed by an exchange of notes in 1991, when the FCO also relinquished its rights to the Voyevodina site.

On the Smolenskaya site, meanwhile, Richard Burton took the lead for Ahrends Burton and Koralek, with Jeremy Peacock as his project architect. OED's project manager was Clive Newey, and Ove Arup and Partners were commissioned as structural engineers, YRM as mechanical and electrical engineers and Hanscomb as quantity surveyors. The design that emerged was in many ways a literal and graphical response to several strict requirements of the brief. The Soviets insisted on a 30-metre height limit; security requirements insisted that the offices be as near to the middle of the site as possible; and the construction strategy envisaged by the draft Building Agreement was for the Soviets to undertake the main building work (and doubtless riddle it with bugs) and for British labour to fit out the offices after the Soviet contractors had left site (and disinter them). The scheme that Burton proposed was two parallel lines of outward-looking flats, at right angles to the river, with a huge covered atrium between them. In this atrium, British contractors would later erect a prefabricated four-storey office building imported from the UK **(Fig. 20.6)**. This scheme was shown to FCO Ministers in January 1990, and to the Moscow City Architect, Leonid Vavakin, and the architectural panel that advised Moscow City Council, in summer 1990. All parties agreed that the scheme was an enterprising and acceptable response to a curious problem but there was alarm in London at the exorbitance of the estimated cost, about £160 million. While the implications of that level of expenditure were sinking in, the Cold War was beginning to thaw and the pressure to take forward such an ultra-high security solution was relaxing.

By early in 1991, it was becoming evident that the brief for the offices should be recast. As a trial of a less stringent security brief and of a greatly reduced budget, the FCO tasked the design team in May 1991 with producing a scheme to an amended brief. Though the scheme was unsatisfactory in itself, the exercise played an invaluable part in re-shaping the brief for the new building that was now, with *perestroika* and rapidly increasing staff numbers in the embassy, becoming imperative. In the interim, a strip of temporary buildings was installed along the back of the main embassy building on Sofiskaya Embankment. The Russians (as they were now being called) were pretty obstructive about this additional building but eventually agreed to it on condition that it was demolished as soon as the offices moved to a new building on Smolenskaya Embankment.

Andrew Wood became chief clerk in 1992: he had served in Moscow twice in his career and may have expected to go back as ambassador. He well understood the looming office problem in Moscow and did much to clear the way for its solution. The design team was tasked, through a feasibility study of 1992, to explore a radically new design which was developed into firm outline proposals in early 1994. As the project became a more normal one, the duke's panel gradually wound itself down and FCO Ministers were content for the new design to be taken forward. It was decided, too, that the FCO should appoint a project manager to lead the team of professional consultants and carry the main load of interfacing with the innumerable involved bodies. Hanscomb, the quantity surveyors, was appointed and it spawned The London Group to carry out the project manager role and keep its distance from the rest of the practice. This arrangement left Burton free enough to be a fully committed design team leader.

The new design comprised three between eight and ten storeys, blocks of flats, and one of classified offices on a podium along the front of the site, with cars and plant rooms beneath, and connected by a long corridor running north-south beside. The classified offices block had an extension reaching eastwards back from the river containing the unclassified offices, with entrance hall and exhibition area beneath. Where this east-west axis crossed the corridor was the crux of the site and of the design. Ancillary accommodation was grouped in the north-east corner. It was an admirably clear, yet subtle, disposition of functions, easily understood, and it appealed to all in London. The layout proved strong enough, and Burton's detailed planning ingenious enough, to cope with the many additional demands that came to be placed on it. The main corridor, the spine of the building, served the offices, the 31 flats and the sports and leisure amenities without compromising the security of any of them. It was rather surprising that the first and only time in the diplomatic estate that staff families could share such a main route with office staff was in this most secure of Posts. This solution, far from being a requirement of the brief, was a felicitous choice by the architect in partial response to Wood's belief that Moscow was still a grim and not particularly healthy posting for most families and that encouraging human contacts and physical exercise was a thoroughly desirable outcome.

The end of the Cold War enabled the laboriously negotiated but still unsigned Building and Lease Agreements to be simplified and loosened. Although the prescribed actions remained broadly reciprocal in Moscow and London, two major requirements of the former arrangements were relaxed. The receiving country could now undertake all of its own building works in the host country, and each side could proceed at its own pace. With the benefit of these relaxations, and of the Treasury's approval in May 1994 of £70 million for the project of about 20,000 square meters, it was time to seek planning approval in Moscow. The hope was that it could be achieved in time for HM The Queen to unveil a commemorative plaque on the site during her State Visit in October 1994.

The resumption of discussions with Vavakin started promisingly but were halted in July 1994 when he reported that his colleagues required certain changes. Vavakin visited London in early August to discuss these with Burton and OED. What was evidently required was a more monumental and less 'frivolous' appearance. Burton, with Patrick Stubbings who had by now succeeded Peacock as project architect, worked fast to bulk up the appearance by raising the podium, increasing the building heights, eliminating some curved roofs, and other adjustments. Three weeks later, Burton and OED called on Vavakin in Moscow to show him the results, as a result of which the Moscow Architectural Council gave the scheme its approval in September 1994, as did the Foreign Secretary, Douglas Hurd.

20.7. Richard Burton's 1994 design for the Moscow embassy on the Smolenskaya Embankment, with the offices and three staff accommodation blocks facing the river on a podium. This winter rendering was produced late in 1995 in a final, and successful, bid to satisfy the Mayor of Moscow.

Nonetheless, when The Queen unveiled the plaque on 4 October, the Mayor of Moscow, Yuri Luzhkov, explained to her that the city architects were still not content with all the details of the design and would no doubt revert to the issue in due course. Luzhkov was known to believe that the front elevation bore too close a resemblance to a block of 'holiday flats in a Black Sea resort' than was appropriate for Moscow but it was a surprise that he brought the matter up on this occasion.

Meanwhile, design development and working drawings were going ahead in London. The frontage design issue was not finally settled until February 1995, when Burton and OED called again on Vavakin in Moscow. They were surprised to find a Russian architect's drawings of how the British embassy should look pinned up on the wall of Vavakin's office, and totally ignored them. Fortunately, Vavakin did the same. Burton won him round to his latest proposals, which included balcony structures that connected the blocks visually at high level, and described the intended materials in terms of their Russian relevance. Vavakin agreed that he would try and persuade Luzhkov when he saw him that afternoon. Burton and OED were summoned to Vavakin's office the next morning. He had met Luzhkov, in the words of Burton's private diary,

in the zoo where Luzhkov was … saying that the zoo wasn't a fit place for animals and needed rebuilding. Between seeing the elephants and the tigers they looked at the drawings. What I had done … was to give Vavakin the drawings of a year ago so they could compare them with what we had now. There was a great difference; … it was in all a better project. The … mayor looked at our drawings and said he liked them and gave Vavakin the job of approving them and the responsibility.

Vavakin handed over a signed copy of the approved drawing there and then.

Mayor Luzhkov returned once more to the charge in December 1995 but Burton managed to satisfy him with sympathetic explanations and graphical representations **(Fig. 20.7)**.

The FCO had decided earlier in the design process that the structure of the unclassified offices wing should be capable of taking another floor for visa-issuing in case the demand should grow so much as to require it. It did, and the extra floor was slipped in just before tenders were invited in May 1996, in which month the Treasury revised its approval to £81.2 million. The simpler, but still hardly simple, Building and Lease Agreements were signed in mid-October 1996, and the construction contract with a Taylor Woodrow/Skanska joint venture, with a value of £59.5 million, later that same month. Within the joint venture, the contract management was British

20.8. Interior of the entrance hall in the new embassy in Moscow. At the top of the stair, and running at right angles to its axis, is the main corridor linking the accommodation blocks and all the communal facilities. Michael Craig-Martin's huge torch painting is on the right.

and the construction management Finnish. The security strategy that had underlain the negotiations with the Russians and was designed into the scheme from the outset was put into full effect. An inner security perimeter was built around the classified offices block into which only vetted British labour ever had access. All of the construction materials and elements for this block were shipped from the UK in containers to Helsinki and driven to the site in Moscow as diplomatic bags, immune from examination or tampering.

The construction period of three years over-ran by six months, and the contract cost out-turned at £82.3 million, including payment of a large contractual claim for extra expenses occasioned by the security regime. The whole project's total out-turn was just under £100 million. The embassy took up occupation in early 2000, having delayed the move until after it was clear that the millennium computer bug had been dealt with. The building was opened by HRH The Princess Royal, with the Foreign Secretary, Robin Cook, in attendance, on 17 May 2000 **(Fig. 20.8)**.

Berlin

Gestation of the Moscow building took over 50 years. For Berlin it was under ten. Germany was formally re-unified on 3 October 1990, and it was announced that the seat of government would return to Berlin before the end of the decade. The FCO did not take long to decide to build a new British embassy on the site of the old one at 70 Wilhelmstrasse, which was bought in 1884 and bombed in 1944. The site, beside the Berlin Wall on the east side, had lain vacant since then. Here, on 21 October 1992, HM The Queen unveiled a plaque recording her visit 'to the site of the future British Embassy to Germany'. The Adlon Hotel was building anew along the north and west boundaries of the site with six or more floors of blank walls, with the result that it would be difficult to design a new large British embassy on the old site alone. There was opportunity, however, to buy the vacant site to the south, No. 71, and combine the two. The ambassador, Sir Nigel Broomfield, and the permanent under-secretary, Sir David Gillmore, met on the site in June 1993 and decided that it was worth trying to persuade the Treasury to agree to its purchase for £6.5 million. They succeeded, and the way became clear for OED to start formulating a design strategy for the new embassy.

Until the previous year, there had been a splendid and defensible alternative to the obvious course of a competition: directly appointing James Stirling, who towered above his British contemporaries and whose Neuestaatsgalerie in Stuttgart had given him a large German following. The appointment would have been as comparably obvious as that of Lutyens for Washington in 1925, and the fact of the former foreign secretary's wife, Elspeth Howe, and Stirling's wife, Mary, being half-sisters intriguingly echoed the family relationship between Sir Lionel Earle and Emily Lutyens. But it was not to be: Stirling had tragically died the previous year, less than two weeks after he had been appointed a Knight.

So an architectural competition it was to be for Berlin. The chief clerk, Wood, was chairman of the assessment panel and the two architectural advisers on the panel were Peter Ahrends and Terry Farrell, both of whose practices were already working for OED and well knew the difficulties and opportunities of embassy design. There were 67 expressions of interest in 1994 in response to a notice in the Official Journal, whittled down to nine by OED, Ahrends and Farrell.[5] The submissions were received in January 1995 and put through a technical assessment. Concurrently, an exhibition of several boards from each submission was held in the FCO and was visited by ministers and the private secretary to the Prince of Wales. Although a difficult site with tall blank walls on three sides, it was wide and deep enough for many courtyard configurations to be explored and the submissions showed a wide range of highly articulated interiors.

The architects' presentations to the panel were held over two days in February 1995 in the FCO's fine Map Room. Immediately after the presentations, the chief clerk invited the eight assessors in turn to summarise their conclusions and indicate their first three preferences. The officials on the panel variously favoured the schemes of Grimshaw, Hopkins, MacCormac and Wilford (Stirling's former partner), while the professionals (including the senior representative from the Berlin planning authority) settled exclusively on the schemes of Wilford and Alsop & Stormer. There was a long and lively discussion, with officials being upbraided for not being brave enough to support the Alsop & Stormer scheme. In many ways, it was a splendid solution, but had little hope of working well as an embassy and was too large and expensive to build and operate: that its main elevation was constituted of recycled glass blocks was not its greatest drawback. The quiet discipline of the Wilford scheme, with an external entrance court and an internal winter garden beside each other, was given exceptional life by several rather provocative elements. The discussion developed to a stage at which the assessors were equally split between these two schemes. The chief clerk was not inclined to use his casting vote, which would have been in favour of Wilford, preferring instead to show both schemes to the Foreign Secretary and to invite Ahrends and Farrell to argue their case direct to him. Douglas Hurd went to the Map Room the next day and looked and listened

20.9. The entrance to the Berlin embassy, designed by Michael Wilford, and completed in 2000. An information centre protrudes through the wide horizontal slot at second-floor level, which also reveals the drum that stands in the winter garden and holds the conference centre.

carefully. He implied that he inclined towards Wilford but wanted to mull on it over the weekend. On the Monday afternoon his private secretary reported that, on balance, Hurd favoured the Wilford scheme. Alsop & Stormer's scheme was awarded a particular commendation.

There were one or two snippets in the press to the effect that the decision had been taken by the Secretary of State and not by the assessment panel. This was, of course, true, but the Secretary of State's careful judgement was a better way for the FCO to reach a considered result for the taxpayer than his chief clerk deploying a casting vote. The minister of state, Alastair Goodlad, announced the result at the Royal Institute of British Architects a couple of weeks later. The Wilford scheme was widely liked. Wood went off to be ambassador in Moscow soon afterwards, and the Prince of Wales's private secretary wrote to his successor in search of a way in the future of factoring the Prince's point of view into the FCO's design deliberations. The FCO, however, was pleased with the result of the competition **(Fig. 20.9)**.

Wilford's scheme adhered scrupulously to the planning guidelines and so planning permission was readily forthcoming from the Berlin authorities. Progress, however, was dislocated in early 1996 when the FCO was given no option by the Treasury but to offer up an estate project for treatment under the Private Finance Initiative (PFI). The choice fell on Berlin, on condition that the Wilford design could survive. The Private Finance Panel Executive took some persuading on this point but agreed to countenance it as, what it called, a prescriptive solution. After an advertisement in the Official Journal for appropriate consortia, OED received 27 serious investor responses which it distilled to a list of nine consortia, each comprising a financier, a contractor and a team of professional building and legal consultants. Each consortium gave a presentation to a panel of FCO officials and advisers in October 1996 to outline its background, ideas and approach to Private Finance Initiative solutions. A short-list of three was derived with whom to negotiate, on the basis of what was called an output specification, in pursuit of a preferred bidder. The specification was divided, in the prescribed manner, into primary services like construction, secondary services like building maintenance, and tertiary services like cleaning the building and providing office support facilities. The detail required to govern payments over 30 years for numerous different services and to reflect varied changes of circumstances defied belief. The outcome then had to be compared with what was termed the Public Sector Comparator, in other words, the guesstimate of what it would cost without going down the Initiative route. The preferred bidder, selected in July 1997, was Arteos, a consortium comprising Bilfinger and Berger as contractors and equity financiers, Dresdner Bank as loan financiers, and Johnson Controls as facilities managers. Michael Wilford's commission from the FCO was novated, much to his understandable chagrin, to Arteos, which immediately reduced the building specifications.

Construction started in mid-1998 when the FCO minister of state,

20.10. The main stair from the reception area to the winter garden atrium in the Berlin embassy. A wrought-iron gate salvaged from the bombed former embassy on the same site is fixed above the head of the stair.

Derek Fatchett, performed a ground breaking ceremony by planting a 45-year-old English oak, grown in Hamburg, in the middle of the future open courtyard. The National Audit Office published a lukewarm report of its enquiry into the Private Finance Initiative contract in June 2000, shortly before completion. It concluded that the FCO had 'managed the process effectively' and would 'obtain a suitable building at a price comparable with a traditional procurement' **(Fig. 20.10)**.[6]

Her Majesty The Queen opened the new Berlin building on 18 July 2000: a fitting point at which to conclude this account of 200 years of permanent British diplomatic buildings.

Postscript

The decade since the opening of the new embassy in Berlin in 2000 saw a quickening of changes in the management of the FCO against a background of benign financial times followed by the worst crunch since the 1970s. For the diplomatic estate, the defining event of the decade was the bomb explosion at Pera House in Istanbul on 20 November 2003. The consul-general, Roger Short, and his assistant, Lisa Hallworth, and eight local staff lost their lives in what was the most deadly assault on a British mission since the Boxer siege in Peking in 1900. The result of subsequent reviews was a significant increase in the capital budget for new buildings to replace ones that were assessed as insecure and for additional defences at Posts where weaknesses were identified.

The biggest debate was about whether to remain in some city centres. This is where most diplomatic activity is best performed but also where it is impossible to achieve adequate 'stand-off' distance between roadside and building. The alternative was to move, as the Americans had been doing since the bombing of their embassies in Nairobi and Dar es Salaam in 1998, towards 'fortresses' in suburbs, where the land for sufficient stand-off was affordable but the negativity of the message to the host country was conspicuous. On the whole, the British diplomatic presence has remained in city centres but the appearance around embassy buildings of barriers, gates, guards and road closures is off-putting to visitors and infuriating for local residents.

The FCO, bolstered by additional money from the Treasury to strengthen its defences, undertook a large capital programme of new embassy office buildings that included Algiers, Colombo, Dar es Salaam, Doha, Harare, Kampala, Manila, Rabat, Sana'a and Warsaw. The costs rocketed as sufficient land was bought, greater blast resistance was built into building structures and envelopes, and the FCO sought to shift more of the construction risks to

447

its contractors. On the other hand, the pursuit of good architectural design for these new buildings had never been more energetic, thanks also to the stimulus of the government's Better Public Buildings campaign and the advocacy of the Commission for Architecture and the Built Environment (which succeeded the Royal Fine Art Commission).

The good financial times, including the strength of sterling, could not be expected to last, and nor did they. Matters were made worse in 2007 by the withdrawal of a foreign currency pricing mechanism that had long insulated the FCO from adverse exchange movements, and by rules that forced the FCO to charge rent from its tenants from other government departments at full economic cost, with the absurd result that the FCO was unable to fill the space that became surplus as a result of its new methods of working. The Berlin Private Finance Initiative also proved far less attractive than had been anticipated because the scope for the FCO to make efficiency savings was limited by being locked into a 30-year contract.

While building itself out of security trouble, and managing successful sales transactions in Bangkok and Madrid, the FCO did not press on with the next generation of estate rationalisations. This is mainly confined to the 'land and sand' inheritance: large compounds acquired when land, in Tokyo for example, or sand, in Abu Dhabi say, had practically no value at all and now has a latent value disproportionate to the embassy uses it sustains. Unlocking and sharing some of that value still lies ahead, and will require skill and time: though less time, perhaps, than the hundred years that it has taken to decide what to do about the site at Tarabya on the Bosphorus where the summer residence burned down in 1911.

The fears of the Public Accounts Committee and others at the time of Vote Transfer in 1983 that the FCO diplomats might be wayward estate managers proved groundless because they worked out a *modus operandi* that balanced the diplomatic and professional inputs to the management of the estate. This balance was upset during the last decade, to the detriment of the professional contribution, by the under-regulated devolution of estate responsibilities and budgets to Posts undermining the estate as a corporate asset that required central direction and oversight. The fragmentation of responsibility led to widespread inconsistencies, some injudicious uses of resources, and a drift away from strategic estate direction. The dialogue between diplomats and professionals at the centre was weakened and mutual frustrations resulted, exacerbated by the inability of buildings to respond to change as quickly or as flexibly as change managers thought they should. At the end of the decade, a new and different type of estate management regime was installed. It faces the tasks of upgrading the professional contribution to strategic estate direction and bringing the inputs back into constructive balance at a financially difficult time. Its success will not become clear for a few years yet.

There is no doubt that the estate must adapt and develop. The hope must be that, in doing so, some of the lessons of its history are taken into account.

Notes

Abbreviations:

ER - FCO estate register

FCO – Foreign and Commonwealth Office

HP - FCO estate files at Hanslope Park

IO - India Office Records at the British Library

MB - author's collection

ODNB - Oxford Dictionary of National Biography

TNA - The National Archives

Chapter 1 First Ownerships 1800-1815

1. Trevelyan, *Diplomatic Channels*, p.122.
2. Horn, *British Diplomatic Service*, pp.16, 54.
3. TNA, FO78/35 (p.13, Elgin to Hawkesbury, 5 January 1802).
4. TNA, FO78/33 (p.247, Elgin to Hawkesbury, 22 November 1801).
5. Ibid.
6. TNA, FO78/35 (p.86, Elgin to Hawkesbury, 25 January 1802).
7. Walsh, *Residence at Constantinople*, p.232.
8. Gurney, *Legations and Gardens*, p.204.
9. Ibid.
10. TNA, T1/4067, Long Papers, bundle 556, includes the deeds and inventory.
11. ER, Register of Properties, 2 vols, pp.131-2.
12. Platt, *Cinderella Service*, p.85, note 3.
13. Toplis, *Foreign Office*, p.164 for origin of quotation.

Chapter 2 Enter the Office of Works 1824-1856

1. Crook, *British Museum*, p.78, quoted in *ODNB* entry for Sir Robert Smirke.
2. TNA, T1/4067.
3. Leveson Gower, *Letters of Harriet,* vol. 1, p.314.
4. TNA, T1/4067.
5. Decimus Burton, *Letterbook 1841-3*, V&A National Art Library, MSL/1908/1883.
6. TNA, WORK10/27/1.
7. Crook, *The King's Works*, vol. 6, p.634, note 2.
8. TNA, WORK10/27/4.
9. Walsh, *Residence at Constantinople*, p.321

and ff.

10. TNA, WORK10/1.
11. Ibid. (11 June 1841).
12. Ibid. (12 March 1842).
13. Ibid.
14. Ibid. (25 April 1842).
15. Ibid. (4 May 1842).
16. TNA, WORK11/1/2, f.159. The widespread belief that Barry designed Smith's building derives from the exaggerations of his son, Alfred, in his biography of his father. He made two references to his father's contribution: on p.124, 'In the same year [referring, clearly erroneously, to 1847] he modified the design for the Ambassador's palace at Constantinople, to an extent which greatly determined its general effect': on p.357 he included 'Ambassador's Palace at Constantinople 1842' in his list of Barry's architectural designs.
17. Crinson, *Empire Building*, p.128.
18. TNA, WORK10/2 (17 September 1844).
19. Ibid (ff.401, 504).
20. TNA, WORK10/3 (17 September 1846).
21. TNA, WORK10/4 (26 August 1848).
22. TNA, WORK10/3 (17 March 1848).
23. TNA, WORK10/4.
24. TNA, WORK10/5 (18 February 1852).

Chapter 3 The Treasury Tightens its Grip 1852-1876

1. TNA, 22/2/14, Report upon the Office of Works, 14 June 1854.
2. Port, *Imperial London*, p.37.
3. Ibid., p.61.
4. *ODNB* entry for Mitford.
5. Morris, *Stones of Empire*, p.37.
6. Sheil, *Glimpses of Life and Manners in Persia*, p.162.
7. TNA, FO60/395 (Treasury to Foreign Office, 21 July 1862).
8. Ibid (f.153).
9. TNA, WORK10/34/1 (April 1869).
10. Ibid. (April 1871).
11. Ibid.
12. TNA, FO78/1714 (including

succeeding quotes).

13. TNA, FO78/2212 (19 May 1865).
14. Ibid.
15. TNA, FO78/3205A (29 August 1831).
16. TNA, FO78/3208 (24 April 1866).
17. Brassey, *Sunshine and Storm in the East,* 1880, entry at 22 October 1874.
18. TNA, WORK10/43/5.
19. TNA, FO78/3209 (13 June 1870).
20. TNA, WORK10/43/7.
21. TNA, WORK10/44/6 (17 July 1870).
22. TNA, FO78/3209.
23. TNA, WORK43/7 (Elliot to Derby, 22 July 1875).

Chapter 4 Consulates 1850-1900

1. Platt, *Cinderella Service*, p.13.
2. Dickie, *British Consul*, p.32: Supply Debate, 14 April 1856.
3. Platt, *Cinderella Service*, p.156.
4. Michie, *The Englishman in China*, p.115.
5. TNA, WORK10/430 (26 February 1866).
6. Ibid. (24 August 1866).
7. *Who's Who* entry for R.H. Boyce (1834-1909).
8. TNA, WORK10/756.
9. Report from the Select Committee on Diplomatic and Consular Services, printed 16 July 1872: Appendix no.2, Memorandum no.1, p.134.
10. Ibid., Minutes of Evidence, p.40, para.770.
11. Cortazzi, *Victorians in Japan*, p.40.
12. Wood, *Consul in Paradise*, pp.33, 130.
13. Hoare, *Embassies in the East*, p.121.
14. TNA, WORK10/389 (Boyce to Primrose, 3 August 1892).
15. Wright, *The English amongst the Persians*, p.82.
16. TNA, FO27/3246 (Maclean to Foreign Office, 11 January 1895).
17. TNA, FO27/3284 (7 April 1896).
18. TNA, WORK10/49/1 (18 October 1890).
19. TNA, FO27/3284.
20. TNA, FO27/3637 (27 May 1903).
21. TNA, WORK10/47/6 (Downer to Secretary).
22. TNA, WORK10/350.
23. TNA, FO687/1 (21 October 1851).

Chapter 5 Legation Houses 1850-1900

1. MB. 8 November 1860. Chinese version at TNA, FO 682/1993/84.
2. Hoare, *Embassies in the East*, p.19.
3. Report published 23 July 1861.
4. TNA, WORK10/25/1 (24 April 1879).
5. Ibid.
6. TNA, WORK10/609 (14 April 1875).
7. TNA, WORK10/202 (Codrington to Winter 17 April 1950, quoting letter 3 April 1882).
8. TNA, WORK10/488.
9. Ibid.
10. *ODNB* entry for Buchanan.
11. TNA, T1/7306B.
12. Ibid. (5 April 1873).
13. Ibid.
14. Ibid.
15. Ibid.
16. Ibid.
17. TNA, WORK10/293 (21 July 1886).
18. Ibid.
19. Ibid.
20. Ibid. (1 July 1887).
21. Ibid. (25 March 1889).

Chapter 6 Order and Disorder 1875-1900

1. Horn, *British Diplomatic Service*, p.54.
2. TNA, WORK10/255 (26 September 1877).
3. Ibid.
4. Ibid. (10 December 1878).
5. Ibid.
6. *The Builder*, 43, 8 July 1882, p.39.
7. TNA, WORK10/33/1 (Cowan to Secretary, 19 September 1900).
8. *Royal Engineers Journal*, 1 April 1901, pp.66-9.
9. TNA, WORK10/33/1 (Cowan to Secretary, 19 September 1900).
10. Hoare, *Embassies in the East*, p.33.

Chapter 7 Early Twentieth Century Houses 1900-1915

1. Crinson, *Empire Building*, p.132.
2. TNA, WORK10/25/1 (10 August 1901).
3. Ibid. (16 September 190).
4. TNA, WORK10/182 (15 April 1904).
5. TNA, WORK10/287.

6. Ibid. (14 May 1908).
7. Howard, *Theatre of Life*, pp.169-70.
8. TNA, WORK10/206 (27 May 1910).
9. Ibid.
10. Ibid.
11. Ibid.
12. Howard, *Theatre of Life*, p.203.
13. TNA, WORK10/393 (17 January 1913).
14. Ibid.
15. Howard, *Theatre of Life*, pp.203-4.
16. TNA, WORK10/552.
17. Ibid. (12 January 1909).
18. Ibid.
19. TNA, WORK10/292.
20. McKinstry, *Rosebery*, p.131.
21. Rodd, *Social and Diplomatic Memories 1902-19*, pp.125-6.
22. TNA, WORK10/375 (15 October 1909).
23. Earle, *Turn over the Page*, p.95.
24. TNA WORK22/8/5 (April 1911).
25. TNA, WORK22/39 (Holmes Committee Report 1913, p.28, recommendation v.(f)).
26. Ibid. (Holmes Committee Report, p.32, II, para.2).
27. Ibid. (Earle minute, 3 December 1913).

Chapter 8 Post-War and the 1920s
1. TNA, WORK10/487 (1 March 1915).
2. TNA, WORK10/235.
3. Tilley and Gaselee, *Foreign Office*, p.199.
4. TNA, FO366/799.
5. TNA, WORK22/37 (Eggar Report, 26 April 1919).
6. Earle, *Turn over the Page*, pp.250-1.
7. TNA, WORK10/378 (Loraine to Earle, 21 February 1931, and reply 12 March 1931).
8. *ODNB* entry for Earle.
9. Jones, *Diary with Letters*, p.47.
10. TNA, FO366/780.
11. TNA, WORK10/196.
12. TNA, WORK10/197.
13. Ibid.
14. TNA, WORK10/198 (11 June 1925).
15. Ibid. (13 January 1926).
16. Earle, *Turn over the Page*, pp.201-2.
17. TNA, FO366/844.
18. TNA, WORK10/263.
19. TNA, FO366/2958 (Helm, Beginnings of the Ankara Embassy, 4 April 1952).

20. TNA, WORK10/211.
21. TNA, WORK10/212.
22. TNA, WORK10/292 (20 May 1912).
23. TNA, WORK10/388 (4 April 1925).
24. TNA, WORK10/171.
25. TNA, WORK10/216.
26. Ibid. (12 November 1925).
27. Ibid.
28. Ibid.
29. Ibid.
30. E.R. Himsworth, 'A History of the British Embassy in Kabul', unpublished FCO account, 1976.

Chapter 9 Tokyo and Washington 1923–1932
1. All the direct quotations in the Tokyo part of this chapter are taken from TNA, WORK10/638-40.
2. All the direct quotations in the Washington part of this chapter, except as identified below, are taken from TNA, WORK10/100-106. The FCO presented the full set of Lutyens' contract drawings to the British Architectural Library's Drawings Collection in 2006.
3. Howard, *Theatre of Life*, p.560.
4. Ibid.
5. TNA, WORK67/2 (Allison scrapbook).
6. Earle, *Turn over the Page*, p.192.
7. The eight donors, as recorded in the pergola, were: SIR DOUGLAS ALEXANDER Bart, HENRY M J BUCKNALL, CHARLES H HOLLAND, W H JONES CBE, DR R FOSTER KENNEDY, GEORGE O MAY, SAMUEL AGAR SALVAGE, SIR ASHLEY SPARKS KBE.

Chapter 10 Buildings 1930-1940
1. TNA, WORK10/345.
2. TNA, FO366/824.
3. TNA, WORK10/346.
4. TNA, FO366/874 (10 January 1930).
5. Ibid.
6. TNA, FO366/875.
7. TNA FO366/887 (19 February 1931).
8. TNA, WORK10/81.
9. Ibid. (10 December 1929).
10. TNA, WORK10/200 (22 October 1937).
11. Ibid. (26 November 1937).

12. TNA, WORK10/96.
13. The plaque reads: 'This house was
presented to His Majesty's Government
in the United Kingdom by Charles
Maggs, who built and lived in it from
1912 until his death in 1937, in token
of his affection for the country of his
birth and with the desire that, in
the country of his adoption, the High
Commissioner for the United Kingdom
should be worthily housed for the
discharge of his functions as a link
between His Majesty's Governments in
the United Kingdom and in the Union
of South Africa.'
14. Earle, *Turn over the Page*, p.152.
15. TNA, WORK10/213 (9 April 1936).
16. Ibid. (17 April 1936).
17. Ibid. (18 April 1936).
18. Ibid. (4 May 1936).
19. Ibid. (23 June 1936).
20. Ibid.
21. IO, L/P+S/12/3637 (7 and 9 March
1929).
22. Ibid. (7 November 1929).
23. TNA, FO366/1022 (28 January 1938).
24. TNA, WORK10/380.

**Chapter 11 Second World War and
Aftermath 1940-1950**
1. TNA, FO370/588 (19 September 1939).
2. FCO Historians, *Retreat from Moscow – the
British Embassy 1941,* June 2006.
3. Norwich, *Duff Cooper Diaries*, p.320.
4. Ibid., p.327.
5. Paterson, *Tired and Emotional*, p.62.
6. TNA, WORK10/736.
7. TNA, WORK10/489 (10 December
1943).
8. TNA, WORK10/351 (2 November
1945).
9. TNA, FO366/1535.
10. TNA, WORK10/748 (26 July 1943).
11. Ibid.
12. Ibid.
13. Ibid. (15 January 1943).
14. Ibid. (10 March 1944).
15. Ibid.
16. TNA, WORK10/380.
17. Ibid.
18. John Brewster in *News Chronicle*, 30

September 1947.
19. TNA, WORK10/379.
20. TNA, WORK10/591 (26 May 1960).
21. TNA, WORK10/748.
22. TNA, WORK10/239.
23. TNA WORK10/411.
24. TNA, WORK10/9/2.
25. HP, EO 1263/1 pt 1 (November 1952).
26. Ibid. (Addis to Steel, 28 June 1955).
27. HP, EO 1263/1 pt 2 (December 1957).

Chapter 12 Cold War 1946-1983
1. TNA WORK10/122 (25 March 1947).
2. Ibid.
3. TNA WORK10/289.
4. Ibid (19 August 1947).
5. HP, EO1 23802/7 pt 2.
6. Hoare, *Embassies in the East*, p.75.
7. TNA, WORK10/757 (typescript, R.G.
Scott, 'Peking Diary: an Account of Day-
to-Day Activities and Personal
Impressions of a Mechanical and
Electrical Engineer stationed at Peking,
February 1958 – May 1960').

**Chapter 13 New Commonwealth 1947-
1983**
1. TNA, WORK10/229 (Croft to
Monteath, 22 May 1946).
2. TNA, WORK10/226 (Nye to Liesching,
28 January 1950).
3. Ibid.
4. TNA, WORK10/228.
5. Ibid. (meeting 10 November 1954).
6. TNA, BP1/10 (meeting 9 February
1955).
7. HP, EO2 40703/7 (meeting 4 October
1948).
8. TNA, DO142/463 (16 August 1947).
9. TNA, WORK10/219.
10. HP, EO 1255/1 pt 3.
11. TNA, WORK10/536 (Oliver to Wilby,
July 1956).
12. TNA, WORK10/366.
13. TNA, WORK10/537 (19 May 1958).

**Chapter 14 Roles, Rules and Rations,
1950-1970**
1. TNA, WORK10/746 (Bevin to Key, 11
July 1949).
2. Ibid.

3. Ibid. (3 August 1949).
4. TNA, WORK10/674 (12 June 1950).
5. TNA, WORK10/115.
6. Ibid.
7. TNA, WORK10/704 (27 March 1962).
8. Ibid. (minutes of meeting of Committee on Publicity, 9 & 14 March 1961).
9. TNA, WORK10/515 (de Normann to Marshall, 21 February 1953).
10. Part, *The Making of a Mandarin*, pp.108-9.
11. TNA, WORK10/672 (Turner to Newis, 18 February 1960).
12. Ibid. (4 March 1960).
13. Ibid. (Turner to Jenkins, 15 July 1960).
14. Ibid.
15. TNA, WORK10/380.
16. TNA, WORK10/683.
17. Ibid.
18. TNA WORK10/684.
19. Plowden Report, Cmnd. 2276, February 1964, para.541.
20. TNA, WORK10/711 (Tour of Diplomatic Missions Abroad, 1966).

Chapter 15 In-house Production Line 1950-1970

1. TNA, BP1/10 (3892, 13 October 1954).
2. TNA, WORK 10/418 (Bedford to Cunliffe, 5 November 1954).
3. TNA, BP1/10 (4030, 9 February 1955).
4. TNA, WORK10/418 (Crawford to Birch, 13 February 1955).
5. Ibid. (Cunliffe to Muir).
6. Ibid. (Crawford to Birch, 12 March 1955).
7. TNA, FO366/3135.
8. TNA, BP1/11 (4302, 9 November 1955).
9. TNA, FO366/3136.
10. TNA, WORK10/659.
11. Trevelyan, *Diplomatic Channels*, p.136.
12. MB, British Information Services press leaflet: *The New British High Commission Building*.
13. TNA, WORK10/182 (May 1961).
14. Ziegler, *Diana Cooper*, p.296.
15. Trevelyan, *Diplomatic Channels*, p.136.
16. TNA, WORK10/757 (Scott 'Peking Diary': see Ch.12, note 7).
17. HP, EO1 23802/7 pt 2.
18. TNA, WORK10/516 (3 February 1953).
19. Carrington, *Reflect on Things Past*, p.122.

20. TNA, WORK10/313.
21. Ibid. (25 May 1954).
22. TNA, BP1/11 (4623, 10 October 1956; 4649, 14 November 1956; 4762, 13 February 1957).
23. MB, British Embassy, Belgrade, Residence Manual, March 1977.
24. TNA, WORK10/709 (24 May 1963).

Chapter 16 Lagos, Rome and Brasilia 1957-1970

1. Hansard, HC Deb. 01 July 1958, vol. 590 cc1043-4.
2. TNA, BP1/11 (5548, 8 October 1958).
3. Brett, *Our Selves Unknown*, p.111.
4. TNA, WORK10/699 (Hope to Muir, 12 April 1961).
5. *The Guardian*, 30 January 1961.
6. TNA, CO554/2552.
7. Hunt, *On the Spot*, p.127.
8. TNA, BP1/13 (7562, 13 June 1962).
9. HP, EO1 22803/3 pt 5 (4 October 1962).
10. HP, EO1 22803/2 pt 2 (25 November 1964).
11. TNA, WORK10/597 (Muir to Pannell, 25 January 1965).
12. Hansard, PQ written answer, 28 July 1966.
13. HP, AC 10138/28 pt 2 (Cloake to Knight, 11 July 1967).
14. Ibid. (Spence to Knight, 28 February 1968).
15. Sir Evelyn Shuckburgh, 'The British Presence', *Architectural Review*, 150, September 1971, pp.155-6.
16. TNA, WORK10/608 (Shuckburgh to Roberts, 19 November 1968).
17. Ibid.
18. TNA, WORK10/505.
19. Ibid.
20. HP, EO1 15600/19 pt 1.
21. Ibid.
22. Alison and Peter Smithson, *Architectural Review*, 158, October 1975, pp.222-8.
23. TNA, BP1/15, 9259 (12 January 1966).
24. HP, EO1 15600/19 pt 2 (Alison Smithson to Pannell, 23 March 1966).
25. TNA, WORK10/504 (Diamond to Mellish, 1 September 1967).
26. *The Times*, 15 September 1967.
27. TNA, WORK10/504 (Kennet to Mellish,

20 March 1968).

28. *The Times*, 1 June 1968.

29. *Architectural Review*, 144, August 1968, p.79.

30. Alison and Peter Smithson, *Architectural Review*, 158, October 1975, pp. 224-5.

31. HP, XA 3082/8/1 (Smithson to Dodson, 30 April 1976).

Chapter 17 Internals and Externals

1. TNA, WORK10/56/6.

2. TNA, WORK10/699. The two ladies were Miss W.J. Matcham and Miss S. Vigor.

3. Ibid. (Hope to Lloyd, 7 July 1960).

4. Ibid. (record of initial meeting, 1 December 1960).

5. Ibid.

6. Ibid. (28 August 1964).

7. 'British Art for Foreign Eyes', *Country Life*, 183, 9 Nov. 1989, pp.82-5.

8. *The Connoisseur*, August 1982, p.48.

9. HP, EO 1451/1 pt 1 (Vinter to Root, 29 July 1966).

10. David Manning, 'A Miraculous Survival: the Zamoyski Furniture at the Royal Castle, Warsaw', *Country Life*, 157, 23 January 1975, pp.208-9.

11. TNA, FO366/792.

12. TNA, WORK10/410 (24 September 1921).

13. Ibid. (Russell memorandum, 17 December 1946). Mary Henderson wrote an account, 'The Beresford Hope Silver' in *Apollo*, January 1974, pp. 34-7, and Michael Llewellyn Smith in a 1996 unpublished FCO paper 'British Embassies to Poland and the British Embassy Warsaw'.

14. TNA, FO366/759.

15. Government Art Collection, *The Twentieth Century*, 1997, introduction by Dr Wendy Baron, p.x.

16. Ibid., p.xiii.

17. TNA, WORK10/663.

18. MB, correspondence with Halter.

19. TNA, WORK10/231 (Mann to Kelt, July 1952).

20. HP, EO1 23802/7 pt 2 (Clutton to Kaye, 11 November 1963).

Chapter 18 Reforms and Upheavals 1968-1983

1. HP, XA 1/1/3.

2. Hansard, PQ written answer, 11 November 1971.

3. HP, XA 1/3 pt F.

4. HP, XA 1/3 pt B.

5. Ibid.

6. Ibid. (Wright to Scott, 1 May 1972).

7. Ibid.

8. Ibid.

9. HP, XAA 1/1 (Brimelow to Cox, 3 April 1975).

10. HP, XAA 360/11, 20 May 1977.

11. Ibid.

12. CPRS, *Review of Overseas Representation*, HMSO, 1977.

13. Ibid., para.18.13, p.289.

14. HP, XAA 360/2 (Owen to Shore, 8 March 1978).

15. Ibid.

16. Ibid. (Shore to Owen, 11 April 1978).

17. Ibid. (Barnett to Owen, 28 April 1978).

18. MB, 'Joint Review of Diplomatic Estate Management', typescript report of the Steering Group, 19 February 1981.

19. Ibid., para.11.1.

20. *Architectural Review*, 144, August 1968, p.79.

21. TNA, WORK10/507 (Richards to Gibson, 9 September 1968).

22. *Architectural Review*, 150, September 1971, pp.149-51.

23. HP, XAA364/3082/4 (Casson to Shore, 24 November 1976).

24. MB. DOE Press Notice 15/71, 27 January 1971.

25. Philip Powell's sketch scheme is in the British Architectural Library Drawings Collection, PB481/1.

26. Hansard, HC Deb. 27 November 1967, vol. 755 cc19-20.

27. TNA, WORK10/518 (Wright to Cloake, 2 August 1967).

28. Ibid. (27 November 1968).

Chapter 19 Diplomats in Control 1983-2000

1. Statutory Instrument 1983 no.146, under Section 2 of the Ministers of the Crown Act 1975.

2. House of Commons, *Fifth Report from the Committee of Public Accounts*, Session 1983-84 (HC106), Minutes of Evidence, para.1612.
3. Ibid., para.31.
4. *Management of the Diplomatic Estate from the Mid 1980s*, November 1983, Pt III, para.1. The paper was reproduced as Appendix A to the Memorandum by the C & AG in the published Minutes of Evidence taken on 6 March 1985.
5. MB, 'Farewell to 123 Years of History', letter Mansfield to Howe, 16 October 1984.
6. Hurd, *Memoirs*, p.275.
7. The competitors were: Montgomerie Oldfield and Denn (winner), Norman and Dawbarn, and Peter J. Palmer.
8. The full membership of this committee was: Sydney Chapman MP (and architect), John Cornforth (*Country Life*), Dennis Marler (managing director, Capital and Counties), Alan Moore (Lloyds Bank International), John Partridge (partner, HKPA), Idris Pearce (Richard Ellis), and Sir Donald Tebbit (former chief clerk and director-general, British Property Federation).
9. The competitors were: John S. Bonnington Partnership, De Brant Joyce and Partners, Brian Clouston and Partners with Kampulan Akitek (winner), GMW Partnership, Percy Thomas Partnership, Raglan Squire and Partners, and Sheppard Robson Architects.
10. MB, 'Residence for BHC Kuala Lumpur: Architectural Competition: Conditions and Design Brief', issued 4 November 1985.
11. The competitors for Nairobi were: Cullum and Nightingale (winner), Denton Scott Associates, and Troughton

McAslan. For Dublin: Ahrends Burton and Koralek, Allies and Morrison (winner), Forum Architects, and Percy Thomas Partnership. For Muscat: Huckle Tweddell Partnership, YRM Architects and Planners (winner), and another.
12. MB, Howe PM84/85, 24 May 1984.

Chapter 20 Hong Kong, Moscow and Berlin 1986-2000
1. The competitors were: Terry Farrell and Company (winner), Leigh & Orange/John R Harris Partnership, Llewellyn-Davies Weeks HK, Palmer and Turner, Property Services Agency, and RMJM HK.
2. The other members of the Moscow design panel were: Ralph French (ICI), Sydney Chapman MP (also an architect), Idris Pearce (Richard Ellis), and Kathleen Berton Murrell (historian).
3. The competitors were: Allies and Morrison, Julian Bicknell (winner), Cambridge Design, Chipperfield Associates, Edward Cullinan, Barry Gasson, Nicholas Hare, and Maguire and Murray.
4. *Architects' Journal*, 14 December 1988, p.33.
5. The competitors were: Allies and Morrison, Alsop and Stormer, Arup Associates, Clelland Associates, Nicholas Grimshaw, Michael Hopkins and Partners, MacCormac Jamieson and Prichard, Ian Ritchie, and Michael Wilford (winner).
6. Report by the Comptroller and Auditor General, *The New British Embassy in Berlin*, HC 585 Session 1999-2000, published 30 June 2000 (wording taken from Executive Summary sub-headings).

Illustration Credits

The National Archives: 1.2. MPK1/396; 2.2. WORK10/43/7; 3.6. FO925/3017, FO925/3011, FO925/3012, MPK1/433; 3.7. FO925/3010; 3.8. FO925/3376; 4.4. WORK40/340; 4.5. WORK10/56; 4.10. WORK40/358; 4.15. WORK10/184; 4.17. MPK1/139; 4.18. WORK40/273; 5.1. WORK40/88; 5.4. MFQ1/1015; 5.7. MPD1/53; 5.11. WORK40/469; 6.3. WORK40/93; 7.9. MPK1/349; 7.11. WORK55/17; 9.1. WORK10/638; 9.3. WORK55/5; 10.2. WORK40/397; 10.9. WORK55/1; 10.10. WORK10/354; 12.6. WORK10/374; 12.7. WORK55/17; 15.1. WORK10/660; 16.6-7. WORK10/601; 16.9. WORK10/506; 17.3. WORK10/663.

Foreign and Commonwealth Office: 2.1; 3.1-2; 3.10; 4.2-3; 4.6; 4.7-9; 4.11-14; 4.16; 5.2-3; 5.5-6; 5.8; 6.2; 7.1-8; 8.1-9; 9.2; 9.5-6; 9.9-12; 10.3-8; 11.1-8; 12.1-5; 12.8; 13.1; 13.3-10; 15.2-13; 17.1-2; 18.2; 18.5-6; 19.1-6; 20.1; 20.6.

Peter Cook and the Foreign and Commonwealth Office: 19.9-10; 20.2-3; 20.8-10.

Others: 1.1 Walsh, *A Residence at Constantinople*, vol.2, frontispiece; 1.4 Jean Nérée Ronfort, *À l'ombre de Pauline*, p.17; 1.5 Day, *At Home in Carthage*, p.8; 3.3 RIBA Library Drawings and Archives Collections, SD89/19; 6.1 *Royal Engineers Journal*, 1 April 1901; 10.1 John Freeman, frontispiece in Berton *British Residence, Moscow*; 15.14 Family of Eric Bedford; 16.1-4. *Country Life*; 16.8 The Frances Loeb Library, Harvard Graduate School of Design; 19.7 Lady Ruth Hawley; 20.5 Julian Bicknell.

Bibliography

General

Arbuthnott, Hugh, Terence Clark and Richard Muir, *British Missions around the Gulf, 1575-2005: Iran, Iraq, Kuwait, Oman,* Folkestone: Global Oriental, 2008.

Barry, Alfred, *The Life and Works of Sir Charles Barry CB RA FRS,* London: Murray, 1867.

Berridge, G.R., *British Diplomacy in Turkey, 1583 to the Present: a Study in the Evolution of the Resident Embassy,* Leiden and Boston: Nijhoff, 2009.

Black, Jeremy, *A History of Diplomacy,* London: Reaktion Books, 2010.

--------- *British Diplomats and Diplomacy 1688-1800,* University of Exeter Press, 2001.

Boyce, R.H., *Report on Her Majesty's Legation and Consular Buildings in China, Corea, Japan and Siam,* London: HMSO, 1899.

Brassey, Annie, *Sunshine and Storm in the East: or, Cruises to Cyprus and Constantinople,* New York: Henry Holt, 1880.

Brett, Lionel, *Our Selves Unknown: an Autobiography,* London: Gollancz, 1985.

Carrington, Lord, *Reflect on Things Past,* London: Collins, 1988.

Coates, P.D., *The China Consuls: British Consular Officers 1843-1943,* Oxford University Press, 1988.

Cortazzi, Hugh, *Victorians in Japan: in and around the Treaty Ports,* London, and Atlantic Highlands, NJ: Athlone Press, 1987.

Crinson, Mark, *Empire Building: Orientalism and Victorian Architecture,* London and New York: Routledge, 1996.

--------- *Modern Architecture and the End of Empire,* Aldershot: Ashgate, 2003.

Crook, J. Mordaunt, and M.H. Port, *History of the King's Works, vol. 6 1782-1851,* London: HMSO, 1973.

Curzon, George Nathaniel, *Persia and the Persian Question,* London: Longmans Green, 1892.

Dickie, John, *The British Consul: Heir to a Great Tradition*, London: Hurst, 2007.

--------- *The New Mandarins, How British Foreign Policy Works,* London: Tauris, 2004.

Earle, Sir Lionel, *Turn over the Page,* London: Hutchinson, 1935.

Emmerson, Sir Harold, *The Ministry of Works*, London: Allen and Unwin, 1956.

Fairweather, Maria, *Pilgrim Princess: a Life of Princess Zinaida Volkonsky,* London: Constable, 1999.

Fiddes, Sir George V., *The Dominions and Colonial Offices,* London and New York: Putnam, 1926.

Finn, Dallas, *Meiji Revisited: the Sites of Victorian Japan,* New York: Weatherhill, 1995.

Garner, Joe, *The Commonwealth Office 1925-68,* London: Heineman, 1978.

Goode, James W., *Capital Losses: a Cultural History of Washington's Destroyed Buildings,* Smithsonian Institution Press, 1979.

Gore-Booth, Paul, *With Great Truth and Respect: the Memoirs of Paul Gore-Booth,* London: Constable, 1974.

Loeffler, Jane C., *The Architecture of Diplomacy: Building America's Embassies*, New York: Princeton Architectural Press, 1998.

Henderson, Sir Nevile, *Failure of a Mission: Berlin 1937-1939,* London: Hodder and Stoughton, 1940.

Henderson, Nicholas, *Mandarin: the Diaries of an Ambassador,* London: Weidenfeld and Nicolson, 1994.

Hickman, Katie, *Daughters of Britannia: the Lives and Times of Diplomatic Wives,* London: HarperCollins, 1999.

Hoare, James E., *Embassies in the East: the Story of the British and their Embassies in China, Japan and Korea from 1859 to the Present,* Richmond: Curzon, 1999.

Horn, D.B., *The British Diplomatic Service 1689-1961,* Oxford: Clarendon Press, 1961.

Howard, Esme, *Theatre of Life: Life seen from the Stalls 1903-36,* Boston: Little, Brown, 1936.

Hunt, Sir David, *On the Spot: an Ambassador Remembers,* London: Peter Davies, 1975.

Hurd, Douglas, *Memoirs,* London: Little, Brown, 2003.

Irving, Robert Grant, *Indian Summer: Lutyens, Baker and Imperial Delhi,* New Haven and London: Yale University Press, 1981.

Jeffries, Sir Charles, *The Colonial Office,* London: George Allen and Unwin, 1956.

Johnson, Penny, *The Oil Paintings in Public Ownership in the Government Art*

Collection, London: Public Catalogue Foundation, 2007.

Jones, Raymond, *The Nineteenth-Century Foreign Office: an Administrative History,* London: Weidenfeld and Nicolson, 1971.

--------- *The British Diplomatic Service 1815-1914,* Gerrards Cross: Colin Smythe, 1983.

Jones, Thomas, *A Diary with Letters 1931-1950*, Oxford University Press, 1954.

Kelly, Sir David, *The Ruling Few, or the Human Background to Diplomacy,* London: Hollis and Carter, 1952.

King, Anthony D., *The Bungalow: the Production of a Global Culture,* Oxford University Press, 1995.

Leveson Gower, F., *Letters of Harriet, Countess Granville 1810-45*, vol. 1, London: Longmans, Green, 1894.

McKinstry, Leo, *Rosebery: Statesman in Turmoil,* London: John Murray, 2005.

Michie, Alexander, *The Englishman in China during the Victorian Era as Illustrated in the Career of Sir Rutherford Alcock,* Edinburgh: William Blackwood, 1900.

Morris, Jan, with Simon Winchester, *Stones of Empire: the Buildings of the Raj,* Oxford University Press, 1983.

Norwich, John Julius, *The Duff Cooper Diaries,* London: Weidenfeld and Nicolson, 2005.

Part, Antony, *The Making of a Mandarin*, London: Andre Deutsch, 1990.

Paterson, Peter, *Tired and Emotional: the Life of Lord George Brown,* London: Chatto and Windus, 1993.

Phillips, Sir Horace, *Envoy Extraordinary: a Most Unlikely Ambassador,* London and New York: Radcliffe Press, 1995.

Platt, D.C.M., *The Cinderella Service: British Consuls since 1825,* London: Longman, 1971.

Port, M.H., *Imperial London: Civil Government Building in London 1851-1915,* New Haven and London: Yale University Press, 1995.

Rodd, Sir James Rennell, *Social and Diplomatic Memories 1902-19,* London: Edward Arnold, 1925.

Saint, Andrew, *Architect and Engineer: a Study in Sibling Rivalry,* New Haven and London: Yale University Press, 2007.

Seldon, Anthony, *The Foreign Office: an Illustrated History of the Place and its People,* London: HarperCollins, 2000.

Sheil, Mary, *Glimpses of Life and Manners in Persia: with Notes on Russia, Koords, Tookromans, Nestorians, Khiva and Persia,* London: John Murray, 1856.

Smedley, Beryl, *Homewood and its Families: a Story of Wellington,* Wellington: Mallinson Rendel, 1980.

--------- *Partners in Diplomacy,* Ferring, West Sussex: Harley Press, 1990.

Smithson, Alison and Peter, *The Charged Void: Architecture*, New York: Monacelli Press, 2001.

Strang, Lord, *The Foreign Office*, London: George Allen and Unwin, 1955.

Swenarton, Mark, *Building the New Jerusalem: Architecture, Housing and Politics 1900-1930*, Bracknell: Brepress, 2008.

Tilley, Sir John, and Stephen Gaselee, *The Foreign Office*, London: Putnam, 1933.

Toplis, Ian, *The Foreign Office: an Architectural History*, London and New York: Mansell Publishing, 1987.

Trevelyan, Humphrey, *Diplomatic Channels*, London: Macmillan, 1973.

Walsh, R., *A Residence at Constantinople during a Period including the Commencement, Progress and Termination of the Greek and Turkish Revolutions*, London: Westley and Davis, 1836.

Weiler, John Michael, 'Army Architects: the Royal Engineers and the Development of Building Technology in the Nineteenth Century', Ph.D. thesis, University of York, 1987.

Wood, Frances, *No Dogs and Not Many Chinese: Treaty Port Life in China 1843-1943*, London: John Murray, 1998.

Wood, W.A.R., *Consul in Paradise: Sixty-eight years in Siam*, London: Souvenir Press, 1965.

Wright, Denis, *The English amongst the Persians: Imperial Lives in Nineteenth-Century Iran*, London: Tauris, 2001.

Ziegler, Philip, *Diana Cooper*, London: Hamilton, 1981.

Post-specific monographs, articles and papers

Addis Ababa
Campbell, Margaret, *A Short History of the British Embassy: Addis Ababa*, 1972.

Alexandria
Smith, Gordon, *El 'Onsuleya: the Former British Consulate-General, Alexandria*, Harpocrates, 2010.

Ankara
Helm, Sir Knox, 'The Beginnings of the Ankara Embassy', 4 April 1952 (typescript at TNA, FO366/2958).

Athens
Llewellyn Smith, Michael, *The British Embassy, Athens*, British Embassy, 1998.

Bandar Seri Begawan
Watson, A.C., 'Notes on the History of Bubongan Dua-Belas, the British High Commissioner's Residence in Brunei', *Brunei Museum Journal*, 1981.

Banjul
Le Breton, D.F.B., 'History of "Admiralty House", Cape St Mary, British High Commissioner's Residence, The Gambia', unpublished FCO typescript, 1984.

Canberra

Barder, Jane, 'Canberra House – Westminster House 1931-1993', unpublished FCO typescript, 1993.

Copenhagen

Johansson, Ejner, 'The British Ambassador's Residence in Bredgade', *Berlingske Tidende*, 21 May 1957.

Dakar

Snoxell, David, 'British Representation in Dakar 1872–1945 and the Rebuilding of the British Residence', unpublished FCO typescript, 2000.

Helsinki

Falla, Gordon, *The British Ambassador's Residence at Helsinki*, British Embassy, 2002.

Kabul

Himsworth, Katherine, 'A History of the British Embassy in Kabul, Afghanistan', unpublished FCO typescript, 1976.

Kingston

Reid, Jane, 'Trafalgar House: its History and its Contents', unpublished FCO account, 1984. Appeared in a slightly different form in *Jamaica Journal*, 18, no. 2, May 1985.

Kuala Lumpur

Hawley, Ruth, 'Carcosa: an Outline of its History', *Malaysian Historical Magazine,* 1979.

Lagos

Girouard, Mark, 'New Look on a Lagoon', *Country Life*, 131, 15 March 1962, pp. 582-4.

Lisbon

Bull, T.A., *The Residence of the British Ambassador at Lisbon*, The British Historical Society of Portugal, 1995.

Calado, Maria, 'The British Ambassador's Residence in Lisbon: Historical Study', unpublished typescript, 1992.

Moscow

Berton, Kathleen, *The British Embassy Residence, Moscow*, British Embassy, 1991.

Melvin, Jeremy, *The British Embassy, Moscow*, London: FCO, 2000.

Muscat

Hawley, Ruth, *The British Embassy in Muscat: A Short History*, 1974.

Oslo

Tschudi-Madsen, Stephan, *The British Ambassador's Residence at Oslo*, British Embassy, 2001.

Ottawa

Reddaway, Norman, *Earnscliffe: Home of Canada's first Prime Minister and since 1930 Residence of High Commissioners for the United Kingdom in Canada*, Commonwealth Relations Office, 1955.

Paris

Beal, Mary, and John Cornforth, *British Embassy, Paris: the House and its Works of Art*, London: Government Art Collection, 1992, (reprinted with amendments, 1996).

Craig, Maurice J., *Report on the British Embassy, Paris*, Ministry of Public Building and Works, November 1958.

Friedman, Joseph, *British Embassy, Paris. The History of a House 1725-1985*, four vols, and *Catalogue of Bonaparte-Borghese Collection*, two vols, 1986. A summary, *Short History of the British Embassy, Paris*, was published by the FCO in 1990.

Middleton, Robin D., *Her Britannic Majesty's Embassy, Paris: an Historical Report*, Ministry of Public Building and Works, 1961.

Ronfort, Jean Nérée, and Jean-Dominique Augarde, *À l'ombre de Pauline: la Résidence de l'Ambassadeur de Grande-Bretagne a Paris*, Editions du Centre de Recherches Historiques, 2001.

Prague

Willan, Edward Gervase, *A History of the British Embassy Prague*, British Embassy, 1976.

Tehran

Gurney, John, 'Legations and Gardens, Sahibs and their Subalterns', *Journal of the British Institute of Persian Studies*, 40, 2002, pp.203-32.

The Hague

Garran, Sir Peter, 'Westeinde 12 – The Embassy Story', 1968 (typescript of speech, at TNA, WORK10/523).

Tunis

Day, Stephen and Philippa, *At Home in Carthage: the British in Tunisia*, Tunis: Trustees of St George's Church, 1991.

Warsaw

Llewellyn Smith, Michael, 'British Embassies to Poland and the British Embassy Warsaw', unpublished FCO typescript, 1996.

Washington

Hussey, Christopher, 'The New Embassy at Washington', *Country Life*, 62, 24 December 1927, pp.943-6.

--------- 'The British Embassy, Washington', *Country Life*, 85, 14 and 21 January 1939, pp.38-42, 64-8.

Stamp, Gavin, and Allan Greenberg, '"Modern Architecture as a Very Complex Art": the Design and Construction of Lutyens's British Embassy in Washington DC', Chapter 11 in Andrew Hopkins and Gavin Stamp (eds), *Lutyens Abroad: the Work of Sir Edwin Lutyens outside the British Isles*, London: British School at Rome, 2002.

Zanzibar

Crofton, R.H., *The Old Consulate at Zanzibar*, Oxford University Press, 1935.

Index

Bold denotes pages with illustrations.